THE
BRITISH
POLITY

Other Books by Philip Norton:

Dissension in the House of Commons 1945–1974 (1975)

Conservative Dissidents (1978)

Dissension in the House of Commons 1974–1979 (1980)

The Commons in Perspective (1981)

Conservatives and Conservatism (with A. Aughey) (1981)

The Constitution in Flux (1982)

Law and Order and British Politics (editor) (1984)

Parliament in the 1980s (editor) (1985)

The Political Science of British Politics (coeditor) (1986)

Parliament in Perspective (1987)

Legislatures (editor) (1990)

Parliaments in Western Europe (editor) (1990)

New Directions in British Politics? (editor) (1991)

Politics UK (with others) (1991, 2nd ed., 1994)

Back from Westminster (with D. Wood) (1993)

Does Parliament Matter? (1993)

Parliamentary Questions (coeditor) (1993)

THE BRITISH POLITY

THIRD EDITION

PHILIP NORTON
The University of Hull

Longman
New York & London

Evans

The British Polity, Third Edition

Copyright © 1994, 1991, 1984 by Longman
All rights reserved.
No part of this publication may be reproduced,
stored in a retrieval system, or transmitted
in any form or by any means, electronic, mechanical,
photocopying, recording, or otherwise,
without the prior permission of the publisher.

Longman, 10 Bank Street, White Plains, N.Y. 10606

Associated companies:
Longman Group Ltd., London
Longman Cheshire Pty., Melbourne
Longman Paul Pty., Auckland
Copp Clark Pitman, Toronto

Acquisitions editor: David Shapiro
Development editor: Susan Alkana
Production editor: Professional Book Center
Cover design: Kevin C. Kall
Production supervisor: Richard Bretan

JN
231
.N669
1994

Library of Congress Cataloging-in-Publication Data

Norton, Philip.
    The British polity / by Philip Norton.—3rd ed.
        p.   cm.
    Includes bibliographical references and index.
    ISBN 0-8013-1169-1
    1. Great Britain—Politics and government. I. Title.
JN231.N669   1993
320.941—dc20
                                    93-14317
                                     CIP

2 3 4 5 6 7 8 9 10-MA-97969594

To Mr. and Mrs. R. A. Bradel

Contents

Illustrations and Tables

FIGURES

Preface

The second edition of this book was written when Margaret Thatcher was prime minister and at a time when the Labour party enjoyed a substantial lead in the opinion polls and looked set to form the next government of the United Kingdom. Political developments since then have been nothing if not dramatic. In November 1990, Margaret Thatcher was toppled as leader of the Conservative party and replaced by John Major, a politician little known in the United Kingdom and unknown outside it. The following year saw British involvement in the Gulf War in January and the successful negotiation of a new European treaty, the Maastricht Treaty, in December. In 1992 the Conservative party was unexpectedly victorious in a general election, a victory not foreshadowed by the opinion polls, and the party was returned for an unprecedented consecutive fourth term. Prime Minister Major appeared at the height of his power, an apparently "Teflon" prime minister. Within six months, the government's policy toward the European Community was in disarray, with a sterling crisis forcing British withdrawal from the Exchange Rate Mechanism of the European Monetary System and a "no" vote to the Maastricht Treaty in Denmark encouraging growing opposition to the treaty within Conservative ranks in Britain. An attempt to close most of Britain's remaining coal mines proved widely unpopular, including within Parliament, the government being forced to concede a review of its policy. By November 1992, there was talk of the prime minister resigning.

The same year saw growing public discussion about the role of the royal family and about the marital difficulties of the prince and princess of Wales and the duke and duchess of York. Media coverage of the private lives of various members of the royal family fueled speculation about divorce and even about the future of the monarchy. The celebration of the queen's fortieth anniversary as monarch was a relatively low-key affair. Other central institutions of the state have not escaped criticism and crises, including—following the revelation of several highly publicized miscarriages of justice—the courts and the police force. All these developments took place against a backdrop of economic recession, with no clear signs of recovery.

Though events in eastern and central Europe were far more momentous—with Margaret Thatcher vying with President George Bush to take credit for them—the developments within the United Kingdom created a political environment very different from the one that had existed in the 1980s. A "feel good" mood had given way to a "feel bad" one. Britain's apparent ills lent themselves to differing analyses and competing solutions.

I have therefore taken the opportunity of this new edition to detail and explain the changes that have taken place. To accommodate this, some dated material has been excised and some chapters recast and re-written. Changes also have been made in structure and content, in part reflecting helpful suggestions made by readers. The theme of earlier editions has been that of continuity and change. Although this edition incorporates the dramatic changes of recent years, the importance of continuity remains central. Contemporary British politics can be explained only in the context of a notable continuity of values and institutions.

In preparing this edition, I have incurred a number of debts. I am especially grateful to Andrew Griffin, who has done sterling work in researching data. I am grateful to colleagues in the United States for observations on earlier editions and also to those readers who responded to my invitation to write with their comments. A number of changes in this edition are a consequence of the helpful suggestions that have been made. I am again happy to invite readers' comments. Also, the following individuals reviewed the manuscript for this edition and provided helpful suggestions:

Shaun Bowler, University of California at Riverdale

Thomas W. Casstevens, Oakland University

Harold Clarke, University of Texas

Michael Curtis, Rutgers University

Mary-Jane Deeb, The American University

Ronald Francisco, University of Kansas

Gary Freeman, University of Texas at Austin

Arthur Gunlicks, University of Richmond

Michael Jogerst, University of Iowa

Anthony Messina, Tufts University

Glen Mitchell, Florida State University

Jerrold Rusk, University of Arizona

Donald Searing, University of North Carolina, Chapel Hill

Since the second edition, exchange rates have again fluctuated, sometimes dramatically. In this edition, dollar equivalents are based on the exchange rate prevailing in November 1992 of £1 = $1.55.

As ever, responsibility for any errors, misjudgments, or omissions is entirely mine.

THE
BRITISH
POLITY
THIRD EDITION

PART I
Introduction

CHAPTER 1

The Contemporary Landscape

Continuity and change are features of every political system. What makes each significant is the nature and the extent of that change. Some systems are characterized by rapid and sometimes revolutionary change. Others are noted for continuity with past experience and structures. The task of the student of politics is to discern the distinctive features of that continuity and change; to generate concepts; and, if possible, to construct models and theories that will aid understanding of and serve to explain those distinctive features and the relationship among them.

The distinctive features of a political system can be recognized by comparing that system with another or, better still, with many others. In discussing the merits of comparative politics, a student in a class of mine once objected to the whole exercise. "There's no point in comparing one country with another," he argued. "Every country is unique." As others in the class were quick to respond, the only way by which one knows that a country is unique is by comparing it with others. Just as one can know whether one is short or tall only by comparing oneself with others, so one can know whether one's own political system is "short" or "tall" only by putting it alongside other systems and noting the differences.

Space and resources preclude an exhaustive or even an extensive comparative study in this work. Instead, I will illustrate the distinctive nature of the British polity by comparing it, where appropriate, with the American. They are similar in many respects, with a shared language; advanced industrial economies; similar but not always identical political, social, and economic values; and some mutual needs. Each has a sense of affinity with the other. As we shall see, however, there are significant dissimilarities, which make a comparative exercise useful. Such an exercise will serve not only to sensitize the American reader to the distinctive features of the British polity but also to make readers more aware of the features of their own polity. That, at least, is the hope.

To help the reader understand continuity and change within the British polity, I will stress the significance of the political culture. This emphasis will form the basis of the next chapter as well as the book's conclusion. Before we proceed to an analysis of that culture, a brief sketch of the salient features of contemporary Britain is necessary. This outline is especially pertinent for comparative purposes. There are important dissimilarities between the United States and Britain in terms of geography, demography, and social hsitory. Britain is a small, crowded island, largely oriented in terms of industry and population to England (and especially the southeast of England), with a class-based society that has superseded, but by no means discarded altogether some of the characteristics of, a feudal society. The purpose of this chapter is to highlight those features. Such a study is a prerequisite for a consideration of the political culture and the institutions and processes that culture nurtures.

LAND AND POPULATION

From the perspective of land distribution and usage, Great Britain could be described as a predominantly agricultural kingdom based on the three countries of England, Scotland, and Wales. (The United Kingdom comprises these three countries plus Northern Ireland: See Map 1.1.) In terms of the distribution and activities of the population, it is predominantly English, nonagricultural, and town- or suburban-based.

Great Britain occupies a total area of 88,798 square miles. This compares with an area of 3,615,123 square miles for the United States. Within the United States, ten states each have a greater land area than Britain, Alaska (586,412 square miles), Texas (267,339), and California (158,693) being the most notable. England has approximately the same land area as New York State, Scotland the same as South Carolina, and Wales the same as Massachusetts.

The disparity in population size is not quite so extreme. In 1990 the United Kingdom population was 57.4 million, up from 38.2 million at the turn of the century. The United States population in 1989 was almost 249 million, up from 76 million in 1900 (see Table 1.1). There is a more significant difference, though, in population growth. Between 1970 and 1990, the United Kingdom population increased by only 3%. (A continuation of the slow growth rate is anticipated, with the population projected to be no more than 59 million in 2001.) Between 1970 and 1989 the United States population increased by 21%. Much higher increases have been recorded in third-world countries. In South Asia over the same period, for example, the population increase was more than 40%.

When the population is put in the context of land size, Britain emerges as a crowded island. The number of people per square kilometer in 1986 was 233. By European standards, this is high but not exceptional: The Netherlands, Belgium, and Germany are even more densely populated. The number of people per square kilometer in the United States in 1987 was less than 28. By worldwide standards, this is a low but not exceptional figure. Russia, Brazil, New Zealand, Australia,

MAP 1.1   The United Kingdom

TABLE 1.1   United States and United Kingdom populations, 1900–1990

Year	United Kingdom Population (millions)	United States Population (millions)
1900	38.2	76.1
1910	42.1	92.4
1920	44.0	106.4
1930	46.1	123.1
1940	48.3	132.4
1950	50.6	152.3
1960	53.0	180.7
1970	55.7	205.0
1980	56.0	227.7
1990	57.4	248.8*

*1989 figure
SOURCES: Adapted from Central Statistical Office, *Social Trends 22* (Her Majesty's Stationery Office, 1992); *Statistical Abstracts of the United States 1988,* 108th ed. (U.S. Department of Commerce, Bureau of the Census, 1988); *Population Trends 68* (Her Majesty's Stationery Office, 1992).

and Canada were among the nations with lower population density. In Australia and Canada there were fewer than 3 people per square kilometer.

Within the United Kingdom, the population is heavily concentrated in one country. In 1990 almost 48 million people lived in England, compared with a little over 5 million in Scotland, 2.9 million in Wales, and 1.6 million in Northern Ireland. The number of people per square kilometer in England in 1987 was 363—the highest population density of European countries and greater even than that of Japan. Within England, the greatest concentration of inhabitants is in the southeast of the country (that is, Greater London and the surrounding counties); just under one-third of the population of the United Kingdom resides there.

The population resides predominantly in areas classified, for local government purposes, as urban. About 80% of the population in England, and more than 70% in Scotland and Wales, live in urban areas. One-fifth of the population lives in the ten largest cities (see Table 1.2). The shift from rural to urban areas has been marked in England, the proportion of the population living in nonurban areas declining from a little over 35% in 1951 to not much more than 20% twenty years later.

Although approximately three-quarters of the land surface is used for agriculture, very few people are employed in the agricultural industry. There has been a persistent drift from land work since industrialization in the eighteenth and nineteenth centuries, a trend that continues. More than 700,000 people were employed in agriculture, forestry, and fishing in 1961. By 1990, the figure was below 300,000. Increased efficiency and greater mechanization have in part facilitated this development. (Britain has one of the heaviest tractor densities in the world.) There are more than 250,000 farm holdings in Britain, with three-fifths of the full-time farms being devoted mainly to dairying or beef cattle and

TABLE 1.2 The ten largest cities in the United Kingdom, 1988

City*	Population (thousands)
Greater London	6,735.4
Birmingham	993.7
Leeds	709.6
Glasgow	703.2
Sheffield	528.3
Liverpool	469.6
Bradford	464.1
Manchester	445.9
Edinburgh	433.5
Bristol	377.7

*For locations, see Map 1.1.
SOURCE: *Britain 1990: An Official Handbook* (Her Majesty's Stationery Office, 1990).

sheep. Farms devoted to arable crops are predominant in the eastern part of England. Sheep and cattle rearing is a feature of the hills and moorland areas of Scotland, Wales, and northern and southwestern England.

Although Britain exports agrochemicals, agricultural equipment, and some agricultural produce and food products, it nonetheless has to import a substantial portion of its food supply.[1] Indeed, Britain is heavily dependent on imports of raw materials. Compared with other large industrialized (and some developing) nations, Britain is notably lacking in natural resources. The exception is energy resources: It is a major world producer of oil and natural gas. However, it is largely dependent on other nations either wholly or in part for products such as cotton, rubber, lead, tin, phosphates, rice, corn, silk, coffee, and tobacco. The list is by no means exhaustive. The United States, by contrast, is self-sufficient in most of these products, with surplus supply in several cases. Among other things, the United States is the world's largest producer, and consumer, of lead. France, Germany, Canada, Japan, and India also are more self-sufficient than Britain. This lack of raw materials is important not only for an understanding of comtemporary Britain but also in providing a partial explanation of Britain's internationalist and imperialist history.

LINGUISTIC AND RACIAL DIFFERENCES

The population is predominantly English in birth as well as residence. It also is predominantly white and English-speaking. It is not, however, totally homogeneous. Not only is there a division in Britain between the English, the Scots, and the Welsh; there is also a division in Scotland between those who do and do not speak Gaelic, and in Wales between those who do and do not speak Welsh. In both cases, those who speak the traditional native languages are in a small minority. In Wales, only about one in five inhabitants can speak Welsh. Only about 80,000 Scots are believed to speak the indigenous Scots Gaelic, most of them concentrated in the Scottish highlands and islands. Looking beyond Britain to Northern Ireland, a few families in the province still speak the Irish form of Gaelic. However, as we shall see in chapter 9, the absence of homogeneity in the province extends far beyond linguistic differences.

The influx of immigrants into Britain, especially in the 1950s and early 1960s (numbers have been limited since the passage of the Commonwealth Immigrants Act of 1962), also has added to the diversity of the population and to linguistic differences. Immigration has resulted in a significant increase in the number of nonwhite citizens, though they constitute a small proportion of the population. The number of nonwhite people in Britain is now just over 2.5 million—up from more than 1 million in 1968—with the largest single nonwhite community being the Indian (see Table 1.3). Of the ethnic minority population, just over 40% is U.K.-born. As a proportion of the total population, the nonwhite community is small: less than 5% of the total. It is, though, relatively heavily concentrated—a factor often claimed to exacerbate racial tension—in a number of urban areas, notably London, Leicester, Birmingham, Bradford, and various towns in the West Midlands and Yorkshire.

The United States has experienced analogous problems of concentration but has a much larger nonwhite population, African Americans accounting for more than 12% of the population. (There are also more than 7 million other nonwhite Americans.) There is also another significant difference. The African-American population is as indigenous as the white. (Native Americans now account for well under 1% of the population.) As such, it is unusual for an African American to be asked, ''Where do you come from?''—meaning, ''What is your country of

TABLE 1.3   Minority ethnic groups, 1981–1989

	Estimated Population (thousands)	
Ethnic Group	*1981*	*1989*
West Indian or Guyanese	528	482
African	80	127
Indian	727	779
Pakistani	392	433
Bangladeshi	51	112
Chinese	92	132
Arab	53	72
Mixed	217	284
Other	60	149
All ethnic minority groups	*2,092*	*2,569*

SOURCE: *Population Trends 54, 1986* (Office of Population Censuses and Surveys 1988), p. 29; *Social Trends 22* (Her Majesty's Stationery Office, 1992), p. 28.

origin?''—whereas such a question is often asked of nonwhite Britons. The United States also has a far greater ethnic mix than the United Kingdom. The combined noun is common in discussions of that mix (German Americans, Polish Americans); there is no equivalent use in the United Kingdom.

RELIGION

Britain, like the United States, is a predominantly Protestant country. There the similarity largely ends. Britain has an established church, the United States does not. There is no separation of church and state in the United Kingdom. Religious assemblies are held in schools, mangers are displayed on public land at Christmas, and various official occasions—such as the enthronement of a new monarch— are held in church. Disputes over prayers in school occur but are unrelated to the principle of whether or not prayers should be held: The dispute is over whether they have to be predominantly Christian. (Some schools have a majority of non-Christian pupils.) Such a link between church and state says little, however, about religious dedication. Few Britons are regular churchgoers; in the United States, church attendance is widely practiced. ''Less than a tenth of the English people are zealous Christians. . . . Between 40% and 50% of Americans are in church on a typical Sunday. Nearly two-thirds of Americans say a strong religious commitment is 'absolutely essential' or 'very important'.''[2]

The Anglican Church of England is ''by law established'' the official church in England. (The Presbyterian Church of Scotland is the established church there.) As such, it is variously involved in the affairs of state. The monarch is the supreme governor (temporal head) of the church, and archbishops, bishops, and deans are appointed by the queen on the advice of the prime minister. The coronation of a new monarch is conducted by the senior churchman in the Anglican faith (the archbishop of Canterbury), and services of national celebration, or grief, are conducted in one of the principal Anglican churches, usually St. Paul's Cathedral of Westminster Abbey in London. The monarch is required by statute to be a member of the Church of England and must promise to uphold the faith. The senior figures in the church—two archbishops and 24 bishops—sit in the House of Lords. Various measures affecting the governing principles of the church require parliamentary approval.

A broad Protestant church, the Church of England was founded by King Henry VIII in the sixteenth century following his break with the Roman Catholic church.[3] It comprises two provinces: Canterbury, headed by the archbishop of Canterbury (titled primate of all England), with 30 dioceses, and York, headed by the archbishop of York (primate of England), with 14 dioceses. Within the dioceses, there are more than 13,000 parishes. Though about half of the population claim to be Anglicans, fewer than 2 million are actually members of the church. The membership is lower than that of the Roman Catholic church and—in common with most, though not all, Christian churches—is declining (Table 1.4). It is set to decline further. In recent years the church has faced a schism on the issue of women priests. In 1992, the General Synod (the central governing body,

TABLE 1.4 Church membership in the United Kingdom, 1975–1990

Churches	Adult Members (millions)	
	1975	*1990*
Trinitarian Churches		
Church of England	2.27	1.84
Presbyterian	1.65	1.29
Methodist	0.61	0.48
Baptist	0.27	0.24
Other Protestant churches	0.53	0.70
Roman Catholic	2.53	1.95
Orthodox	0.20	0.27
Total	8.06	6.77
Nontrinitarian Churches		
Mormons	0.10	0.15
Jehovah's Witnesses	0.08	0.12
Spiritualists	0.06	0.06
Other nontrinitarian	0.09	0.13
Total	0.33	0.46
Other Religions		
Muslims	0.40	0.99
Sikhs	0.12	0.39
Hindus	0.10	0.14
Jews	0.11	0.11
Others	0.08	0.23
Total	0.81	1.86

SOURCE: *UK Christian Handbook 1992–93* (MARC Europe, 1992).

comprising bishops, clergy, and lay members) voted to admit women to the priesthood, a move bitterly opposed by traditionalists, many of whom—clergy included—vowed to leave the church.

The Roman Catholic church, the "out" and often legally discriminated against church for most of the period since the Reformation in the sixteenth century, now enjoys the same freedoms as other religions. It is divided into seven provinces in Britain, each headed by an archbishop; the premier archbishop is the archbishop of Westminster. There are 30 Episcopal dioceses, and 6 more in Northern Ireland. The church places particular emphasis on religious education as well as devotion, though the proportion of church members who attend services on a typical Sunday is not much different from the proportion of Anglican church members. As with the Church of England, membership is declining, as is regular attendance at church. It is estimated that between 1979 and 1989 attendance fell by some 14%. The equivalent figure for the Church of England was 9%.

Membership of other trinitarian churches (those believing in the union of the Holy Trinity under one Godhead) also has fallen in recent years. Increases have come in membership of the nontrinitarian churches and, more significantly, in the Hindu, Sikh, and Muslim religions. Both the Jewish and Muslim faiths are large communities by European standards. The Jewish community in Britain—about 400,000, with about one-quarter constituting adult members of the faith—is the second largest in Europe. Most are Orthodox Jews, with about 20% being members of the Reform or Liberal and Progressive movements. There are about 300 Jewish congregations in the country. Muslims are served by over 1,000 mosques and prayer centers, the Islamic Cultural Center (and London Central Mosque) on the edge of London's Regent's Park constituting the most important Muslim institution in the Western world.

Though religion remains politically and socially central to the life of Northern Ireland, its importance in Britain has declined throughout the twentieth century. In significance, it has been displaced by class.

CLASS

The United States does not have a feudal history. The significance of this fact was well described by Louis Hartz in his incisive work on the Lockean basis of U.S. society.[4] Britain, by contrast, does have a feudal past. Furthermore, unlike some of its European neighbors, it has witnessed no revolutionary break with past experience. As a result, the class patterns of a capitalist society have been superimposed on the hierarchical social structure of a departing feudal society.

Status derives from the tendency of people to accord positive and negative values to human attributes and to distribute respect accordingly. In feudal society, a superior status was accorded to the landowning aristocracy and gentry. They were deemed to have breeding and to be the best people to govern the land. They were deferred to as a socially superior body. It was a status that was passed on by inheritance, not one that could be acquired by merit or work.

Whereas status is essentially the product of a social system, class is the product of the economic.[5] Defining the concept of class is not an easy task. Marx distinguished two classes, bourgeois and proletarian, based on the ownership of the means of production. This is not a particularly useful definition given the significant distinction between ownership and control.

The problem is compounded by the fact that there is a difference between attempts at objective measurement and subjective self-assessment. In other words, how social scientists measure class—and there are an increasing number of measures used—and how others perceive it (particularly in terms of self-ascription) often are far from congruent. Though there are now several definitions of class, the most used is that of groups formed on the basis of occupational difference. In Britain there are essentially two classes, the middle and the working; as A. H. Halsey has observed, it is a characteristically British distinction.[6] Within each of the two classes, there are further divisions. Table 1.5 provides a simple delineation of them.

Class grew out of industrialization and the development of a capitalist economy. It did not displace status; it usurped it. In the nineteenth century, the upper class comprised the traditional landed aristocracy, but it was an aristocracy that had absorbed largely, if not wholly, the new men of wealth who had made

TABLE 1.5 Social classes in Britain

Class	Market Research Designation	Encompassing
Middle class		
Upper-middle	A	Higher managerial and professional
Middle	B	Lower managerial and administrative
Lower-middle	C1	Skilled or supervisory nonmanual, lower nonmanual
Working class		
Upper-working	C2	Skilled manual
Working	D	Unskilled manual
	E	Residual, pensioners

their money from trade and industry. These new men were drawn into this class until, eventually, they overwhelmed it.[7]

This combination of class and status was carried into the twentieth century. In recent decades, however, it has been weakened. Some of the features of a status society, such as peerages, can be passed from father to son: The inheritance is founded in law. Class can be inherited but it is an inheritance based on the market, which is less predictable than the law. Recent years have witnessed a growing social mobility. The children of many working-class parents have been upwardly mobile socially. The children of some middle-class parents have taken up working-class occupations. Indeed, a few members of that institutional survivor of a feudal era, the House of Lords, pursue manual occupations. Writes Halsey, "Men and women, moving and marrying between different occupational levels, both over the generations and also within their own working lives or careers, have become an increasingly common feature of British social life in the past half century."[8] The general pattern of change has been one of upward mobility. Greater mobility and affluence have eroded the claims to status. Mobility deprives one of claims to breeding. Acceptance of the principle of meritocracy is discordant with claims of inherited worth. Status remains important but it is no longer the central feature of British society that it was in preceding centuries.

The importance of class in contemporary society has been confirmed by a number of studies. In their 1970 survey, Butler and Stokes asked respondents to name the main social classes and the class to which they would ascribe themselves. They found that "virtually everyone accepted the conventional class dichotomy between middle and working class"[9] with 77% spontaneously ascribing themselves to one or the other. According to Butler and Stokes: "It is difficult not to see this as evidence of the acceptance of the view that British society is divided into two primary classes. This is much more than a sociologist's simplification: It seems to be deeply rooted in the mind of the ordinary British citizen."[10] Though increased social mobility and changes in the occupational profile of the nation appear to have reduced the significance (or, perhaps more accurately, the measurability) of class, most citizens continue to consider themselves members of a particular class. Surveys in 1987 and 1989 found only 3% of respondents giving a "don't know" answer when asked to identify the social class they belonged to,[11] and, as in the Butler and Stokes survey of 20 years before, most identified themselves with the class of their parents (Table 1.6). Insofar as there is a difference between the class of self and parents, the figures in Table 1.6 reinforce the thesis of upward mobility.

Though measured principally in terms of occupation, class connotes significant differences in lifestyles. A whole range of interests and pursuits are associated with each particular class. The middle class, bolstered traditionally by higher incomes, have been able to afford their own homes—usually semi-detached or detached houses—and to take holidays in exotic climes. They have encouraged children to do well educationally and to go to university. They have pursued a range of leisure interests such as golf, tennis, squash, and skiing. They belong to country clubs and chambers of commerce. They are more likely than working-class families to be theatergoers and to be joiners of civic organizations and pressure groups. Working-class families traditionally have lived in terraced, often rented, housing; taken holidays—when they can afford them—at seaside resorts in the United Kingdom and, more recently, in Spain; been less able to provide a supportive environment for children to pursue education to degree level; and been more likely than the middle class to pursue interests such as football and snooker and to be more inclined to spend more time drinking in the local public house, or "pub." These are broad, possibly overly crude, generalizations, but they point to the very real differences of lifestyles that are essentially ingrained and that often remain unaffected by significant changes in income.

The importance of class is political as well as social. For most of the twentieth century, there has been a significant relationship between class and politics. The Labour party has attracted largely but not wholly the support of the working class, and the Conservative party that of the middle class. The significance of the class-party nexus will be explored in more detail later. There is recent evidence of a decline in class identification and in the correlation between class and party. Such decline, though, has been relative. Class remains a feature of British society. Most Britons continue to ascribe themselves to a particular class. Politicians analyze their support in class terms, and sociologists would be lost without it.

TABLE 1.6   Social class by self-ascription, 1989

If you had to make a choice, would you call yourself middle class or working class?

	Self (%)	Parents (%)
Middle class	30	21
Working class	67	75
Don't know	3	4

SOURCE: E. Jacobs and R. Worcester, *We British* (Weidenfeld & Nicolson, 1990), pp. 138–139.

EDUCATION

Education in Britain is best seen in pyramidal terms. All children receive a primary and secondary school education. Thereafter, only a minority proceed to institutions of higher education. For children receiving education at private schools, the structure is less pyramidal: A greater proportion of those educated at private schools proceed to university than those attending state schools. After entering primary school at the age of 5, children in England receive a common education until the age of 11, when they enter secondary schools. In the two decades following the passage of the 1944 Education Act, secondary schools were divided into grammar and secondary modern schools. The former were essentially academic institutions, oriented to scholastic skills with a large proportion of pupils achieving university entrance. The latter taught more practical skills, some pupils going on to a technical college but with very few achieving admission to university. Selection for entry to grammar schools was made by examination taken at age 11. Labour politicians came to view the bifurcation of grammar and secondary modern schools as socially divisive, with those attending secondary modern schools being unable to shake off the perception of being failures and unable to achieve the occupational opportunities of grammar school pupils. Following the return of a Labour government in 1964, a new scheme of education was introduced, selection and the dual school system being replaced by a nonselective, all-encompassing system of comprehensive education. Comprehensive schools were introduced over the next 20 years, under both Conservative and Labour governments. In 1971, 38% of secondary schoolchildren in England attended comprehensive schools; by 1990, the proportion had reached 92%. In Wales and Scotland, it was 99% and 100%, respectively.

From the mid-1980s onward, Conservative governments have introduced other changes, largely designed to ensure that basic subjects are not ignored and that parents have a greater influence over their children's schools. The reforms have included the introduction of a national curriculum, with three core subjects (English, science, and mathematics) and seven foundation subjects (history, geography, technology, art, physical education, music, and a modern foreign language), each with attainment targets and assessment arrangements. Greater powers also have been given to school governors. Funding remains publicly provided but school governing bodies now have power to determine the spending priorities for most of their budget and a school can seek to take full control of its own budget and admissions policy through opting out of the existing framework of control. Many of these changes—especially the power for schools to opt out—have proved contentious, the Conservatives seeing them as means of raising educational standards and Labour critics claiming they are attempts to restore some of the features of the system that existed in the 1950s.

Although secondary education is compulsory, parents are not required to send their children to state schools but can choose instead to send them to private schools. Private schools tend to stress academic achievement and concentrate on developing the ability to pass examinations and on building self-confidence. Believing that their children will receive a better and more disciplined education, with a greater prospect of university entry than from a state school, many parents who can afford it send their children to such private institutions, known (confusingly) as "public schools." Fees at such schools vary. The more prestigious, such as Eton, Harrow, and Winchester, can afford to charge annual fees in excess of £10,000 ($15,500), whereas some less prestigious day schools may charge less than £4,000 ($6,200). Fewer than one in ten schoolchildren (7% in 1990) attends private schools, though more than one-quarter of entrants to the older universities are drawn from such schools.

From secondary school, a minority of students proceed to institutions of further and higher education. Only a small proportion achieve the examination success necessary for admission to universities. Recent years have seen both a change in the structure of higher education as well as an increase in the proportion of those going on to study beyond secondary school. Until 1992, institutions of higher education were divided into universities and polytechnics. The former were more academic, whereas the latter—first established in 1967—were more vocationally oriented, often providing "sandwich" courses (part study, part practical job experience) for their students. In 1992, the formal dividing line, known as the binary line, between universities and polytechnics was abolished, allowing polytechnics to acquire university titles, and a common funding agency established. Even with the addition of the polytechnics to the ranks of the universities, the number of universities remains small by U.S. standards: less than 80.

The sector of higher education, though, is growing. At the turn of the century, England had only 7 universities, Scotland had 4, and Wales had 1. Relatively few were founded in the first few decades of the century. Recent decades have seen a significant expansion. Of the 46 universities that existed before 1992, 28 were founded after 1945. As we have seen, polytechnics were first created in 1967: By the time the binary line was abolished, there were 30. (The 1960s also saw the creation of the "open university," a nonresidential university requiring no formal academic qualifications for admission and offering tuition by correspondence and through special radio and television programs.) At the end of 1992, an expansion of further education—colleges offering subdegree courses—also was announced. By comparison with the United States, the number studying beyond secondary school is small. Less than one in three of those aged 18 to 24 go on to any form of further and higher education. Only one in ten go on to university. By comparison with the past, though, the figure has grown rapidly. By the end of the twentieth century, most school leavers are expected to go on to some form of further study.

A university education continues to provide occupational advantage. More than 80% of graduates have ended up in the professional and managerial classes. They constitute fewer than one-third of those in these classes, but it is these classes that will provide more children than any other for university entry. The likelihood that a person will go to university, especially the older (nonpolytechnic) universities, remains strongly linked to social class. "Roughly speaking, the lower the socioeconomic group of someone's father, the more likely it is that his or her full-time education ended in school, rather than college or university."[12]

Recent decades have seen no major change in the proportion of students drawn from working-class families going to the older universities.

MARRIAGE AND FAMILY

Although much emphasis is placed on the individual, the family remains the most important social unit in Britain. There remains strong attachment to the ideal of marriage and having children. Despite a high divorce rate, marriage—and remarriage—remains popular. As Jowell, Witherspoon, and Brook have noted in their survey of British social attitudes, "In their attitude towards marriage and other family matters, the British emerge as highly and consistently conventional."[13]

Nonetheless, there have been important changes in recent years. There has been some variation in the number of people getting married and in the number getting divorced. The number of marriages has declined in the past two decades. There were 58,000 fewer marriages in 1989 than in 1971. At the same time, the number of divorces has increased, doubling in number between 1971 and 1989. In 1989, the number of marriages per 1,000 of the eligible population was 6.8, compared with 7.1 at the beginning of the decade. The number of divorces was 12.6 per 1,000 population, compared with 11.9 at the beginning of the decade.[14] This gave the United Kingdom the second highest divorce rate (after Denmark) in the European Community (EC), though still well below that of the United States.[15]

Households also have been getting smaller. In 1971, 18% of households in Britain comprised one person, and 35% of households comprised a couple with dependent children. The same percentage comprised couples with no children or nondependent children. By 1991, the percentage of one-person households had increased to 26%. The percentage of households comprising couples with children had fallen to 24%. In 1961, the average household size was 3.09 people. By 1971, the number had fallen to 2.89, and by 1991 to 2.46.

The decrease in the number of families with children reflects a fall in the birthrate, a feature common to all EC countries. The increase in the number of one-person households is in part explicable by the increase in the size of the elderly population. In 1971, 12% of households comprised one person of pensionable age, compared with 6% under pensionable age. By 1991, the largest number of one-person households was still accounted for by people of pensionable age, but the gap was not so great: 15% of households comprised one person of pensionable age but 11% comprised an individual under pensionable age. The largest increase in the period was of men under pensionable age.

There also has been a change within the nature of family groupings, recent years seeing a marked increase in the number of unmarried couples living together. In 1984, one in ten births registered were of children born to unmarried couples. By 1990, the proportion had increased to one in five.

Within these trends, there also are some variations correlated to region and class. In terms of births outside marriage, the percentage is greater in the northern regions of England (north, northwest, Yorkshire, and Humberside) than in southern regions. There is some correlation between household size and socioeconomic grouping. In 1989–1990, one in three households headed by someone in the professions or management had a child age 15 or under. For those headed by semi-skilled or unskilled workers, the proportion was one in four.[16]

The traditional attitudes toward marriage remain. The decrease in the number of marriages was sharpest in the 1970s. The numbers showed relatively little change in each year in the 1980s: just over a quarter-of-a-million marriages a year. In comparative terms, the marriage rate in relation to the eligible population remains high. The United Kingdom has the third highest marriage rate, after Portugal and Greece, in the EC. Nonetheless, the past 20 years have shown a considerable shift in patterns of living, with smaller and relatively less stable households.

EMPLOYMENT

Britain was the first major nation to experience industrialization. Most of the population in the nineteenth century moved from the land to find jobs in manufacturing industries in the towns and cities. The north of England in particular witnessed the growth of major industrial conurbations. "Mill towns" became common features. So, too, did mining communities. Most of the economically active population came to be employed in primary industries and manufacturing. In the twentieth century, especially in the period since 1945, more and more workers have moved into service industries.

The growth of service industries has been particularly marked in London and the southeast, where almost 75% of employees are now in the service sector. There has been a corresponding decline in employment in manufacturing, especially in the north. As Table 1.7 shows, the decline in manufacturing employment continued in the 1970s and on an even greater scale in the 1980s. The closure of local factories, mills, and coal mines has been met in some cases by diversification and attracting new firms, but otherwise by migration and higher levels of unemployment than elsewhere. Today, Britain can be described as having a predominantly service economy (Table 1.7) with the southeast of England enjoying a preeminent position in that economy. That preeminence is now consolidated by British membership in the European Community and the increased trade with EC countries. The southeast of England forms part of a "golden triangle" within the Community, with access to the continent not enjoyed by more distant parts of the United Kingdom.

Within employment, recent years have seen a growth in the number of female workers and in the number of self-employed. There also have been major changes in the proportion of the adult population in employment.

In all categories other than service industries, male employees outnumber females. The extractive industries have been traditionally male preserves. In the service industries, more than half the workers are women and much of the increase in service jobs in the 1980s was accounted for by part-time jobs taken by women. Between 1971 and 1990, the number of male workers in employment

TABLE 1.7   Employment by industry, 1971–1990

Industry	Number in Employment (thousands)		
	1971	*1979*	*1990*
Agriculture, forestry, and fishing	450	380	298
Energy and water supply	798	722	451
Construction	1,198	1,239	1,087
Manufacturing			
Extraction of minerals and ores other than fuels, manufacture of metals, mineral products and chemicals	1,282	1,147	728
Metal goods, engineering, and vehicle industries	3,709	3,374	2,316
Other	3,074	2,732	2,106
Total Manufacturing	8,065	7,253	5,150
Services			
Distribution, hotels, catering, and repairs	3,686	4,257	4,824
Transport and communication	1,556	1,479	1,374
Banking, finance, insurance, business services, and leasing	1,336	1,647	2,734
Other	5,049	6,197	6,936
Total Services	11,627	13,580	15,865
All Industries and Services	**22,138**	**23,174**	**22,854**

SOURCE: *Social Trends 22* (Her Majesty's Stationery Office, 1992), p. 75.

actually decreased (from 13.7 million to 12 million) whereas the number of female workers increased from 8.4 million to 10.8 million. Reflecting in part government encouragement for people to start their own businesses, the number of self-employed people in Britain increased by 60% between 1981 and 1990. In 1981, 2 million were self-employed; in 1990, the number was 3.2 million.[17] The self-employed also constitute one of the categories most vulnerable to recessions in economic performance. The early 1990s witnessed a record number of businesses, particularly among the self-employed, go bankrupt.

Unemployment increased in the early 1980s and peaked in 1986, when just over 3 million people—11% of the work force—were out of work. With economic recovery, unemployment rates fell and were below 6% by 1990. Recession then pushed the numbers up again and by the end of 1992 more than 2.6 million—more than 8% of the work force—were unemployed. Though unemployment rates remained highest in the northern half of England, the increase in 1991 and 1992 was greatest in the southern half of the country. In the southeast, the unemployment rate in 1990 was under 4%. By the end of 1992 it was 9%. Within the United Kingdom, the highest unemployment rate remains that of Northern Ireland, where the percentage of people unemployed is consistently well above 10%: In 1986 it was above 17% and in 1992 it was just over 14%.

In international comparison, unemployment levels in the United Kingdom rank behind the United States, Germany, and Japan, though they are no longer the worst—as they were in the early 1980s—of the seven major countries of the Organisation for Economic Cooperation and Development (OECD). In 1990, most West European countries had higher rates of unemployment than the United Kingdom.

PERSONAL WEALTH AND TAXATION

The country has thus witnessed some notable shifts in social behavior as well as in patterns of employment. There has been less significant change in the distribution of wealth.

The distribution of marketable wealth is skewed in favor of a minority. Marketable wealth comprises stocks and shares, cash, bank deposits, consumer durables, buildings, trade assets, land, and dwellings net of mortgage debt. In 1976, the total marketable wealth of the country was estimated to be £280 billion ($434 billion): just over one-fifth of it was owned by 1% of the population; half of it was owned by 10% of the population (Table 1.8). Insofar as there has been any trend in the pattern of ownership it has been away from the top 1% in favor of the 10% to 50% of the population owning most of the wealth. Of the country's marketable wealth in 1989—estimated at £1,578 billion ($2,446 billion)—more than half was owned by the top 10% and three-quarters by the top 25%. The trend predates 1976 but has not been marked. The least wealthy half of the population owns under 10% of the country's marketable wealth.

When occupational and state pension rights are added to marketable wealth, there is a change in the pattern of distribution (Table 1.8). Over the past 20 years the proportion of this wealth owned by 1% of the population has declined; the decline was most marked in the 1970s but continued in the 1980s. Most of this wealth continues to reside in the hands of the most wealthy half of the population—indeed, slightly more in 1989 than in 1976—but one-fifth of it is owned by the least wealthy half. Most wealth clearly remains in the hands of a minority, more than 60% being owned by the most wealthy 25% of the population.

TABLE 1.8 Distribution of marketable wealth, 1976–1989

Percentage of Population	Percentage Owned of Marketable Wealth		Percentage Owned of Marketable Wealth plus Occupational and State Pension Rights	
	1976	*1989*	*1976*	*1989*
1	21	18	13	11
5	38	38	26	26
10	50	53	36	38
25	71	75	57	62
50	92	94	80	83

SOURCE: *Social Trends 22* (Her Majesty's Stationery Office, 1992), p. 101.

Taxation is progressive, though the various rates have been reduced to two: a basic rate of 25% (with a lower rate of 20% for the lower paid) and a top rate of 40%. (At one stage there was a maximum rate of 83%.) The reduction—with a shift of emphasis from direct to indirect taxation—also has resulted in income tax constituting a smaller proportion of the gross domestic product (GDP): from 11.2% in 1979 to 10.3% in 1991. Despite the reduction in the number and level of rates, the proportion of tax paid by the highest 5% of taxpayers has increased, from approximately one-quarter in 1979 to more than 30% in 1991.

Though the most wealthy in the country remain very wealthy, the nation as a whole lags behind other West European countries, with a GDP per head that is lower than the Scandinavian countries and ahead only of Belgium, Spain, Portugal, and Ireland. In 1990, the GDP per head in the United Kingdom was $16,070. In each of the Scandinavian countries it was in excess of $22,000, in France it was more than $19,000, and in Germany more than $18,000. In Ireland and Portugal, it was less than $10,000.[18]

CONCLUSION

Britain constitutes a small and crowded island with relatively few natural resources, with wealth and population heavily concentrated in the southeast of England. It is a largely secular society and one in which class remains important. These features distinguish it from the United States, which shares none of these features. Though some of these features are shared with other European countries, in combination they render Britain distinct from its neighbors.

Compared with the United States and most European countries, Britain is notable for the absence—certainly since the seventeenth century—of invasion or revolution. Continuity in both institutions and many social traditions is a feature that underpins many of the structures and political relationships that form the basis of discussion in later chapters. Nonetheless, some change has taken place. That is apparent from the brief description offered in this chapter. We have touched upon some of the social changes that have occurred. We will later draw out the extent of political change. Some of that change has been significant and dramatic, especially in recent decades. Observing change can nonetheless obscure the extent of continuity. This volume is designed to ignore neither. It seeks to explain both. Hence our theme of the two C's: continuity and change.

NOTES

1. In 1987, food accounted for 10% of the nation's imports by value. Central Office of Information, *Britain 1989: An Official Handbook* (Her Majesty's Stationery Office, 1989), p. 305.
2. "Bagehot: The Worst of Worlds," *The Economist,* December 26, 1992, p. 30.
3. Henry VIII was excommunicated by the pope in 1533, following the crowning of Anne Boleyn as queen, the pope having refused to annul Henry's previous marriage

to Catherine of Aragon. Parliament responded with various acts establishing Henry's position as head of the church. By the Act of Supremacy of 1534, the king was recognized as "the only supreme head of the Church of England, called *Anglicana Ecclesia.*"

4. L. Hartz, *The Liberal Tradition in America* (Harcourt, Brace & World, 1955).
5. See A. H. Halsey, *Change in British Society,* 2nd ed. (Oxford University Press, 1981). This section draws heavily on this work.
6. Ibid.
7. Ibid., p. 47.
8. Ibid., pp. 53–54.
9. D. Butler and D. Stokes, *Political Change in Britain,* 2nd ed. (Macmillan, 1974), p. 69.
10. Ibid.
11. R. Jowell, S. Witherspoon, and L. Brook, *British Social Attitudes: The Fifth Report, 1988–1989* (Gower, 1988), p. 227; E. Jacobs and R. Worcester, *We British* (Weidenfeld & Nicolson, 1990), pp. 138–139.
12. J. Statham and D. MacKinnon, with H. Cathcart, *The Education Fact File* (Hodder & Stoughton, 1989), p. 160.
13. R. Jowell, S. Witherspoon, and L. Brook, *British Social Attitudes: The 1987 Report* (Gower, 1987), p. 140.
14. *Social Trends 22* (Her Majesty's Stationery Office, 1992), p. 43.
15. In 1988, the divorce rate in the United States was almost two-thirds higher than in the United Kingdom. The disparity was greatest among the under-25 age group. The duration of marriages ending in divorce also was shorter in the United States than in the United Kingdom. *Population Trends,* Autumn 1991 (Her Majesty's Stationery Office, 1991), p. 2.
16. *Social Trends 22,* p. 41.
17. Ibid., p. 75.
18. "Survey: The European Community," *The Economist,* July 11, 1992, p. 26.

CHAPTER 2

The Political Culture

Political culture is a vague, abstract concept that has been subject to various definitions.[1] In its simplest form, it may be described as denoting the emotional and attitudinal environment within which a political system operates.[2] If we are to understand how a political system is formed and operates, we have to understand the environment that produced and nurtures it.

The focus of this chapter is the political culture of Britain and the means through which individuals are socialized into that culture. As I shall seek to show, that culture cannot be divorced from the constraints of history and of physical and spatial resources. Each has had a significant impact on the other. The collection of emotions and attitudes that form the political culture has served to shape actions and hence affect the nation's history. Conversely, those actions, as well as the country's geographic location and limited resources, have had consequences that have affected elite and mass attitudes.

A number of problems have to be borne in mind. There is the danger especially of tautology and, as may be inferred from the preceding paragraph, the "chicken and egg" problem—which came first?—in attempting to discern the cause-and-effect relationships among culture, history, and resources. The existence of a stable political culture in Britain has been ascribed by some to the effectiveness of government in being able to implement programs of public policy. But what has enabled government to be effective? Has it been a distinctive political culture, citizens accepting the legitimacy of government to act in the way that it does? If so, what explains the existence of such a culture? Is not a partial explanation the effectiveness of government? The problem is an acute one in Britain given the absence of any clear point of departure. Where do English, Scottish, and Welsh history begin? At what point is a political culture discernible? The basic conundrum is insoluble. It is important, though, to bear it in mind, with an awareness of it informing our study.

What, then, are the basic components of the British political culture? And by what process are the values and attitudes that form that culture imbued by Britons?

POLITICAL SOCIALIZATION

The various values and beliefs that coalesce to create, maintain, and variously modify the political culture are not generated in a vacuum; they are acquired through a process of socialization. In that process, the most important influences usually are family, education, occupation, geographic location, and to a lesser extent, the mass media. For illustrative purposes, we shall consider their impact in shaping class and partisanship, before considering the basic underlying values that form the political culture.

Family

It is primarily from parents that children acquire particular values and habits. It is largely the parents who shape the child's view of society, including one's status in that society. It is also parents who significantly influence political perceptions and partisan support.

Perceptions of social class are derived not only from objective position but also often from inherited class orientations. Most children, as we have seen (Table 1.6) ascribe themselves to the same social class as their parents. The self-ascription is important and does not always correlate with objective assessments derived from socioeconomic conditions. Jacobs and Worcester also found a relationship between those who were upwardly mobile and those who believed their parents were upwardly mobile. "46% of those who described themselves as upwardly mobile middle-class described their parents in the same terms and so did 44% of those who called themselves upwardly mobile working-class."[3] As they note, with possibly a greater degree of insight than they realize, the claim to upward mobility may be an inherited characteristic.

Political habits and values are passed from parent to child. Children tend to inherit their parents' interest in politics (or, as appropriate, lack of it) and their partisan preferences. The influence is strongest when both parents share the same preference and that preference is known to the child.[4] There is evidence of decline in the class-party nexus,[5] and in recent general elections a substantial minority of electors have voted for parties their parents could not have supported, such as the Social Democrats and the Greens. Nonetheless, parents' preferences remain a significant predictor of partisan preference.[6]

The influence of parents on partisanship is relevant for our study in later chapters. Of more immediate relevance for the political culture is the wider impact of parents: the fact that, whatever divergent influences may serve to modify or undermine particular values, it is mother and father who remain the first and foremost points of reference in defining the political and social environment.

Education

Formal education is important in political socialization, less for its effect on partisan support (family remains the predominant influence) than for helping shape awareness of the political system and explicitly or, more often, implicitly the values that underpin it. In their classic but now dated study of the civic culture, Almond and Verba found that there were differences in attitude toward government between those with different levels of education, and between those who had received some formal education and those who had received none. The more extensive the education, up to university level, the greater the perceived significance of government action.[7] Nonetheless, the overwhelming majority of those with some formal education, primary or above, considered that national government had some effect.

It would thus seem plausible to hypothesize that the increase in educational provision in postwar years, and in the raising of the school-leaving age, will have raised political awareness and perceptions of political efficacy. Indeed, expanded educational opportunities and the development of the broadcast media have been identified as generating greater involvement in civic activity, a process that Inglehart has termed *cognitive mobilization.*[8] The disparity in the levels of education continues to correlate with levels of political activity. As the 1987 edition of *British Social Attitudes* found, those with educational qualifications, and graduates in particular, were more confident in their ability to understand politics and more inclined to participate in political activity than those without such qualifications; they also were more likely to be liberal in their moral values.[9] A further study not surprisingly found a relationship between the study of politics by students and greater political awareness and ideological sophistication.[10]

Types of education also can serve to reinforce values and behavior. Public schools tend to reinforce middle- and upper-middle-class norms and expectations. Conservative members of Parliament, for example, are drawn disproportionately from public schools and the universities of Oxford and Cambridge. At such schools, leading public figures frequently are invited to speak and pupils are encouraged to engage in activities appropriate for later public service (for example, taking part in school debates), an environment maintained at Oxford and Cambridge. No such environment or traditions are provided in state comprehensive schools. In most cases, the school environment tends to reinforce the influence of the home background.

Occupation

Occupation and class, as we have seen (chapter 1), are closely related. The former usually is employed as the primary criterion for determining the latter. Both are important in the context of political socialization. The nature of the occupation can affect values and perceptions of society. Having a poorly paid, mundane, and personally unrewarding job—or, indeed, having no job at all—is likely to invoke a greater sense of alienation than pursuing a well-paid and satisfying position. It would seem plausible to assume a broad correlation between these two positions and class, with those in the working class more likely to have more mundane, less well paid jobs and the middle class to have better paid and probably more varied jobs. There also appears to be a broad correlation with perceptions of political efficacy. Those in the working class are more likely than those in the middle class to consider that governments are not particularly able to change things.[11]

There also is a significant, and much charted, relationship between class and partisan support: The middle class has traditionally preferred the Conservative party and the working class the Labour party. The relationship is not exact and is declining, but—as we shall see in later chapters—remains important. The relationship is not that surprising, given that those in the middle class are more likely to occupy better paid jobs and consequently able to pursue a preferred lifestyle than those in working-class positions; hence, as the "haves" in society, they are more likely to prefer the party that is more oriented to maintaining the status quo. The "have-nots" are more likely to support a party favoring a change to the existing system. This hypothesis has largely been borne out by the empirical evidence,[12] though the relationship—as we shall see—is not as strong as it once was.

The nature of particular jobs also may influence other values. Those who are employed as part of a large factory work force are more likely to imbue values of social and political solidarity than those who occupy isolated positions, with little contact with fellow workers. Those employed in the armed services are taught the importance of discipline. Those employed in the private sector are more likely to acquire an attachment to private enterprise than those employed in the public sector.

In many, if not most, cases the experience of occupation serves to reinforce values acquired through family, children seeing themselves occupying the same social stratum as their parents and taking up jobs that maintain them in that same social stratum. Again, though, as we have noted, there is some change, with a degree of class mobility, especially upward mobility.

Location

Location also can be important in the process of political socialization. Living in an area of expensive detached houses can serve to reinforce one's sense of being middle class. The area provides a social milieu that reinforces that awareness. Conversely, living in an area of terraced public accommodation can reinforce one's identification with the working class. Within such areas, there is often a particular lifestyle.

The independent influence of location is borne out when correlated with partisan support. As Miller found: "At a minimum, the class characteristics of the social environment have more effect on constituency partisanship than class differences themselves, perhaps much more. The partisanship of individuals is influenced more by where they live than what they do."[13] As we shall see in chapter 5, there also is a correlation between party support and urban and rural locations and between party and region.

The values that may be reinforced or shaped by location are not confined to political partisanship and class. People living in small, self-sufficient rural communities are likely to have different values than those confined to overcrowded and largely transient urban areas. Those living in areas of high ethnic concentration are more likely to exhibit overt racist traits than those not living in such areas. Those who live in small, tightly-knit communities for decades are more likely to have a different view of life than those who lead a peripatetic existence. Britain, as we have seen, occupies a relatively small land mass but nonetheless exhibits a number of significant regional variations.

Mass Media

The mass media of communication—principally television, radio, and news-papers—also are important agents of socialization. They constitute the most used sources for acquiring knowledge of what is going on in society. As in the United States, television in Britain constitutes the most used source.[14] Perceptions of the reliability of the different media also are similar in both countries: One survey of Americans in the 1980s found that, given conflicting reports from different media, 53% of respondents would consider television the most believable; a similar survey in the United Kingdom found 57% giving the same response.[15]

The media can serve, deliberately or otherwise, to reinforce, and possibly even change, values. Reinforcement is more likely given evidence that readers and viewers are likely to engage in a process of selective retention, selecting those items that reinforce existing beliefs (see chapter 14). That reinforcement also can take the form of bolstering the legitimacy of existing institutions and processes. As we shall see, media exposure also can serve to have a "magnetizing" effect on partisan preferences. Most newspaper readers choose a paper whose partisan stance is in line with their own partisanship or, for young people, with that of their parents. Butler and Stokes, in their seminal but now dated study, found that when the children absorbed and accepted the preferences of their parents, they continued to read the same newspaper.[16]

A Complex Mix

The process of socialization is a complex and continuous one. The influences just outlined are the most important but they are not the only influences, nor are they mutually exclusive. Usually the reverse: They clearly interact and, more often than not, will reinforce one another. Parents remain the most important influence. Parental influence usually will be reinforced by the choice of newspaper and often by the choice of school and job. However, the influences are not always reinforcing: Social mobility, marriage into a family with different values, and exposure to certain programs or stories in the media may challenge received parental wisdom. Parental values may conflict with prevailing social norms: the belief in arranged marriages in traditional Indian families, for example, in a society where the belief in free choice for individuals prevails. Nor are the influences themselves necessarily static. Educational opportunities have changed during the twentieth century, economic conditions have changed, and the mass media have developed, with the broadcast media assuming a new and central significance.

The importance of various of these changes, especially for partisan support, will be touched upon later in this volume. However, the changes we have mentioned are relative. In terms of the basic values being transmitted, the most significant feature is not change but continuity. There are differences in social and political values. We have illustrated the media of socialization in terms particularly of structuring social class and partisanship. There is, though, some convergence on a number of basic values. It is that convergence that provides the essential British political culture. In identifying the media of socialization, we have not identified those basic values. To know the media through which values and beliefs that coalesce to form the political culture are transmitted is useful but does not serve to identify the culture itself.

THE POLITICAL CULTURE

In his work on political oppositions in Western democracies, Robert Dahl observed that patterns of opposition may have something to do with widely shared cultural premises. He noted that four kinds of culturally derived orientations toward politics seem to have a bearing on the pattern of opposition.[17] Those four orientations can usefully be employed not only to help one understand and explain attitudes toward political opposition in Britain but also to identify the fundamental characteristics of the political culture. They enable one to draw out the distinctive features of that culture and to consider the impact of both history and resources. Those four orientations, listed not in the order provided by Dahl but in the order I believe to be most significant to an understanding of the British political culture, are toward (1) problem solving, (2) the political system, (3) cooperation and individuality, and (4) other people.

Orientation toward Problem Solving

Giovanni Sartori has distinguished two approaches to problem solving: the empirical and the rational.[18] The empirical approach is concerned with what is and what can be seen and touched, proceeding on the basis of testing and retesting and largely rejecting dogma and abstract or coherent grand designs for change. The rationalist approach, by contrast, is concerned with abstraction rather than facts, stressing the need for deductive consistency and tending to be dogmatic and definitive. According to Dahl, ''While the empirical approach takes the attitude that if a program does not work in practice there must be something wrong about the theory, the rationalist will retort that what is true in theory must also be true in practice—that it is the practice, not the theory, that is wrong.''[19]

France has been identified as employing a rationalist approach. Germany and Italy, to some extent, also tend to find such an approach useful. Britain and the United States, by contrast, are seen as the exemplars of an empirical approach.

Indeed, it is my contention that this approach is *most* marked in the British case and that it constitutes the most significant aspect of British political culture.

Although oriented more toward an empirical approach, the United States has exhibited some elements of the rationalist. Although tempered by experience and (according to Beard) self-interest, the framers of the U.S. Constitution were informed by Lockean values and sought to impose a political framework in line with a Lockean conception of society.[20] Those values and that conception of society have permeated the American consciousness, so much so that they have largely gone unstated. They have been so pervasive and so self-evident that there has been little point in articulating them. Hence, the United States might be described as being oriented toward a mix of the empirical and the rationalist, albeit with the former being clearly the more dominant of the two.

Britain, by contrast, has a distinct orientation toward the empirical approach. Even the political system, however strong the attachment to it, tends to be justified in pragmatic terms. Democracy, having been implemented in largely pragmatic fashion, has been lauded on the grounds that "it works." The point has been well put by Vivien Hart in comparing U.S. and British approaches: "In America the emphasis has been on what democracy is and *should* be, while Britain has been characterised by a more pragmatic and less urgent emphasis on what democracy is and *can* be."[21] Empiricism seems appropriate to the English consciousness. Instinct, trial and error, and incremental change are the essence of the English approach to problem solving. "I believe in the instinctive wisdom of our well-tried democracy," declared Churchill in 1945—shortly before going down to election defeat.[22]

Such an orientation to problem solving has been a distinctive feature of *English* political culture for many centuries, discernible, I would suggest, since at least the thirteenth century. It is an approach that has informed political actions and hence the political history of the country. An empirical orientation in turn has been reinforced by the experience of history—it is the approach that has always been employed and no external constraints have managed to force themselves on the nation to generate conditions in which a rationalist approach would be possible. In the wake of the War of Independence, Americans were able to sit down and generate a political system from first principles. Invasions by foreign powers and subsequent liberation (or absence of liberation) have put other states in similar positions. England, by contrast, never has been faced with or sought such an opportunity. The closest it came was during the Protectorate of Oliver Cromwell in the seventeenth century. When that failed, the country resorted as far as possible to the conditions prevailing prior to its creation. English history is scattered with philosophers generating theories that have failed to find congenial soil in the nation's consciousness. Ideologies have been either discarded or else molded to fit with the experience of history. Prevailing theories, once they no longer seem appropriate, have been dispensed with. The act of dispensing with them has not always met with common assent nor has it always been smooth—the English historical landscape is scattered with periods of violence and upheaval—but once the dispensing process is achieved, it has largely been accepted. Hankering after the old order is congenial to some minds, but seeking to revert by force or civil unrest to the *status quo ante* is not. In the English perception, empiricism is both a descriptive and a prescriptive term. To the Briton, it is both what is and what he or she believes always has been.

Orientation toward the Political System

Orientation toward the political system may be classified as allegiant when attitudes, feelings, and evaluations are favorable to the political system; apathetic or detached when feelings and evaluations are neutral; and alienated when such feelings and evaluations are unfavorable.[23] Italy and France have been cited as examples of political cultures that generate alienation and a large measure of apathy. The former West Germany has been put forward as having a culture that generated detachment. In contrast, Britain and the United States are among those countries cited as exhibiting a strong allegiant orientation.[24]

Almond and Verba found that evaluation of the political system in Britain was the product of a mix of participant and deferential orientations. A participant orientation developed in Britain (citizens being oriented to the input as well as the output side of the political system, believing that they enjoyed access to it), but it was one adapted to the existing deference to the independent authority of government. The participant orientation did not displace the deferential;[25] deference remained important.

The participant orientation finds expression in citizens' beliefs that they can influence government at both national and local levels. Although Almond and Verba found few people in their survey who actually sought to exert such influence, the proportion who believed they *could* do so was significant. Of British respondents, approximately three out of five believed they could influence government. (Only the United States managed to produce a higher proportion.) The proportion believing they had no influence was only one in five. A 1974 survey by Barnes and Kaase showed that high levels of political efficacy remained in the 1970s,[26] and evidence from the 1985 and 1987 British Social Attitudes Reports suggested continuing high levels in the 1980s.[27] The level is important in absolute terms as well as relative terms: Almond and Verba found significantly lower levels in Germany, Italy, and Mexico, and Barnes and Kaase lower levels in the Netherlands and Austria.[28]

Deference to the authority of government has found expression in a number of ways. It has been shown in a voluntary compliance with laws passed by Parliament. Criminal acts tend to be antisocial rather than conscious acts against the state.[29] Indeed, the concept of the state is not well entrenched in English consciousness. (It is, though, important to stress *English* consciousness: As we shall see in chapter 9, a proportion of the citizenry in Scotland and Wales has expressed resentment toward what is seen as an "English" state, and in Northern Ireland some inhabitants do engage in explicit and violent antistate activity.) Recent decades have seen relatively little overt opposition, at least in Britain (as distinct from the United Kingdom), to the parliamentary form of government that exists. Some may want to modify its form but do not challenge the principle that underpins it, nor do they seek to change its form through unlawful or violent means. When government authority has been challenged, citizens have expressed themselves in favor of maintaining that authority.

Such deference often has been seen as allied with a social deference, citizens according certain skills of government to those drawn from a particular group. Walter Bagehot, in his classic work *The English Constitution,* identified England as a "deferential nation," one that had a structure of its own. "Certain persons," he wrote, "are by common consent agreed to be wiser than others, and their opinion is, by consent, to rank for much more than its numerical value."[30] Such deference, though in diluted form, survived into the era of mass suffrage and the democratic ideal. It has been seen as a significant feature of twentieth-century Britain and has been variously offered as a partial explanation of the continuing success of the Conservative party and its socially atypical leadership.[31]

Such deference, though, has been contingent rather than certain. It has been built on a reciprocity between governors and governed. The populace has deferred to the independent authority of government and to those who occupy government in return for the satisfaction of expectations. Those expectations have covered the substance of policies as well as the form and practices of government. Almond and Verba, for example, found that an overwhelming majority of Britons expected equal treatment from politicians and from bureaucrats.[32]

Conversely, those to whom citizens accord deference have been characterized as having a sense of duty and as recognizing their responsibility to others. A stress on responsibilities as well as rights has been seen as a significant characteristic of the British political elite and has been associated with a particular and often predominant tradition within the party that has been in government longer than any other party during the past century, the Conservative party (chapter 6).

The greater the perception of public service, exercised impartially, the greater the level of public trust. Confidence traditionally has been—and remains—high in the armed services and the police force. In 1991, for example, more than 90% of those questioned in a Gallup poll expressed "a great deal" or "quite a lot" of confidence in the armed forces; 75% expressed a great deal or quite a lot of confidence in the police. The percentage of respondents expressing no confidence at all did not exceed 10% for any of the institutions of the state mentioned (Parliament, civil service, the legal system), whereas for trade unions and the press the percentages were 24% and 28%, respectively.[33]

Orientation toward Cooperation and Individuality

Some cultures emphasize the values of cooperating with others, conciliating opposing views, and being prepared to compromise and submerge personal ideas in a broader and more popularly acceptable solution. Others, by contrast, stress the virtues of maintaining the distinctiveness, ideas, and integrity of the group or the individual, such virtues being considered superior to those of compromise and cooperation.[34]

Various countries and regions have been cited as exhibiting a noncooperative orientation, with the maintenance of group and individual integrity being stressed in both the general culture and political life. Dahl, for example, cited France and

Italy.[35] Highly visible examples in the 1990s include large parts of the Middle East, the Balkans, and, indeed, one part of the United Kingdom: Northern Ireland. Northern Ireland stands out as an atypical part of the United Kingdom. Britain, along with the United States, is among those countries in which the political culture emphasizes the virtues of compromise and conciliation, without threatening personal integrity. The Anglo-American perception was well expressed by Edmund Burke in 1775. "All government, indeed every human benefit and enjoyment, every virtue, and every prudent act," he declared, "is founded on compromise and barter."[36]

Given the relatively weak emphasis on what should be, as opposed to what can be, we would suggest that this orientation is more marked in Britain than in the United States. In Britain, there is an almost instinctive distaste for conflict, both in personal relationships and in political life. An adversarial relationship between political parties—the partisanship that we have already discussed—has tended to mask a general acceptance of the rules of the game under which that relationship operates. Though industrial relations often have been marked by a similar adversarial relationship, resolving disputes through bargaining has generally formed part of the culture of industrial life. There is almost a penchant for resolving disputes by discussion, by sitting around a table and ironing out differences. It is an orientation compatible with the others we have identified and is congenial to a society that stresses the responsibilities as well as the rights of the citizen. It is a predominant orientation: There are certainly exceptions, not least—as we have mentioned—in a particular part of the United Kingdom, but it is an orientation that remains a feature of British society, one that constitutes for many Britons a source of pride.

Orientation toward Other People

A belief that one can have confidence in others has been put forward as a culturally rooted phenomenon, with potentially important implications for political life. Research in the 1950s by Morris Rosenberg found that "faith in people" was related to democratic and internationalist values and attitudes.[37] In their study, Almond and Verba found that Americans and Britons "tend to be consistently more positive about the safety and responsiveness of the human environment."[38] The Germans and the Italians, by contrast, were found to be more negative, and the Mexicans inconsistent.

Surveys in recent years have shown that Britons retain a fairly positive view of themselves. A 1985 Gallup poll found that they regarded themselves as friendly, polite, hard-working, fun-loving, and with a sense of humor.[39] Eighty percent declared themselves to be very or quite proud of being British; the proportion was fairly well spread throughout different groups in society. Only 4% were not at all proud to be British. An earlier survey also found levels of pride to be higher in Britain than in other West European countries.[40]

Various surveys have found that Britons tend to regard other Britons as fairly trustworthy,[41] though trust in one's own nationality tends to be a feature of most countries of western Europe.[42] There are, though, some differences in levels of trust in other nationalities, though again a similar feature exists in other European countries. Britons tend to be more trusting of northern Europeans (Scandinavians, Danes, Germans, and Dutch) and Americans than southern Europeans (Spanish, Italians, and Greeks).[43] Britain's old historical enemy, the French, fall into the latter category. There are strong emotional ties to old Commonwealth countries such as Canada, New Zealand, and Australia. The positive orientation toward the United States and a number of Commonwealth countries is hardly surprising, partly for reasons of history and partly for reasons of language. Britons have tended to look toward the English-speaking world rather than to countries whose languages they have been reluctant to learn. The English and the Scots, as Anthony King has observed, have tended not to think like Europeans nor to think of themselves as Europeans.[44] This is relevant for understanding both the British political culture and the difficulties of Britain in adjusting to membership in the European Community. As we shall see (chapter 10), the United Kingdom has more often looked like a semidetached member of that Community than a fully integrated one.

Brtitons thus tend to have faith in themselves and a relatively discriminating faith in others. This is an important component of the political culture, though not one that renders Britain distinctive. It is the combination of orientations that renders the country distinct from the United States and from its European allies.

A DECLINING CIVIC CULTURE?

The political culture of Britain may then be characterized, in broad terms, as having the four orientations identified: empirical in terms of problem solving and change, allegiant in terms of the political system, cooperative in making decisions, and trusting in relation to fellow citizens and allies. These, it is important to stress, are generalizations. There are various subcultures that deviate from these orientations and some that do not share them all. Nor is the list of orientations exhaustive. There is a richness of cultural diversity not encompassed by these four principal orientations. A more detailed study would differentiate the political cultures of England, Scotland, and Wales. Furthermore, it is important to stress that it is the British political culture under discussion. As we shall see in chapter 9, it does not encompass the political culture of Northern Ireland. What is important for our purposes, though, is that the four orientations remain the orientations of *most* Britons, at both the mass and the elite levels.

The strength of the culture may be said to lie in the convergence of these orientations—that is, they are compatible with and reinforce one another, and similarly are compatible with and are reinforced by the experience of history. The stress on cooperation and compromise, an emphasis compatible with an empirical approach to change, has facilitated the integration of groups and individuals into the political system. Such integration may be seen as reinforcing an allegiant rather than a neutral or alienated orientation to the political system. History has been kind: The country has staved off invasion by its enemies, and the resources have been available for government to make and meet commitments in response to changing demands and expectations. As a result, it has been possible to interpret the experience of history as justifying or reinforcing an attachment to empirical problem solving and to the virtues of cooperation and trust. The interplay of these variables generated what Almond and Verba characterized as "the civic culture," "a pluralistic culture based on communication and persuasion, a culture of consensus and diversity, a culture that permitted change but moderated it."[45]

What of the contemporary civic culture? There are two conflicting analyses. One is that the civic culture is in decline. The other is that there has been no fundamental decline in the culture, but rather a misperception of that culture.

The argument that the civil culture is in decline has gained ground over the past 20 years. It was articulated especially by Samuel Beer in the 1980s and has been taken up since by a number of groups commited to constitutional reform. On the basis of some survey evidence, Beer concluded in 1982 that "it is no exaggeration to speak of a decline in the civic culture as a 'collapse'."[46] The orientations of the culture—the positive orientation toward institutions and cooperation—were diminishing, reflected in a conflict between elite and popular behavior. For Beer, as for constitutional reformers in the 1990s, a dysfunctional constitutional system is both cause and effect of this decline. Old institutions have been unable to meet expectations and to harness popular support. As institutions fail to meet those expectations, so trust in the effectiveness and equity of government diminishes. The greater the lack of trust, the greater the lack of cooperation, and hence the more government has to centralize power in order to meet its policy goals.

Empirical support for this thesis is found in a decline in political participation: Since the 1950s, the membership of political parties has declined and voter turnout has declined, as has the percentage of the population voting for the two main parties. Single-party governments have been elected on smaller percentages of the poll than before, sometimes no more, and on occasion even less, than 40%. The number of people believing the system of government does not work, or does not work well, has grown. In one survey in 1991, almost two-thirds of respondents said the system needed "quite a lot" or a "great deal" of improvement.[47] The existing system, according to the constitutional reform body, Charter '88, is locked into a spiral of decline. The civic culture can be restored only through a new constitutional settlement, with existing structures swept away and replaced by a political system that engages the participatory energies of citizens.[48]

The counter argument is that what has changed radically over the past 20 years or so is not the culture itself, but perceptions of that culture. Analyses of the political culture have swung, pendulum fashion, from one extreme to the other. At times of apparent stability, contentment, and political success, there has been a tendency to see the political culture in idealized terms, to hold it aloft as a culture to be admired, even envied. Although Almond and Verba drew attention to some of the inconsistencies and problems inherent in the civic culture, it was nonetheless difficult not to ascribe positive connotations to that culture.

At times of economic difficulty, there is a tendency to see it in a different light. Popular discontent with government starts to shade into discontent with the system of government itself. Evidence of discontent can then be read as suggesting a decline in the civic culture, a decline that can be reversed only by radical change to existing structures and relationships.

Concentration on immediate difficulties and on shifts, sometimes small shifts, in popular opinions and attitudes are—on this counterargument—given undue attention, masking the fact that the essential orientations of the culture remain strong. Far from participation declining, the cognitive mobilization identified by Inglehart has resulted in a population far more active than before. A massive growth in the number of organized groups has offered citizens new outlets for participation. And survey data, rather than proving the thesis of decline, can be utilized to demonstrate the continuing strength of that culture. Eight out of every ten citizens, according to one British Social Attitudes Survey, believe the democratic system works well and needs little or no change.[49] A similarly large number continue to think that Britain is an open society and that citizens' rights are very or fairly well protected.[50] And, as we have already seen in discussing the orientation toward the political system, there is survey data that would not suggest a "collapse" in confidence in existing institutions.

These competing analyses are basic to any study of contemporary British politics. They underpin, respectively, calls for—and a rejection of—a new constitutional settlement for the United Kingdom. We will variously have cause to refer to them in later chapters. They will form the basis of the concluding chapter, which will address the question, "Which is the most plausible analysis?"

NOTES

1. See D. Kavanagh, *Political Culture* (Macmillan, 1972), pp. 10–11.
2. Ibid., p. 10.
3. E. Jacobs and R. Worcester, *We British* (Weidenfeld & Nicolson, 1990), pp. 143–144.
4. See especially M. Franklin, *The Decline in Class Voting in Britain* (Oxford University Press, 1985), pp. 69–71, 78–79.
5. R. Rose and I. McAllister, *Voters Begin to Choose* (Sage, 1986), pp. 104–106.
6. Franklin, pp. 69–71, 78–79.
7. G. Almond and S. Verba, *The Civic Culture* (Princeton University Press, 1963), pp. 86–87.
8. R. Inglehart, *The Silent Revolution* (Princeton University Press, 1977).
9. R. Jowell, S. Witherspoon, and L. Brook, *British Social Attitudes: The 1987 Report* (Gower, 1987), p. 65.
10. D. Denver and G. Hands, "The Effects of 'A' Level Politics: Literacy, not Indoctrination," *Social Studies Review*, 4 (1), 1988, p. 40.
11. R. Jowell and S. Witherspoon, *British Social Attitudes: The 1985 Report* (Gower, 1985), p. 18. See also R. Jowell, S. Witherspoon, and L. Brook, *British Social Attitudes: Special International Report* (Gower, 1989), pp. 132–133.
12. R. J. Johnston, C. J. Pattie, and J. G. Allsopp, *A Nation Dividing?* (Longman, 1988), p. 49.
13. W. L. Miller, *Electoral Dynamics* (Macmillan, 1977). See also Johnston, Pattie, and Allsopp, pp. 61–63.
14. Jowell and Witherspoon (1985), p. 46.
15. Ibid., p. 47.
16. D. Butler and D. Stokes, *Political Change in Britain* (Penguin, 1971), pp. 281–300.
17. R. A. Dahl (ed.), *Political Opposition in Western Democracies* (Yale University Press, 1966), p. 353.

18. G. Sartori, *Democratic Theory* (Wayne State University Press, 1962), p. 233, cited in Dahl, p. 354.
19. Dahl, p. 355.
20. L. Hartz, *The Liberal Tradition in America* (Harcourt, Brace & World, 1955). For the analysis by Charles Beard, see C. Beard, *An Economic Interpretation of the Constitution* (Macmillan, 1913).
21. V. Hart, *Distrust and Democracy* (Cambridge University Press, 1978), pp. 202–203.
22. Eve of election broadcast, July 4, 1945.
23. Dahl, p. 353.
24. Almond and Verba, ch. 14.
25. Ibid., pp. 455–456.
26. Reproduced in D. P. Conradt, "Changing German Political Culture," in G. Almond and S. Verba (eds.), *The Civic Culture Revisited* (Little, Brown, 1980), p. 232.
27. Jowell and Witherspoon (1985), p. 12; Jowell, Witherspoon, and Brook (1987), p. 58.
28. Barnes and Kaase in Conradt; Almond and Verba, p. 186.
29. See R. N. Berki, *Security and Society* (Dent, 1986).
30. W. Bagehot, *The English Constitution* (first published 1867; Fontana, 1963 edition).
31. See, e.g., R. McKenzie and A. Silver, *Angels in Marble* (Heinemann, 1968); though see also P. Norton and A. Aughey, *Conservatives and Conservatism* (Temple Smith, 1981), pp. 176–177.
32. Almond and Verba, p. 108.
33. *Gallup Report 368,* April 1991.
34. Dahl, p. 354.
35. Ibid.
36. Speech on conciliation with the American Colonies, March 22, 1775.
37. M. Rosenberg, "Misanthropy and Political Ideology," *American Sociological Review,* 21, pp. 690–695; and "Misanthropy and Attitudes towards International Affairs," *Journal of Conflict Resolution,* 1, 1957, pp. 340–345, cited in Almond and Verba, p. 266.
38. Almond and Verba, p. 268.
39. G. Heald and R. J. Wybrow, *The Gallup Survey of Britain* (Croom Helm, 1986), p. 277.
40. Ninety-three percent of Britons, according to a 1983 Eurobarometer survey, were "very" or "quite proud" to be British, against an average in EC countries of 77%. *Eurobarometer,* June 1983.
41. N. Webb and R. Wybrow, *The Gallup Report* (Sphere Books, 1981), pp. 103–104; *Eurobarometer,* No. 33, June 1990, Table 14.
42. *Eurobarometer,* No. 33, June 1990, Table 14.
43. Webb and Wybrow, pp. 103–104; *Eurobarometer,* No. 33, June 1990, Table 14.
44. A. King, *Britain Says Yes* (American Enterprise Institute, 1977), p. 6. See also L. Barzini, *The Impossible Europeans* (Weidenfeld & Nicolson, 1983).
45. Almond and Verba, p. 8.
46. S. H. Beer, *Britain Against Itself* (Faber, 1982), p. 119.
47. P. Dunleavy and S. Weir, "Ignore the People at Your Peril," *The Independent,* April 25, 1991.
48. See especially D. Marquand, *The Unprincipled Society* (Fontana, 1988).
49. R. Jowell, S. Witherspoon, and L. Brook, *British Social Attitudes: Special International Report* (Gower, 1989), p. 133.
50. *The Guardian,* November 20, 1991, reporting the findings of the Eighth Report of the British Social Attitudes Survey.

CHAPTER **3**

Past and Present
Historical Perspective
and Contemporary Problems

A number of introductory texts on British politics do not have chapters devoted specifically to political history. The omission is a surprising one. When the proposal for this book was under consideration by the publishers, a number of U.S. professors were asked for their comments. One responded with this advice: "Make sure you incorporate as much historical detail as possible. American students don't know much about British history." The need for historical detail, however, is not confined to Americans interested in the subject; it encompasses all those who seek to make some sense of the institutions and complex relationships that form the British polity.

The country has witnessed continuous and sometimes dramatic change. In the past 300 years alone, the nation has experienced industrialization, the advent of democracy, and the introduction and growth of the welfare state—yet the changes have been built upon and have adapted that which already existed. The body politic may have undergone radical surgery and it may have aged considerably, but it has continued to endure.

What, then, are the significant features of British history that help us understand the contemporary political system and the political culture? Limitations of space preclude a lengthy dissertation on what is a vast subject. That vastness is apparent when put in comparative perspective. The *Magna Carta,* for instance, was signed more than two centuries before Christopher Columbus set sail. Parliament was summoned more than 500 years before the United States Congress first assembled. And a U.S. president, unlike a British monarch, cannot trace his forebears in office back more than 1,000 years. Nonetheless, it is possible to provide a brief but structured sketch that furthers our understanding of contemporary British politics. This can be done under two headings: the emergence of parliamentary government, and the development of the welfare state and managed economy. Under the latter can be subsumed the more recent challenge to the managed economy posed by Thatcherism.

HISTORICAL PERSPECTIVE

The Emergence of Parliamentary Government

One of the essential features of the British Constitution is a parliamentary government under a limited, or symbolic, monarchy. The formal elements of this type of government will be more fully outlined in the next chapter. For the moment, what concerns us is that this government is the product of change extending over several centuries, coming to fruition only in the past century. Its development sometimes has been characterized as being evolutionary, but in practice it is the outgrowth of piecemeal change.

Let us begin in the thirteenth century. Traditionally, the sovereign power in England resided in the monarch. Nonetheless, the king was expected to consult with his tenants-in-chief (the earls, barons, and leading churchmen of the kingdom) in order to discover and declare the law and to have the counsel before any levies of extraordinary taxation were made. This expectation was to find documented expression in the Great Charter (*Magna Carta*) of 1215, by which the king recognized it as a right of his subjects "to have the Common Council of the Kingdom" for the assessment of extraordinary aids—that is, taxation. Such consultation was undertaken through a Great Council, from which evolved what was to be recognized as a *parlement* or Parliament. The Great Council itself was essentially the precursor of the House of Lords. The House of Commons evolved from the summoning to council, in the latter half of the thirteenth century on a somewhat sporadic basis, of knights and burgesses as representatives of the counties and towns. At various times in the fourteenth century the Commons deliberated separately from the Lords, and there developed a formal separation of the two bodies.

During the period of the Tudor monarchs in the sixteenth century, Parliament acquired enhanced status. It was generally supportive of the monarch but became more powerful because the monarchs depended upon it for that support, especially during the reign of Elizabeth I. The relationship between Crown and Parliament under the subsequent Stuart dynasty was one of conflict. The early Stuart kings James I and Charles I sought to assert the doctrine of the divine right of kings and to deny many of the privileges acquired or asserted by Parliament. This conflict was to lead to the civil war and the beheading of Charles I in 1649. With the abolition of the monarchy came a brief period of rule by a Council of State elected by what was termed the Rump Parliament. (Some attempts were actually made to formulate what amounted to a written constitution, but they came to nothing.)[1] Rule by the Council of State was succeeded by Oliver Cromwell's unsuccessful military dictatorship, and in 1660 Charles's son returned to assume the throne as Charles II. The period between 1642 and 1660 proved an aberration in British history. The Restoration witnessed an attempt to return, unconditionally, to the country's position as it was at the beginning of 1642.[2] Through this attempt, the Restoration lent itself to a repetition of the earlier struggle between king and Commons. Relations between the two gradually deteriorated during the reign of Charles II and became severe in the reign of his successor, James II. James sought to reassert the divine right of kings, and Parliament combined against him. In 1688 James fled the country. At the invitation of Parliament, the throne was taken by William and Mary of Orange, James's son-in-law and daughter. The new occupants of the throne owed their position to Parliament, and the new relationship between them was asserted by statute in the Bill of Rights. Although the Bill of Rights was important for enumerating various "Liberties of this Kingdom" (some of which were to be similarly expressed during the following century in the Bill of Rights embodied in the United States Constitution),[3] its essential purpose was to assert the position of Parliament in relation to the Crown. The raising of taxes or the dispensing of laws without the assent of Parliament was declared to be illegal. The monarch was expected to govern, but to do so only with the consent of Parliament. The Act of Settlement of 1701, which determined the succession to the throne, affirmed that the laws of England "are the Birthright of the People thereof and all the Kings and Queens who shall ascend the Throne of this Realm ought to administer the Government of the same according to the said Laws and all their Officers and Ministers ought to serve them respectively according to the same."

The monarch thus became formally dependent on Parliament for consent to the raising of taxes and for the passage of legislation. In practice, he or she became increasingly dependent also on ministers for advice. The importance of ministers grew especially in the eighteenth century. The Hanoverian kings were not uninterested in political life but they had difficulty comprehending the complexities of domestic and foreign affairs. According to the historian J. H. Plumb, both George I and George II were "crassly stupid" and "incapable, totally incapable, of forming a policy."[4] During the period of their reigns, the leading body of the king's ministers, generally known as the cabinet, began to meet without the king being present.[5] The period also witnessed the emergence of a minister who was to become popularly known as the prime minister. (Not until the twentieth century, though, was the office of prime minister to be mentioned in a statute.) The relationship among Crown, ministers, and Parliament in the century was one in which the king relied on his ministers to help formulate policy. Those ministers were chosen by the king on the basis of his personal confidence in them, and they remained responsible to him. They also were responsible to Parliament in order to achieve their ends, a fact recognized by both the king and his ministers. Nonetheless, parliamentary support was not difficult to obtain; the king and his ministers had sufficient patronage and position usually to ensure such support. A ministry that enjoyed royal confidence could generally take the House of Lords for granted, and provided it did not prove incompetent or seek to impose excessive taxation, "its position was unassailable in the Commons."[6] The position was to change significantly in the nineteenth century.

Britain underwent what has been popularly referred to as an industrial revolution from the middle of the eighteenth century to the middle of the nineteenth. Seymour Martin Lipset has characterized the United States as the "first new nation," but Britain has been described as "the first industrial nation."[7] Industry became more mechanized, improvements took place in agricultural production techniques, and there were improvements in transport and the organization of trade and banking. There was a notable growth in the size of cities, particularly in the early part of the nineteenth century. Men of industry and commerce began to emerge as men of some wealth. In 1813 Robert Owen referred to the "working class," a term brought into common speech by Lord Brougham.[8] By the 1830s, a nonlanded middle class, artisans, and an industrial work force were important constituents of the country's population.

Parliament remained dominated by the aristocracy and by the landed gentry. Representation in the House of Commons was heavily weighted in favor of the rural counties. Some parliamentary constituencies had only a handful of electors: Known as "rotten boroughs," they were often in the pocket of an aristocrat or local landowner.[9] Pressure for some parliamentary reform, with a redistribution of seats and a widening of the franchise, began to develop. It was argued that a Parliament full of men of wealth and property was unlikely to view industry, trade, and agriculture from the point of view of the laboring classes. Rotten boroughs were criticized as being used by the ministry to help maintain a majority. Unrest in a number of areas, both agricultural and industrial, and the French Revolution of 1830 (a spur to radical action) increased the pressure for change. One political group in particular, the Whigs, who had been the "outs" in politics for the 25 years prior to 1830, began to see the need for some response to this pressure. The concession of some parliamentary reform was seen as necessary in order to prevent worse happenings. The result, following the return of the Whigs to power, was to be the Reform Act of 1832.

The Reform Act, introduced, ironically, by the most aristocratic government of the century, reorganized parliamentary constituencies and extended the franchise. The electorate increased in size from a little under 500,000 to 813,000 electors.[10] Although much remained the same as before—the new electorate constituted but one-thirtieth of the population, 31 boroughs still had fewer than 300 electors in each, voting remained by open ballot (secret ballots were considered rather un-English), and the aristocracy still held great sway politically— the act precipitated important changes both within and outside the House of Commons.

The redistribution of seats and the extension of the franchise helped loosen the grip of the aristocracy and of ministers on the House of Commons. The size of the new electorate encouraged the embryonic development of political organizations. Members of Parliament (MPs) became less dependent on aristocratic patrons without acquiring too great a dependence on the growing party organizations. The result was to be a House of Commons with a greater legitimacy in the eyes of MPs and electors and with an ability to assert itself in its relationship with government. The House proved willing to amend or reject legislation put before it as well as to remove individual ministers, and on occasion the government itself. In his classic work on the constitution, Walter Bagehot attached much importance to this "elective function"; the House of Commons, he declared, was "a real choosing body: it elects the people it likes. And it dismisses whom it likes too."[11] Debates in the House really counted for something and, with the exception of the period from 1841 to 1846, party cohesion was almost unknown. The House of Commons did not itself govern, but government was carried on within the confines of its guidance and approval.

The period after 1832 also witnessed important changes in the relationships within and among the different elements of Crown, government, and Parliament. The monarch retained the formal prerogative power to appoint the prime minister, but the changed political circumstances essentially dictated that the person chosen should be able to command a majority in the House of Commons. Royal favor ceased to be an essential condition for forming the government. Within Parliament, the relationship between the two Houses also changed. Members of the House of Lords sat by virtue of birth, holding hereditary peerages. The acceptance of the Commons as the "representative" chamber undermined the authority of the peers to challenge or negate the wishes of the other House. After the 1830s, the Lords tended to be somewhat restrained in their attacks on government measures. "This," as Mackintosh noted, "followed from the view that while a ministry retained the confidence of the elected representatives it was entitled to remain in office. The peers on the whole accepted these assumptions, though many found the explicit recognition of the situation hard to bear."[12] The Lords' remaining authority was in practice to be removed in consequence of the 1867 Reform Act, though not until the twentieth century was the House forced formally to accept its diminished status.

Whereas the 1832 act helped ensure the dominance of the House of Commons within the formal political process, the passage of the Reform Act of 1867 began a process of the transfer of power from Parliament to ministers. The act itself was the product of demands for change because of the limited impact of the 1832 act and because of more immediate political considerations.[13] Its effect was to increase the size of the electorate from 1,358,000 to 2,477,000. (The number had grown since 1832 because of increased wealth and population.) Other significant measures followed in its wake. Secret voting was introduced by the Ballot Act of 1872. Other acts sought to prohibit as far as possible corrupt practices and limited the amount of money a candidate could spend on election expenses. Single-member districts (known in Britain as constituencies) of roughly equal electoral size were prescribed as the norm.[14] The 1884 Representation of the People Act extended the franchise to householders and tenants and to all those who occupied land or tenements with an annual value of not less than 10 pounds. The effect of the act was to bring into being an electorate in which working men were in a majority. The consequence of these developments was to be party government.

The size of the new electorate meant that the voters could be reached only through some well-developed organization, and the result was to be the growth of organized and mass-membership political parties. The Conservative National Union and the National Liberal Federation were formed to facilitate and encourage the support of the new electors. However, contact with the voters was insufficient in itself to entice their support. Not only had a large section of the population been enfranchised, but also it was a notably different electorate from that which had existed previously. The new class of electors had different and greater demands than those of the existing middle-class electors. If the votes of working men were to be obtained, the parties had to offer them something. And the parties could fulfill their promises only if they presented a uniform program to the electorate and achieved a cohesive majority in the House of Commons to carry through that program. What this was to produce was a shift of power away from the House of Commons to the cabinet and the electorate, with political parties serving as the conduit for this transfer.

The electorate proved too large and too politically unsophisticated to evaluate the merits of an individual MP's behavior. Political parties provided the labels with which electors could identify, and elections became gladiatorial contests between parties rather than between individual candidates. The all-or-nothing spoils of an election victory and the method of election encouraged (if not always produced) a contest between two major parties.[15] And having voted for party candidates, the electors expected the members returned to Parliament to support the program offered by their leaders at the election. Party cohesion soon became a feature of parliamentary life.[16] The House of Commons in effect lost two of the most important functions ascribed to it by Bagehot, those of legislation and of choosing the government: The former passed to the cabinet and the latter to the electorate. The cabinet constituted the leaders of the party enjoying a parliamentary majority. It assumed the initiative for the formulation and introduction of measures of national policy and became increasingly reluctant to be overruled by the House. The growth in the number and complexity of bills further limited the influence of the individual MP. Increasingly, his role became one of supporting his leaders. The cabinet previously had rested its authority on the support of the House; now it derived its authority from the electors. As Mackintosh states, ''The task of the House of Commons became one of supporting the Cabinet chosen at the polls and passing its legislation. . . . By the 1900s, the Cabinet dominated British government.''[17]

Further modifications and addenda took place in the first half of the twentieth century. The House of Lords was forced by statute in 1911 to accept its diminished status. The franchise was variously extended, most notably to half the population previously excluded because of their sex. (The first female MP to take her seat in the House of Commons did so in 1919.) The monarch's political influence further receded. The growth and increasing economic weight of groups generated more extensive and complex demands of government. And the size of government grew as its responsibility expanded.

Basically, though, the essential features of the political system were those established in the preceding century. The responsibility for making public policy rested with the government, a government derived from and resting its support upon a political party. That same party's majority in the House of Commons ensured that the government's measures were approved. Formal and political constraints limited the effect of any opposition from the House of Lords. The monarch gave formal assent to any legislative measure approved by the two houses. Thus, within the formal framework of deciding public policy, the government was dominant. The role of Parliament became largely but not wholly one of legitimating the measures put before it. For the monarch, that became the exclusive role (that is, in respect of legislation). Government, as we shall see, operated within a political environment that imposed important constraints, but the limitations imposed formerly by Parliament and the monarch were largely eroded. Britain retained a parliamentary form of government, but what that meant was not government by Parliament but government through Parliament.

The Welfare State and the Managed Economy

To comprehend some of the problems faced by contemporary British government, it is necessary to know not only the structure and relationships of the political system but also the popular expectations and the burden of responsibilities borne by government. Those expectations and responsibilities have not been static. Just as the governmental structure has been modified in response to political demands, so the responsibilities of government have grown as greater social and economic demands have been made of it.

Toward the end of the nineteenth century and more so in the twentieth, the responsibilities of government expanded. In part this expansion was attributable to the growth of the empire. (As prime minister in the 1870s, Benjamin Disraeli had played the "imperial card," the British empire expanding rapidly: By 1900 it covered virtually a quarter of the globe.) It was also attributable to the increasing demands and expectations of the newly enfranchised working population. Government began to conceive its duties as extending beyond those of maintaining law and order and of defending the realm. The statute book began to expand, with the addition of measures of social reform. Various such measures were enacted prior to 1867, though the most notable were to be enacted in the remaining decades of the century. They included measures to limit working hours for women and children, to improve housing and public health, to make education for children compulsory, to provide for the safety of workers (including the payment of compensation by employers in the event of accidents at work), and even to extend the right to strike.[18] Such measures, exploited for electoral advantage, were within the capabilities of the government to provide. They did not create too great an economic burden; they were not themselves economic measures.

The growth of expectations and the greater willingness of government to intervene in areas previously considered inviolate was to be continued and become more marked in the twentieth century. The general election of 1906 was something of a watershed in British politics. It was the first election to be fought essentially on national issues and it witnessed the return not only of a reforming Liberal government but also, and in some respects more significantly, of 27 Labour MPs. The Labour party had been created for the purpose of ensuring working-class representation in Parliament, and from 1906 onward class became a significant influence in voting behavior. The nature of electoral conflict changed as the Labour party succeeded the Liberal as the main opposition party to the Conservatives. The franchise was further extended, notably in 1918 and 1928, and new expectations were generated by the experience of the two world wars.

During the First World War (1914–1918), socialists within the Labour party argued the case for the conscription of wealth (public ownership) to accompany the conscription of labor (the drafting of men into the armed forces). Politicians fueled rather than played down the belief that Britain should become, in the words of one politician, "a land fit for heroes" once "the war to end all wars" was won—in other words, that provision should be made for those who had fought for king and country. The period of the Second World War (1939–1945) witnessed a significant shift of attitudes by a sizable fraction of the electorate. One informed estimate was that by December 1942 about two out of the five people had changed their political outlook since the beginning of the war.[19] Opinion was moving toward the left of the political spectrum. There was a reaction against (Conservative) government unpreparedness for war in the 1930s and against those who had not done more to solve the nation's problems during the depression. There was support for calls for equality of sacrifice. There was some degree of goodwill toward the Soviet Union as a wartime ally. There was also, very importantly, the enhanced position of the Labour party. It had entered into coalition in 1940 (its leader, Clement Attlee, became deputy prime minister to Churchill) and had demonstrated its claim to be a capable partner in government. As the 1940s progressed, there developed a notable movement, including within the Conservative party, for a greater degree of social and economic intervention by government. This was to find some authoritative expression during the war years themselves and especially in the years after 1945, when a general election resulted in the return of the first Labour government with a clear working majority in the House of Commons. The 1940s and the 1950s were to produce what Samuel Beer has referred to as the welfare state and the managed economy, or what some commentators have referred to as the period of the social democratic consensus.

The welfare state and the managed economy did not suddenly emerge full-blown in this period. The preceding decades had not witnessed governments unresponsive to electoral expectations and the nation's problems. The Liberal government before the First World War had made the first tentative steps in the introduction of old-age pensions (1908) and national health and unemployment insurance (1911). The interwar years had seen the introduction of a number of significant measures of social reform, especially those associated with a Conservative, Neville Chamberlain, as minister of health. He proposed to the cabinet 25 measures and secured the enactment of 21 of them. These included unemployment insurance, public health and housing, and the extension of old-age pensions. Much of this legislation, as one biographer noted, "has an important place in the development of the Welfare State."[20] The Conservative government also began to engage in certain measures of economic management. It embarked on a protectionist policy and, in return for the grant of a tariff to an industry, demanded that its major producers reorganize themselves. Such producers were encouraged to reduce capacity and maintain prices. The gold standard was abandoned, the pound was devalued, and interest rates were lowered. The government even proved willing to take certain industries into public ownership: broadcasting, overseas airways, and the electricity-generating industry. By indulging in such policies, Beer has contended, government was beginning to move in the direction of a managed economy.[21] The movement, though, was modest. Government adhered to the prevailing orthodoxy that balanced budgets were necessary and desirable and that deficit financing was neither. Ministers showed little desire to emulate the innovative approach adopted in the United States by Franklin Roosevelt during the period of the first New Deal. (Indeed, Conservative leader Stanley Baldwin commented at one point that the United States Constitution had broken down and was giving way to dictatorship.)[22] Britain and the United States were similar, though, in that both were to be brought out of the depression of the 1930s not by government economic policies but by rearmament and the Second World War.

Two major documents published in the war years provided the planks for the final emergence of the welfare state and managed economy. These were the Report on Social Insurance and Allied Services by Sir William Beveridge (the so-called Beveridge Report), published in November 1942, and the White Paper on Full Employment, published in 1944. The former proposed a comprehensive scheme of social security, one to provide "social insurance against interruption and destruction of earning power and for special expenditure arising at birth, marriage or death."[23] The latter was significant because of its opening pledge: "The Government accepts as one of their primary aims and responsibilities the maintenance of a high and stable level of employment after the war." There was also one particularly significant measure of social reform enacted during wartime: the 1944 Education Act, pioneered by R. A. Butler. It provided for the division among primary, secondary, and higher education—and, within secondary education, between secondary modern and grammar schools—that was to form the basis of the educational system for almost a generation.

The welfare state was brought to fruition by the establishment of the National Health Service (NHS) in 1948, entailing the nationalization of hospitals and the provision of free medical treatment, and also by the passage of the 1945 Family Allowance Act, the 1946 National Insurance Act, and the 1948 National Assistance Act. The principle enunciated by the Beveridge Report was largely put into practice. National insurance ensured a certain level of benefit in the event of unemployment or sickness. For those who required special help there was "national assistance," the provision of noncontributory benefits dispensed on the basis of means-testing. There were family allowances for those with children. The state now provided something of a protective safety net from the cradle to the grave. It was still possible to pay for private treatment in the health service, but for most people it was a case of having treatment "on the national health." The NHS became a feature of some pride at home and of considerable interest abroad.

Acceptance and usage of techniques pioneered by the economist J. M. Keynes ushered in the managed economy. Government accepted responsibility for keeping aggregate monetary demand at a level sufficient to ensure full employment or what was considered as far as possible to constitute full employment (an unemployment rate of 1% or 2% was considered acceptable), and the annual budget was to be used as the main instrument of economic policy. The Labour government proved unwilling to pursue a more overtly socialist approach; physical controls acquired during wartime were eventually discarded and those industries that were nationalized, such as steel, the mines, and the railways, were basically essential and loss-making concerns. Government was prepared to pursue a managed rather than a controlled economy.

The Conservative party was returned to office in 1951 and was to remain there until 1964. It accepted, or appeared to accept, both the welfare state and Keynesian models of demand management. Indeed, it gave the impression of making a success of both. As heir to the Disraelian belief in elevating the condition of the people and as a party seeking to enhance its image among working-class voters, the Conservative party could claim both a principled and a practical motive for maintaining the innovations of its predecessor. At the same time, it was reluctant to pursue policies that would increase the tax burden or the public sector of the economy. Good fortune was with the government: World economic conditions improved and heralded a period of sustained growth in industrial output and trade. Government revenue was such that not only was it possible to sustain and indeed expand expenditure on the National Health Service, but also it was possible to do so without substantial increases in taxation. Indeed, reductions rather than increases in tax rates were a feature of the period. There was an extensive and successful house-building program. Economic prosperity allowed government to maintain peace with the labor unions by allowing high wage settlements. It was also possible finally to abandon many of the controls maintained since wartime. Government was able to claim to have maintained full employment, an expanding economy, stable prices, and a strong pound. Despite the agonies of withdrawing from the imperial period of empire and various undulations in economic performance, the 1950s was seen more than anything as "an age of affluence."[24] In July 1957 Prime Minister Harold Macmillan was able to declare that, for most of the people, "You've never had it so good."

The 1960s witnessed a downturn in economic performance and a growing realization that, in comparative terms, Britain was faring less well than many of her continental neighbors. The Conservative government of Harold Macmillan responded with various novel proposals, including indicative economic planning and an application to join the European Economic Community. The succeeding Labour government of Harold Wilson, returned to office in 1964, sought a more comprehensive method of national economic planning as part of its grand design of modernization. Inflation and unemployment became more visible problems.

Despite the economic problems and some unrelated political problems of the 1960s, the country remained a relatively prosperous one. Living conditions continued to improve. The rise in wages exceeded the rise in inflation. Where economic conditions impinged on the ability to maintain the welfare state, it was essentially at the margin: Government imposed nominal charges for medicines obtained on NHS prescriptions. Parties tended to argue more about means rather than ends. The consensus that developed in the 1950s remained intact.

The Era of Thatcherism

The first attempt to break away from that consensus was made by the Conservative government of Edward Heath, which was returned to office in 1970. There was an emphasis on the withdrawal of government from economic activity and an attempt, ultimately unsuccessful, to curb trade union power. The aim was to force British industry to be more competitive. This goal also provided some of the motivation for British membership in the European Community, which Heath achieved in 1972. However, the government's measures failed to stem a rise in inflation, and when unemployment reached record levels, the government embarked on a new interventionist policy, including the imposition of a pay and prices policy. The government lost office in 1974.

The return of another Conservative government five years later saw a more determined effort by Heath's successor as party leader, Margaret Thatcher, to achieve a free-market economy and to move away from, indeed dismantle, the postwar consensus. The Thatcher government heralded a break with its predecessors both in terms of style and substance. The prime minister in particular adopted a combative style of government in pursuit of her goal: a rolling back of the frontiers of the state. Government intervention was seen as economically harmful, stifling initiative and the creative forces of the market. Various policies were pursued in an attempt to achieve this goal.

In terms of substantive changes, the most significant was the reduction in the size of the public sector. Various utilities and companies previously taken into public ownership were privatized (that is, sold back to the private sector), a policy also pursued by the government of Thatcher's successor, John Major. Between 1979 and 1992, 46 major companies were privatized, including the telephone, gas, water, and electricity utilities. Among them, the 46 companies employed almost 1 million workers. The size of the public sector thus contracted.

The emphasis on a market economy also led to reductions in income tax (to the basic rates detailed in chapter 1); to curbs on trade union power; to ensuring wider private ownership (not only of shares but also of housing); to the introduction of a greater market orientation for bodies remaining in the public sector, including local government and the national health service; and to greater autonomy in policy making by government. Organized economic interests that previously had been effectively co-opted in economic policy making were kept at arm's length. By the end of Margaret Thatcher's tenure of office in 1990, the nature of government and of public debate and the division between public and private sectors had changed significantly. Political parties were forced to work on the basis of a new political agenda.

Yet the Thatcher government was as important for what it tried to do as much as for what it did do. It sought to achieve what amounted to a "cultural revolution." "The public had to be persuaded to lower its expectations of, and dependence on, the state; the social democratic consensus had to be replaced by a new neoliberal consensus."[25] In practice, the Thatcher government failed to achieve a free-market economy and a new popular attitude that would sustain such an economy. The economy became more market oriented than before, but that was the extent of the achievement: No fundamental shift of attitudes occurred.

Margaret Thatcher, despite periods of tremendous strength during her 11.5 years as prime minister, was never able to mold a party and a cabinet completely committed to her neoliberal philosophy (see chapter 6). Many of the government's policies were not as radical as she wanted. Subsidies to public sector industries were maintained. Mechanisms for controlling the money supply were less than adequate to the task. When the economy went into recession, the Conservative government under Thatcher's successor opted for budget deficits and a shift of emphasis from fighting inflation to pursuing growth.

There was no social revolution, resulting in established social position being displaced by a new meritocracy, nor in a paradigmatic shift of attitudes. A survey by the *Economist* in 1992 found little change, compared with the position 20 years before, in the dominant position of public school and Oxbridge graduates in the top posts in business, the arts, and the professions. In some areas, a number of people had made it to the top from humble backgrounds, including Prime Minister John Major. "But change has not just been slow. It has been almost non-existent."[26]

There was similarly little move toward values espoused by Margaret Thatcher—if anything, the reverse. Ten years after Mrs. Thatcher came to power, a survey of popular attitudes found that, asked to choose between a Thatcherite and a "socialist" society, respondents opted for the Thatcherite model on only two out of five dimensions, and then only by slender majorities. Indeed, over the decade, opinion on some issues had moved away from a Thatcherite position: Asked to chose between cutting taxes and extending public services, opinion in 1979 was equally divided; ten years later, those favoring extending services outnumbered tax cutters by a margin of seven to one.[27] Where Margaret Thatcher carried, and sometimes increased, support was on issues on which she already had prevailing public support when she entered office.

Margaret Thatcher thus failed to create a new polity. She had brought about significant changes in British society, but the most significant feature of British society in 1990 was not so much change but, given what Thatcher had set out to achieve, continuity. Political pressures resulted, as we shall see, in Thatcher's loss of the premiership (chapter 6). Her successor as Conservative prime minister continued a number of her innovative policies, including those on privatization, but sought neither to emulate her style nor to pursue her particular vision of future society.

THE CURRENT DEBATE

In the 1950s and 1960s, Britain, as we have noted, experienced relative economic decline. Given that it was relative rather than absolute, the implications were hazily rather than fully grasped. Since 1970, there has been greater awareness of Britain's problems. During the 1970s, inflation reached record levels (peaking at 27%) and the country had the lowest growth rate of the major industrialized nations. Despite a relative improvement in the 1980s, the annual growth rate still trailed behind the average for the big industrial seven and the nation's manufacturing base declined (see chapter 1). In 1991, the "growth" rate was a negative one (-2% compared with 1990), worse than the figure for the United States, which also experienced negative growth (almost - 1%); Italy, France, and Germany experienced growth rates of between 1% and 4%. The United Kingdom also had the highest unemployment rates.

The past 20 years have seen a major debate as to the cause of the nation's failure to catch up with, and surpass, the performance of its international competitors. The diagnoses have been several, but can be grouped under three, albeit not exclusive, heads: economic, sociological, and structural.

Economic

Three explanations can be subsumed under this particular head: the legacy of the empire, the legacy of the Second World War, and the legacy of the post-war consensus.

Some economists have laid the blame for economic failure at least partially on the emphasis given by successive governments to maintaining a balance of payments surplus in order to fund overseas military commitments and foreign investments, a policy pursued at the expense of economic growth.[28] A consequence of the empire has been that Britain has tended to retain a number of overseas commitments beyond what many regard as its financial capacity to do so, and to continue to harbor international pretensions. Despite a reduction in overseas commitments, the United Kingdom retains interests beyond those of the North Atlantic alliance, resulting in various occasions in the committal of troops: as in the Falkland Islands in 1982, in the Gulf War in 1991, and in Bosnia in 1992.

Another economic explanation for poor economic performance is a failure to modernize. There has been a tendency to retain old plants and to rely on traditional but declining industries, such as textiles. There is a popular view that the Second World War was, for Britain, a military success but an economic disaster. The country was left in serious debt, primarily to the United States,[29] and with a large portion of its industrial plant still intact. There was neither the capacity nor the incentive to start afresh; a number of other countries had no option but to begin anew, both politically and economically.

The third explanation is compatible with the second. This views the economic policies pursued by postwar governments as creating a dependency culture as well as maintaining, indeed strengthening, vested interests and restrictive practices. Under this analysis, government has not been part of the solution but rather part of the problem. This analysis, as we have seen, found favor with the Conservative party under Margaret Thatcher and provided the basis for the neoliberal economic policy pursued in the period of Thatcher government from 1979 to 1990.

All three explanations remain current. Despite diversification and inward investment, with many new Japanese car plants and high-technology industries, there remains much old plant and residual attachment to established industries. An attempt to close most of Britain's remaining coal pits in 1992, for example, evoked an angry public and parliamentary response, forcing the government to compromise. When attempts were made, following the collapse of the Iron Curtain, to reap the "peace dividend" by reducing the size of Britain's armed services, there was sustained opposition from many politicians who believed the cuts threatened Britain's capacity to maintain its global influence. And, following Margaret Thatcher's departure from the premiership in 1990, there were various claims by her supporters that her policies, far from failing to produce the desired results, had shown what could be achieved in tackling inflation and an overgrown state and that what was required was not less, but rather more, of the same. Opponents claimed that the era of Thatcherite economics, far from solving the nation's problems, had eroded the nation's manufacturing base, leaving it less well equipped than ever before to face the economic challenges of its international competitors.

Sociological

Some explanations of decline have been primarily sociological. As we have seen in chapter 1, class did not displace status in British society. Preindustrial aristocratic attitudes were carried over into an industrial age. These attitudes included looking down on the pursuit of "trade" as somewhat socially inferior. Low priority was given to industry and science and, so this analysis goes, a tendency grew for those with wealth to favor professions such as the law.[30] Such attitudes are less pronounced but still apparent today. An allied perception, still pronounced, is that breeding—meaning principally status by inheritance—and a good general education constitute the basis for positions of eminence. The top positions in business and elsewhere are, as was found in the 1992 survey already mentioned, still likely to be held by men (rarely women) with a public school and Oxbridge education—or, indeed, no university education. Whereas nine out of every ten senior managers in the United States and Japan will be graduates, often with specialist degrees, the proportion in the United Kingdom is only about one in four. Top management has thus often been notable for having no particular training for the task, the "old school tie" proving more valuable than a particular degree for advancing up the career ladder.

Some blame for sluggish economic performance also has been imputed to the egalitarianism of the labor movement, harboring dislike of profits and risk taking as well as the values of thrift and self-reliance that underpin the operation of the free market. This view has been argued by some of those who were close to Margaret Thatcher during her leadership of the Conservative party.[31] Unlike the case in the United States, there is no culture that favors ambition among blue-collar workers to achieve a junior managerial post and then a post above that. In some industries, it is not just management positions that have been seen as having passed from father to son but the manual jobs as well.

In short, bringing the two sociological explanations together, the attitudes of both the social elite and the labor movement—generating an "us" and "them" mentality in industrial relations—have hindered economic growth. Both sides have been content to maintain that relationship, with attempts to break it down coming from outside, from government legislation or from the influx of working practices of those, such as the Japanese, responsible for establishing new factories in U.K. sites.

Structural

Structural explanations, like the economic, can be subsumed under three heads: adversary politics, centralization, and pluralist stagnation.

The adversary politics thesis contends that attempts to generate long-term solutions to problems are thwarted by a system that encourages an adversary relationship between the two main political parties, with those parties vying with one another for the all-or-nothing spoils of a general election victory.[32] To win, one party has to outbid the other, making promises that are difficult to fulfill once in office. Competing claims mean that, if one party ousts another from office, the new government reverses the policies of its predecessor and introduces a new program. The result is policy discontinuity and uncertainty, with investors and managers unable to plan ahead.

The adversary politics thesis was developed in the 1970s, achieved some prominence in the debate in the latter half of the decade, and has achieved renewed prominence in recent years. In part, this is attributable to the view that an adversary relationship has meant that government, despite large parliamentary majorities, has been unable to mobilize a consensus in support of its policies, and with uncertainty generated by claims by the Labour opposition that, if returned to power, it would reverse many of the government's radical programs. For those who advance this thesis, the political system does not offer the means of resolving the nation's problems; rather the way the system is structured is seen as part—a very central part—of the problem.

The thesis of centralization dovetails to some extent with that of adversary politics. As government responsibilities in the twentieth century have expanded, so government has become increasingly centralized in Whitehall; the centralization has been both political (Whitehall as the center of the executive) and geographical (Whitehall being in the heart of the nation's capital). The problem, according to a number of observers, was exacerbated by the election of a Conservative government under Margaret Thatcher in 1979. To implement the goal of a free-market economy, the government had to strengthen its own powers, creating what Andrew Gamble termed "the Strong State."[33]

This further centralization of power is seen as part of a vicious circle. The government, by virtue of a political system that allows it largely unfettered law-making power (through a parliamentary majority), is able to extend its formal powers. However, the adversarial nature of that same system militates against its mobilizing the support of disparate groups—and the population generally—to tackle economic problems. Consequently, to tackle these problems, the government takes more powers. The more powers it takes, the more distant it becomes from those groups it needs to mobilize; hence a government with strong legal powers vested by Parliament but an increasingly limited capacity to mobilize support. That, on this analysis, has been the dilemma, indeed the paradox, of the years of Conservative government since 1979.

The thesis of pluralist stagnation asserts that the problem lies with the growth of groups in Britain, each group pursuing its own interests and bringing pressure to bear on government to provide resources or pursue policies to the benefit of its members. Government for its part has been unwilling to pursue policies that would arouse opposition from well-entrenched groups, resulting in inertia.[34] The problem has been exacerbated by the growth in the number of organized groups. Because there are so many, self-restraint would bring no discernible benefit to any particular group. As a result, even though recognizing the need for restraint, a group is tempted to maintain or increase existing demands. Other groups then compete by raising their demands. Government is then overwhelmed by the multiplicity of self-serving demands.

This thesis was prominent in the 1970s but less so in the 1980s. The Conservative government demonstrated a willingness to pursue single-mindedly its own policy agenda, eschewing the tendency of its predecessors to arbitrate between competing demands. The government adopted an arm's length relationship, especially with peak economic groups. Certain groups, such as the trade unions, were essentially marginalized. The thesis, nonetheless, retains some relevance. Government departments continue to arbitrate between competing group demands; groups remain significant, primarily self-serving, actors in the political system, and the replacement of Margaret Thatcher by a more emollient figure as prime minister has reduced some of the perceived animosity of government toward contact with bodies such as the Trades Union Congress.

These various explanations remain current, though some have enjoyed greater prominence in political debate than others. Those that have both wider and the greatest salience for our purposes—given our focus on the British political system—are those derived from the pursuit of a Thatcherite free-market economy and the theses of adversary politics and centralization. As we shall see, the pursuit of particular economic policies and the structure of the political system constitute two principal, and competing, explanations for the decline in support for the two main political parties in recent years (chapter 6). Pluralist stagnation, and, more especially, the attempts by government to break out of a cycle of stagnation, are important for explaining the activity of pressure groups in the 1980s and 1990s (chapter 7). Structural—and sociological—analyses underpin current debate on government and the civil service (chapter 8) and, most important of all, the combination of adversary politics and centralization are at the heart of the thesis advanced by Samuel Beer and contemporary advocates of a new constitution. As we have seen (chapter 2), these advocates posit a decline of the civic culture in Britain. On their argument, a restoration—indeed, a revitalization—of that culture is possible only with the introduction of a new constitution for the United Kingdom. That argument, as promised in the preceding chapter, will be put to the test in our concluding chapter.

NOTES

1. See A. H. Dodd, *The Growth of Responsible Government* (Routledge & Kegan Paul, 1956), pp. 43–44.
2. B. Kemp, *King and Commons 1600–1832* (Macmillan, 1957), p. 3.
3. Its provisions included, for example, "That excessive Baile ought not to be required nor excessive Fines imposed nor cruell and unusuall Punishments inflicted." Compare this with the Eighth Amendment to the United States Constitution, which prescribes that "Excessive bail shall not be required, nor excessive fines imposed, nor cruel and unusual punishments inflicted."
4. J. H. Plumb, *England in the Eighteenth Century* (Penguin, 1950), p. 50.

5. J. Mackintosh, *The British Cabinet,* 3rd ed. (Stevens, 1977), pp.50–51.

6. Ibid., p. 64.

7. S. M. Lipset, *The First New Nation* (Heinemann, 1964); P. Mathias, *The First Industrial Nation* (Methuen, 1969).

8. Sir L. Woodward, *The Age of Reform 1815–1870,* 2nd ed. (Oxford University Press, 1962), p. 3.

9. A table compiled in 1815 revealed that 144 peers, along with 123 commoners, controlled 471 seats (more than two-thirds of the total number) in the House of Commons. M. Ostrogorski, *Democracy and the Organisation of Political Parties,* Vol. 1: England (Macmillan, 1902), p. 20.

10. J. B. Conacher (ed.), *The Emergence of British Parliamentary Democracy in the Nineteenth Century* (Wiley, 1971), p. 10. Different authors cite different figures.

11. W. Bagehot, *The English Constitution* (first published 1867; Fontana ed., 1963), p. 150.

12. Mackintosh, p. 113.

13. See Conacher, pp. 68–69, for a summary.

14. See H. J. Hanham, *Elections and Party Management,* 3rd ed. (Harvester Press, 1978), p. xii.

15. Similarly, in the United States the all-or-nothing spoils of presidential victory have encouraged two rather than many parties. See M. Vile, *Politics in the USA* (Hutchinson, 1976 ed.), pp. 62–63.

16. A. L. Lowell, *The Government of England,* Vol. 2 (Macmillan, 1924), pp. 76–78.

17. Mackintosh, p. 174.

18. Many of the reforms were introduced by Conservative governments. See C. E. Bellairs, *Conservative Social and Industrial Reform* (Conservative Central Office, 1977).

19. P. Addison, *The Road to 1945* (Quartet, 1977), p. 127.

20. I. Macleod, *Neville Chamberlain* (Muller, 1961), p. 123.

21. S. H. Beer, *Modern British Politics* (Faber, 1969 ed.), pp. 278–287.

22. Addison, p. 29.

23. *Social Insurance and Allied Services—Report by Sir William Beveridge,* Cmnd. 6404 (Her Majesty's Stationery Office, 1942), para. 17, p. 9.

24. Based on the title of Vernon Bogdanor and Robert Skidelsky (eds.), *The Age of Affluence 1951–1964* (Macmillan, 1970).

25. I. Crewe, "The Thatcher Legacy," in A. King (ed.), *Britain at the Polls 1992* (Chatham House, 1993), p. 18.

26. "The Ascent of British Man," *Economist,* December 19, 1992, p. 21.

27. Crewe, pp. 19–22. See also P. Norton, "The Conservative Party from Thatcher to Major," in A. King (ed.), *Britain at the Polls 1992* (Chatham House, 1993), pp. 32–33.

28. See, for example, A. W. Manser, *Britain in Balance* (Penguin, 1973).

29. This fact is resented by part of the political elite in Britain. This was reinforced in 1945 by the terms of the loan to Britain by the United States. Some Conservative members of Parliament saw the terms as part of an attempt to open up world markets to the benefit of the United States and some Labour members feared that it would, in the words of one of them, hitch the nation "to the American bandwagon." See P. Norton, *Dissension in the House of Commons 1945–74* (Macmillan, 1975), p. 3. Further resentment was caused by the active opposition of the U.S. government to Britain's attempt to occupy the Suez Canal zone by force in 1956.

30. See, e.g., M. Postan, *An Economic History of Western Europe 1945–64* (Methuen, 1967).

31. As, e.g., Sir K. Joseph, *Stranded on the Middle Ground* (Centre for Policy Studies, 1976).

32. See especially S. E. Finer (ed.), *Adversary Politics and Electoral Reform* (Wigram, 1975); D. Coombes, *Representative Government and Economic Power* (Heinemann, 1982); and A. M. Gamble and S. A. Walkland, *The British Party System and Economic Policy 1945–1983* (Oxford University Press, 1984).

33. A. Gamble, *The Free Economy and the Strong State* (Macmillan, 1988).

34. See I. Gilmour, *The Body Politic,* rev. ed. (Hutchinson, 1971); and J. E. S. Hayward, *Political Inertia* (University of Hull Press, 1975).

PART II

The Political Environment

CHAPTER **4**

The Uncodified Constitution

A constitution may be defined as the body of laws, customs, and conventions that define the composition and powers of organs of the state and that regulate the relations of the various state organs to one another and to the private citizen.[1]

The United States has a constitution; so does the United Kingdom. Expressed in purely formal terms (Table 4.1) there is very little similarity between them. Indeed, the differences are such that to the student weaned on a study of the U.S. Constitution, the British Constitution is nearly incomprehensible. Even to the student of British politics it is not well understood. Nonetheless, the differences should not be emphasized to the exclusion of certain common features. Both Constitutions are strong in that they reflect their respective political cultures.

The U.S. Constitution is considered by Americans to embody the principles of a higher law, to constitute "in fact imperfect man's most perfect rendering of what Blackstone saluted as 'the eternal immutable laws of good and evil, to which the creator himself in all his dispensations conforms: and which he has enabled human reason to discover, so far as they are necessary for the conduct of human actions.' "[2] As the embodiment of a higher law, it thus not only needs to be distinguished from ordinary law but also needs to be protected from the passing whims of politicians—hence the introduction of extraordinary procedures for its amendment.

By contrast, the British Constitution is admired by Britons for reflecting the wisdom of past generations, as the product of experience—in short, a constitution that stipulates what should be on the basis of what has proved to work rather than on abstract first principles. The empirical orientation to change that underpins such a constitution also favors flexibility in amendment: As conditions change, so some amendment may be necessary. Formal extraordinary procedures for its amendment have not been found necessary.

TABLE 4.1   U.S. and British constitutions

	Constitutions	
Characteristics	*United States*	*United Kingdom*
Form of expression	Written	Part written but uncodified
Date and manner of formulation	1787 by a constitutional convention	No one date of formulation; no precise manner of formulation
Means of formal amendment	By two-thirds majorities in both houses of Congress and by ratification of three-quarters of the states, or by conventions	No extraordinary provisions for amendment
Location of its provisions	The written document (also judicial decisions, custom usage, works of authority)	Statute law, common law, conventions, works of authority
Bodies responsible for interpretation of its provisions	The judiciary primarily (can be overridden by constitutional amendment)	The judiciary (statute and common law), scholars, and politicians (conventions)
Main provisions	Document as "supreme law," judicial review, separation and overlap of powers, federal system, bill of rights, republican form of government	Parliamentary sovereignty, "rule of law," unitary system, parliamentary government under a constitutional monarchy, membership in the European Community
Public promulgation of its provisions (in textbooks, etc.)	Extensive	Infrequent

The differences in political culture have thus produced somewhat different constitutions, but the attachment to them is similar in the two countries. Also, as we shall see, there are certain similarities in sources and in the means of interpretation.

FORMS OF EXPRESSION

New nations from the eighteenth century onward have found it both necessary and useful to codify their constitutions. At the time that the founding fathers promulgated the U.S. Constitution in Philadelphia, a written constitution was exceptional. Today it is the norm. Having lacked the opportunity to create a new constitutional framework afresh from first principles, Britain now stands out as one of the few nations lacking such a document.

The absence of a written constitution similar to that of the United States and other nations has led to the British Constitution being described as unwritten, but such a description is misleading. As we shall see, various elements of the Constitution find expression in formal, written enactments. What distinguishes the British Constitution from others is not that it is unwritten, but rather that it is part written and uncodified. The lack of codification is of special importance. It makes it difficult to identify clearly and authoritatively what constitute the provisions of the Constitution. Certain principles clearly are at the heart of the Constitution, parliamentary sovereignty being the prime example, but there are many provisions, be they expressed through statute law or the writings of constitutional experts, that are of constitutional significance but on which there is no clear agreement that they are core provisions of the British Constitution. It is this lack of codified certainty that makes a study of the Constitution so fraught with difficulty.

SOURCES

Because one cannot have recourse to one simple authoritative document to discover the provisions of the British Constitution, one has instead to research four separate sources: statute law, common law, conventions, and works of authority. Such sources are also relevant in analyses of the U.S. Constitution. Congress may pass measures of constitutional significance, such as certain stipulations of electoral law or the War Powers Act. Provisions of the Constitution are developed and molded by judicial decisions. In seeking to interpret the Constitution, the courts may have recourse to works by constitutional experts. The difference between the two countries is that in Britain such sources are primary sources, and in the United States the primary source is the written document.

Of the four sources, statute law is perhaps the best understood and, nowadays, the most extensive. It provides the main source for the part-written element of the British Constitution. It comprises acts of Parliament and subordinate legislation made under the authority of the parent act. Many acts of Parliament that have been passed clearly merit the title of constitutional law. Acts that define the powers of the various state organs (for example, the 1911 and 1949 Parliament Acts) and acts that define the relationship between Crown and Parliament (notably the Bill of Rights of 1689), between the component elements of the nation (the Act of Union with Scotland of 1707, for example), between the United Kingdom and the European Communities (the 1972 European Communities Act and European Communities [Amendment] Acts of 1986 and 1993), and between the state and the individual (as with the Habeas Corpus Act of 1679 or the Police and Criminal Evidence Act of 1984) clearly constitute important provisions of the Constitution. They are published in authoritative, written form and, as acts of Parliament, are interpreted by the courts. This is the most important of the four sources both in quantitative and qualitative terms. It has increasingly displaced common law as the most extensive form of law in Britain and it is the most definitive of the four. It takes precedence over any conflicting common law and is superior to the conventions of the Constitution and to works of authority. Its precedence derives from the concept of parliamentary sovereignty.

Common law constitutes rules and customs of ancient lineage that are so well established that they have been upheld as law by the courts in cases decided before them. Once a court has upheld a provision as being part of common law, it creates a precedent to be followed by other courts. In past centuries, when few statutes were enacted, common law constituted the main body of English law; today, it has been largely but not wholly displaced by statute law. Certain principles derived from common law remain fundamental to the Constitution, and these include the principle of parliamentary sovereignty.

Under the heading of common law comes also prerogative powers—the powers and privileges recognized by common law as belonging to the Crown. Although many prerogative powers have been displaced by statute, many matters at the heart of government are still determined under the authority of the prerogative. These include the appointment of ministers, the making of treaties, the power of pardon, the dispensing of honors, and the declaration of war. By convention, such powers are normally exercised formally by the monarch on the advice of ministers (the ministers, in practice, make the decisions). There is no formal requirement that Parliament assent to such decisions. This is in stark contrast to the position in the United States, where Congress alone has the formal power to declare war and the Senate's consent is necessary for the ratification of treaties and the appointment of federal public officers. (In practice, the differences are not that great: "presidential wars" have been waged without a congressional declaration of war, and in Britain a government taking military action abroad will seek the consent of Parliament.) In 1972 the Treaty of Accession to the European Community was signed under prerogative powers. In 1982 a naval task force was dispatched to the Falkland Islands under the same authority. Although diminishing in number, prerogative powers clearly remain of great importance.

Generally included under the generic heading of common law is the judicial interpretation of statute law. Unlike those in the United States, British courts have no power to hold a measure unconstitutional. They are limited to the interpretation of provisions of acts of Parliament. Even in exercising their power of interpretation, they are limited by rules of interpretation and by precedent. (The exception is the House of Lords, the highest domestic court of appeal, which is not now bound by its previous decisions.) Nonetheless, judges retain the power to distinguish cases, and by their interpretation they can develop a substantial body of case law. In interpreting acts of Parliament, they traditionally have assumed Parliament to have meant what, on the face of it, the words of an act appear to mean. However, following a decision of the House of Lords (in its judicial capacity) in 1992, it is now possible for courts, where they consider it necessary, to look at the proceedings of Parliament in order to determine what Parliament really meant.

The third and least tangible source of the Constitution is that of convention. Conventions of the British Constitution are most aptly described as rules of behavior that are considered binding by and upon those who are responsible for making the Constitution work, but rules that are not enforced by the courts or by the presiding officers in either house of Parliament.[3] They derive their strength from the realization that not to abide by them would make for an unworkable Constitution. They are, so to speak, the oil in the formal machinery of the Constitution. They help fill the gap between the constitutional formality and the political reality. For example, ministers are responsible formally to the monarch. Because of the political changes wrought in the nineteenth century, they are by convention responsible now also to Parliament. By convention, the government of the day resigns or requests a dissolution of Parliament if a motion of no confidence is carried against it in the House of Commons. By convention, the monarch gives the Royal Assent to all legislative measures approved by Parliament. The last time a monarch refused assent was in 1707, when Queen Anne vetoed a Scottish Militia Bill. Queen Victoria in the nineteenth century contemplated refusing her assent to a measure but wiser counsels prevailed.

No formal, authoritative documents set forth these rules, and they find no embodiment in statute law. The courts may recognize them but have no power to enforce them. They are complied with because of the recognition of what would happen if they were not complied with. For the queen to refuse her assent to a measure passed by the two houses of Parliament would draw her into the realms of political controversy, hence jeopardizing the claim of the monarch to be "above politics." A government that sought to remain in office after losing a vote of confidence in the House of Commons would find its position politically untenable: It would lack the political authority to govern. For ministers to ignore Parliament completely would prove equally untenable.

Some conventions may be described as being stronger than others. Some on occasion are breached, whereas others are adhered to without exception. On three occasions in this century, the convention of collective ministerial responsibility has been suspended temporarily by the prime minister of the day. In contrast, no government has sought to remain in office after losing a parliamentary vote of confidence. The point at which a useful and necessary practice is accorded the status of a constitutional convention is not clear. Once a practice has become well established in terms of the relationship within or between different organs of the state, finding recognition in works of authority and by those involved in its operation, then it may be said to have reached the status of a convention. At any one time, though, a number of relationships may be said to be in a constitutional haze. Is it a convention of the Constitution that the government of the day must consult with interested bodies before formulating a legislative measure for presentation to Parliament? A noted constitutional lawyer, Sir Ivor Jennings, once argued that it was.[4] Prime Minister Harold Wilson appeared to give some credence to this view in 1966 when he said in the House of Commons that it was the *duty* of the government to consult with the Trades Union Congress and the Confederation of British Industry.[5] Few other authorities have supported Jennings's assertion and it has not found acceptance by most practitioners of government. It is usual for governments to engage in such consultation, but it is not a convention of the Constitution that they do so.

The fourth and final source of the Constitution is that of works of authority. These have persuasive authority only. What constitutes a "work of authority" is rarely defined. Various early works are accorded particular standing by virtue of the absence of statutes or other written sources covering a particular area. The statements of their writers are presumed to be evidence of judicial decisions that have been lost and are therefore accepted if not contrary to reason.[6] Among the most important early sources are Fitzherbert's *Abridgment* (1516) and Coke's *Institutes of the Law of England* (1628–1644). More recent works have been called into aid on those occasions when jurists and others have sought to delineate features of the contemporary Constitution; this has been the case especially in determining the existence or otherwise of conventions. Given that conventions are prescribed neither by statute nor by judicial interpretation, one must study instead scholarly interpretations of political behavior and practice. Especially important authoritative works in the nineteenth century were those by John Austin and A. V. Dicey. Important names in the twentieth century have included Sir Ivor Jennings, Sir Kenneth Wheare, O. Hood Phillips, and E. C. S. Wade.[7]

Given the disparate sources of the British Constitution and the fact that important relationships within and between organs of the state are not laid down in any one formal or binding document, it is not surprising that one must have recourse to books by constitutional scholars to discover the extent and nature of those relationships. Works of authority tend to be consulted more frequently in the field of constitutional law than in any other branch of English law.

MEANS OF AMENDMENT

Given the disparate primary sources of the British Constitution and the difficulty in determining where the Constitution begins and ends, it is perhaps not surprising that there are no extraordinary procedures for its amendment. Statute and common law of constitutional significance are subject to amendment by the same process as that employed for other legislative enactments. Conventions can be modified by changes in behavior or by reinterpretations of the significance of certain behavior. Works of authority can be rewritten or subjected to different interpretations in the same way as can other texts.

Much the same can be said about constitutionally significant statute law, judicial decisions, and works of authority in the United States. Even the provisions of the formal document, the U.S. Constitution, may be amended by judicial decisions and custom usage. The difference between the two countries is that the formal wording of the U.S. Constitution can be amended only by an extraordinary process, that is, one that goes beyond the provisions employed for amending the ordinary law. (Because of the extraordinary procedures necessary for amendment, the provisions of the Constitution are commonly referred to as ''entrenched.'') No such formal amending procedures exist in Britain, where there is no formal document.

INTERPRETATION

As may be surmised from the foregoing, there is no single body endowed with the responsibility for interpreting the provisions of the Constitution. As in the United States, statute and common law are subject to judicial interpretation, but there is no power of judicial review, at least not as the term is understood in the United States. The courts cannot declare a legislative measure or an executive action contrary to the provisions of the Constitution.

The courts can influence and to some extent mold certain provisions through their interpretation of statute and common law. Indeed, their use of common law has been of special importance in outlining and protecting certain rights of the individual. However, at the end of the day they are subject to the wishes of Parliament. Judicial interpretation of statute law can be overridden by a new act of Parliament. By virtue of the concept of parliamentary sovereignty, the act would be definitive. The judges serve to enforce and interpret such acts: They cannot strike down an act.

Identification and interpretation of conventions have little to do with the courts. Conventions arise as a result of changes in the relationships within and between different organs of the state. Their delineation rests with scholars, and their enforcement rests with those at whom they are aimed.

The Constitution, in short, is subject to interpretation by different bodies, the most prominent being politicians, judges, and scholars. The same can be said of the U.S. Constitution, but in Britain there is no body that stands in a position analogous to that of the U.S. Supreme Court. This is an important difference, reflecting the differences in political culture. The Lockean basis of constitutional interpretation in the United States—a higher law cognizable by independent, rational magistrates operating free of outside interests[8]—finds no parallel in Britain.

MAIN PROVISIONS

The central provisions of the British Constitution are listed in Table 4.1: parliamentary sovereignty, the rule of law, a unitary (as opposed to a federal) system, what I have termed parliamentary government under a constitutional monarchy, and membership in the European Community. Although there is some dispute as to whether it should remain so, the preeminent provision is that of parliamentary sovereignty. In the nineteenth century the great constitutional lawyer A. V. Dicey identified it as being one of the two main pillars of the Constitution, the other being the rule of law.[9] Dicey's work has had a major and lasting impact. Despite subsequent criticisms, the two pillars identified by Dicey still stand. Although some critics have considered them weak and (in the case of parliamentary sovereignty) unnecessary pillars, supporting a crumbling edifice, they remain crucial to an understanding of the British Constitution.

Parliamentary Sovereignty

The most succinct definition of parliamentary sovereignty was offered by Dicey. Paliamentary sovereignty, he wrote, means that Parliament has "the right to make or unmake any law whatever; and, further, that no person or body is recognized by the law of England as having a right to override or set aside the legislation of Parliament."[10] An act passed by Parliament will be enforced by the courts, the courts recognizing no body other than Parliament as having authority to override such an act. Parliament itself can substitute an act for an earlier one. One of the precepts derived from the principle is that Parliament is not bound by its predecessors. Once Parliament has passed an act, it becomes the law of the land. It is not open to challenge before the courts on the grounds of being unconstitutional.

Although Dicey claimed more ancient lineage for it, the principle of parliamentary sovereignty became established as a judicial rule in consequence of the Glorious Revolution of 1688 and subsequent Bill of Rights, which established the relationship between the Crown and Parliament (see chapter 3). It was the product of an alliance between Parliament and common lawyers and of the intimidation of judges by the House of Commons. Assertion of the principle served to do away with the monarch's previously claimed powers to suspend or dispense with acts of Parliament and it served to deny judges the power to strike down measures. It came to occupy a unique place in constitutional law. The principle finds no expression in statute or any other formal enactment. It exists in common law but enjoys a special status beyond that enjoyed by other principles of common law. Its underpinnings are not only legal but also political and historical. Judicial obedience to it constitutes what H. W. R. Wade referred to as "the ultimate political fact upon which the whole system of legislation hangs."[11] No statute can confer the power of parliamentary sovereignty, for that would be to confer the very power being acted upon. It is therefore considered to be unique. As Hood Phillips states, "It may indeed be called the one fundamental law of the British Constitution."[12]

The Rule of Law

The second pillar identified by Dicey was that of "the rule of law." Identifying what is meant by the term is extremely difficult. Few students of the Constitution would deny the importance of the tenet. Dicey himself argued that it comprised "at least three distinct though kindred conceptions": "that no man is punishable or can be lawfully made to suffer in body or goods except for a distinct breach of law established in the ordinary legal manner before the ordinary courts of the land"; that "no man is above the law [and] every man, whatever be his rank or condition, is subject to the ordinary law of the realm and amenable to the jurisdiction of the ordinary tribunals"; and that "the general principles of the constitution [are] the result of judicial decisions determining the rights of private persons in particular cases brought before the courts." These three conceptions have been subject to various criticisms: among them, that many discretionary powers are vested in officials and public bodies, that many officials and bodies have immunities that the ordinary citizen does not have, and that certain rights have been modified by or enacted in statute. Furthermore, it is not clear why Dicey's third conception should be considered "kindred" to the other two. Some students of the Constitution find Dicey's analysis useful, and others tend to be dismissive; even Dicey later revised his own definition. The important point for our purposes is that there is no agreed-upon definition.

The rule of law, then, stands as a central element of the British Constitution, but no one is sure precisely what it means. It remains "one of the most elusive of all political concepts.''[13] Some writers, especially in recent years, have tended to accord it a wide definition, encompassing substantive rights. On their argument, the rule of law cannot be said to exist unless basic human rights are protected. Others have adopted a narrow and more long-standing definition, contending that the concept entails certain procedural (or ''due process'') rights, that government must be subject to the law, and that the judiciary must be independent. The problem is one of determining what those rights are, how they are to be protected, and how the independence of the judiciary is to be maintained.

There is a further problem. The concept of the rule of law is not logically compatible with that of parliamentary sovereignty. Parliament could if it so wished confer arbitrary powers upon government. It could fetter the independence of the judiciary. It could limit or remove altogether certain rights presumed to exist at common law. The rule of law, in short, could be threatened or even dispensed with by parliamentary enactment. Dicey himself recognized this problem and sought to resolve it. He argued, in essence, that the rule of law prevented government from exercising arbitrary powers. If government wanted such powers, it could obtain them only through Parliament (Parliament itself has never sought to exercise executive powers) and the granting of them could take place only after deliberation and approval by the triumvirate of monarch, Lords, and Commons.[14]

Such an argument serves to explain potential impediments to a government intent on acquiring arbitrary powers. It does not deny the truth of the assertion that Parliament could, if it wished, confer such powers upon government. Indeed, many observers would argue that given the growth of cabinet government, the potential for government to seek and receive such powers is significantly greater now than was the case at the time when Dicey was writing. For many critics of the existing Constitution, parliamentary sovereignty no longer constitutes an encouragement to the rule of law but rather exists as an impediment to its attainment. So long as parliamentary sovereignty remains ''the one fundamental law'' of the Constitution, there is no way in which substantive rights can be entrenched and put beyond the reach of Parliament.

Unitary System

The third feature of the Constitution that I have listed—that the United Kingdom is a unitary state—is a less difficult one to comprehend. The United States is a federal nation. The power vested in the federal government is that delegated in the U.S. Constitution: All other powers not delegated rest with the states or the people. In the United Kingdom, no powers are reserved to national or regional bodies. If they were, Parliament would not be omnicompetent. Parliament exercises legal sovereignty. It can confer certain powers and responsibilities upon regional and local authorities, and it also can remove those powers.

The unitary nation is that of the United Kingdom of Great Britain and Northern Ireland. Wales was integrated with England in 1536 by act of Parliament (the Laws in Wales Act), and Scotland and England were incorporated in 1707 by the Treaty of Union and by the Act of Union with Scotland. Ireland entered into legislative union in 1801. Following an armed uprising, the emergence of the Irish Free State was recognized in 1922 and given the status of a self-governing dominion. (The Irish Constitution of 1937 declared the country to be a sovereign independent state, a position recognized by the Westminster Parliament in 1949.) Excluded from the Irish Free State were the northern six counties of Ireland, forming part of the traditional region of Ulster. The Protestant majority in Ulster wished to remain part of the United Kingdom, and the province of Northern Ireland has so remained.

Parliamentary Government under a Constitutional Monarchy

The fourth element of the Constitution is one that I have described as a parliamentary government under a constitutional monarchy. It is this element that is especially important in terms of the current relationships among the different organs of the state and the one in which conventions of the Constitution are predominant. It constitutes an assembly of different relationships and powers, the product of traditional institutions being adapted to meet changing circumstances. The developments producing this form of government were sketched in chapter 3. The result, as we have seen, was parliamentary government in the sense of government *through* Parliament rather than government *by* Parliament, with a largely ceremonial head of state. The essentials of this form of government may be adumbrated as follows.

In the relationship among government, Parliament, and the monarch, the government dominates. Although lacking formal powers, the cabinet is recognized by convention as being at the heart of government. It is responsible for the final determination of policy to be submitted to Parliament, for the supreme control of the national executive in accordance with the policy prescribed by Parliament, and for continuous coordination and delimitation of the interests of the several departments of state.[15] It is presided over by the prime minister. The prime minister is appointed by the monarch. By convention, the monarch summons the leader of the party with a majority of seats in the House of Commons. (In the event of a party having no overall majority, the monarch summons whoever he or she believes may be able to form an administration.) The prime minister then selects the members of his or her cabinet and other government ministers and submits their names to the monarch who, by convention, does not deny the prime minister's choice. By convention, ministers are drawn from Parliament and, again by convention, predominantly from the elected house, the House of Commons. Although the government no longer is chosen by the Commons, it nonetheless is elected through the House of Commons: There is no separate election of the executive. There is a separation and overlap of powers between the government and the House of Commons in Britain but no equivalent separation of personnel. Government ministers are drawn from, and remain within, Parliament.

Legally, ministers are responsible to the monarch. Politically, they are responsible for their policies and actions to Parliament. Ministers are responsible to Parliament through the convention of individual ministerial responsibility, which assigns to them control of their departments, for which they are answerable to Parliament. The cabinet is similarly responsible to Parliament through the convention of collective ministerial responsibility. This convention, one scholar writes, ''implies that all cabinet ministers assume responsibility for cabinet decisions and actions taken to implement those decisions.''[16] It also has begotten two other conventions. It is a corollary of collective responsibility that any minister who disagrees publicly with a cabinet decision should resign and that a government defeat in the House of Commons on a vote of confidence necessitates either the resignation of the government or a request for a dissolution of Parliament (there is no convention as to which of these alternatives the government should select). Party cohesion ensures that the cabinet usually enjoys a parliamentary majority, but political parties remain unknown to the Constitution.

The cabinet approves government bills to be presented to Parliament. (In drawing up measures, it is aided primarily by its officials—that is, civil servants—and will consult normally with interested bodies: Such consultation, though, enjoys no formal recognition in constitutional terms.) Within Parliament, the most important house is the Commons. It is expected to submit bills to sustained scrutiny and debate before giving its assent to them (or not giving its assent to them, but the influence of party usually precludes such an outcome). Formally, the Commons is free to pass or reject bills as it wishes. The House of Lords is more constrained (see chapter 3); it was forced to accept a restricted role under the terms of the 1911 and 1949 Parliament Acts. Under the provisions of the 1911 act (a measure to which the Lords acquiesced under threat of being swamped with a mass of new Liberal pro-reform peers), the Lords could delay passage of nonmoney bills for only two successive sessions, such bills being enacted if passed by the Commons again in the succeeding session. Money bills, those certified as such by the speaker of the House of Commons, were to receive the Royal Assent one month after leaving the Commons, whether assented to by the House of Lords or not. The only significant power of veto retained was that over bills to prolong the life of a Parliament. (The delaying power over nonmoney bills was reduced by a further session under the terms of the 1949 Parliament Act, itself passed under the provisions of the 1911 act.) In practice, it is rare for the Lords to reject government measures, and there is a gentleman's agreement among the parties in the House that a bill promised in a government's election manifesto should be given an unopposed second reading (see chapter 11).

Once a bill has received the assent of both houses, it goes to the monarch for the Royal Assent. By convention, this assent is always forthcoming. As was already mentioned, not since Queen Anne's reign has a monarch refused assent. Queen Victoria contemplated such refusal but was persuaded otherwise. By convention, the queen exercises her powers on the advice of her ministers. In certain extreme circumstances, Her Majesty may find herself in a position in which she is called on to use her discretion in making a political decision. Such cases are rare, though the queen would probably prefer them to be nonexistent. The strength and the value of the contemporary monarchy derives from being above and avoiding political decisions.

The moment a bill receives the Royal Assent it becomes an act of Parliament. It is then enforced and upheld by the agencies of the state. It is binding and, by virtue of the doctrine of parliamentary sovereignty, cannot be challenged by the courts, nor can it be overridden by any other authority. The development of a form of representative democracy in the nineteenth century led Dicey to distinguish between legal sovereignty, which continued to reside with the triumvirate of the monarch, Lords, and Commons, and political sovereignty, which he deemed to rest with the electorate. This somewhat clumsy distinction has a certain utility. The electorate may have the power to choose the members of the House of Commons, but the will of the electorate is not something formally recognized by the courts. The courts recognize and will enforce only acts of Parliament.

Under the provisions of the 1911 Parliament Act, the maximum life of a Parliament is five years. (Previously, the period was seven years.) Within that period, the prime minister is free to recommend to the monarch a dissolution—in effect, to call a general election. Unlike the United States, Britain has no fixed-term elections at a national level. The ability of a prime minister effectively to call a general election has been regarded by some writers as the most important weapon in ensuring parliamentary support. The prime minister can threaten to recommend a dissolution if he or she does not receive the necessary support to get a measure through. Such a threat may constitute a bluff in that the prime minister would have more to lose if an election was called than would most MPs (the prime minister could lose office: Most seats are safe seats and so most MPs could expect to be reelected), but nonetheless it has proved a potent influence in determining parliamentary behavior. It would be exceptional, albeit not unknown, for MPs of the government party to vote against their own side on a vote of confidence. No government in the twentieth century has lost a vote of confidence as a result of dissent by its own supporters[17]—hence the dominance of government.

In summary, then, the fourth element of the Constitution—parliamentary government under a constitutional monarchy—may be seen to comprise different relationships and powers, which are the product of traditional institutions being adapted to meet changing circumstances and are prescribed by a variety of measures of statute and common law and by convention. The working of the various relationships within the framework established by law and convention is made possible by the operation of bodies not formally recognized by the Constitution, namely political parties. To understand contemporary British politics, one has to understand this framework.

European Community Membership

To understand British politics fully, one now has also to go beyond this framework. This brings us to the fifth and most recent constituent of the Constitution, one for which there is no parallel in North America: membership in a supranational body, the European Community (EC). The United Kingdom became a member of the Community on January 1, 1973, and the effect of membership has been to add a new dimension to the formulation, approval, and enforcement of measures of public policy.

By virtue of Community membership, decision-making competence in a number of sectors has passed from the British government to the principal executive institutions of the Community: the Council of Ministers, comprising the relevant ministers drawn from the member states, and the Commission, the permanent bureaucracy headed by a College of Commissioners. (The commissioners are appointed by, but required to be independent of, the member states.) The council is the ultimate decision-making body; the Commission alone has the power to propose legislation.

British ministers thus form part of a wider, collective decision-making body. Under the terms of the treaties forming the Community, the council and Commission can issue different forms of Community legislation (see chapter 10). Under the terms of the European Communities Act of 1972, which provides the legal basis necessary for membership, the force of law is given in the United Kingdom to EC legislation. Such legislation has immediate and general applicability. The assent of Parliament is not required: It has, in effect, been given in advance under the provisions of the 1972 act. In the event of any conflict between domestic (known as municipal) law and EC law, EC law is to prevail. Disputes concerning Community law are to be treated by British courts as matters of law, and cases that reach the highest domestic court of appeal—the House of Lords—must, under the provisions of the Treaty of Rome, be referred to the Community's Court of Justice for a definitive ruling. Requests also may be made from lower courts to the Court of Justice for a ruling on the meaning and interpretation of Community treaties.

Membership in the Community has thus had profound constitutional implications for the United Kingdom. These implications are even more pronounced now as a result of the implementation of the Single European Act, which constitutes an amendment to the treaties of the EC and came into force on July 1, 1987. (As a treaty amendment, it required parliamentary approval and this was given under the provisions of the European Communities [Amendment] Act of 1986.) The effect of the act was to change the power relationship *between* the institutions of the Community and the member states, and *within* the Community among the different institutions. The act extended the provision for weighted majority votes in the Council of Ministers: This means one or a small minority of ministers can be outvoted by the ministers from the other countries. (Each minister enjoys a stipulated number of votes, depending on the size of the country, with a total of 54 votes out of 76 being necessary for a measure to be adopted; the British minister has 10 votes.) A measure thus can be opposed by the British government and Parliament and yet, if it achieves the necessary number of votes in the council, be enforced as law in the United Kingdom. Within the institutions of the Community, the act also accorded a stronger role to the European Parliament (a 518-member body, directly elected since 1979, in which the United Kingdom has 81 seats); it now is more directly involved in the discussion and amendment of council proposals and, in certain circumstances, can fulfill a significant blocking role. Its powers have been further strengthened under the Maastricht Treaty (see chapter 10).

Membership in the Community has been added on, and as far as possible, integrated with the existing provisions of the British Constitution. The "fit" has not necessarily been complete. The doctrine of parliamentary sovereignty has been undermined, especially as a result of a ruling by the EC Court of Justice in 1990 (the *Factortame* case—see chapter 14), but remains intact in that Parliament retains the power to repeal the original EC Act of 1972. (To do so would be a breach of the nation's treaty obligations, under which membership is in perpetuity, but the courts would enforce the act of repeal.) The British government retains its autonomy in several significant sectors. Most significant measures of public policy arise from the domestic process of lawmaking. There is, though, a capacity for tension between the established national institutions and those grafted on at a supranational level. Two provisions of statute law—the European Communities Act of 1972 and the Amendment Act of 1986—may be seen as constituting a Trojan horse, allowing the introduction of a new layer to the British Constitution. Existing institutions and procedures have not yet become fully accommodated to this new dimension.

CONCLUSION

The shifting and complex web of relationships and powers that forms the British Constitution is not an easily discernible one. Some powers and relationships recognizably fall within the rubric of the Constitution. Others are less easy to classify. Sometimes a feature of the Constitution is discerned as such only at the time when it has just ceased to have much relevance. Walter Bagehot's *The English Constitution,* published in 1867, constituted a classic description of a Constitution that had not previously been so well sketched, yet a Constitution that was to undergo significant modifications as a result of the passage that very same year of the Second Reform Act. Bagehot's work continued to be regarded as an authoritative work long after the Constitution had undergone fundamental change.

Grasping the essentials of the Constitution at any given moment is clearly a demanding and confusing task. It is confusing even to those charged with its interpretation and to those who seek to make it work. To the student of the subject, the British Constitution appears complex, confusing, ill defined, and in many respects amorphous. Such a reaction is both natural and understandable: The Constitution does exhibit those very characteristics.

At the heart of the difficulty of delineating clearly the essential features of the Constitution is its ever-changing nature. Statute law, as we have seen in the case of membership in the European Community, can introduce new bodies of government. Constitutional norms serve to influence and mold political behavior. Conversely, political behavior helps influence the contours of the Constitution. As we have seen, such changes are made possible by the assimilating influence of conventions. "The conventions of the constitution," as Professor LeMay observed, "have meaning only when they are looked at against a background of continuous political change. It is very difficult to say with certainty what they were at any particular moment. Above all, they cannot be understood 'with the politics left out.' ''[18]

The Constitution has proved adaptable to changing political conditions. In recent years, however, its relevance has been questioned. The patchwork quilt of powers and relationships has been criticized for no longer being either useful or relevant. There is, as we shall see, pressure from many influential sources for the Constitution not only to be further amended but also to be radically altered. In some cases there are calls for a new constitutional settlement. It is this pressure for change and its implications that subsequent chapters will explore.

NOTES

1. O. Hood Phillips, *Constitutional and Administrative Law,* 6th ed. (Sweet & Maxwell, 1978), p. 5.
2. C. Rossiter, prefatory note to E. S. Corwin, *The "Higher Law" Background of American Constitutional Law* (Cornell University Press, 1979 ed.), p. vi.
3. See G. Marshall and G. Moodie, *Some Problems of the Constitution,* 4th rev. ed. (Hutchinson, 1967), p. 26.
4. I. Jennings, *The Law and the Constitution,* 5th ed. (University of London Press, 1959), p. 102.
5. A. H. Hanson and M. Walles, *Governing Britain,* rev. ed. (Fontana, 1975), p. 156.
6. Phillips, p. 25.
7. P. Norton, *The Constitution in Flux* (Basil Blackwell, 1982), p. 9.
8. See L. Hartz, *The Liberal Tradition in America* (Harcourt, Brace and World, 1955), p. 9.
9. A. V. Dicey, *An Introduction to the Study of the Law of the Constitution,* 10th ed. (first published 1885; Macmillan, 1959).
10. Ibid., pp. 39–40.
11. H. W. R. Wade, "The Basis of Legal Sovereignty," *Common Law Journal,* 1955, cited by E. C. S. Wade in his introduction to the 10th ed. of Dicey, p. lvi.
12. Phillips, p. 46.
13. "The Rule of Law in Britain Today," *Constitutional Reform Centre: Politics Briefing No. 6* (Constitutional Reform Centre, 1989), p. 1.
14. See Norton, pp. 16–17.
15. As listed by *The Report of the Machinery of Government Committee* (His Majesty's Stationery Office, 1918).
16. S. A. de Smith, *Constitutional and Administrative Law* (Penguin, 1971), p. 176.
17. The government of Neville Chamberlain effectively fell in 1940 because of dissent by its own backbenchers, though it retained a majority in the parliamentary vote that took place. The government, in effect, got the message without having to be defeated formally. On three occasions in this century, government has actually lost a vote of confidence—in 1924 (twice) and 1979—but in each instance the government party did not enjoy an overall parliamentary majority.
18. G. LeMay, *The Victorian Constitution* (Duckworth, 1979), p. 21.

CHAPTER 5

The Electoral System
Fair and Workable?

In the United States, citizens are presented with the opportunity to go to the polls at frequent and fixed intervals to elect at national, state, and local levels a host of legislators, executive heads, councilpersons, officials, and even, in some states, judges. It has been estimated that there are approximately 1 million elective offices to be filled. In any given year, 120,000 or 130,000 elections may be held, most of them for local school boards.[1] Before polling day, the citizen is faced with a lengthy election campaign: There are primary campaigns, the primary elections, the general election campaign, and the general election itself. The presidential election campaign lasts for nearly a year; with all the preplanning, advance publicity, and fund-raising, it lasts for much longer. Given the short interval between elections, campaigns for the U.S. House of Representatives are virtually continuous. Once in the polling booth, the voter is faced with a daunting array of candidates: Given the number of offices to be filled and the number of people seeking to fill them, the number of names may be a three-figure one. Voting and its subsequent tabulation are much eased by the use of voting machines. Choosing between Republican and Democratic candidates is not always an easy task, and ticket splitting is a well-recognized phenomenon.[2] Such characteristics of U.S. elections are well known. They have little in common with those of British elections.

In the United Kingdom, a citizen may have the opportunity to vote in the election of a national body only once every five years. That election is for the House of Commons and the House of Commons alone. The members of the House of Lords are not elected: They serve by virtue of birth or, for life peers, by appointment for life. There is no separate election of the executive: The leader of the party with a majority of seats in the House of Commons is invited to form a government. (The choice of party leaders is a matter for the parties themselves.) The date of an election is not known until approximately four weeks before the event, when the prime minister recommends to the queen a dissolution of Parliament. Although there is much anticipatory planning, the election campaign proper extends over approximately three weeks. There are no primaries: Candidate selection is an internal matter for the parties. The campaign is fought on a national, and party, basis. Funding and organization in the constituencies as well as nationally is undertaken by the established parties, not by individual candidates or campaign organizations created by the candidates. The amount of money spent on electioneering during this period, at least at constituency level, is strictly limited by law. On polling day the elector is faced with a small ballot slip on which are printed the names usually of only three or four candidates. (Six or more candidates standing in any one constituency would be unusual.) The voter places his or her cross next to the name of one of them. With each elector having only one vote to cast for only one candidate, there is no such thing as ticket splitting. At the close of polling, the votes are collected in one central area in each constituency and counted by hand. The process of counting is an efficient one, and a sufficient number of results are usually announced within a few hours of the close of the polls to know which party has won the election. If the party in office has lost, the prime minister goes to Buckingham Palace to tender his or her resignation. The leader of the party newly returned with a majority of seats is then summoned. The new cabinet and other ministerial appointments are announced within a matter of days, sometimes within a matter of hours. Within a month of an election being called, Britain may find itself with a new government.

Since 1979, British electors have also had an opportunity to vote in a supranational election, electing the United Kingdom's 81 members in the European Parliament (see chapter 10). Britain is exceptional in that, unlike every other country in the European Community, it employs (other than for the three seats in Northern Ireland) the plurality, first-past-the-post method of election. There are consequently similarities to elections to the House of Commons: Candidates of the main parties compete in single-member constituencies, each elector having just one vote to cast. Though the elections are held on a fixed-term basis once every five years, election campaigns are short.

For elections to national and supranational bodies, the demands made on British electors are thus not onerous. Coupled with the shortness of election campaigns, they do not impinge upon electors' lives on any extensive basis. Greater opportunities to vote exist in local elections. An elector can vote for members of councils at district and county levels and sometimes at parish level as well (see chapter 9). However, only council members (councillors) are elected; no executive officers are subject to election. Councils choose their own chairmen or chairwomen, and the chief administrative officers are appointed professionals. There is no election of any local official, be it police chief, register of wills, city auditor, or judge. The one similarity between local elections in Britain and the United States is the turnout. Normally two-thirds of electors stay away from the polls.

The essential characteristics of national elections in the United States and the United Kingdom are contrasted in Table 5.1. Let us consider in a little

TABLE 5.1   United States and United Kingdom national elections

Characteristics	United States	United Kingdom
Bodies elected	President and vice-president Senate House of Representatives	House of Commons
Constituencies	President: national Senate: state House: single-member districts (435)	Single-member districts (constituencies) (651)
Terms of Office	President: 4 years (two-term maximum) Senator: 6 years (one-third elected every 2 years) Representative: 2 years (limits to seeking reelection by senators or representatives vary by state)	Maximum of 5 years (no limit to MPs seeking reelection)
Eligibility for candidature	President: native-born citizen, age 35 or over, 14 years resident in U.S. Senator: age 30 or over, 9 years a citizen, inhabitant of state Representative: age 25 or over, 7 years a citizen, inhabitant of state	Citizen age 21 or over (certain exceptions)
Fixed-term or irregular elections	Fixed-term	Irregular (but must not go beyond 5-year intervals)
Mode of election	Plurality vote for Senate and House, popular vote and electoral college for president	Plurality vote
Date of election determined by	Acts of Congress	Recommendation of prime minister to monarch (within limits of 1911 Parliament Act and subject to certain qualifications)
Franchise	Citizens age 18 and over (certain exceptions)	Citizens age 18 and over (certain exceptions)
Registration procedures	Generally required to register in person at stipulated times and places (certain state exceptions)	Head of household required by law to complete annual registration form, submitted by mail
Turnout at elections	Less than 60% post-1968 (40% or less in midterm elections)	Regularly over 70%

more detail some of the main features of national elections in Britain—that is, to the House of Commons—and of electoral behavior before proceeding to a consideration of the current controversy surrounding the electoral system. Elections to the European Parliament and to local councils are considered in later chapters.

THE ELECTORAL STRUCTURE

Electors

As we have seen (chapter 3), the franchise was variously extended in the nineteenth century. The basis on which the vote was given was that of property. Not until 1918 was universal manhood suffrage introduced on the basis of (six months') residence. In the same year, women age 30 and over, if already local government electors or married to such electors, were given a vote in general elections. The vote was extended to all women aged 21 and over in 1928. It was extended to 18- to 20-year-olds in 1969. The various extensions of the franchise during the course of the twentieth century, much more radical in numerical terms than the various extensions of the previous century, and the growth in population have resulted in the electorate growing from 6,730,935 in 1900 to 43,181,321 in 1987. The 1949 Representation of the People Act effectively brought to final fruition the principle of "one person, one vote." The only people excluded from the franchise are peers (they have their own house), imprisoned criminals, those of unsound mind, people convicted of certain election offenses, and aliens.

To exercise one's right to vote, it is necessary to be on the electoral register, which is compiled annually. Each year every household receives an electoral registration form. The head of the household is required to complete it and to list all those who are resident in the dwelling on October 10 of that year and are eligible for inclusion, including those who will attain the age of 18 years during the period that the new register comes into effect. These forms are returned by mail to the registration officer for the constituency. Once the register is compiled, it is open for inspection; it takes effect the following February, and is in force for one year. Electors who move to another constituency during the course of the year are entitled to apply to vote by post in the constituency in which they are registered.

Compared with registration procedures adopted previously in most U.S. states,[3] the British practice is efficient and effective. Completing the registration forms is a legal requirement. Supplementary registers are published every month to allow registration officers to include people wrongly omitted. Even so, it has been estimated that something like 2 million people who are eligible are not included. Some voters fill in registration forms incorrectly or fail to complete them. In 1991, the Office of Population Censuses and Statistics found that electoral registration was the lowest since 1976, the earliest year for which it had comparable data.[4] One explanation offered was that many voters were seeking to evade paying the "poll tax" (see chapter 9).[5] In registration, there is no procedure analogous to the U.S. practice of registering as a Republican, Democrat, or Independent; given the absence of primary elections in Britain, there is no logical reason that one should exist.

Constituencies

The United Kingdom is divided into single-member constituencies. There are currently 651, though the number can and does vary. From 1974 until 1983 there were 635, and at one time earlier in the twentieth century there were over 700.

The drawing of boundaries is the responsibility of bodies known as boundary commissions: There is a commission each for England, Scotland, Wales, and Northern Ireland. Each commission is chaired by the speaker of the House of Commons (a nonparty figure) and each has a judge as deputy chairman. Assistant commissioners, usually lawyers, are appointed to supervise local inquiries, and the staff of the commissions includes the country's main officials dealing with population and geographic surveys.

In redrawing boundaries the commissions are guided by rules laid down by act of Parliament. They are supposed to ensure that constituencies are as equal as possible in the size of their electorates. However, they are permitted to deviate from this equality if special geographic considerations (for example, the size, shape, and accessibility of a constitutency) appear to render such a deviation desirable. Other rules further complicate the position. The commissioners are enjoined not to cross local authority boundaries in creating parliamentary constituencies. They also have to work within the context of regional disparities.[6] To compensate for the absence of its own national assembly, Scotland has a greater number of constituencies allocated to it than its population strictly allows, and the same exception applies to Wales. Hence, the electoral quota (the national electorate divided by the number of seats) is greater in England than in Scotland or Wales.

Under existing legislation, the commissioners are required to review electoral boundaries every 10 to 15 years. (It used to be at more frequent intervals, but this was found to be too disruptive.) Before making their recommendations, the commissioners consider submissions from interested bodies, primarily the local political parties. If a proposed change has the support of the local parties, it is usual for the commissioners to accept it. Once they have completed their work, their recommendations are presented to a government minister, the home secretary, who is then required to lay them before the House of Commons for approval. They are rarely free of criticism. Boundary reviews in 1948 and 1955 were the subject of protests, and in 1969 the Labour home secretary advised his supporters in the House to vote against the commission's recommendations, which they did. As a result, the 1970 general election was fought on the basis of the old boundaries. The commission's recommendations were implemented in the new Parliament. The next review by the commission was completed in 1982 and challenged unsuccessfully in the courts by the Labour party. The recommendations were subsequently approved by Parliament, and the 1983 general election was fought on the new boundaries. The next review should be completed by the end of 1994.

A combination of population shifts (about three-quarters of a million people move every year in Britain), the disparity among constituency electorates recommended by the commissioners in favor of other criteria (maintaining local government boundaries and the like), the lapse of time between reviews, and the disparity in the number of seats allocated to the different countries in the United Kingdom has meant that marked differences often exist among the sizes of electorates. In the 1970s, some constituencies had electorates in excess of 100,000 and some had fewer than 25,000. Before the boundary revisions made in 1983, 39% of seats deviated from the electoral quota by ± 20%. Even after the revisions, 5% of the seats still deviated from the quota by the same margin. In 1987, the proportion had increased to 15%. By 1990, one seat—Milton Keynes—had an electorate of 107,000. The Boundary Commission took the unusual step of recommending, outside of its periodic review of boundaries, the creation of a new seat to deal with the situation. As a result, the number of seats increased in the 1992 general election from 650 to 651. Separate recommendations resulted in marginal changes to a number of constituency boundaries.

Campaigns

Election campaigns are short, sharp, and dominated by the political parties. The formal campaign extends over a period of three to four weeks. In 1992, for example, Parliament was dissolved on Monday, March 16, and the general election held on Thursday, April 9. This short campaign contrasts with the two-month campaign in U.S. presidential elections—from Labor Day to polling day—and the preceding months of primary elections. For U.S. politicians, there are essentially four stages in an election campaign: profile raising, fund-raising, the primary campaign, and the general election. For British politicians, only the first and the last stages apply. Incumbents and challengers in Britain do not have to contest primary campaigns, and fund-raising is the task of the local party organizations. Activity in the constituency—and, for the incumbent, in the House of Commons— is important for gaining visibility with electors. However, only in the event of a formal election campaign are the resources of the local party mobilized on an extensive scale.

In British elections, unlike those in the United States, the personalities of candidates (except for national leaders) and their personal wealth play but a marginal role. The campaign is fought in practice on a national level between the two main parties, the candidates and the local campaigns serving to reinforce the national campaigns of their leaders. Candidates are selected locally by the parties, and the parties provide the finance and the organization for the campaign. Election expenses in each constituency are limited by statute and have been since 1883. Expenditure is permitted only where authorized by the candidate, the candidate's election agent, or a person authorized in writing by the agent. The maximum permitted expenditure is calculated on the basis of a fixed sum plus a limited amount based on the number of electors: in 1992, £3,648 ($5,654) plus 4.1p per voter in each county (predominantly rural) constituency and £3,648 plus 3.3p per voter in borough (urban, and smaller in area) constituencies. Certain types of expenditure are illegal (for example, paying an elector to exhibit a poster or paying for voters to be taken to and from the polling booths), and separate committees to promote a candidate are not permitted. Even with the modest expenditure that is permitted, most candidates fail to spend the maximum allowed.[7] Some devices for keeping costs low are employed and these can, where required, provide up to an extra 20% of expenditure:[8] A popular ploy is to purchase stationery in advance and then resell it cheaply to the candidate as second-hand stock. Few candidates, though, are prepared to run too many risks for fear of having their elections challenged and declared void: Expenses have to be declared and opponents keep a wary eye open for any infringements of election law. There is, in any event, a major practical constraint: The parties have difficulty raising sufficient money to fight campaigns.

Each candidate is permitted one postage-free mailing of one piece of election literature. Other literature is distributed by the unpaid party activists. The main item of literature is the candidate's election address. This will usually incorporate a summary of the main points of the party's national election manifesto. The candidate will spend most of the campaign making speeches throughout the constituency, not infrequently at thinly attended meetings, and canvassing door to door where possible. He or she will be aided by volunteers who do doorstep canvassing to try to determine where supporters live: On election day they will keep a running tab on who has voted in order to ensure that support is maximized.

The main focus of the campaign is national. The party leaders will make regular and well-publicized appearances throughout the country, ensuring that the national press and television reporters follow in their wake, as well as holding daily press conferences. The national party organizations increasingly also make use of press advertising. As long as expenditure cannot be said to apply in support of specific candidates, national party campaigns do not fall foul of the election finance restrictions. In the 1992 election the Conservative, Labour, and Liberal Democratic parties spent a total of £19 million ($29 m.) centrally, about twice the amount expended by their candidates in the local campaigns.[9] The largest single item of expenditure was advertising. The parties also enjoyed the benefit of free but limited television time. Paid political advertising on television is not allowed: Each party is allocated a set number of 10-minute party political broadcasts that are transmitted on all television channels. The allocation of the number of broadcasts to the parties is a somewhat contentious one. The broadcasts themselves are often regarded by voters as the least appetizing part of election campaigns.[10]

The basis of the parties' appeal to the country is the election manifestos that they issue. In recent elections these have become increasingly lengthy and specific documents, detailing the intended policies and measures to be pursued by a party if returned to office. They constitute a topic of some controversy. It has been argued that very few electors actually read them and that many of the commitments made do not enjoy widespread support among voters, even among those voting for the parties that issued them.[11] They also are viewed by some observers as hostages for the future, parties in office being perceived as often doing the reverse of what was promised in their manifestos.[12] In practice, they constitute something of a guide to interested bodies and provide a framework for the main items of legislation introduced by an incoming government in the first session or two of a new Parliament: Most manifesto promises are usually implemented.[13] A more relevant criticism is that manifesto promises may not address themselves to the country's real problems. Some would argue that, by virtue of the manner of their complilation and their utilization as a means furthering the adversary relationship between the parties, manifestos add to those problems rather than offering solutions.[14]

Candidates

Any citizen age 21 years or over is eligible to be a candidate for election to the House of Commons. There are certain limited exceptions. Precluded from serving in the House of Commons are those who are disqualified from voting, as well as policemen, civil servants, judges, members of the boards of nationalized industries, undischarged bankrupts, members of the armed services, and clergy of the Churches of England, Scotland, Ireland, and the Roman Catholic Church. The exclusion of public servants has an acceptable rationale to reinforce it; they are free to resign their positions should they wish to stand for election. The exclusion of certain clergy is less easy to justify (a relic of the time when religious disputes were at the heart of national affairs), as is the exclusion of 18- to 20-year-olds: When the voting age was lowered in 1969, the age of eligibility for candidature was not.[15] To be a candidate one has to obtain the signature of ten electors in the constituency and submit a deposit of £500 ($775), returnable in the event of receiving 5% of the votes cast. (From 1918 to 1985 the deposit was £150, returnable in the event of receiving one-eighth of the votes cast.) Unlike in the United States, there are no residence requriements: Hence, parties enjoy a wider range of choice in the selection of candidates.

In practice, candidates are party candidates. As a result of a change in the law in 1969, this fact is now more formally recognized: Candidates are permitted to include their party designation on the ballot paper. It is generally assumed that an individual candidate has little influence on voting behavior. Party is the decisive factor, though the candidate can have some impact. In recent general elections there have been examples of locally popular candidates holding their marginal seats against the national swing (even in some instances increasing their majorities) and recent research has suggested that the "personal vote" achieved by candidates may be higher than was previously assumed.[16] Such personal votes can make a difference in some marginal seats, but the instances are limited. Party remains the primary and almost exclusive influence. Since 1950, only four MPs have been elected in Britain (excluding Northern Ireland) without the support of a major party, and those four were all incumbent party members who had broken with their parties.

All constituencies in Great Britain are contested by Conservative and Labour candidates. In the 1970s there was an increase in the number of Liberal candidates, and in the general elections of 1983 and 1987 the Liberal/Social Democratic Alliance fielded candidates in all 633 seats in Britain; their successors, the Liberal Democrats, contested all but 2 of the British seats in 1992, the exceptions being the 2 seats being defended by independent SDP incumbents. In 1992, the Conservative party also ventured into Northern Ireland, contesting (unsuccessfully) 11 of the 17 seats in the province.

In Scotland there is the challenge of the Scottish National Party (the SNP), which witnessed a notable growth in the 1970s and a relative decline in the 1980s and early 1990s. In February 1974, it won 7 seats and increased the number to 11 in the second election of that year. That constitited the high point of its parliamentary representation. Though remaining an electoral force in Scotland, its representation in the House slumped to 2 in the 1979 and 1983 elections. In 1987, it improved its position marginally, winning 3 seats. Despite a remarkable by-election victory in the supposedly ultra-safe Labour seat of Glasgow Govan in 1988, and an increase of almost 50% in its vote, it could still only manage to take 3 seats in 1992. Its activity and electoral support nonetheless renders Scotland a four-party battleground, each party enjoying parliamentary representation (see Map 5.1). In Wales, there is Plaid Cymru (the Party of Wales), which since 1974 has won between 2 and 4 seats in the province (see Table 5.2); its 4 seats in 1992 constituted the best performance in its history. In Northern Ireland, the dominant force is the Ulster Unionists, though it is now divided into different parties. In 1992, Unionists of different hues, committed to the union with Britain, won—as they had in 1987—13 of the province's 17 seats. The remaining 4 seats were won by candidates of the Social Democratic and Labour party (SDLP), an increase of 1 over 1987: It won Belfast West, the seat previously held by Gerry Adams, the Sinn Fein candidate who had refused to take his seat in the House of Commons. The seats won by regionally based parties in the 1992 election— 24—constituted less than 4% of the seats but meant that the total number of parties represented in the House was 9.[17]

Other parties, or fringe groups, also ostensibly are keen to be represented in the House of Commons. The 1970s and early 1980s witnessed a growth in the number of candidates contesting seats. The 1951 general election was fought

TABLE 5.2   General election results, 1945–1992

General Election (Winning Party in Capital Letters)	Votes Cast[a]		Seats Won[b]	
July 1945				
LABOUR	11,995,152	(47.8%)	393	(61.4%)
Conservative	9,988,306	(39.8%)	213	(33.3%)
Liberal	2,248,226	(9.0%)	12	(1.9%)
Others	854,294	(2.8%)	22	(3.4%)
Turnout: 72.7%	25,085,978	(99.4%)	640	(100.0%)
February 1950				
LABOUR	13,266,592	(46.1%)	315	(50.4%)
Conservative	12,502,567	(43.5%)	298	(47.7%)
Liberal	2,621,548	(9.1%)	9	(1.4%)
Others	381,964	(1.3%)	3	(0.5%)
Turnout: 84.0%	28,772,671	(100.0%)	625	(100.0%)
October 1951				
CONSERVATIVE	13,717,538	(48.0%)	321	(51.4%)
Labour	13,948,605	(48.8%)	295	(47.2%)
Liberal	730,556	(2.5%)	6	(1.0%)
Others	198,969	(0.7%)	3	(0.5%)
Turnout: 82.5%	28,595,668	(100.0%)	625	(100.1%)
May 1955				
CONSERVATIVE	13,286,569	(49.7%)	344	(54.6%)
Labour	12,404,970	(46.4%)	277	(44.0%)
Liberal	722,405	(2.7%)	6	(0.9%)
Others	346,554	(1.2%)	3	(0.5%)
Turnout: 76.7%	26,760,498	(100.0%)	630	(100.0%)

(continued)

TABLE 5.2 (continued)

General Election (Winning Party in Capital Letters)	Votes Cast[a]		Seats Won[b]	
October 1959				
CONSERVATIVE	13,749,830	(49.4%)	365	(57.9%)
Labour	12,215,538	(43.8%)	258	(40.9%)
Liberal	1,638,571	(5.9%)	6	(0.9%)
Others	142,670	(0.8%)	1	(0.2%)
Turnout: 78.8%	27,746,609	(99.9%)	630	(99.9%)
October 1964				
LABOUR	12,205,814	(44.1%)	317	(50.3%)
Conservative	12,001,396	(43.4%)	304	(48.2%)
Liberal	3,092,878	(11.2%)	9	(1.4%)
Others	347,905	(1.3%)	0	(0.0%)
Turnout: 77.1%	27,647,993	(100.0%)	630	(99.9%)
March 1966				
LABOUR	13,064,951	(47.9%)	363	(57.6%)
Conservative	11,418,433	(41.9%)	253	(40.2%)
Liberal	2,327,533	(8.5%)	12	(1.9%)
Others	422,226	(1.2%)	2	(0.3%)
Turnout: 75.8%	27,233,143	(99.5%)	630	(100.0%)
June 1970				
CONSERVATIVE	13,145,123	(46.4%)	330	(52.4%)
Labour	12,179,341	(43.0%)	287	(45.6%)
Liberal	2,117,035	(7.5%)	6	(0.9%)
Others	903,299	(3.2%)	7	(1.1%)
Turnout: 72.0%	28,344,798	(100.1%)	630	(100.0%)
February 1974				
LABOUR	11,639,243	(37.1%)	301	(47.4%)
Conservative	11,868,906	(37.9%)	297	(46.8%)
Liberal	6,063,470	(19.3%)	14	(2.2%)
Others (Great Britain)	1,044,061	(3.4%)	11	(1.7%)
Others (Northern Ireland)[c]	717,986	(2.3%)	12	(1.9%)
Turnout: 78.7%	31,333,666	(100.0%)	635	(100.0%)
October 1974				
LABOUR	11,457,079	(39.2%)	319	(50.2%)
Conservative	10,464,817	(35.8%)	277	(43.6%)
Liberal	5,346,754	(18.3%)	13	(2.0%)
Scottish National Party	839,617	(2.9%)	11	(1.7%)
Plaid Cymru	166,321	(0.6%)	3	(0.5%)
Others (Great Britain)	212,496	(0.8%)	0	(0.0%)
Others (Northern Ireland)	702,904	(2.4%)	12	(1.9%)
Turnout: 72.8%	29,189,178	(100.0%)	635	(99.9%)

TABLE 5.2 (continued)

General Election (Winning Party in Capital Letters)	Votes Cast[a]		Seats Won[b]	
May 1979				
CONSERVATIVE	13,697,690	(43.9%)	339	(53.4%)
Labour	11,532,148	(36.9%)	269	(42.4%)
Liberal	4,313,811	(13.8%)	11	(1.7%)
Scottish National Party	504,259	(1.6%)	2	(0.3%)
Plaid Cymru	132,544	(0.4%)	2	(0.3%)
Others (Great Britain)	343,674	(1.2%)	0	(0.0%)
Others (Northern Ireland)	695,889	(2.2%)	12	(1.9%)
Turnout: 76.0%	31,184,015	(100.0%)	635	(100.0%)
June 1983				
CONSERVATIVE	13,012,602	(42.4%)	397	(61.1%)
Labour	8,457,124	(27.6%)	209	(32.1%)
SDP/Liberal Alliance	7,780,577	(25.4%)	23	(3.5%)
Scottish National Party	331,975	(1.1%)	2	(0.3%)
Plaid Cymru	125,309	(0.4%)	2	(0.3%)
Others (Great Britain)	198,834	(0.6%)	0	(0.0%)
Others (Northern Ireland)	764,474	(2.5%)	17	(2.6%)
Turnout: 72.7%	30,670,895	(100.0%)	650	(99.9%)
June 1987				
CONSERVATIVE	13,760,525	(42.3%)	376	(57.8%)
Labour	10,029,944	(30.8%)	292	(35.2%)
SDP/Liberal Alliance	7,341,152	(22.6%)	22	(3.4%)
Scottish National Party	416,873	(1.3%)	3	(0.5%)
Plaid Cymru	123,589	(0.4%)	3	(0.5%)
Others (Great Britain)	127,329	(0.4%	0	(0.0%)
Others (Northern Ireland)	730,152	(2.2%)	17	(2.6%)
Turnout: 75.3%	32,529,564	(100.0%)	650	(100.0%)
April 1992				
CONSERVATIVE	14,092,235	(41.9%)	336	(51.6%)
Labour	11,559,735	(34.4%)	271	(41.6%)
Liberal Democrat	5,999,384	(17.8%)	20	(3.1%)
Scottish National Party	629,555	(1.9%)	3	(0.5%)
Plaid Cymru	154,390	(0.5%)	4	(0.6%)
Others (Great Britain)	445,612	(1.3%)	0	(0.0%)
Others (Northern Ireland)	731,782	(2.2%)	17	(2.6%)
Turnout: 77.7%	33,612,693	(100.0%)	651	(100.0%)

[a]Percentages do not always add up to 100% because of rounding.
[b]The Speaker, where seeking reelection, is included with original party.
[c]Prior to 1974, Ulster Unionists were affiliated with the Conservative party. Thereafter they sat as a separate parliamentary party.

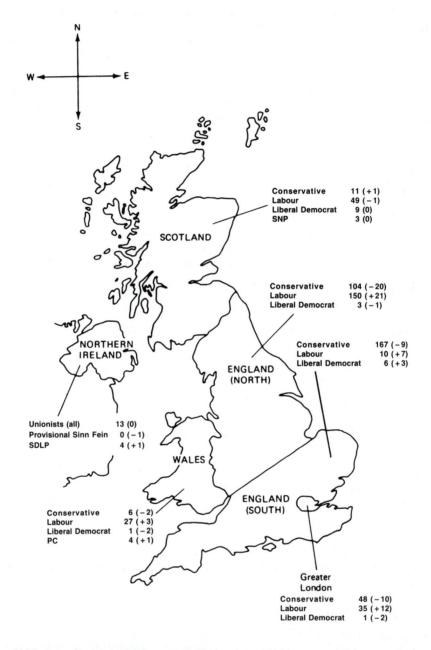

MAP 5.1 General election results by region, 1992

Note: Net gains and losses from 1987 are shown in parentheses.
Note: South of England comprises Avon, Bedfordshire, Berkshire, Buckinghamshire,
Cambridgeshire, Cornwall, Devon, Dorset, Essex, Gloucestershire, Hampshire, Hertfordshire,
Isle of Wight, Kent, Norfolk, Northamptonshire, Oxfordshire, Somerset, Suffolk, Surrey, Sussex,
and Wiltshire.

by 1,376 candidates, that of 1983 by 2,579, an average of 4 per seat. It was in order to deter nonserious candidates that the deposit for candidature was raised to £500 in 1985, but the deterrent effect was short-lived and modest. Though the right-wing National Front (which had fielded 303 candidates in 1979) gave the increased deposit as the reason it did not contest any seats in 1987, the number of candidates in 1987 was not much fewer than in 1983: a total of 2,325. In 1992, the figure was a record 2,948. The increase was the result principally of the usual array of fringe candidates being supplemented by 309 candidates standing for a new and eccentric pseudoscientific and quasi-religious party, the Natural Law party, and by an increase in the number of Green party candidates (256, compared with 133 in 1987). There also were 73 Liberal candidates, representing those traditional Liberals who opposed the 1988 merger of the Liberal and Social Democratic parties (see chapter 6). Other party labels included those of the Anti-Federalist party; the far right British National party and the National Front; the Islamic party of Great Britain; and—representing the rather endearing, and enduring, fringe of British politics—the Official Loony and Loony Green Giant parties. Only the Liberal candidates achieved a mean vote in excess of 1.5%.[18] (Green candidates achieved a mean vote of 1.3%.) Loony candidates achieved better results than those standing under the Natural law banner. Of all the candidates standing under these assorted party labels, only one—the leader of the Liberals—managed to retain his deposit. In one Scottish seat, Glasgow Pollock, a maverick candidate standing under the label of Scottish Militant Labour not only managed to retain his deposit but also, with just under 20% of the poll, achieved second place. Other lone candidates had no such impact. The experience of the range of fringe candidates contesting the prime minister's seat in 1992, shown in Table 5.3, is typical of how they fared.

Candidate Selection

The candidates of the main parties are selected locally, though the national party in each case retains some veto power. In Britain, unlike in the United States, there are no primary elections and the selection of a candidate is in practice determined by the party activists. Given that more than 70% of seats are safe for one party or another, this selection is usually tantamount to election.

In the Conservative party, aspiring candidates have to be on the party's Candidates List maintained by the party's national headquarters.[19] Achieving a place on the list was previously done through an interview with the party vice-chairman and the national committee responsible for candidates. In recent years, the procedure has been extended and more professional methods of selection employed. Aspiring candidates are required to attend a vigorous weekend selection process in which they are put through a series of exercises (for example, taking part in debates, writing and discussing essays); about half of those taking part make it through to the Candidates List.[20]

A local Conservative association seeking a candidate will invite applicants and will be sent the names of those on the Candidates List wishing to be considered for the seat. In a safe Conservative seat, the number of applicants will usually

TABLE 5.3 Selected constituency results, 1992

Blaneau Gwent

Electorate: 55,638		
L. T. Smith (Labour)	34,333	(78.98%)
D. Medling (Conservative)	4,266	(9.81%)
A. Burns (Liberal Democrat)	2,774	(6.38%)
T. A. R. Davies (Plaid Cymru)	2,099	(4.83%)
LABOUR MAJORITY	30,067	(69.16%)
Total vote: 43,472		
Turnout: 78.13%		

In the heart of the traditional mining area of Wales, an area of particular Labour strength and Conservative weakness, Blaneau Gwent was Labour's safest seat in 1992.

Huntingdon

Electorate: 92,913		
J. Major (Conservative)	48,662	(66.16%)
H. A. Seckleman (Labour)	12,432	(16.09%)
A. N. Duff (Liberal Democrat)	9,386	(12.76%)
P. Wiggin (Liberal)	1,045	(1.42%)
D. Birkhead (Green)	846	(1.15%)
D. Sutch (Loony)	728	(0.99%)
M. Flanagan (Conservative Thatcherite)	231	(0.31%)
Lord Buckethead (Gremloids)	107	(0.15%)
C. Cockell (FTM)	91	(0.12%)
D. Shepheard (Natural Law Party)	26	(0.04%)
CONSERVATIVE MAJORITY	36,230	(49.26%)
Total vote: 73,554		
Turnout: 79.16%		

Huntingdon, in the east of England, produced the largest Conservative majority, both in absolute terms and expressed as a percentage of the poll. The seat is held by the prime minister, John Major. It was because of having such a high visibility incumbent that it attracted such a range of fringe candidates.

Inverness, Nairn, and Lochabar

Electorate: 69,468		
Sir R. Johnston (Liberal Democrat)	13,258	(26.05%)
D. Stewart (Labour)	12,800	(25.15%)
F. S. Ewing (Scottish National Party)	12,562	(24.68%)
J. Scott (Conservative)	11,517	(22.63%)
J. Martin (Green)	766	(1.50%)
LIBERAL DEMOCRAT MAJORITY	458	(0.90%)
Total vote: 50,903		
Turnout: 73.28%		

A large rural constituency in the north of Scotland, the seat is held by the president of the Scottish Liberal Democrats. It is a classic example of a four-way split between four serious challengers, the gap between the winning candidate and the one coming fourth constituting less than 4% of the poll.

run into the hundreds. The association will appoint a selection committee, usually comprising the association officers and representatives from its different branches and associated groups such as the Young Conservatives, to draw up a short list and then recommend three or more names to the executive council, the main decision-making body of the association. The council may then recommend one name for approval to a general meeting of the association or it may put forward more than one name and leave it to the general meeting to decide.

Traditionally, Conservative selection committees have been less concerned with the political views of applicants than have Labour committees.[21] (In the 1950s and 1960s, applicants were more likely to be asked their views on capital punishment than their views on economic policy.) Selection committees have tended to be influenced by an applicant's knowledge of the constituency (and willingness to live in it if selected), his or her stature and delivery of speech, and whether or not he or she has the makings of a good constituency member or, in some cases, a national figure. On occasion, more esoteric considerations may apply. When this author served on a committee, one question asked during the short-listing process was "Can't we interview him? He has a nice name." (The response: a polite "no.") Other influences can include, in some areas, religion and quite often age and sex: Local parties are reluctant to adopt women candidates (the folklore being that women voters dislike voting for them) and anyone under 30 or over 50 years of age. There also is a tendency to prefer married men (single men over 30 are considered somewhat suspect), and wives are often asked to appear before selection committees. Because wives are looked on as surrogates for their husbands while the latter are at Westminster, their attitudes to constituency work are considered important. In recent years, the party nationally has been urging local associations to adopt more female candidates and in 1992 it also signalled a desire for a broader age range. In the 1992 election, the party fielded 59 female candidates, 13 more than in 1987. Of the 59, 20 were elected.

Although the Labour candidates selected are increasingly similar in background to Conservative candidates, the selection procedure in the Labour party differs from that of the Conservatives. It also has undergone a number of recent changes. A local Labour party will seek a candidate by inviting nominations. Nominations may be made by local ward committees, party groups such as the women's section, and affiliated organizations, principally trade unions. (An aspiring candidate can approach such groups to solicit a nomination.) Once nominations are received, the executive committee, responsible for the day-to-day running of the party, will draw up a short list. Since 1989, the selection had been made by an electoral college in which at least 60% of the votes are allocated to local party members and up to 40% to affiliated organizations.[22] Before 1989, the selection had been made by the General Management Committee, comprising representatives from the different ward committees and affiliated organizations.

The successful candidate has to be endorsed by the party's National Executive Committee (NEC). The NEC has variously used its power to refuse endorsement to certain candidates and also to block attempts by local parties to replace sitting MPs. It also has acquired, and uses, the power to determine the short list for candidates in by-elections.

In 1980, the Labour conference approved the principle, confirmed in 1981, of mandatory reselection of sitting Labour MPs. What this meant was that sitting MPs could no longer be reselected automatically by local parties just before a general election was held. Instead, a full selection procedure had to be gone through during the lifetime of a Parliament, thus allowing other challengers to be considered. It was a contentious issue and generally seen as an attempt by the party's left wing to remove some right-wing Labour MPs. By 1986, a total of 14 MPs had been ousted through this route. The selection procedure introduced in 1989 for selection by electoral colleges was designed to reduce the influences of the activists who monopolized the General Management Committees. In the 1987–1992 Parliament, only two MPs were successfully removed by their local parties, with most encountering little difficulty in achieving reselection.[23] Conservative MPs do not have to face mandatory reselection, but on occasion a sitting MP has nonetheless been denied reselection—be it for reasons of age, laziness, unpopularity, or personal scandal—and replaced by a new candidate.[24]

The principle of local selection is also a feature of the other national parties in Britain with parliamentary representation. However, there is a difference in that whereas Conservative and Labour local parties usually have to choose from many eager applicants, other parties often have difficulty in recruiting candidates. At the 1989 Liberal Democrat conference, an appeal was made for activists to offer themselves as candidates. Consequently, there is often a willingness by the national leadership to accept whomever the local party has managed to recruit.

The candidates selected by the major parties tend to be middle class, middle aged, male, and white. Female and nonwhite candidates are exceptional, but not as exceptional as they used to be. In the 1992 election, a record number of women were elected to the House of Commons—60, compared with 41 in 1987—as were 6 blacks, compared with 4 in 1987 and none before 1987. The successful candidates more than the unsuccessful ones tend to be middle aged, university educated (and, in the case of Conservative MPs, products of public schools), and drawn from business and the professions (see chapter 11). In postwar years, there has been a tendency for MPs to be even more middle-class than previously.[25] Recent decades also have seen the emergence of more career-oriented MPs, devoted to politics and a lifetime of service in the House of Commons.[26]

Elections

In each of the 651 single-member constituencies, the method of election employed is the plurality or ''first-past-the-post'' method, with the candidate who wins the largest single number of votes—even though it may not be an absolute majority—being declared the winner. It is the same method as that employed in the Senate and House elections in the United States. However, whereas most contests in the United States are straight fights between Democrats and Republican candidates, thus producing a victor with more than 50% of the votes cast, the three- or four-way fights that are now common in U.K. seats can result in the winning candidate achieving way below 50% of the vote. Indeed, in hotly contested four-way fights it is actually possible to win with less than 30% of the vote, as the remarkable example of Inverness, Nairn, and Lochabar in the 1992 election demonstrates (Table 5.3). The result in the constituency was exceptional, though not unique.

In practice, most seats are safe seats for one or the other of the two main parties—that is, the winning candidate has achieved a margin that constitutes 10% or more of the total poll. More than 70% of seats are safe seats. Some are deemed to be very safe. In the 1992 election, more than 150 seats were held by Conservative or Labour candidates with margins that represented 30% or more of the poll (77 Conservative, 85 Labour).[27] In some of these seats the margin constituted more than 50% of the poll, and in Blaneau Gwent, as Table 5.3 reveals, the winning candidate's margin constituted almost 70% of the poll.

It is in the remaining minority of seats that general elections are effectively fought. In the 1987 election, there were 80 marginal seats. The 1992 election produced more, with 92 Conservative, 60 Labour, and 11 Liberal Democrat and 6 other marginal seats. The outcome in these seats in the next general election—likely to be held in 1996 or 1997—will determine which party forms the next government.

The electoral system, as we shall see, has facilitated the return of governments enjoying an overall majority of seats in the House of Commons. In all but one of the general elections since (and including) 1945, one party has won an absolute majority of seats and the leader of that party has formed a government. The Labour party has achieved an overall majority in five elections, on three occasions by slim margins (in 1950, 1964, and October 1974). The party also formed the government following the Februray 1974 election, in which it won more seats than any other party but did not obtain an overall majority (see Table 5.4). The Conservatives have won overall majorities by clear margins in eight elections since 1945, four of them consecutively since 1979.

TABLE 5.4   Parliamentary majorities, 1945–1992

Parliament	Party Returned to Office	Overall Majority*
1945–1950	Labour	146
1950–1951	Labour	5
1951–1955	Conservative	17
1955–1959	Conservative	60
1959–1964	Conservative	100
1964–1966	Labour	4
1966–1970	Labour	98
1970–1974	Conservative	30
1974	Labour	–33
1974–1979	Labour	3
1979–1983	Conservative	43
1983–1987	Conservative	144
1987–1992	Conservative	101
1992–	Conservative	21

*Overall majority following general election. The speaker, where seeking reelection, is included in the original party. A negative number indicates that a minority government was returned to office.

VOTING BEHAVIOR

Recent decades have seen some significant shifts in the nature and pattern of electoral support for British political parties. In the 1950s and 1960s, Britain displayed the characterics of a stable two-party system.[28] During that period:

1. There was a high turnout of electors.
2. Of those who voted, virtually all voted for either the Conservative or the Labour party.
3. The most significant predictor of party voting was class.
4. The class base of voting produced stable blocks of voting support, with changes in government being determined by small shifts of voting support from one party to another.

The first two generalizations are borne out by the data in Table 5.2. In every general election held from 1950 to 1966 inclusively, more than three-quarters of those on the electoral register turned out to vote and, of those who did so, 87% or more voted for either the Conservative or Labour candidates. In the 1950 election, turnout reached 84%. In the election of the following year, almost 97% of those who voted cast their ballots for one of the two main parties.

The third generalization is drawn from survey data, which demonstrate the close relationship of class and party in this period. In the general elections held in the 1950s, 70% or more of middle-class voters cast their votes for the Conservative party. In the 1960s, 60% or more of working-class voters cast their votes for the Labour party.[29] Party support was most marked at the two extremes of the social scale. In 1951, 90% of the upper middle class voted Conservative. In 1966, 72% of the "very poor" voted Labour.[30] Class was not an exclusive predictor of voting behavior, nor was the relationship between class and party symmetrical: The middle class was more Conservative than the working class was Labour. One-third of working-class voters regularly voted Conservative. Nonetheless, class remained the most important predictor of how an elector might vote— so much so that one writer, Peter Pulzer, was to declare in 1967 that "class is the basis of British party politics: all else is embellishment and detail."[31]

The class basis of electoral behavior provided each party with a substantial base of support. Small shifts in support could turn one party out of government at an election and replace it with another, but the period of the 1950s in particular did not witness major shifts in voting intentions between elections. This was reflected in by-election results. In the period from 1945 to 1959, there were 168 by-elections: Only 10 of them resulted in losses by the incumbent party. Stability seemed a feature of the two-party system.

The period since the end of the 1960s has produced a very different picture. Turnout since 1966 has been more variable. In the four general elections held from 1950 to 1959, the average turnout was just over 80%. In the elections from 1964 onward, the average has been 5% lower, with turnout in three falling below 73%. In the six elections since, and including, February 1974, the percentage of voters casting their ballots for the Conservative or Labour parties reached 80%

TABLE 5.5 Turnout and two-party voting, 1959–1992

General Election	Percentage Turnout	Of Those Voting, % Voting Con. or Lab.
1959	78.8	93.2
1964	77.1	87.5
1966	75.8	89.8
1970	72.0	89.4
1974 (Feb.)	78.7	75.0
1974 (Oct.)	72.8	75.0
1979	76.0	80.8
1983	72.7	70.0
1987	75.3	73.0
1992	77.7	76.3

in only one election, that of 1979 (Table 5.5). In the remaining five elections, the percentage has averaged just under 75%. This is approximately 20% lower than the average achieved in the four elections from 1950 to 1959. The 1983 general election marked the low point in terms of turnout and two-party support.

The explanation for this change generally has been ascribed to a decline in the class-party nexus. The two main parties can no longer rely on their "natural" class support. The relative decline in this support is borne out by survey data from the 1987 and 1992 general elections (Table 5.6). Labour failed to achieve even half of the working-class vote. Even among trade unionists, it attracted the support of only 46%. Almost a third of trade unionists (31%) voted Conservative; 19% voted for the Liberal Democrats. The Conservatives made no significant inroads among their traditional class supporters, the swing against the Conservatives in 1992 actually being greatest among the upper middle class. Although social class continues to structure party choice, it is not a predictor of party choice to the extent that it was in the 1950s and 1960s.

Also of declining significance have been the variables of gender, age, and religion. Traditionally, women have been somewhat more likely to vote Conservative

TABLE 5.6 Vote by social class, 1992

Party	Professional and Managerial (AB) %	Office and Clerical (C1) %	Skilled Manual (C2) %	Semiskilled, Unskilled, Residual (DE) %
Conservative	56 (57)*	52 (51)	39 (40)	31 (30)
Labour	19 (14)	25 (21)	40 (36)	49 (48)
Liberal Democrat	22 (26)	19 (26)	17 (22)	16 (20)

*1987 percentages in parentheses.
SOURCE: MORI.

TABLE 5.7 Party support by gender, 1974–1992

	Oct. 1974		1979		1983		1987		1992	
	M %	*W* %	*M* %	*W* %	*M* %	*W* %	*M* %	*W* %	*M* %	*W* %
Conservative	32	39	43	47	42	46	43	43	41	44
Labour	43	38	40	35	31	26	32	32	37	34
Liberal/Liberal Democrat	18	20	13	15	25	27	23	23	18	18

SOURCE: MORI.

than men. In most postwar elections, more men have voted Labour than have voted Conservative whereas more women have voted Conservative than voted Labour. However, the bias was a slight one. According to Gallup, the bias disappeared in 1983 and according to MORI it disappeared in 1987, returning in 1992 (Table 5.7). However, the bias was not consistent among age groups, with Labour achieving a notable lead among females ages 18–24, an age group in which the Conservatives achieved a slight lead among male voters. Gender, then, cannot be drawn upon as a reliable predictor of voting behavior.

Age, as the foregoing suggests, also shows some variation, but again, as a predictor of voting behavior, is of limited utility. The older the voter, the greater the likelihood of voting Conservative (Table 5.8). Among those aged 55 or over who voted, the Conservatives enjoyed a 15-point lead over Labour in the 1987 election and a 12-point lead in 1992. Labour, in contrast, had a 3-point lead among the 18–24 age group in 1987 and a 4-point lead in 1992. However, in 1983, the Conservatives enjoyed a 9-point lead in this age group. It is possible that this shift reflects a generational cohort change; Butler and Stokes found in their survey that it is not age as such that influences voting behavior but rather the period at which one becomes politically aware. Those voting for the first time in 1983 are likely to have been able to recall the period of Labour government and especially the "winter of discontent" of 1978–79 that severely undermined

TABLE 5.8 Party support by age, 1992

	Age							
	18–24 %		*25–34* %		*35–54* %		*55 +* %	
Conservative	35	(37)*	40	(39)	43	(45)	46	(46)
Labour	39	(40)	38	(33)	34	(29)	34	(31)
Liberal Democrat	19	(21)	18	(25)	19	(24)	17	(21)

*1987 percentages in parentheses.
SOURCE: MORI.

Labour's credibility as a governing party. In 1987 and more especially 1992, first-time voters would have had no salient perceptions other than those of a period of Conservative government. Even so, the differences are not great, and as a predictor of voting behavior, the generational cohort thesis is of little value.[32]

Religion, once an important variable in explaining voting behavior, is no longer the force it was. It was a significant influence in the nineteenth century but declined rapidly in the twentieth, as class became more important. Butler and Stokes found the relationship between religion and party of declining relevance with each generation. In some areas where religious loyalties remain strong, such loyalties can still alter the pattern of class voting. An obvious example is Northern Ireland (see chapter 9), though mainland examples can be found in certain cities, notably Glasgow and Liverpool. In such cities, there is a sizable Irish Catholic vote, and that swells the Labour vote in elections.[33] Liberal Democrats also tend to maintain support in areas of traditional strength of nonconformist religions. Overall, though, the impact of religion is marginal and that marginality is reflected in the fact that it no longer figures in analyses of general elections.

Class, then, is of declining relevance as a predictor of voting behavior, and it has not been displaced by the other variables we have identified. The waning of the class-party nexus would appear to explain a greater volatility in voting intentions. Though the Conservative party won four consecutive general elections from 1979 onward, each time with roughly the same share of the national poll, this does not reflect a stability in support among the electorate. By-election results and opinion polls reveal a high level of volatility. In the 99 by-elections held between 1966 and 1979, 31 (31% of the total) resulted in a defeat for the defending party. Of the 56 held between 1979 and 1992, 19 (34%) were lost by the defending party. This compares with less than 6% in the period from 1945 to 1959. Opinion polls during the period of Conservative government from 1979 onward also revealed significant shifts in voting intentions. According to the polls, if an election had been called in 1981, early 1986, or 1990, the Conservative party would have gone down to defeat, in some cases of disastrous proportions. At one point in 1981 (the year the Social Democrat party was formed), the Conservatives actually fell to third place in the opinion polls. In March 1990, the party trailed Labour in the polls by more than 20 points. It was fear of an electoral disaster that encouraged Conservative MPs to replace their leader in 1990 with one more likely to restore party fortunes in the polls.[34]

Electoral behavior has thus changed significantly. The class-party nexus has waned, though not disappeared. Both main parties have substantial bodies of commited supporters, but not to the same extent as before. Voters do not identify with parties to the same degree as in earlier decades.[35] The Conservative and Labour parties still dominate in the parliamentary arena but no longer enjoy the monopoly they enjoyed in the 1950s and 1960s. Recent election outcomes suggest that the change in electoral behavior has been more at the expense of the Labour party than the Conservative party, but with volitility in voting intentions suggesting the need for caution in drawing that conclusion.

Explanations of Voting Behavior

Is it possible, then, to provide any clear explanation of contemporary voting behavior? The analysis of electoral behavior has been a significant growth industry in British social science. Butler and Stokes's pioneering study dominated in the 1970s. Since then, there have been several, often competing, models of electoral behavior. The most significant have been those to explain voting in terms of (1) class, (2) consumption, (3) location, (4) issues, and (5) performance evaluation.

Class.   The class-party nexus, as we have seen, declined in the 1970s and 1980s. Class became a less useful predictor of voting behavior, apparently because of changing social patterns— rendering class itself less relevant—and because of class dealignment, those within a class being less likely to vote for their "natural" class party. Class, nonetheless, has not ceased to be relevant. As we have seen, middle-class voters are more likely to vote Conservative than Labour; the more one moves up the social scale the greater the propensity to vote Conservative. Those at the bottom of the social scale remain more likely to vote Labour. In the 1992 election, in only one of the three social groupings shown in Table 5.6 is the difference between Conservative and Labour support less than 18%.

Some students of electoral behavior have sought to demonstrate that there has not been a significant decline in class-based voting. They have done so through a redefinition of class. Instead of relying on the occupation of the heads of households, they have utilized more sophisticated criteria. Heath, Curtice, and Jowell, for example, take into account authority at work and those who are self-employed.[36]

The problem with these new variables is that those with the greatest predictive value cover but a small proportion of the population. In the analysis of Heath and his associates, only about one in three voters are in categories where as many as half of the voters support one party.[37] The explanatory value of this approach is thus extremely limited.

A more recent analysis suggests the continuing relevance of class polarization, but only in a particular part of the country. Political geographers Johnston and Pattie contend that class divisions have persisted in the north of England but declined substantially in the south.[38] Class thus has some continuing relevance but not to the same extent as before. It is necessary to identify other influences that have become more salient.

Consumption.   One of the more controversial of recent studies has been that advanced by Patrick Dunleavy.[39] He contends that not only has there been a class dealignment but also that there has been a realignment: The cleavage based on production has been replaced by one based on consumption. In other words, class voting—derived from one's stance in relation to the means of production—has been replaced by voting based on public and private consumption. Those who rely on services provided by the state (housing, education, health, transport) are most likely to vote Labour; those who rely on services provided by the private sector are most likely to vote Conservative. The greater the degree of private-sector consumption, the greater the likelihood of voting Conservative. Thus, home-owning households with two cars are 4.39 times more likely to vote Conservative than those with no car who rent their homes from the local authority.

The problem with this particular analysis is the same as that with the redefinition of class: The ideal type (home owning, car owning, privately educated, private health care) is very small. One test of the consumption cleavage thesis found that it did not explain anything that could not be explained through existing approaches.[40]

Location.   Various studies have demonstrated the independent influence of location in voting behavior. A middle-class voter in an urban area is more likely to vote Labour than is a middle-class voter in a rural area. A trade unionist in a rural area is more likely to vote Conservative than is a trade unionist in an urban area. One explanation for this phenomenon is the process of socialization. Living for a long period of time in a particular locality, one begins to absorb the predominant values of that community.

Recent decades have witnessed a marked north-south polarization and an urban-rural polarization in party support. Research by Curtice and Steed found that the spatial divisions began to emerge after 1955. "A North-South cleavage began to emerge in the 1955–59 swing . . . while the urban-rural cleavage became clearly more evident in the 1959–64 swing."[41] Conservative support has become more pronounced in the south of England, whereas Labour support has increased in the north and Scotland.

In each of the general elections since 1979, the Conservative party has been carried to victory largely on the votes of the electorate in the southern half of England, below a line drawn from the River Severn to the Wash (see Map 5.1). Labour, despite the challenge of the Scottish National Party and a slight swing to the Conservatives in the 1992 election, has achieved a notable predominance in Scotland. In the general election of 1959, the Conservatives won 31 seats in Scotland and Labour won 38. In 1992, the Conservatives won 11 seats (1 up from the all-time low of 10 in 1987) to Labour's 49. A similar predominance has been achieved by Labour in Wales (27 seats in 1992, compared to 6 for the Conservatives). In contrast, in the southern half of England, Labour has been largely marginalized and displaced by the Liberals, now the Liberal Democrats, as the principal challenger to the Conservative party. As Map 5.1 vividly demonstrates, there is now only one part of Britain that, in terms of competition for seats, can be described clearly as a two-party area.

The urban-rural divide has been equally pronounced. Conservative support in the larger cities has been declining for 30 years. By 1983, the number of seats it was winning in the larger cities was half that achieved in 1959. The position became more pronounced in the elections of 1987 and 1992. In 1959, in the three large cities of Glasgow, Liverpool, and Manchester, the Conservatives won 15 seats. In 1983, they won just 1 and in both 1987 and 1992 none at all. Of the nine British cities, excluding Greater London, listed in Table 1.2, the Labour party holds a majority of seats in all but one; in the one exception (Bristol), both parties have two seats each. Within London, Labour's strength lies in inner London, with a Conservative dominance being achieved in outer, suburban London.

The explanations for the spatial polarization are to be found in mobility and economic change. The north of England has continued to rely on many old traditional industries, characterized by mass unionized work forces and relatively little mobility. It has thus retained an environment conducive to established class politics, as identified by Johnston and Pattie. Economic decline in recent years has hit the traditional manufacturing industries hardest, producing high unemployment. The area has thus been the one area in which Labour has been able to maintain a strong base. The south has been characterized by a growing service industry, less tied to traditional trade unionism than the north, and by greater mobility in the work force. A similar development has characterized urban and suburban areas, inner cities being characterized often by economic decline, with the more prosperous white-collar workers moving to the suburbs. There is thus a growing correlation between location and party support, with location being both an independent as well as a dependent variable in explaining that support.

Issues.   As class was perceived to have declined as a determinant of voting behavior, various analysts asserted the increasing significance of issue-based voting. The most sophisticated analysis has been that offered by Mark Franklin in *The Decline of Class Voting in Britain*. He charts the decline in class voting since 1964, which he contends is a consequence of changing social structures and a reduced appeal of the Labour party to its traditional class groups. "The decline in the class basis of voting amounts to a weakening of constraints on volatility and self-expression and the consequence was to open the way to choice between parties on the basis of issue preferences."[42] As the constraint of class has declined, so attitudes—reevaluated in the light of changing conditions—have played a greater role in shaping voting choice. Voters have been more willing to vote on the basis of issue preference and that has generated greater volatility in electoral behavior. Even though the Conservative party has won four successive elections since 1979 it has done so on the basis of a relatively low share of the poll and, more important, despite wide swings in party preferences in between elections.

To win, the Conservatives have had to run hard in order to stand still, in other words, to work hard to tap issues that are salient in electoral terms. In the 1983 and 1987 elections—especially the former—the issue of defense was an electoral plus for the Conservatives. In the 1992 election, with the end of the cold war, defense did not figure prominently in voters' evaluations. Instead, salient issues were those of health care, unemployment, replacing the poll tax, education, and housing (all electoral pluses for Labour) along with management of the economy, taxation, law and order, and—at the bottom end of the scale in voters' ranking of importance—Europe and Northern Ireland (electoral pluses for the Conservatives).[43] Issue voting, as Franklin recognized, makes for uncertainty in electoral outcomes. Though the Conservatives were returned to office in 1992, the result of the election was uncertain until the results were announced.

The issue-voting approach has been the subject of both challenge and defense.[44] It contributes an important but not the only part of the jigsaw for explaining electoral behavior. Were issue voting the sole determinant of electoral behavior in Britain, survey data suggest that Labour would have won the general election in 1992. "Sixty-three per cent of those who considered unemployment important favoured Labour's ability to handle it, yet only 47 per cent of them actually voted Labour."[45] Similar disparities were found on other issues. Other explanations thus have to be sought.

Performance Evaluation.   Class, however important as a variable in shaping voting behavior, has never been an exclusive influence. If it were, elections would have demonstrated a more consistent outcome. Instead, class was identified as important at a time when political scientists were claiming the existence of a "pendulum effect" in politics, with some rotation in office between the two main parties. Other variables served to make the difference between success and failure in general elections. Various studies have reinforced the accepted wisdom that evaluation of performance in office has been crucial. With the decline in the class-party link, this instrumental variable becomes more important.

One of the most important analyses in the 1980s was that of Paul Whiteley. According to his research, retrospective evaluation (of how parties have performed in office) and prospective evaluation (of how parties are likely to behave in office) are, along with social attributes, important influences on voting. Utilizing data drawn from the 1979 Election Study, he concluded that subjective judgements were better predictors of voting behavior than objective factors, and that of retrospective and prospective evaluations, the former were more significant than the latter for explaining support—and the decline in that support—for the Labour party. "This is consistent with the performance hypothesis in which voters are passing judgement on Labour's record in office, rather than on its future policy proposals. The dealignment is explained by the failure of the party to represent adequately the objective and subjective interests of its supporters."[46]

The problem with this particular hypothesis is that it presupposes a reasonably high level of political awareness and an intellectual capacity to assess specific performance in office, whereas the largest switch away from the Labour party in an earlier election that it lost, in 1970, came from the least educated of its supporters.[47] Data drawn from the 1992 general election also question the plausibility of Whiteley's thesis while reinforcing the relevance of performance evaluation as an important determinant of voting behavior. By 1992, a large section of the voting population could no longer engage in retrospective evaluation of a Labour government. Survey data also reveal that evaluations were prospective rather than retrospective. Despite being in the throes of an economic recession, voters believed that they would be worse off under a Labour government than under a Conservative one. According to the analysis of David Sanders, unemployment and levels of economic optimism were not such negative factors as might have been supposed for the Conservatives, with electors willing to blame a worldwide recession rather than the government. The Conservatives, for their part, were able to convince a substantial number of electors that Labour would make a worse job of economic management than the present government; the numbers so convinced were sufficient to secure the government's reelection. In the days immediately preceding the election, there was a shift in voters' perceptions of the parties' capacities to deal with the economy and a range of other issues; the shift was not issue specific but across the board. "The fact that perceptions shifted so markedly in all fourteen areas simultaneously suggests that the observed responses were largely rationalizations. They derived from decisions—to support the Conservatives—that had already been taken and that themselves reflected fears about personal economic well-being and the general ability of Labour to govern."[48] By the end of the campaign, almost half the electorate believed they would be worse off under Labour's tax policies.

The Conservatives thus benefitted from a prospective evaluation of Labour's likely performance in office. That was sufficient to ensure the government's reelection. However, the election nonetheless showed a swing to Labour. That swing was marked in areas where electors appear to have engaged in retrospective evaluation. There was a correlation between a decline in Conservative support and the areas hit hardest by recession, though the correlation—when measured in terms of unemployment levels—was far from total.[49]

Evaluation of performance emerges as a highly plausible explanation of both the Conservative victory and the swing to Labour in the 1992 general election, though even its principal proponents concede that other important variables were at work. Indeed, most of the explanations we have considered appear to offer some insight into electoral behavior, and changes in that behavior, over the past 20 to 30 years, but with none offering a sole explanation. Most serve to explain some degree of behavioral change. Rose and McAllister found that about 80% of voting variance could be explained by five influences: pre-adult socialization, socioeconomic interests (class), political principles, current performance of parties, and party identification.[50] What is significant about this finding is, first, the number of variables and, second, the fact that— despite that number—20% of the variance remains unexplained. Elections in Britain, to quote Rose and McAllister, have become more open. As they have, the study of them has become more extensive and increasingly sophisticated.

THE CURRENT DEBATE

Electoral behavior, then, has been the subject of extensive academic analysis. That behavior occurs within the context of a particular electoral system, and in recent years that system itself has been the subject of public debate. The debate became prominent in the latter half of the 1970s and has reemerged since the end of the 1980s as part of a wider discussion about Britain's constitutional arrangements. The electoral system, according to its critics, is a dysfunctional one, in need of replacement. The view is not one that enjoys universal support.

A Dysfunctional Electoral System?

By the middle of the twentieth century, Britain had developed an electoral system whose basic characteristics were delineated above: single-member constituencies, first-past-the-post election to determine the winner in each, and each adult citizen having the right to cast a vote. That system was both perceived and expected to perform three related functions: Through election to the House of Commons it was expected to produce a government;[51] through a purportedly democratic franchise and mode of election, it was expected to confer legitimacy upon the government to govern, subject to the approval of Parliament; and through facilitating a choice between parties propounding specific programs, it was expected to influence public policy, the party in government carrying through the promises embodied in its election manifesto. In the 1950s and 1960s such expectations were assumed to have been met. Governments were returned with overall majorities. There were few complaints about the mode of election. Governments appeared to carry out their promises. The electoral system appeared to form an intrinsic part of a stable polity.

In the 1970s, and especially in the wake of the two general elections of 1974, the extent to which the electoral system was capable of fulfilling such functions became a matter of controversy. In the February 1974 election no party was returned to office with an overall majority of seats. In the election of October of the same year the Labour party achieved an overall majority of only three seats: By the end of the Parliament, as a consequence of by-election losses and defections, it was in a minority by 17 seats. The Conservative party achieved a swing of 5.2% in its favor in the May 1979 election, being returned with a majority of 43 seats. In previous decades a similar swing would have produced a much higher majority. Shifts in the distribution of party support within the country were, according to one important study, likely to increase the likelihood of "hung" Parliaments, no one party being returned with an overall majority.[52] The ability of the electoral system to produce a government in the way previously expected of it was thus called into question. This analysis appeared to lose some of its persuasive appeal in the wake of the three subsequent elections. The results of those elections, though, gave greater force to another criticism. The system came under attack as being unfair—hence undermining consent by calling into doubt the legitimacy of both the mode of election and the government produced by it—and for facilitating the adversary relationship between the parties, a relationship that significantly influenced public policy but that did so in a manner harmful to the interests of the country.

The accusation that the electoral system is unfair is not new. It has been advanced for some time by both the Liberal—now the Liberal Democratic—party and the Electoral Reform Society. It gained ground as a result of the election results of the 1970s and the development of the adversary politics thesis. The first-past-the-post plurality method of election in single-member constituencies, it is argued, does not allow realization of the principle of "one person, one vote, one value." Each adult citizen may have one vote but each vote is not of equal value. The disparity in the size of constituency electorates means that a vote cast in a constituency with a small electorate is worth more than one cast in a constituency with a large electoral roll. Furthermore, the extensive number of safe seats means that many electors cast "wasted" votes. What is the point of voting Conservative in a constituency such as Blaneau Gwent, for example, where the Labour candidate has a majority in excess of 30,000? An elector consistently voting Conservative in the constituency would never contribute toward the election of an MP.

The two most central criticisms, though, have been directed at the aggregate effects of such a method of election. Given the difference in the spread of support between the parties, it is possible for one party to get more votes than its opponent party but receive fewer seats. For example, party A could win two marginal seats by the barest of margins while party B won one seat with an overwhelming majority; the aggregate vote for party B in the three seats could well exceed that of party A, but party A has won twice as many seats. (A similar spread of support among states in the U.S. presidential election may result in a president obtaining a majority in the electoral college without obtaining a majority of the popular vote.) On two occasions in postwar elections, such a situation actually occurred. In the 1951 general election, the Conservatives won a majority of seats but the Labour party won more votes (see Table 5.2). In the February 1974 election, the position was reversed, the Conservatives winning more votes nationally than Labour but Labour winning more seats. In terms of forming a government, it is the number of seats that count: The Conservatives formed the government in 1951, the Labour party in 1974.

The other major and related criticism, the one emphasized most often, is that the plurality system of voting works against national third parties. Those who benefit most from such a system are the two largest parties and those with regionally concentrated support. This is as true in the United States as it is in Britain. In presidential elections, a third-party candidate with concentrated support, such as George Wallace in 1968, can carry some states and hence win some electoral college votes. A candidate with support that is broad but not deep, such as Ross Perot in 1992, can amass several million votes but carry no state at all. The system favors the Republican and Democratic parties. Similarly in Britain, a party can win several thousand votes in each constituency yet not come out top of the poll in any; in consequence, it amasses a large popular vote but no seats in Parliament. This is almost the position in which the Liberal party found itself in the 1970s (see Table 5.2). In 1979, for example, it won in excess of 4 million votes yet topped the poll in only 11 seats, less than 2% of the total. This phenomenon was even more marked in the case of the SDP/Liberal Alliance in the 1980s: In both 1983 and 1987 it achieved more than 20% of the votes cast yet won less than 4% of the seats in Parliament. The largest party, by contrast, can top the poll in most constituencies with, say, 40% of the poll, the remaining votes split among the other party candidates, thus achieving a majority of seats without receiving an absolute majority of the votes cast. Indeed, at no election since 1935 has a party obtained more than 50% of the votes cast, yet at only one election since that time has a government been returned without a majority of seats. In the election of October 1974 the Labour party obtained a bare majority of seats for fewer than 40% of the votes cast. Not surprisingly, the Liberal Democratic party, formed by a merger of the Liberal party and SDP in 1988, is in the vanguard in arguing for a reform of the electoral system to eliminate such anomalies. It has been joined by the Green party. As it appears increasingly disadvantaged by the present system, the Labour party also has adopted a less supportive stance toward the existing arrangements. The Conservative party, by contrast, retains a preference for the system as it stands.

The other more recent criticisms of the electoral system have derived from the characterization of the existing political system as an adversary one. The "adversary politics" thesis was developed following the 1974 elections by a number of academics, led by S. E. Finer (see chapter 3). The essence of their argument was that the electoral system encouraged a polarized contest between two parties for the winner-take-all spoils of a general election. One party would be returned to office with an overall majority and implement its manifesto program, a program neither known nor supported by most electors and one drawn up on the basis more of party dogma than of a dispassionate and well-informed analysis of Britain's problems. The other party would then win at a subsequent election, enter office, and largely undo the work of its predecessor, implementing instead its own program. Given that the two parties were perceived as representing different poles of the political spectrum, government policy would lurch from being right of the political center under one administration to being left of center under another. The results, in short, were unrepresentative governments—pursuing policies more politically extreme than those favored by the more centrist electorate—and policy discontinuity. Policy discontinuity frustrated industrialists and investors who wished to engage in forward planning: They could not anticipate stability in government programs. Adversary politics and changes in government may make for "exciting politics," but they produced "low-credibility Government strategies, whichever party is in power."[53]

Indeed, the conditions created by the electoral system were seen as being the heart of Britain's problems. To win an election, a party would make extravagant promises, doing so to outbid the other party. In office, it would find it could no longer raise the resources to meet those promises. It therefore had to change tack, further adding to confusion in governmental policy making. However, it also had to act in a way that would not jeopardize its chance of winning the next election. Hence it was reluctant to take the unpopular measures deemed by some to be necessary to tackle Britain's long-term problems. Even when, as in the 1980s, a government gained reelection, the adversary relationship militated against its being able to mobilize popular support in order to achieve its goals. The response of the Conservative government, according to critics, has been to strengthen its own power, thus further reducing its capacity to mobilize necessary, and voluntary, support. The result, in short, has been a vicious circle.[54]

The solution to the problem, or at least a partial one, was perceived by these critics as the introduction of a new electoral system, one that introduced a method of proportional representation (PR). Proportional representation, it was argued, would be fairer than the existing electoral system, ensuring that a party received the share of parliamentary seats equivalent to its national vote. Furthermore, given existing voting behavior, it would deprive any one party of an overall majority of seats. Forming a government with an overall parliamentary majority would thus necessitate a coalition. This would likely involve one of the main parties having "to co-operate with a party or parties taking a more central stance," hence leading to greater moderation in policy.[55] Given that such a coalition would enjoy the support of more than 50% of electors and that the turnover of seats under PR is small, the coalition would most likely remain in office for the foreseeable future and hence be in a position to ensure a degree of policy continuity. The overall effect of PR would thus be to put an end to the worst features of adversary politics and its unfortunate consequences.

Of the systems of proportional representation, the one favored by Liberal Democrats and the Electoral Reform Society is the single transferable vote (STV) system. This is the method of election currently employed in the Republic of Ireland, in Tasmania, and in Malta and for elections to the Australian Senate. Under STV there are multi-member constituencies, with each elector able to indicate a preference on the ballot paper, putting the number 1 beside the name of the candidate most preferred, 2 against the name of the elector's second choice, and so on. A quota is established by the formula of dividing the number of valid ballots cast by the number of seats, plus one: to the resulting figure, one is added. Thus in a five-member constituency in which 120,000 ballots are cast, the formula would be

$$\frac{120,000}{5 + 1} + 1$$

Hence the quota (the number of ballots required to elect one member) would be 20,001. Any candidate receiving this number of votes is declared elected. The second preferences of any of the candidate's surplus votes, plus those of the candidate at the bottom of the poll, are then redistributed, and so on until the necessary number of candidates reach the quota.

The other main system that has been advocated is the additional member system, similar to that employed in Germany. Under this system, single-member constituencies would be retained, with the first-past-the-post method of election retained in each—in other words, the same as at present. However, additional seats would be allocated to parties on a regional basis, a minimum of 5% of the vote in any area of allocation being necessary to obtain additional seats. Additional seats would go to the parties on the basis of the proportion of votes received in the region. Under a scheme proposed by the Hansard Society for Parliamentary Government, there would be 480 single-member constituencies and 160 seats allocated on a regional basis.[56] Proponents of this system and of STV argue that the effect would be a representative House of Commons, the proportion of seats going to parties being the same as the proportion of the votes won in the election.

Support for a new electoral system has developed since the mid-1970s, encompassing academics and politicians. The Conservative and Labour parties have witnessed the creation of bodies within their own ranks favoring such reform. Various attempts were made in the 1974–1979 Parliament to introduce PR throughout the United Kingdom for elections to the European Parliament and to the proposed assemblies in Scotland and Wales. The attempts failed, but they helped keep the issue of electoral reform on the agenda of political debate. The outcome of the elections since 1979 added a further spur to the reform movement. Electoral reform is a central plank of the Charter '88 reform movement (see chapter 15). Liberal Democratic MPs now regularly introduce bills in the House of Commons to utilize a system of PR in local elections.

Despite this pressure for reform, the existing system retains its supporters. A majority of MPs, especially on the Conservative benches, prefer the first-past-the-post method of election. One keen defender is the present prime minister, John Major. In recent years, supporters have been more vigorous in advocating retention of the present system.[57] The arguments deployed against the reformers' case are varied. The essential line of argument is that a reformed electoral system could constitute a greater threat to the maintenance of political authority than any defects of the existing system. The STV system, it is argued, could threaten the essential link between an elector and her or his MP, given that it would necessitate in rural areas constituencies of massive size. Given the reformers' argument that PR would enhance the likelihood of coalition government, consent could be undermined if government were to result from post-election bargaining between parties, or by a small center party holding the balance of power and hence wielding undue influence over government policy, or by the alienation of voters who support a party excluded on a long-term basis from becoming a partner in coalition.[58] Such rebuttals are based on accepting the assumption made by PR advocates about the likely consequences of electoral reform. Some observers have drawn attention to the fact that such assumptions themselves rest on flimsy foundations, however. The reformers argue their case on the assumption that voting behavior experienced under the current mode of election would most likely continue under a new mode: This is, as Geoffrey Alderman has pointed out, a most unlikely hypothesis.[59] Arguments that PR works well in countries such as Germany are countered by pointing to the experience of Italy, where turnover in governments is rapid and a significant fraction of the population vote for a party that is consistently excluded from government. Given the different political cultures that exist, seeking to anticipate what would happen in Britain on the basis of experience abroad is an undertaking of limited usefulness.

The adversary politics thesis developed by the reformers has also been variously challenged. Two mutually exclusive arguments are deployed against it. One line of argument accepts the notion of an adversary relationship between the parties but considers this a beneficial rather than a harmful process: It offers a clear choice to the electorate and it results in one party with a mandate from the people getting on with the job of governing. If the electorate disapproves of the policies or their outcomes, it has the opportunity to replace the government at the next election.[60] There may be some discontinuity in policy occasioned by governments of different political persuasions pursuing different paths, but that is the price—an acceptable price—one has to pay for the advantages offered by the existing system. Proportional representation, it is feared, would facilitate a blurring of choice and prevent a party from being returned with a mandate clearly approved by the people.

The other argument deployed against the adversary politics thesis calls into doubt the relevance of the notion itself. The rhetoric of adversary politics, it is argued, hides a more consensual substance. In terms of government legislation, empirical research has indicated that a consensual model is indeed more applicable.[61] In this view, parties are seen as being not quite as central to formulation of public policy as both reformers and the politicians themselves believe. The external demands on government are such that it can often act only as arbiter between competing demands and respond, under guidance from civil servants, to international events and trends over which it has no direct influence. Whichever party is in power makes some but not a great deal of difference. This particular argument received considerable reinforcement in 1992 as a result of research commissioned, ironically, by the Electoral Reform Society. Undertaken by Richard Rose, the analysis was of the relationship between electoral systems and economic performance in 21 advanced industrial nations. The finding was that there was no consistent link. "Differences in economic performance," declared Rose, "cannot be explained by differences in electoral systems."[62] His conclusion undermined a central tenet of the reformers' case.

The electoral system in the United Kingdom thus constitutes the subject of considerable debate. In terms of the participants in that debate, the stance taken correlates with electoral performance. The principal beneficiary of the system is the Conservative party, which remains wedded to the present arrangements. While the electoral pendulum swung from one party to another, the Labour party remained a supporter of the first-past-the-post system. After its third successive election defeat in 1987, the party began to witness a number of leading figures advocating proportional representation. The party leader, Neil Kinnock, established a party commission to report on the subject (the Plant Commission) and in the 1992 election his own commitment to the present system appeared to be faltering. In 1993, the commission recommended a change to the existing system (see chapter 6). The Liberals, now the Liberal Democrats, are the "outs" in British politics and their advocacy of change has been as long-standing as their marginalization in British politics, a marginalization facilitated by the first-past-the-post electoral system.

In terms of the effects of the present system, it can be said to provide the means by which a government is chosen but, despite the results of recent general elections, the extent to which it will continue to be capable of providing a government remains in question; a "hung Parliament" was a very real possibility for much of the 1992 election campaign. The consistency of recent results masks an underlying and significant electoral volatility. The system operates on the principle of "one person, one vote," but there is now some dispute as to its legitimacy and that of the government it produces given that the principle of "one person, one vote, one value" has not been fully realized. And there is notable disagreement about the consequences that elections not only do but also should have for public policy. The debate is very much a current one. It revolves around arguments for and against a reform of the electoral system. So long as the Conservative party is returned to government, the chances of electoral reform are minimal; the more it is returned to government, the greater the calls for such reform from other parties.

NOTES

1. M. J. C. Vile, *Politics in the USA* (Hutchinson, 1976 ed.), p. 91.
2. B. Cain, "The American Electoral System," in G. Peele, C. J. Bailey, and B. Cain (eds.), *Developments in American Politics* (Macmillan, 1992), pp. 40–43; H. W. Stanley and

and R. G. Niemi, *Vital Statistics on American Politics,* 2nd ed. (CQ Press, 1990), p. 132.

3. F. F. Piven and R. A. Cloward, *Why Americans Don't Vote* (Pantheon, 1989); D. McSweeney and J. Zvesper, *American Political Parties* (Routledge, 1991), pp. 146–147.
4. D. Cowling (ed.), *The ITN Guide to the Election 1992* (Boxtree, 1992), p. 137.
5. The "poll tax" was a local tax levied on residents rather than on property. Though registers of those eligible to pay the tax were maintained separately from the electoral register, many nonpayers feared they could be identified from the electoral register.
6. On the work of the commission, see R. McLeod, "Reviewing the Situation," *The House Magazine,* 571, November 16, 1992, p. 10.
7. The average expenditure by a Conservative candidate in the 1992 election was £5,840 ($9,052), that by a Labour candidate £5,090 ($7,890), and that by a Liberal Democrat candidate £3,169 ($4,912). D. Butler and D. Kavanagh, *The British General Election of 1992* (Macmillan, 1992), p. 245.
8. M. Pinto-Duschinsky, *British Political Finance 1830–1980* (American Enterprise Institute, 1981), p. 249.
9. Butler and Kavanagh, *British General Election of 1992,* p. 260.
10. See M. Pilsworth, "Balanced Broadcasting," in D. Butler and D. Kavanagh, *The British General Election of 1979* (Macmillan, 1980), p. 229.
11. See S. E. Finer, *The Changing British Party System, 1945–79* (American Enterprise Institute, 1980), pp. 125–126.
12. G. Alderman, *British Elections: Myth and Reality* (Batsford, 1978), pp. 25–27.
13. R. I. Hofferbert and I. Budge, "The Party Mandate and the Westminster Model: Election Programmes and Government Spending in Britain, 1945–85," *British Journal of Political Science,* 22, 1992, pp. 151–182.
14. For a thorough discussion, see D. Kavanagh, "The Politics of Manifestos," *Parliamentary Affairs,* 34 (1), 1981, pp. 7–27.
15. P. Norton, "The Qualifying Age for Candidature in British Elections," *Public Law,* 1980, pp. 55–73.
16. D. M. Wood and P. Norton, "Do Candidates Matter? Constituency-Specific Vote Changes for Incumbent MPs, 1983–1987," *Political Studies,* 40 (2), 1992, pp. 227–238; P. Norton and D. M. Wood, *Back from Westminster* (University Press of Kentucky, 1993).
17. Three of the nine are Northern Ireland Unionist parties.
18. Butler and Kavanagh, *British General Election of 1992,* p. 317.
19. It is possible for a constituency party to select a candidate not on the list, but that candidate must then be approved by the party nationally.
20. Usually three or four such weekends are held each year, attended by up to 48 people seeking to be on the Candidates List.
21. See M. Rush, *The Selection of Parliamentary Candidates* (Longman, 1969) for the period of the 1950s and 1960s. No changes were reported in M. Rush, "The 'Selectorate' Revisited: Selecting Parliamentary Candidates in the 1980s," *Teaching Politics,* 15 (1), 1986, pp. 99–113.
22. However, this procedure has proved unwieldy and there is pressure to move toward a selection procedure based on the principle of one person, one vote. See P. Seyd, "Labour: The Great Transformation," in A. King (ed.), *Britain at the Polls 1992* (Chatham House, 1993), pp. 87–88; and "Labour Moves to End Unions' Role in Choosing Candidates," *Financial Times,* May 28, 1992, p. 22.
23. Butler and Kavanagh, *The British General Election of 1992,* p. 213.
24. See ibid., pp. 217–219.

25. C. Mellors, *The British MP* (Saxon House, 1978); and M. Rush, "The Members of Parliament," in M. Ryle and P. G. Richards (eds.), *The Commons under Scrutiny* (Routledge, 1988), pp. 26–27.
26. A. King, "The Rise of the Career Politician in Britain—and Its Consequences," *British Journal of Political Science,* 2 (3), 1981, pp. 249–285.
27. P. Norton, "The United Kingdom: The Incumbency Paradox," paper presented at the annual conference of the American Political Science Association, Chicago, IL, 1992.
28. See G. Sartori, *Parties and Party Systems: A Framework for Analysis* (Cambridge University Press, 1976), pp. 158–189; P. Norton, "Britain: Still a Two-Party System?" in S. Bartolini and P. Mair, *Party Politics in Contemporary Western Europe* (Frank Cass, 1984), pp. 27–45.
29. B. Sarlvik and I. Crewe, *Decade of Dealignment* (Cambridge University Press, 1983), p. 87.
30. The Gallup Poll, "Voting Behaviour in Britain," in R. Rose (ed.), *Studies in British Politics,* 3rd ed. (Macmillan, 1976), p. 206.
31. P. Pulzer, *Political Representation and Elections in Britain* (Macmillan, 1967), p. 98.
32. See R. Rose and I. McAllister, *Voters Begin to Choose* (Sage, 1986), pp. 68–69.
33. R. Rose, *The Problem of Party Government* (Penguin, 1976), p. 43.
34. See P. Norton, "The Conservative Party from Thatcher to Major," in A. King (ed.), *Britain at the Polls 1992* (Chatham House, 1993), pp. 29–69.
35. See Sarlvik and Crewe, pp. 334–336.
36. A. Heath, R. Jowell, and J. Curtice, *How Britain Votes* (Pergamon, 1985), pp. 22ff.
37. Rose and McAllister, p. 46.
38. R. Johnston and C. J. Pattie, "Class Dealignment and the Regional Polarisation of Voting Patterns in Great Britain, 1964–1987," *Political Geography,* 11 (1), 1992, pp. 73–86.
39. P. Dunleavy, "The Urban Basis of Political Alignment: Social Class, Domestic Property Ownership and State Intervention in Consumption Processes," *British Journal of Political Science,* 9, 1979, pp. 409–444.
40. M. Franklin and E. Page, "A Critique of the Consumption Cleavage Approach in British Voting Studies," *Political Studies,* 32, 1984, pp. 521–536.
41. J. Curtice and M. Steed, "Electoral Choice and the Production of Government," *British Journal of Political Science,* 12, 1982, p. 256.
42. M. Franklin, *The Decline of Class Voting in Britain* (Oxford University Press, 1985), p. 176.
43. Derived from the findings of a MORI poll. See "Issues of Influence," *The Times,* April 11, 1992.
44. See Rose and McAllister, p. 147; and R. J. Johnston, C. J. Pattie, and J. G. Allsop, *A Nation Dividing?* (Longman, 1988), p. 59.
45. D. Sanders, "Why the Conservative Party Won—Again," in A. King (ed.), *Britain at the Polls 1992* (Chatham House, 1993), p. 195.
46. P. Whiteley, *The Labour Party in Crisis* (Methuen, 1983), p. 106.
47. Franklin, p. 161.
48. Sanders, p. 212. See the analysis on pp. 207–213.
49. J. Curtice and M. Steed, "The Results Analysed," in Butler and Kavanagh, *The British General Election of 1992,* pp. 324–331.
50. Rose and McAllister, pp. 128–133.
51. That is, the political apex of the executive formed by ministers. See the comments of A. King, "What Do Elections Decide," in H. Penniman (ed.), *Democracy at the Polls* (American Enterprise Institute, 1980), pp. 295–296.

52. J. Curtice and M. Steed, "Electoral Choice and the Production of Government," *British Journal of Political Science,* 12 (2), 1982, pp. 249–298.
53. M. Shanks, *Planning and Politics* (Political and Economic Planning, 1977), p. 92.
54. See the comments of P. Jay, "Englanditis," in R. E. Tyrell, Jr. (ed.), *The Future That Doesn't Work* (Doubleday, 1977), p. 181; and S. E. Brittan, *The Economic Consequences of Democracy* (Temple Smith, 1977).
55. S. E. Finer (ed.), *Adversary Politics and Electoral Reform* (Wigram, 1975), pp. 30–31.
56. *The Report of the Hansard Society Commission on Electoral Reform* (Hansard Society, 1976).
57. See, for example, J. Patten, *Political Culture, Conservatism and Rolling Constitutional Change* (Conservative Political Centre, 1991); and P. Norton, "In Defence of the Constitution," in P. Norton (ed.), *New Directions in British Politics?* (Edward Elgar, 1991).
58. See P. Norton, "Does Britain Need Proportional Representation?" in R. Blackburn (ed.), *Constitutional Studies* (Mansell, 1992), pp. 136–147.
59. Alderman, p. 39.
60. See Sir K. Popper, " 'The Open Society and Its Enemies' Revisited," *Economist,* April 23, 1988, p. 28.
61. I. Burton and G. Drewry, *Legislation and Public Policy* (Macmillan, 1981); and R. Rose, *Do Parties Make a Difference?* 2nd ed. (Macmillan, 1984).
62. R. Rose, *What Are the Economic Consequences of PR?* (Electoral Reform Society, 1992), p. 17.

CHAPTER 6

Political Parties
More or Less Than a Two-Party System?

In the United States, political parties provide some measure of choice among candidates at election time. They offer a reference point for many electors. They do little else. U.S. parties remain characterized by faction rather than party.[1] Ideological and structural factors militate against them developing as coherent and programmatic bodies. They operate within a broad ideological consensus,[2] rendering differences between parties often largely differences of degree rather than kind. Elections, consequently, are often fought on the basis of trust, personality, or particular issues rather than competing programs. Even if the parties were geared to presenting coherent and competing programs, the structure of the U.S. political system would work against such a program being carried through: A party would need to be cohesive, it would need to capture the White House, and it would need to achieve the return of a majority of its supporters in both houses as well as overcome internal procedural constraints within Congress. The occasions when the conditions of programmatic coherence, party unity, and control of executive and legislative branches have been present—as during the period of the first New Deal and the 1964–1966 Great Society program—are notable for their rarity—and their brevity. It has proved impossible to sustain strong party government in the United States.

Britain lacks those features that have facilitated a weak party system in the United States. A unitary and parliamentary form of government has favored the development of centralized and cohesive parties geared to offering a programmatic choice to the electors and to carrying out that program once the all-or-nothing spoils of a general election have been gained. The executive dominance of the House of Commons ensures legislative approval of the party program: The doctrine of parliamentary sovereignty puts the program's implementation beyond challenge by the courts. It is, in short, the very model of a strong party government. It is a model that has been variously admired. It has variously found favor

struggle. On occasion, such tension has been realized: in the 1840s and again in the first decade of the twentieth century on the issue of tariff reform (the liberal strain within the party favoring free trade, the Tory element favoring the erection of tariff barriers to protect British industry), and in the 1970s and 1980s on the issue of economic policy, to which we shall return shortly. Such occasions, though, are the exceptions rather than the rule. Cohesiveness is a distinguishing feature of the party.

The cohesiveness of the Conservative party may be attributed largely to the fact that, unlike the Labour party, it is a party of tendencies rather than of factions[11]—that is, it lacks permanent factions organized to promote a specific set of beliefs. Rather, it comprises a set of differing but not mutually exclusive stands of thought that are not aligned in consistent opposition to one another. On some issues there may be dissent within the party, but the composition of the dissenting body changes from issue to issue, almost like a chemical reaction. One may be a Tory on one issue and something of a Whig on another. The distinction between Whig and Tory is not so clearly and starkly drawn as to permit a permanent divide. Within each Conservative there is a Tory element and a Whig element, though one element may tend to be more dominant at certain times and on certain issues. In consequence, a party member may disagree with the party on one issue but agree with it on other issues. This is in marked contrast to the Labour party, in which there is a factional divide: Someone on a particular wing of the party on one issue is likely to be on that wing across the whole gamut of current political issues. There is in essence a mutually exclusive struggle between Left and Right.

The Conservative party traditionally has been led by leaders drawn more from the Tory than the Whig strain within the party. The postwar leaders up to 1965—Winston Churchill (1940–1955), Sir Anthony Eden (1955–1957), Harold Macmillan (1957–1963), and Sir Alec Douglas-Home (1963–1965)—were men essentially in the Tory paternalist mold, more concerned with social harmony and order than with the intricacies of economic management. In the 1960s the party's fortunes took a turn for the worse. The economy began to falter, and the party suffered a bitter, public battle for the party leadership in 1963 and seemed unable to offer a young and dynamic leadership to match that which the Labour party was providing. Macmillan had married into the family of the duke of Devonshire and was often photographed on the Scottish moors shooting grouse. Sir Alec Douglas-Home was able to assume the office of prime minister only after renouncing his title as the 14th earl of Home. (The prime minister, by convention, must sit in the Commons, not the House of Lords.) The party seemed to be out of touch with the tenor of the times, and in 1964 it lost the general election.

In July 1965, Douglas-Home resigned the party leadership. Previously the leader had not been elected but had been allowed to "emerge" following private consultations within the party hierarchy. Following the struggle for the leadership in 1963, rules for the election of the leader were adopted in 1964 and first employed in 1965. The electorate was the parliamentary party and the MPs chose as leader Edward Heath in preference to former Chancellor of the Exchequer

Reginald Maudling. Maudling was in the traditional Tory mold, though lacking the aristocratic background of previous leaders. Heath was seen by his supporters as a neoliberal and as capable of challenging the Labour party under the leadership of Harold Wilson. Both Heath and Wilson came from relatively humble origins, they were of similar age, and both stressed the need for economic efficiency.

The first four years of Heath's leadership were inauspicious ones. In 1966 the party was roundly defeated in the general election. Heath was no match for Wilson in parliamentary debates and he had difficulty maintaining party unity on a number of issues, including immigration. However, worsening economic conditions and a rigorous campaign by Heath produced an unexpected defeat for Labour in the 1970 general election. Heath became prime minister and pursued a free-market economic policy. The aim was to force British industry to be more efficient. This goal also provided part of the motivation for British membership in the European Community, which Heath achieved in 1972 (see chapter 10). However, the government's economic policy failed to produce the desired results. Unemployment and inflation spiralled and in 1972 Heath dramatically undertook U-turns in industrial and economic policies: Public money was made available to help regional development and a statutory pay-and-prices policy was introduced.[12]

The government's strategy was dashed by a world energy crisis and by opposition at home from trade unions. The National Union of Mineworkers (NUM) introduced an overtime ban and announced plans for a national strike. Negotiations with the NUM failed and Heath called a general election ostensibly on the issue of "Who governs? The government or the miners?" In practice, a number of issues dominated during the campaign and the election—held in February 1974—failed to produce the decisive mandate Heath had sought. Though the Conservatives got more votes than Labour, they got fewer seats. After seeking unsuccessfully to arrange a deal with the parliamentary Liberal party, Heath resigned. A minority Labour government took office. In October, another general election gave Labour more seats and a small overall majority.

Heath's U-turns had not been popular with a section of the Conservative party, especially neoliberals who saw them as an abandonment of their cherished free-market doctrine. Heath's unpopularity spread following the loss of the two 1974 elections and various calls were made for him to resign or offer himself for reelection. Pressure within the parliamentary party resulted in Heath agreeing to new rules providing for the annual election of the leader. Heath immediately offered himself for reelection. The election was held in February 1975. Heath was confident of victory. His main challenger was Margaret Thatcher, a little-known figure who had served in his Cabinet as education minister. She espoused the rhetoric of the neoliberal wing of the party and offered a new style of leadership. Her campaign was well-organized whereas Heath's was marred by overconfidence. In the first ballot, Mrs. Thatcher got 130 votes to Heath's 119. (A third candidate got 16 votes.) Heath promptly resigned the leadership and in a second ballot—in which new challengers were able to stand—Mrs. Thatcher easily beat her other rivals. The Conservative party had acquired its first female leader, one who was more clearly identified with the neoliberal wing of the party than any of her male predecessors.

Mrs. Thatcher led the party in opposition until 1979, when the Labour government—by that time in a minority in the House of Commons—was defeated in a vote of confidence. A general election ensued, in which the Conservatives capitalized on the unpopularity of the government, its tax policies, and its links with the unions. Margaret Thatcher led her party to victory and she entered Downing Street as Britain's first female prime minister. She was to remain in Downing Street longer than any other prime minister of the twentieth century: a total of 11 years and 6 months. Her premiership went through three distinct periods.

The first was one of bitter conflict. Under her leadership, the government embarked on a rigorous policy of controlling the money supply, reducing direct taxation, and limiting public expenditure in order to combat inflation. The policy ran into trouble. Techniques for controlling the money supply proved inadequate for the purpose. Attempts to reduce public spending proved unpopular in the country and with sections of the Conservative party. The Tory wing proved especially uneasy about the effects the policy was having. Mrs. Thatcher dismissed her party critics as "wets."[13] (Her supporters were then dubbed "dries," though becoming more frequently known by the eponymous title of "Thatcherites.") However, some of those critics were in the Cabinet and, despite the dismissal of various "wets" from the Cabinet between 1981 and 1983, the prime minister failed to persuade her own government to adopt more stringent measures. Subsidies to nationalized industries were continued. Trade union reforms were radical but not as radical as the prime minister wanted.

The effects of government economic policy, at a time of recession, and splits within the party resulted in government unpopularity. The party trailed in the opinion polls. At one point in 1981, following the formation of the Social Democratic party, the party was actually third in the polls. Within the parliamentary party, there were threats of a candidate running against Thatcher for the party leadership. The threat was never carried through but it served to emphasize the leader's political vulnerability.

The second period was that of domination by the leader. It began in 1982. The government's response to the Argentinian invasion of the Falkland Islands—dispatching a military task force to expel the invaders—restored it to popular favor. Following the successful recapture of the islands, the Conservative lead in the opinion polls held until the 1983 general election, sustained by some change in economic indicators (inflation and interest rates both fell) and by disarray within the Labour party. The Falklands campaign also transformed the image of the prime minister. Prior to the campaign, the percentage of electors satisfied with her leadership was less than 30%; afterward, it was nearly 60%.[14] In the 1983 election, the party was swept back to office with the largest majority achieved by any Conservative government since 1935.

Thatcher's ascendancy was maintained in the new Parliament. It faced down a prolonged national miners' strike; after 11 months of bitter conflict, the strike collapsed. The government undertook an extensive program of privatization, a range of public utilities and companies being sold off to the private sector. Some sales, such as those of British Petroleum (BP), proved particularly popular. The proportion of the population owning shares quoted on the stock exchange doubled. Economic conditions improved: Unemployment peaked in 1986 and began to drop; inflation continued its downward trend. Economic improvement generated greater optimism for the future.

During this period, the government suffered a number of setbacks, including a major dispute between senior ministers in 1986, when two ministers clashed over the most appropriate rescue package for Britain's only remaining, and ailing, helicopter company (Westland); the clash resulted in the resignation of both of them, complaints of a directionless Cabinet, and of a cover-up over the leaking of certain documents.[15] Dubbed the Westland affair, it dented the government's popularity, but the unpopularity proved short-lived. The government recovered and was in a sufficiently strong position for Thatcher to lead it to election victory again in 1987. In so doing she achieved an event unprecedented in the history of mass politics in Britain: She was the first leader to lead her party to victory in three consecutive elections. The party was returned to office with an overall parliamentary majority of 101. Margaret Thatcher was at the zenith of her power.

The third period was one of conflict and fall.[16] In the new Parliament, the government embarked on a number of radical legislative measures. These included the replacement of the domestic rates, a local property tax paid annually, with a community charge based not on property but on the number of residents. Popularly dubbed the "poll tax," it was the most unpopular of several unpopular measures. Economic indicators also began to worsen. In 1989, inflation began to rise and Thatcher got into what became a public dispute with her chancellor of the exchequer, Nigel Lawson, over economic policy. In October 1989, he resigned. The party also witnessed internal rifts over the issue of European union. In 1988, Thatcher delivered a speech putting the case against further moves toward political and economic union. The speech generated a clash between opponents (Euro skeptics) and supporters (Euro fanatics) of such union. The clash meant that the party faced the European Parliament elections in June 1989 in disarray. In those elections the party lost 13 of its 35 seats, all to Labour candidates. It was the first time Margaret Thatcher had led her party to an electoral defeat.

Thatcher's stance on Europe propelled one Euro fanatic in the parliamentary party to challenge her in 1989 for the party leadership. Sir Anthony Meyer, a 69-year-old backbencher with no ministerial experience, knew he had no chance of winning but was keen to allow dissidents to make their opposition clear. In the ballot, on December 5, 314 Conservative MPs (84% of the parliamentary party) voted for Thatcher, 33 (9%) voted for Meyer, and 27 (7%) spoiled their ballots or abstained from voting. Sixty MPs had withheld their support from the leader. A number of those who voted for her had written privately to her urging her to moderate her stance, especially on the issue of Europe, if she wanted their support on future occasions. The result was a political embarrassment for Thatcher. A shot had been fired across her bows. At that stage, it was no more than that. Initially, the prime minister appeared to be adopting a conciliatory stance in response to the ballot, but that stance was short-lived.

In the spring of 1990, the introduction of the poll tax in England and Wales resulted in a significant level of nonpayment and demonstrations, some of them violent; London witnessed its worst riot in recent history. Labour led the

Conservatives in the opinion polls by more than 20 points. Some Conservative MPs pressed for a reform, or even abolition, of the tax. Thatcher made clear she was committed to it. In the fall, she reiterated her opposition to further European union: "No, no, no," she thundered in the House of Commons. Those words precipitated the resignation of a senior Cabinet minister, Sir Geoffrey Howe. His resignation speech, delivered on November 13, offered a stunning indictment of the prime minister's leadership. The following day, Michael Heseltine—a former Cabinet minister, out of office since the Westland affair—announced he would challenge Thatcher for the party leadership.

The first ballot in the leadership contest was held on Tuesday, November 20. Heseltine's campaign was effectively run by a team of supporters. Thatcher's campaign was not dissimilar to Heath's in 1975: badly run and overconfident. The prime minister herself was in Paris at a European summit the day of the poll. Her campaign managers misjudged the mood on the back benches. They expected her to get the votes necessary for a clear victory. Under the 1975 rules, to win in the first ballot a candidate had to win an absolute majority and a majority that constituted 15% of those eligible to vote. With 372 Conservative MPs, that meant Thatcher required a 56-vote majority over Heseltine. In the event, she fell 4 votes short. She got 204 votes, Heseltine 152, and 16 MPs abstained. Under the rules, a second ballot was necessary. Thatcher declared her intention to contest that ballot. However, after consulting members of her Cabinet, she decided against doing so. In so deciding, she brought her leadership of the Conservative party—and hence her premiership—to an end.

In the second ballot, two new challengers emerged to contest the leadership against Heseltine: Foreign Secretary Douglas Hurd and Chancellor of the Exchequer John Major. Major was 48 and was little known outside Westminster. Unlike Hurd and Heseltine, he had no extensive past political history that could be used against him and no obvious commitment to any particular ideological tendency within the party. He attracted support very quickly within the parliamentary party, and a highly effective campaign team was put together. His campaign overshadowed the others. In the ballot, held on November 27, Major led the field: He got 185 votes, Heseltine 131, and Hurd 56. Under the rules, an absolute majority alone was necessary on the second ballot. If an absolute majority was not achieved, a third ballot had to be held. Major was 2 votes short of an absolute majority, but as it was obvious he would achieve those votes in a third ballot, the two other candidates immediately conceded defeat and the third ballot was abandoned. John Major was the new party leader and the following day he was summoned to Buckingham Palace to become prime minister.

Major brought in a new leadership style as prime minister. Unlike his predecessor, he did not adopt a confrontational stance, either in the Cabinet or on the public platform. He preferred private, face-to-face meetings to the public arena. It was an approach that proved politically effective. He was more popular than his party. Despite the country slipping deeper into recession, survey data showed that electors blamed global economic conditions and his predecessor rather than John Major. Though the Conservatives trailed Labour in the opinion polls for most of 1991 and early in 1992, Major nonetheless led the Conservatives to victory in a general election on April 9, 1992. His government had the appearance of newness—unlike the old Thatcher government—and electors' unwillingness to trust Labour outweighed their dislike of the government's handling of a range of issues. The Conservatives were returned to office with a reduced parliamentary majority (of 21), but a majority nonetheless.

The election victory proved to be the one bright spot for the Conservatives. In 1992, the party again split badly on the issue of Europe (see chapter 10), a pound sterling crisis in September forced the government to withdraw from the European exchange rate mechanism, and a decision to close most of the country's remaining coal pits generated widespread opposition, including from Conservative MPs; the government was forced to retreat on the issue. The recession continued to generate pessimism rather than optimism. Despite some signs of economic improvement in 1993, the political situation for the party worsened rather than improved. In May, the party suffered disastrous results in local elections—the same day as losing a supposedly "safe" seat in a by-election, with a swing against it (of 28%) not witnessed for more than 20 years. At the end of May, the prime minister dismissed the much-criticized Chancellor of the Exchequer, Norman Lamont. In his resignation speech in the House of Commons, Lamont savaged the government, claiming it was in office but not in power. By July, John Major was the most unpopular prime minister since opinion polling began, and the party slumped to third place in the opinion polls, behind Labour and the Liberal Democrats.

Party Organization.   In terms of internal organization, the party is hierarchical. It brings to bear for its own organization the principles it seeks to apply in society. Weight is given to seniority and experience as well as to the wisdom of past generations. The fount of all policy is the party leader. The party's annual conference as well as other organs of the party (see Figure 6.1) serve in an advisory role only. Ultimately, the leader determines the policy of the party and the contents of the election manifesto. The leader also appoints the leading party officials, including the party chairman, and the members of the party front bench in the House of Commons. Although some authors have sought to apply a monarchial or Hobbesian model of leadership to the party, a traditional family model may be more appropriate, emphasizing as it does the mutual dependence and trust that exists between the head and other members of the household.[17] The leader and the led need each other. As long as the leader appears likely to lead the party to electoral success, the party defers to that leader. If the party looks doomed to electoral defeat, the position of the leader becomes vulnerable. The Thatcher leadership stands as an exemplar of that relationship.

Like other parties, the Conservative party recruits dues-paying members. Unlike the Labour party, the Conservative party has no indirect membership through affiliated bodies. Instead it recruits individuals directly as members. Although no definitive figures are available, the party is believed to have a membership of about 750,000. Members are organized in constituency associations, based on the parliamentary constituencies. Each local association is responsible for holding various fund-raising activities, recruiting new members, and organizing

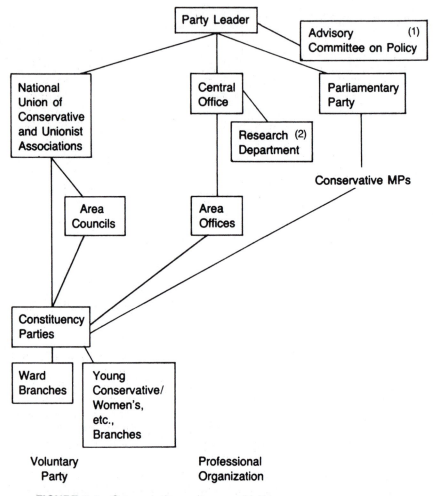

FIGURE 6.1   Conservative party organization

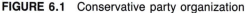

[1] Formally, the Advisory Committee on Policy provides advice on policy, working usually through policy groups composed of MPs and outside experts; in practice, it has been little used in recent years—ad hoc groups being utilized instead—and effectively is now in abeyance.

[2] The Research Department undertakes research for the party, publishes research briefs and pamphlets, assists in drawing up the manifesto, and services the Advisory Committee on Policy and parliamentary party committees. This department was previously independent of Central Office but is now under its roof both organizationally and physically.

election campaigns, both at national and local levels. (The various associations within each European parliament seat also group together to organize the campaign in the Euro-elections.) Almost half of the associations employ full-time agents, paid executive officers responsible for the efficient running of the organization.

Of the political parties, the Conservative is the best financed (see Table 6.1). Its income derives from three sources: business donations, individual donations,

TABLE 6.1 Party income and expenditure, 1982–1987

	Conservative Party		Labour Party	
Year	*Income (£m)*	*Expenditure (£m)*	*Income (£m)*	*Expenditure (£m)*
1982	4.8	4.7	3.9	4.0
1983[a]	9.4	8.6	6.2	6.1
1984	4.3	5.6	4.2	4.2
1985	5.0	5.5	4.9	4.8
1986	8.9	7.5	6.1	6.2
1987[b]	15.0	15.6	10.0	11.3

[a] A Calendar year for the Labour party, financial year (1982–1983, etc.) for the Conservative party.
[b] Election year.
SOURCE: M. Pinto-Duschinsky, "Trends in British Party Funding, 1983–87," *Parliamentary Affairs*, 42 (2), April 1989, pp. 198, 200.

and constituency associations. Each constituency association is given a quota that it is expected to contribute each year to national party funds. Some associations give more than the quota and a number give less (in some cases, nothing at all). Annual income from this source generally has been constant at between £1 million and £1.5 million, forming a decreasing proportion of the total income. The party is seen as the one most sympathetic to the interests of business, and a number of large companies give the party a proportion of their profits each year. Between 1979 and 1992, 12 companies each donated £500,000 ($775,000) or more to the party. Despite a number of leading companies reducing or cancelling their donations in the period of recession in the early 1990s, company contributions continue to contribute a sizable chunk of the party's national income. Estimates vary, but in the early 1990s donations from private and publicly quoted companies are believed to have accounted for almost half of the party's income.[18] Most of the remaining income, possibly as much as one-fifth or one-quarter, comes from private sources: partnerships, bequests, individuals, and in some cases, foreign business tycoons. (Such donations do not have to be declared.) One benefactor revealed in 1991 was a Greek shipping tycoon, who gave £2 million ($3.1 m.). Other contributors include billionaire financier Sir James Goldsmith and composer Andrew Lloyd Webber.[19] The party's receipt of such private donations generated political controversy in 1993, when it was revealed that a disgraced businessman, who had just fled the country while facing charges of fraud, had previously made a large donation to Conservative funds. There were various demands for the party to return the money and calls for new laws requiring greater disclosure of donations to political parties.

Outside of election years, party income is spent on routine administration, salaries, and maintenance of the services the party provides to local associations. In election years, the party regularly outspends its opponents. As Table 6.2 shows, the party in both the 1987 and 1992 elections spent more than the Labour and Alliance parties combined.

TABLE 6.2   Party election expenditure, 1987–1992: Expenditure during general election campaigns

Party	1987 Election		1992 Election	
Conservative	£9.0m	($14m)	£10.1m	($15.6m)
Labour	£4.2m	($6.5m)	£7.1m	($11.0m)
Alliance	£1.9m	($3.0m)	—	
Liberal Democratic	—		£2.1m	($3.2m)

Based on parties' own estimates of expenditure.
SOURCE: D. Butler and D. Kavanagh, *The British General Election of 1992* (Macmillan, 1992), p. 260.

A second tier of fund-raising takes place at the local level. Constituency associations are essentially self-financing bodies (some poorer ones receive support from the central office) and are active fund-raising organizations. They raise about £15 million ($23.25m.) a year, of which—as we have seen—about £1–£1.5 million is sent to party headquarters. More money comes from events such as dinners, coffee mornings, and raffles than from individual subscriptions (there is no minimum subscription and in some associations the recommended subscription is small); the money raised is spent on routine management, primarily the agent's salary and office expenses. Local appeals are normally made to raise money for election campaigns. Conservative associations tend to be more successful than their rival parties' organizations in raising campaign money, though few spend the maximum—and relatively small—sum permitted under election finance laws (see chapter 5). The average expenditure by a Conservative candidate in the 1992 election was approximately 80% of the permitted maximum.[20]

Like its main competitor, the party has had difficulty in recent years in raising funds to meet all its organizational commitments. The party maintains a sizable staff in expensive headquarters close to the houses of Parliament. Even with various attempts at streamlining since the 1970s, costs have continued to exceed income. The party's overall deficit in the period from 1984 to 1988 was estimated at £1.0 million ($1.55m.). By 1992, it exceeded £10 million ($15.5m.), a consequence of the cost of the 1992 election campaign. In the two years to April 1992, the party centrally raised a record £35 million ($54.2m.) but nonetheless spent £45 million ($69.75m.)[21] The party chairman brought in a new chief executive and finance director to address the problem.

The Labour Party

The Labour Party is best described as a coalition of disparate interests. It was formed, in effect, on February 27, 1900, at a conference comprising representatives of the socialist Independent Labour party (the ILP), the Marxist Social Democratic Federation (the SDF), the Fabian Society (which believed in socialism by gradual means), and 65 trade unions. It called for "establishing a distinct Labour Group in Parliament, who shall have their own whips and agree upon policy, which must embrace a readiness to cooperate with any party which for the time being may be engaged in promoting legislation in the direct interest of labour, and be equally ready to associate themselves with any party in opposing measures having an opposite tendency.'' The conference refused to accept an SDF motion linking it with socialism and the class war, and the SDF subsequently withdrew from the movement. An executive committee, the Labour Representation Committee, was set up, consisting of representatives from the different organizations, the trade union representatives being in the majority. There was thus witnessed, in Carl Brand's words, ''an alliance between socialism and trade unionism''; he added, ''It was done in characteristically British fashion: with scant regard for theory, the best tool possible under the circumstances was fashioned. In spite of the fact that for two decades the drive had come from the socialists, they did not insist upon their name or programme.''[22] In the general election of 1906, 29 Labour MPs were elected and the Labour Representation Committee thereupon changed its name to the Labour party. The Labour party had established itself on the British political scene.

The next major event in the party's history was the adoption of a new Constitution in 1918. There was a strong socialist element within the party, notably represented by the ILP, and the First World War had appeared to make socialist principles more relevant than they had been previously. It has also been argued that adopting a socialist program served a functional purpose in differentiating the party from the Liberals.[23] In any event, the party adopted what has been termed a Socialist Commitment and, in clause four of its new Constitution, committed itself to the common ownership of the means of production. (The words ''distribution and exchange'' were added in 1928.) At its subsequent conference it adopted a program, *Labour and the New Social Order,* incorporating four principles: the enforcement of a national minimum (in effect, a commitment to full employment and a national minimum wage); the democratic control of industry, essentially through public ownership; a revolution in national finance (financing of social services through greater taxation of high incomes); and surplus wealth for the common good, using the balance of the nation's wealth to expand opportunities in education and culture. The program was to form the basis of party policy for more than 30 years.[24] At the same time, however, the party amended its own procedures in a way that weakened the socialist element within its ranks: The trade unions, on whom the party depended for financial support, were given greater influence through the decision to elect members of the party's national executive committee at the party conference, where the unions dominated; and the ILP was weakened by the decision to allow individuals to join the Labour party directly. Previously, membership was indirect, through membership of affiliated organizations, and the ILP had been the main recruiting agent for political activists. Socialists within the party were to become increasingly wary of the attitude adopted toward the party's program by those who dominated the party leadership.

At the 1918 general election 63 Labour MPs were returned. In 1922 the number rose to 142, making the party the second largest in the House of Commons. In the 1923 general election the Conservatives lost their overall majority and Labour, with Liberal acquiescence, formed a short-lived minority government under the leadership of Ramsay MacDonald. Given the political constraints, the government achieved little—its main domestic success was the passage of a housing bill—and lasted less than ten months. A second minority Labour government was formed following the 1929 general election. Its domestic program was largely crippled either by the Liberals in the Commons or the Conservatives in the Lords. In response to the depression, it sought international loans, but these were dependent on financial cutbacks at home. The Cabinet was divided on the issue and MacDonald tendered the government's resignation, subsequently accepting the king's invitation to form a coalition, or "National," government incorporating Conservative and Liberal MPs. The new government, though led by MacDonald, was dominated by the Conservatives. Within the Labour party, MacDonald's action was seen as a betrayal of the party's cause and only a handful of Labour MPs followed him into the new government. The majority of the parliamentary party, along with the trade unions, disavowed his action, and he and his supporters were subsequently expelled from the party. The National government, with MacDonald and his supporters standing as National Labour candidates, won a landslide victory in a quickly called general election. The Labour party was returned with only 52 MPs and, though the number increased to 154 in the 1935 general election, spent the 1930s in a political wilderness.

The Second World War, as we have seen (chapter 3), had a significant impact on the fortunes and the appeal of the party. There had been a shift in popular attitudes, conducive to some form of social welfare program, and the party had proved itself a responsible partner of government in the wartime coalition. In 1945 it was returned with a large overall majority. In office, it implemented its election manifesto "Let Us Face the Future," bringing into public ownership various public utilities and introducing a comprehensive social security system and national health service. Much of its program was soon implemented, perhaps too soon. By the end of the Parliament, the party had begun to lose its impetus and there were growing doubts as to the direction in which it should be going. In the general election of 1950 it was returned with a bare overall majority, and in the general election called the following year it lost that majority altogether (despite receiving more votes than any other party), the Conservatives being returned to office.

The 1950s proved to be a period of bitter dispute within the party. The left wing within the party continued to press for greater control of the economy and the taking into public ownership of important industries: It remained committed to clause four of the party's Constitution. Revisionists within the party, influenced by Anthony Crosland and his 1956 seminal work, *The Future of Socialism,* argued that public ownership was no longer necessary because of the absence of large-scale unemployment and primary poverty. Rather, they argued, one should accept the mixed economy and seek instead the goal of equality—equality of opportunity, especially in the sphere of education. Such a goal was possible in an affluent managerial society. Public ownership was seen as largely irrelevant. The dispute between the two sides culminated at the turn of the decade, when party leader Hugh Gaitskell sought to remove clause four from the constitution. The major unions swung against him and he was defeated at the party's 1960 conference.

He then turned his attention to the issue of the British nuclear deterrent, vigorously opposing attempts to commit the party to a policy of unilateral nuclear disarmament, and in so doing instigating another serious internal party dispute.

Conservative unpopularity in the early 1960s and the election of Harold Wilson as party leader in 1963 following the sudden death of Gaitskell helped restore a sense of unity to the Labour party as it sensed electoral victory. The party was returned to office in 1964. However, its periods of office from 1964 to 1970 and later from 1974 to 1979 were not successful ones. The attempt at a national plan in the first Wilson government was effectively stillborn, and both periods of government witnessed generally orthodox attempts to respond to economic crises. The period of Labour government from 1974 onward, in particular, appeared to lack any clear direction, being pushed in different directions by international pressures and the domestic problems associated with trying to stay in office while lacking an overall parliamentary majority. The period witnessed a growing tension within the party between those who adhered to a gradual approach to the achievement of socialists goals, recognizing the constraints imposed by prevailing conditions, and those on the left who pressed for more immediate action and the taking into public ownership of key industries such as the banks. This tension effectively emerged onto the political stage as open and violent political warfare following the election defeat of 1979. It was not only to take the form of a policy dispute but also to be fought largely and ostensibly on the question of the party's Constitution.

The Left within the Labour party argued that the social democratic consensus policies of the 1950s had been tried and had failed. What was needed was a socialist economic policy, one not seriously tried before by a Labour government. The Left sought to increase its influence within the party by arguing for (1) the election of the party leader by a wider franchise than the parliamentary Labour party (the Left was much stronger within constituency parties than it was in the parliamentary party); (2) the compulsory reselection of MPs—that is, for MPs to be subject to a full reselection process by local parties during the lifetime of a Parliament rather than the usual process of automatic readoption when an election was called; and (3) the vesting of the responsibility for writing the election manifesto in the party's National Executive Committee (the NEC), where the Left was strong, rather than jointly by the NEC and the parliamentary leadership. At the party's 1980 conference the Left was successful in achieving two of these three objectives: the widening of the franchise for electing the leader, and MPs being subject to compulsory reselection procedures. At a special conference in January 1981 the party adopted a formula for the election of the leader by an electoral college, the trade unions to have 40% of the votes, constituency parties 30%, and the parliamentary Labour party 30%. (This new method was employed for the first time in 1983 following the resignation of party leader Michael Foot.)

For a number of politicians on the right of the party, already bitterly opposed to the party's policy to withdraw from the European Community, the constitutional changes constituted the final straw. They responded by creating a Council for Social Democracy and then, in March 1981, broke away from the party completely, forming a new party, the Social Democratic party (the

SDP). Others in sympathy with their views remained within the Labour party to fight the battle there.

The next two years proved politically disastrous for the Labor party. In the fall of 1981, there was a bitterly fought contest for the party deputy leadership between the incumbent, Denis Healey, and the candidate of the Left, Tony Benn. Healey won by a tiny margin. More and more Labour MPs defected to join the SDP. The party entered the 1983 general election campaign with a manifesto that called for withdrawal from the European Community, a non-nuclear defense program, a "massive" rise in public expenditure, a wealth tax, and the return to public ownership of assets privatized by the Conservatives. The manifesto was described by one of the party's own leading figures as "the longest suicide note in history." The party faced both a Conservative government buoyed by the success of the 1982 Falklands campaign and the SDP, which was drawing away some of Labour's traditional supporters. The party had a disastrous campaign, with a leader (Michael Foot) whom the media refused to take seriously as a potential prime minister. On election day, Labour suffered its worst result since 1918 in terms of the percentage of the vote obtained. It got 28% of the votes cast, only marginally ahead of the share obtained by the alliance of Liberal and Social Democratic parties.

In the wake of the election defeat, Foot resigned the leadership and was succeeded by Neil Kinnock, a 41-year-old Welshman with no ministerial experience. Despite occasional effective speeches on the conference platform, Kinnock did not shine in the House of Commons and was no match for Margaret Thatcher. He did, however, achieve greater control than his predecessor over the party organization and began to mold it into a more effective body for fighting elections. His performance in the 1987 general election was recognized as highly professional—according to a Gallup poll, 43% of those questioned thought he had campaigned impressively, against 20% so rating Thatcher—and Labour mounted a more polished campaign than the Conservatives. The party's manifesto, however, remained an electoral liability, its defense policy in particular being exploited by its opponents. (It had committed itself to replacing nuclear defense with a conventional force.) In an exit poll on election day, 52% of those questioned said the party's defense policy had made them "less likely" to vote Labour. The party made some gains, especially in Scotland, but was still relegated to the political wasteland of opposition.

Immediately after the election, the party established seven policy groups to review policy. In 1988, the groups produced a broad review of policy and the following year produced specific policy recommendations. The recommendations shifted the party away from the policies that had proved an electoral liability. On defense, for example, it moved the party toward multilateral nuclear disarmament. Neil Kinnock was able to use his control of the party's National Executive Committee and an increasing body of support within the party to achieve endorsement by the party conference of the recommendations.

The party's new policy was embodied in a policy document, *Meet the Challenge, Make the Change* (1989), and in two subsequent documents, *Looking to the Future* (1990) and *Opportunity Britain* (1991). "Overall, two major themes emerged. . . . First, intraparty political debate over the extent of public and private ownership was outdated; and, second, the quality of public service should be improved by putting the needs of the user before those of the producer."[25] The review established a new paradigm for the party, aided in the defense sector by the collapse of the Iron Curtain and the end of the cold war. By 1990, Labour began to appear as a moderate and credible alternative to the increasingly unpopular Thatcher government.

Labour achieved a large lead in the opinion polls early in 1990. That lead receded later in the year and briefly disappeared altogether following the replacement of Margaret Thatcher with John Major as prime minister and in the wake of the 1991 Gulf War. The party reestablished a lead in the polls later in 1991, which it retained into 1992 and the election campaign in March and April. However, the lead was not as large as might have been expected given the severity of the recession and, against general expectations that Labour would win more seats than the Conservatives, Labour failed to pull off an election victory. Though losing several seats, the Conservatives held on to an overall majority in the House of Commons. Despite it being preferred over the Conservatives on most social issues, Labour had failed to shake off a lingering public distrust in its competence to handle the economy and in the qualities of its leader. The party's economic policies—and other manifesto commitments—are shown in Table 6.3. Most voters believed the Conservatives were better able to handle the economy than Labour, that a Labour government would increase taxes, and that John Major was better qualified to be prime minister than Neil Kinnock.[26]

In the wake of the election defeat, Neil Kinnock resigned the leadership. In July, he was succeeded by a 53-year-old Scot, John Smith, who won the leadership contest decisively: He got 91% of the votes (winning easily in each of the three parts of the electoral college), his challenger, Bryan Gould, the candidate of the Left, picking up the remaining 9%. The party also elected a new deputy leader, Margaret Beckett, replacing the previous deputy, Roy Hattersley, who had resigned with Kinnock.

Smith, variously portrayed as looking and sounding like a local bank manager, was seen as a solid, reliable candidate who would be able to consolidate Labour's moderate image and prepare it for victory four or five years later. He had to do so during Labour's fourth consecutive period in the wilderness. In the first few months of his leadership, he was aided by disarray within Conservative ranks, allowing Labour to achieve a lead in the opinion polls. However, some critics within the party pressed for a more proactive approach. Within the House of Commons, Smith rallied his backbenchers with an outstanding first speech as leader, but thereafter failed to shine, with Prime Minister John Major regularly getting the better of their exchanges. Government unpopularity nonetheless ensured that Labour remained ahead in the polls.

Party Organization.   The basic structure of the party is given in Figure 6.2. Formally, the party stresses the concept of intraparty democracy. In the Labour party, the leader is not the fount of all policy. The body formally responsible for determining the party program is the party conference, which meets each

TABLE 6.3 Manifesto promises, 1992 general election

The Issues	Conservative	Labour	Liberal Democrat
Taxation	Continue tax cuts, ambition of 20% basic rate; inheritance tax only for very rich, 40% rate on estates over £500,000; seek one tax-free account for every saver; council tax, revalue homes every three years	Top rate 50%, earnings threshold "well over" £30,000; reverse 1992's budget changes; abolish ceiling on 9% national insurance contributions; new tax on unearned income (pensioners exempt)	Add 1p to basic rate if necessary, increase tax threshold; abolish mortgage relief for new borrowers, replace with "housing cost relief"
Industry	Privatize British Coal, BR; require trade unionists to opt in annually to unions; individuals to sue unlawful strikers in public sector; protection for workers on personal contracts through industrial tribunal	National economic assessment, dual budget-public spending announcement; National Investment Bank, private capital for public projects; tax incentives for investors	Combine Monopolies and Mergers Commission with OFT, power to break up privatized monopolies; BT break-up; more private rail services; new restrictive practices act
Health	Extend opt-out hospitals, fund-holding GPs; increase spending, extra £2.7 billion next year; two-year maximum waiting time for patients; performance league tables; private treatment if NHS inadequate	End GP fund-holding, opt-out hospitals to health authorities; Department of Health and Community Care (renamed); right to smoke-free environment at work; free eye tests, dental checks	End GP fund-holding, NHS trusts; more freedom for doctors to refer patients to chosen hospitals; free eye tests, dental checks; salaried GPs, accredited specialists
Education	Extend city technology colleges, grant-maintained schools, opt-outs; performance-related teachers' pay; teachers, governors to control 80% school budgets by 1994; retain A-level gold standard	Abolish city technology colleges, grant-maintained schools back to council control; review private schools' charitable status, phase out assisted places scheme; reform A-levels	Return city technology colleges, grant-maintained schools to council control; review private schools' charitable status, phase out assisted places scheme; reform A-levels
Training	Tax relief possible for companies improving training schemes	Skills UK, new organization to direct training policy; employers to pay 0.5% of payroll on training; right for 16-year-olds to stay at school or traineeship based on National Training Qualifications	Require working 16- to 19-year-olds to undergo education, training two days a week; return further education colleges to local authorities; adult education fees for fixed period to key groups
Defence	Order fourth Trident, 512 warheads; 6% defence budget over four years; "options for change" review, cut 116,000 soldiers; retain autonomy, subservient to neither NATO nor European Community	Cancel fourth Trident order depending on contractual position and cost; "no first-use" policy for nuclear weapons, end British nuclear testing; Defence Diversification Agency	Limit warheads on four Trident submarines to same (192) or fewer than Polaris; cut £1 billion (50%) from military research, savings to civil research; "significant reduction" in armaments
Law and order	Reorganize police service, nominate police chief for every town; identify potential criminals among children as young as six; monitor police response, satisfaction with service	Increase police numbers over lifetime of parliament; body to investigate miscarriages of justice; Sentencing Council for consistency in punishment orders; prisoners' ombudsman	Extend Court of Appeal powers; regional appeal courts; Judicial Services Commission to nominate judges; public defender to investigate miscarriages of justice; plea-bargaining

The Issues	Conservative	Labour	Liberal Democrat
Environment	Environmental Protection Agency; develop wind, wave, solar power; stabilize carbon dioxide emissions by 2005; phase out CFC emissions by 2000; "green" taxes; extra green-belt protection	Appoint "green minister," Environmental Protection Executive; stabilize then cut carbon dioxide emissions by year 2000; cut VAT on environment-friendly goods; return water companies to public sector	Energy taxes to cut industrial gases; "pollution-added tax" on damaging goods; cut carbon dioxide emissions 30% by 2005, sulphur dioxide by 60% in five years; Environmental Protection Agency
Social policy	Increase pensions, child benefit annually in line with inflation; improve disablement benefits; unemployment, sickness, income support benefits in line with inflation; cut benefit delays	Pensions up £5 a week (single), £8 (couple), linked to average earnings or prices; flexible retirement age; child benefit up to £9.95; minister for children, children's rights commissioner	Priority increases in pensions, £5 (single), £8 (couple); increase child benefit by £1 a week per child
Employment	Extend performance-related public-sector pay; assist people to join union of their choice, union leaders to disclose salaries, stop abuse of "check off" of union dues	Minimum wage, at least half average male earnings (£3.40 an hour), £10,000 fine and three months prison for offending employers; Industrial Court; statutory duty to promote equal treatment	Cut jobless by 400,000 in year; job-creation/training programme costing £3 billion; jobless to improve council homes, other buildings; secondment of redundant executives to small business
Local Government	Replace two-tier system, more unitary local authorities; cabinet-style councils; performance tables for councils; retain uniform business rate	Regional tier in England, elected regional government in second term; strategic authority for London elected by PR; Quality Commissions, "customer contracts" for residents, annual satisfaction surveys	Ombudsman for every council; compensation for sub-standard services; public question times at council meetings, "neighborhood committees"; uniform business rate replaced by site-value rating
Housing	Boost homeownership to 75%; rent-into-mortgage scheme for council tenants; mortgage-rescue schemes, stamp duty relief until August; possibly subsidies for conversions, eg flats above shops	National Housing Bank; phased release council house sale receipts; leaseholders' right to buy freeholds collectively or extend leases; outlaw "gazumping"	Mortgage-to-rent scheme: building societies take ownership, seek rent to get 8% return on capital; support shared ownership; reform housing benefit system, pay claimants in advance of need, lend deposits
Transport	Continue £12 billion roadbuilding, double trunk road programme over 10 years; BR privatization white paper; compensation for delayed travellers	Halt BR privatization moves; transport safety inspectorate; strengthen passenger watchdogs; halt road schemes not yet out to contract; "traffic-calming" bus-priority schemes, cycle routes	Increase petrol prices substantially, fuel taxes linked to pollution emission; phase out vehicle excise duty, "road-pricing"; private rail lines, high-speed link Channel to north and west
Arts and Media	Protect "listed" art works from export; extra finance for museum purchases; support "Millennium Fund" to repair national museums and construct new buildings; devolve Arts Council power	Ministry for Arts and Media; phase out museum, art gallery charges; ownership of TV companies and newspapers to Monopolies and Mergers Commission; abolish Broadcasting Standards Council	Ministry for Arts and Communications, arts spending to 1% GDP; broadcasting act, renew BBC charter responsibilities, abolish Broadcasting Standards Council; lift Sinn Fein broadcasting ban
Constitution	Categorically opposed to proportional representation and devolution to Scotland, Wales or English regions; streamline Whitehall departments	Replace Lords with elected second chamber, proportional representation for Scottish assembly; freedom of information act; Commons committee on security services	PR; incorporate European Convention on Human Rights, move to bill of human rights, written constitution; Senate replaces Lords; home rule for Scotland, Wales; fixed-term parliaments

(table continued on next page)

TABLE 6.3 (continued)

The Issues	Conservative	Labour	Liberal Democrat
Equal Opportunities	Opportunity 2000, encourage promotion of talented women and ethnic minorities, but against positive discrimination	Ministry for Women, cabinet minister; simplify, extend race equality laws; citizenship law to respect "family life"; strengthen laws on rape, domestic violence	Wide-ranging initiatives across all policy areas
Scotland	Oppose devolution or independence but ready to consider higher Westminster profile for Scottish interests; abolish regional authorities; private forestry commission and tourist board	Scottish parliament in Edinburgh in first year, legislative and revenue-raising powers, elected by "additional member" PR, limited power to vary tax, plus contribution from U.K. taxation	Home rule for Scotland; Scottish assembly logical consequence of European union; power over all policy except defence, foreign affairs and large-scale economics
Wales	Oppose devolution or independence but ready to consider higher Westminster profile for Welsh interests; redraw local government map, 23 new all-purpose authorities such as Pembrokeshire	Directly elected Welsh assembly, single-tier "most-purpose" local authorities; Welsh language act, fair treatment of daily users; Welsh-medium schooling for all families wanting it	Welsh language act; offer Welsh-medium schooling to all families who want it
Northern Ireland	Support Anglo-Irish agreement, continue to promote all-party talks suspended in pre-election period	Review prevention of terrorism act; end strip-searching, plastic bullets; support Anglo-Irish agreement; creation of united Ireland by consent	Support Anglo-Irish agreement, reject coalition with Unionists
Europe	Minister for European Affairs of cabinet rank; reject imposition of single currency or European Central Bank removing control of economic policy; retain control of immigration, drugs, anti-terrorist policy	Support single currency development if there is "real convergence" between British and EC economies; sign social charter immediately; develop European environment charter	Single European currency, independent central bank, move to narrow band of ERM soon as possible; political integration, Euro-citizenship; Rapid Response Force, peace-keeping, disaster-relief

SOURCE: *The Sunday Times,* "What the Parties Stand For," Election Guide, March 15, 1992, p. 2.

year in the autumn. Under the party's constitution, a proposal that receives two-thirds or more of the votes cast at conference is adopted as part of the program. Between conferences, the body responsible for party organization and policy discussion is the party's NEC, which will normally bring policy documents forward for approval by the conference.

Complicating the picture, however, is the fact that the party's program is not the same as its election manifesto. Under the party's constitution, the NEC

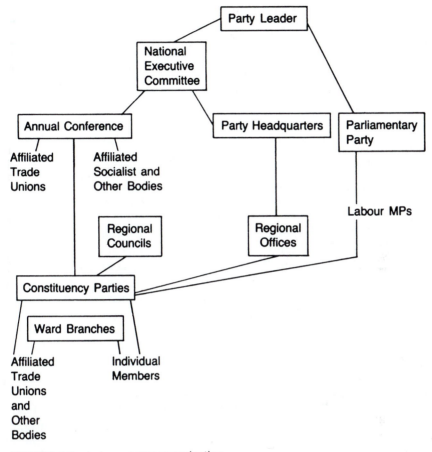

FIGURE 6.2 Labour party organization

in conjunction with the leaders of the parliamentary party decide which items of the program are to be included in the manifesto. In 1983 the program and the manifesto were synonymous, but in practice this has not always been the case. In 1979, for example, party leader James Callaghan blocked the inclusion of the commitment to abolish the House of Lords. Furthermore, when it comes to implementing the program, some latitude is given to the parliamentary leadership, which is expected to give effect to the party's principles "as far as may be practicable." Previously when in office, Labour leaders sometimes did not find it "practicable" to implement party commitments, giving rise to conflict between organs of the party, such as the NEC, and the leadership.

At party conferences, voting is based on an organization's membership, not on the individual votes of those present. Thus the trade unions, with large affiliated memberships, have cast the most votes. In the 1950s, the unions so-called block vote used to be cast regularly in support of the party leadership but became less predictable from the early 1960s onward. Under the leadership of

Neil Kinnock, the unions generally supported his attempts to moderate the party in policy terms but were wary of attempts to reform their own role in party activities. Moves by Kinnock to reduce union influence at conference and in candidate selection in constituencies ran into some union criticism. "No say, no pay" was how one union leader responded to attempts to reform the block vote. At the 1992 conference, it was agreed to cut the union voting strength at conference from 87% to 70%. A party review group was also set up to review the links between the unions and the party. The new party leader, John Smith, had committed himself to achieving change, but union leaders made clear there could be no divorce between the two wings of the movement.[27]

Traditionally, Labour conferences have differed from Conservative conferences in that the latter are advisory and often stage-managed affairs. Labour conferences have often been lively and unpredictable. Recent years have witnessed something of a convergence in that Labour conferences are more geared to the media and Conservative conferences have occasionally proved difficult to manage, but the basic difference remains.[28] Significant differences also exist between the parties in terms of membership. The Conservative party, as we have seen, recruits members directly. Labour, by contrast, has a large indirect membership in addition to a small direct membership. The indirect membership derives from trade unions and other affiliated organizations. Members of unions pay, as part of their union subscription, a "political levy" (unless they explicitly opt out of so doing) and thus become affiliated members of the party. This affiliated membership provides the party with most of its income as well as a large paper membership. The party has almost 5 million affiliated members. In contrast, the number of direct members is under 300,000. Direct membership showed a slight increase in 1990 but has declined since and by the time of the 1992 conference was down to 261,000, roughly one third of the membership of the Conservative party. This low membership is partly explicable by the dependence of the party on trade unions and an absence of professional staff to build up local organizations. Concentrated voting support also has produced many safe seats where the outcome has been assured without too much organizational effort being necessary. The party's internal troubles of the 1980s, and the siphoning off by the SDP of some Labour supporters, also contributed to the problem.

The decline in membership caused a financial crisis for the party. The situation was exacerbated by a fall in the number of affiliated members: almost 6 million in the mid-1980s and less than 5 million in 1990. The bulk of the party's central funds come from trade unions. Of the party's £6.2 million ($9.61m.) income in 1990, for example, £4.1 milliom ($6.3m.) came from the unions. Less than £1 million came from constituency parties and direct membership.[29] By the end of the 1980s, the party had a running deficit of more than £1 million. A reduction in the number of central headquarters staff and an increase in union affiliation fees failed to bridge the gap. The crisis generated by a fall in membership was compounded by the cost of the 1992 general election campaign. Though the unions provide the bulk of the party's election funds, the party had a £2 million deficit at the end of 1992 and the party conference agreed to an increase in membership fees. The rate for individual members was increased from £15 (just over $23) to £18 ($27).

Most of the party's central income is spent on personnel and organization. The same applies to money raised locally. Income raised by local parties varies considerably. Few local parties have full-time agents. Indeed, the party's staff working at regional and local levels is, in total, less than 100. Some local parties receive support from trade unions as a result of candidate sponsorship. Unions can sponsor parliamentary candidates, which means essentially that the candidate has the backing of the union and the union contributes a sum toward the local party's expenses. Of the 271 Labour MPs elected in 1992, 147 were sponsored by trade unions. Union sponsorship bolsters local parties, which, with an average of under 400 members per constituency, have few substantial resources of their own.

THIRD PARTIES

In the postwar years from 1945 to 1970, the principal third party in Britain, and the only one to enjoy parliamentary representation throughout the period, was the Liberal party. Its parliamentary strength was small, but as *the* third party it had no obvious competitors. That ceased to be the case from the 1970s onward.

In the 1970s, the Scottish and Welsh Nationalist parties grew in strength: They had both gained a parliamentary toehold in the 1960s (one seat each) but that grew rapidly in 1974. In 1972, the Ulster Unionists in Northern Ireland, previously affiliated with and, in parliamentary terms, subsumed within the Conservative party, broke away (in protest at the imposition of direct rule in the province) to sit as a separate parliamentary party. The Unionist subsequently witnessed divisions within their own ranks, resulting in the return of MPs representing different Unionist parties.

The situation became even more complicated in the 1980s. In 1981, the Social Democratic party (the SDP), drawing its parliamentary strength from defecting Labour MPs (and one defecting Conservative), was formed. It then entered into an alliance with the Liberal party and it was as an alliance that the two parties contested the 1983 and 1987 general elections. In 1988, the two parties voted to merge. They created the Social and Liberal Democratic party, known popularly as the Liberal Democratic party. A number of SDP members, opposed to the merger, maintained what was known as the Continuing SDP, but the party soon folded. Some disaffected Liberals also refused to merge and maintained the Liberal party, putting forward a number of candidates in the 1992 election.

In 1987, the sole Social Democratic and Labour party (SDLP) MP from Northern Ireland was joined by two more colleagues, thus establishing another new parliamentary party. Its ranks were further swelled in 1992. In 1989 the Green party—formed in 1985 as the successor to the Ecology party—polled unexpectedly well in the European Parliament elections, drawing twice as much support as the Liberal Democrats. In 1992 the field of "third" parties was further swelled by the presence of the new Natural Law party and the more established fringe parties. Figure 6.3 gives some shape to that field in terms of those third parties achieving parliamentary representation.

The Liberal Democrats

The Liberal Democratic party was formed in 1988 by the merger of the long-established Liberal party and the relatively new Social Democratic party (the SDP). By virtue of its age and parliamentary representation, the Liberal party was the senior partner in the merger.

The Liberal party had had a relatively short history as a major political party, spanning less than 60 years. Succeeding the Whigs in the 1860s, it was a major force on the British political scene until the 1920s, when it went into rapid decline. Like the other parties, it as a coalition of interests. The main tenets of Gladstonian Liberalism in the nineteenth century were free trade, home rule for Ireland economy wherever possible, and social reform where necessary. Within the party there was a radical wing, which placed more emphasis on social reform, as well as an imperialist wing.[30] Returned to government in 1906, the party enacted a number of social reforms, but it proceeded on the basis of no coherent program and was divided on a number of important issues. The second decade of the century proved a disastrous one. The party was beset by such problems as division in Ireland, the suffragettes, and the First World War.[31] It was also rent asunder by a rift between Asquith, the party leader until 1916, and Lloyd George, who successfully displaced him. The rift was never really healed successfully. The party's internal problems and its declining electoral appeal were to reduce its parliamentary numbers. In 1918 the election was won by a coalition consisting of Lloyd George Liberals and the Conservatives. The Conservatives were the dominant partner, though Lloyd George remained as premier. In 1922, Conservative MPs brought the coalition to an end. In the ensuing general election 62 National Liberal and 54 Liberal MPs were returned. The position improved temporarily in 1923, when 159 Liberal MPs were returned. In 1924 the number returned was only 40. In subsequent elections the number returned was 59 (1929), 33 (1931, 41 Liberal National MPs also being returned),[32] and 20 (1935). In the general elections between 1945 and 1979 the number of Liberal MPs elected varied from 6 to 14. The only occasion in postwar years when it came close to government was during the period of the Liberal-Labour (known as the Lib-Lab) Pact from 1977 to 1978, when it achieved some concessions and the opportunity to consult in return for sustaining the minority Labour government in office.[33] The pact proved unpopular with party activists and was short-lived.

The fortunes of the party appeared to improve in 1981, when it entered into an alliance with the newly formed Social Democratic party. The Social Democratic party was formed in March 1981 when a number of Labour politicians broke away from the Labour party. The new party was led by four former Labour Cabinet ministers, dubbed by newspapers as "the Gang of Four": Roy Jenkins, Shirley Williams, Dr. David Owen, and William Rodgers. The last two were already in the House of Commons. The other two, both former MPs, were to return later

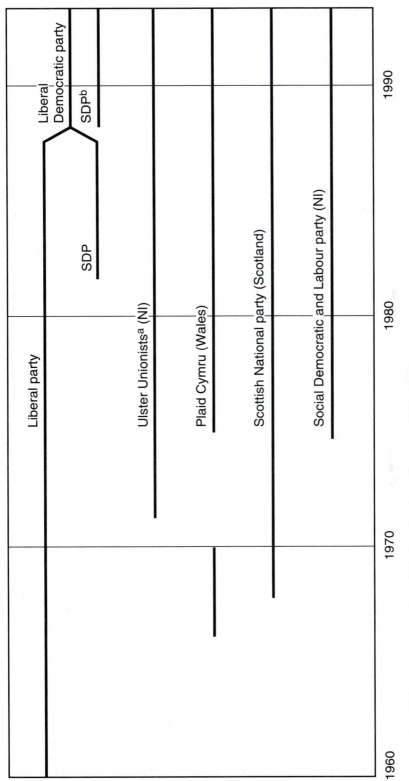

FIGURE 6.3 A growing field: Third parties in parliament, 1960–1993

NI = Northern Ireland; SDP = Social Democratic party

[a] Part of the parliamentary Conservative party until 1972.

[b] Although the Continuing SDP was effectively wound up in 1990, its three MPs continued to sit as independent Social Democratic MPs until the 1992 general election.

135

in by-elections. The party was created with the ostensible aim of "breaking the mold" of British politics.[34] It wanted to get away from the adversary relationships that had characterized British politics, favoring instead consensus government that would represent the center ground of British politics. It favored decentralization, equality, electoral reform, a pay-and-prices policy, and especially membership in the European Community.

The new party attracted support both within the House of Commons and within the country. By the end of 1981, a total of 27 Labour MPs (and 1 Conservative) had defected to join it. It attracted over 70,000 members, and by December its support in the Gallup poll exceeded that of any other party. It formed an alliance with the Liberal party, and alliance candidates began to score some notable victories in by-elections: Croydon North-West in October, Crosby in November (won by Mrs. Williams), and Glasgow, Hillhead the following March (won by Mr. Jenkins). Within a year of its formation, it posed a threat to the two main traditional parties.

During 1982 it began to develop its internal organization and to formulate policies. It also witnessed a decline in support. The former may provide a partial explanation for the latter. As the party committed itself to specific policies and as it selected a leader with a distinctive leadership style and appeal, so it began to shed its "catchall" appeal. A contest for the party leadership and a dispute with the Liberals over the allocation of alliance candidatures produced some loss of support. The Falklands campaign also served to rob it of much-needed publicity.

A consequence of these developments was that the alliance entered the 1983 election campaign in third place in the opinion polls. As the campaign progressed and the Labour campaign faltered, alliance support increased. It became a topic of media speculation as to whether Labour or the alliance would come in second to the Conservatives in the number of votes cast. In the end, despite its worst share of the poll for almost 70 years, the Labour party retained second place in the polls and benefitted from the concentration of its support. The alliance obtained 26% of the votes but suffered from the broadness of its support: Only 23 alliance MPs were returned, 17 of them Liberals and 6 SDP.

In the wake of the election, SDP leader Roy Jenkins resigned and the party elected Dr. David Owen. The two parties remained in alliance but, with a limited parliamentary base, failed to make a dent on public consciousness during the new Parliament. Both alliance partners entered the 1987 election campaign hoping to improve on their 1983 result: The two party leaders—known as "the two Davids" (David Owen and David Steel)—toured the country together to rally support. However, the two parties, and their leaders, failed to make much impact and both parties were showing internal unease by the end of the campaign. In the election, alliance candidates garnered just under 23% of the vote and 22 seats.

Immediately following the 1987 election, Liberal leader David Steel pressed for a merger of the two parties, believing that such a move was necessary if the alliance were to maximize its impact. The move was opposed by David Owen, who decided to step down as SDP leader; he was replaced by SDP MP Robert Maclennan, who began negotiations with Liberal leaders. Agreement was reached eventually on a merged party: In January 1988 a special Liberal Assembly voted,

2,099 to 385, in favor of a merger. The Council of the SDP followed suit by a vote of 273 to 28. Both parties then held a mail ballot of all members: Liberals voted in favor by 46,376 to 6,365 and the SDP, less decisively, by 18,722 to 9,929. Many SDP members, including David Owen, abstained. The new party was formed with the support of all 17 Liberal MPs but only 2 SDP MPs; the remaining 3 SDP MPs refused to join.

The new party immediately encountered a problem of nomenclature: Liberals were insistent that the name "Liberal" should not be lost. Finally the party chose the name of the Social and Liberal Democratic party. It was not a popular choice, especially with Liberal MPs, and the name was believed to contribute to confusion on the part of electors about the nature of the party. The new party also proceeded to elect a leader. David Steel decided not to stand and David Owen was no longer available. The party elected a relatively new MP, Paddy Ashdown, a candidate with a reputation for dynamism (and some degree of erraticism), in preference to a longer serving MP, Alan Beith, regarded as solid and reliable but lacking in charisma.

The combination of new name and leader appeared to leave electors confused as to what the party was and what it had to offer. The party did badly in local elections in 1988 and 1989 and trailed the Green party in the 1989 European Parliament elections. In the 1989 European election, the party got a little over 6% of the vote. That performance represented the nadir of the party's fortunes. The party then decided to be called by the name of Liberal Democrats. In 1991, Paddy Ashdown had a "good Gulf war": the only ex-serviceman (he had served in the marines) among the party leaders, he appeared frequently on television to provide authoritative comments. Party fortunes appeared to improve. In the 1992 general election, the party got just under 18% of the vote: down on the alliance performance in 1983 and 1987 but better than might have been expected two or three years before. Though it clearly was relegated to third-party status— rather than competing with Labour for second place—the performance of other third parties ensured that it was *the* third party, at least in English politics.

Scottish and Welsh Nationalists

Prior to the 1960s the nationalist parties in Scotland and Wales had not proved to be politically important. Their main achievement had been "simply to survive."[35] In the 1960s they began to have some electoral success: The Plaid Cymru (Party of Wales) won a seat at a by-election in 1966, and the Scottish National party won one in 1967. Their achievements were to be greatest in the 1970s. Favoring independence for Scotland, though being prepared to accept an elected national assembly as a step on that path, the Scottish National party was able to exploit dissatisfaction with Westminister government and to make use of an issue that became salient during this period: North Sea oil. It argued that the oil was Scottish oil and that revenue from it could make an independent Scottish government viable. In the February 1974 election it won 7 seats. In the October 1974 election it won 11 and came second in 35 out of 41 Labour-held seats. In Wales, the Plaid argued more for self-government than for independence and was able to play on the fears of the indigenous Welsh population, which felt its heritage to be threatened by English encroachment. In the 1974 elections it won 2 seats in February (out of 36 Welsh seats) and 3 in October. Responding to the nationalist threat, especially in Scotland, the Labour government introduced a scheme for elected assemblies in the two countries, which subsequently was put to the peoples of Scotland and Wales in referendums. The Welsh referendum resulted in an overwhelming vote against the government's proposals. In Scotland 1,230,000 people voted for the scheme and 1,153,000 voted against it. Under the rules laid down by Parliament, the "yes" vote was not sufficiently large for the scheme to be implemented (see chapter 9).

The referendum results and apparent decline of interest in devolution took much of the wind out of the sails of the nationalist parties, though both retained significant support among a section of the electorate. In Scotland, the SNP won 2 seats in 1979 and 1983 and increased the number to 3 in 1987. In 1988 it had a spectacular by-election success, winning the previously ultrasafe Labour seat of Glasgow Govan. It lost the seat in the 1992 election, but nonetheless increased its share of the vote by an average of almost 8% in the seats it contested. Though having far fewer seats, its share of the poll was actually not much below that of 1974. It has also polled well in local elections. SNP strength in the highlands and islands resulted in it winning a Euorpean Parliament seat in 1979. It retained the seat in both the 1984 and 1989 elections. It is the only third party to hold a seat on the British mainland. In the 1989 European elections, it not only retained its seat but also came second in five of the remaining seven constituencies.

In Wales, Plaid Cymru has not achieved the same proportion of the poll as the SNP in Scotland but its more concentrated support (in predominantly Welsh-speaking constituencies) has ensured that it continues to enjoy parliamentary representation. It won two seats in 1979 and 1983, three in 1987, and four in 1992. In the 1992 election, the extra seat was a gain from the Liberal Democrats, thus consolidating the Plaid's position as the third party in Wales, the Liberal Democrats being left with only one seat in the principality.

Northern Ireland Parties

In Northern Ireland the main party is the Unionist party, which stands for the maintenance of the union with Britain. Originally a united party tied to the British Conservative party, it disassociated itself (though in organizational terms not totally) from the Conservative party following the imposition of direct rule in the province by a Conservative government in 1972. It also divided within itself, the two main Unionist parties being the Ulster Unionists, holding 9 of the 17 seats in the province, and the Democratic Unionists, holding 3 of the seats. The Ulster Unionists tend to be more middle class and Anglican and Methodist, whereas the Democratic Unionists, led by fundamentalist Protestant clergyman Ian Paisley, appeal more to working-class Protestants and are more heavily Presbyterian. A further seat in the province is held by a lone Unionist, Sir James Kilfedder, who stands under the banner of the Ulster Popular Unionist party.

Within the province, there is also the predominantly Catholic party, the Social Democratic and Labour party (the SDLP). The party has gradually increased its parliamentary representation. It won three seats in the 1987 election and increased the number to four in 1992 when it captured the seat of West Belfast from the Sinn Fein candidate, Gerry Adams. Adams had been elected for the seat in 1983 and was reelected in 1987 but refused to take his seat. The loss of the seat was a serious political blow to Sinn Fein, the political wing of the IRA. In 1983, Sinn Fein had received 13.4% of the votes cast in the province; it received 11.4% in 1987 and 10% in 1992. The SDLP, by contrast, increased its share of the vote in 1992 to almost 24%.

The Alliance party, unconnected to the former British SDP/Liberal alliance, is a nonsectarian party that seeks to bridge the gap between the two communities. However, it has never achieved any parliamentary representation and looks unlikely to do so. It won only 10% of the votes in 1987 and just under 9% in 1992. Also contesting seats in the province in 1992 were, as we have already noted (chapter 5), a number of Conservative candidates. Only one, in North Down, attracted a significant share of the vote but the candidates nonetheless served to draw off some of the traditional Unionist support, reducing the total vote for Unionist parties to a new low. That low, however, constituted just over 50% of the votes cast in the province.

Other Parties

Various other parties contest parliamentary election in the United Kingdom. Toward the end of the 1980s, two achieved particular prominence: the Continuing SDP and the Green party.

The Continuing SDP comprised those members of the Social Democratic party who opposed the party's merger with the Liberal party, believing that the SDP had common aims with the Liberals but different emphases and traditions. They attempted to maintain the SDP as a continuing entity. They were aided by the fact that their number included three MPs, including the former party leader Dr. David Owen, and by a good performance in a parliamentary by-election in a rural Yorkshire seat in 1989. However, the party had problems raising funds and did badly in local elections in 1988 and 1989. Its limited resources meant it was able to contest only 16 seats in the 1989 European elections, its best result being to come in fourth place in one seat. Following a disastrous by-election result in Bootle in May 1990, in which the SDP candidate came in seventh place behind a candidate of the fringe Loony party, the decision was taken to wind up the party. A few activists tried to keep it going, but it effectively faded from the political scene. The three SDP MPs sat as independent Social Democrats until the 1992 election. In that election, two sought reelection and were defeated; the third, Dr. Owen, stood down.

The Green party was founded as the People's party in 1973, changed its name to the Ecology party in 1975, and took its present name in 1985. Ecology candidates contested 109 seats in the 1983 general election, achieving a total of only 54,000 votes. Green candidates contested 133 seats in 1987 and made little impact: They achieved 89,000 votes in total—an average of less than 700 votes per seat. Party membership was also low, though increasing: The party is believed to have had about 3,000 members at the beginning of the 1980s and about 8,000 by 1989.

However, the party achieved prominence as a result of an unexpectedly good performance in the 1989 European Parliament elections. It appeared to benefit from the disarray within the ranks of the newly formed Social and Liberal Democratic party and from a growing public concern about the environment. The party contested all 78 seats in Britain, doing especially well in England and Wales: In the 70 English and Welsh seats, it took second place in 6 and third place in 61. (It was fourth in every seat in Scotland.) It achieved 14.5% of the votes cast. It achieved more than 20% of the poll in the southeast of England.

Its performance gave the party new visibility and an increase in membership (up to 15,000 in the year following the Euro-elections), but it failed to achieve any political momentum. Its performance had been unexpectedly good but even in those seats in which it came in second it was not within striking distance of winning. It was immediately attacked by its opponents for being dangerously left-wing. Though focusing on environmental issues, the party was committed to withdrawal from the North Atlantic Treaty Organization (NATO), unconditional nuclear disarmament, a levy on land values, and the disengagement of the United Kingdom from international money markets. The criticism appeared to stunt the party's appeal. It failed to make much headway in the opinion polls. It was hit by internal wranglings and by one of its best-known leading figures—a former TV presenter—declaring himself in 1991 to be the son of God. The party contested 253 seats in the April 1992 election, achieving on average just over 1% of the vote in each seat. In local elections the following month, its candidates achieved an average of 4% of the vote. In September, the chair of the party, Sara Parkin, was forced to resign after earlier declaring that the party had become "a liability to Green politics." Membership declined to the level it was at in 1989. The party had failed to become the serious force that it looked like it was becoming just three years before.

Several other parties contest parliamentary elections, though without achieving quite the same prominence. Among the newer parties are the continuing *Liberal party* and, almost certainly a temporary phenomenon in British politics, the *Natural Law party*. The Liberal party comprises Liberals who opposed the merger with the SDP in 1988 and who have sought to continue the traditional identity of the Liberal party. As we saw in chapter 5, they had little success in the seats they contested in 1992, though their leader—Michael Meadowcroft, a former MP—did at least manage to retain his deposit. That was a better performance than any of the candidates of the Natural Law party. The party contested 309 seats and lost its deposit in every one; only two candidates actually managed to get more than 1% of the votes cast. The party expounded the "vedic science" of Maharishi Mahesh Yogi and issued a largely incomprehensible election manifesto. The candidates, some of whom were flown in from abroad, did no campaigning. The candidates of the fringe *Loony* parties (chapter 5) have variously added a touch of color to election campaigns, and in 1992 their candidates actually outperformed those of the Natural Law party.

Longer established parties include the *Communist party* and the *National Front,* but neither constitutes a significant political force. The British Communist party, founded in 1921, has had little impact in electoral terms. One Communist MP was elected in 1924, one in 1935, and two in 1945. Since then the party has achieved no parliamentary representation and has never come close to doing so. What power it had in the 1970s and 1980s was through some of its members holding office in certain trade unions.[36] The demise of communism in Europe at the end of the 1980s undermined an already weak party. The National Front is a right-wing neofascist party that attracts support largely on the basis of opposition to immigration by nonwhites. It has proved a disruptive force, organizing rallies and attracting counterdemonstrations. It achieved some attention in the 1970s and in the 1979 election contested 300 seats. It lost its deposit in all of them and got 0.6% of the votes cast nationally. Following a split within its ranks, it contested only 60 seats in 1983, getting less than 0.1% of the vote; a breakaway movement, the British National party, suffered a similar fate. The Front contested no seats in 1987 and made no impact in those seats it contested in 1992.

There are various other fringe parties, some of them consisting of little more than their founders. None has had any significant or sustained electoral impact.

DECLINE IN PARTY SUPPORT

The past two decades have witnessed major changes in electoral behavior and in support for the two main parties. On the surface, two-party politics appear to have given way to one-party domination. That, though, masks the most important underlying feature of change: the decline in support for both parties. The Labour party has suffered a greater decline in support than the Conservative party, hence its lengthy and continuous period in opposition, but both main parties are suffering from a fall in support. That fall in support is demonstrable at three levels: voting support, party identification, and membership. Our purpose in this section is to sketch this decline and address the basic question: Why has it happened?

The decline in voting support for both parties has been sketched in the preceding chapter. Ever since the peak of two-party support reached in the 1950s, electors have shown a relative desertion of both main parties. The percentage of turnout has declined, as has the proportion of those who cast their vote for the Conservative or Labour parties. In each of the general elections of 1983, 1987, and 1992, more than 20% of those who voted cast their ballots for candidates other than Conservative and Labour candidates, in 1950 the figure had been less than 2%. As we have already noted, the Labour share of the poll in 1983 was its lowest since 1918. Though achieving victory, the Conservative party received a lower share of the poll in the four general elections from 1979 onward than in any of its previous postwar election victories. Indeed, it was their lowest share producing victory since the general election of 1922.

A decline in party identification was detected in the 1970s. What was termed partisan dealignment was especially marked among Labour supporters. The proportion of "very strong" Labour identifiers declined from 50% in 1966 to 27% in 1979.[37] Low and declining levels of support were also a feature of the 1980s. By 1985, less than 8% of Conservative identifiers and less than 10% of Labour identifiers claimed to be "very close" to their party. More than 50% of identifiers in both parties claimed that they were "not close to any party."[38] Low levels of identification, though, were not confined to the two largest parties. Only 3% of Liberal/SDP identifiers gave a "very close" response.

Both parties have witnessed a dramatic decline in membership. The Conservative party claimed a membership of 2.8 million in 1952. That was a high watermark, but it was still able to claim a membership in excess of 2 million in 1958. The figure declined in the 1960s and 1970s and was probably around the 1 to 1.5 million mark in the early 1970s. A further erosion since has resulted in a membership of fewer than 1 million. One estimate put the figure in the late 1980s at just under the 750,000 level.[39] The party's youth movement showed an even more severe decline in membership, though remaining the largest political youth movement in the country. The Labour party reached its peak in membership at about the same time as the Conservatives, claiming a membership of just over 1 million in 1952. By 1992, as we have seen, its membership was approximately 260,000, the lowest membership figure since 1929.

Clearly, on all three indicators the two parties have witnessed a decline in support in recent years though the decline under all three heads did not commence at the same time: Party membership, on the face of it, appears to have dropped prior to a drop in voting support, and voting support declined prior to a marked decline in partisan identification.

Also, declining support for the two main parties is not a phenomenon peculiar to Britain. It has been witnessed elsewhere, including in the United States. Both main parties in the United States have witnessed a decline both in terms of the number of votes cast and party identification. (Given the absence of party membership on a scale similar to that in the United Kingdom, a strict comparison of membership decline is not possible.) The proportion of the adult population turning out to vote for Republican or Democratic candidates in presidential elections has declined over the past 30 years. Voting turnout in presidential elections reached a peak in 1960. Then, almost two out of every three adult Americans went to the polls. In the presidential elections of 1984, 1988, and 1992, the proportion was down to roughly one out of two. And of those voting, not all have cast their ballots for Republicans and Democrats, third-party candidates siphoning off a significant vote in 1968, 1980, and, most especially, 1992.

Identification with both parties also has declined. By the mid-1970s, less than two-thirds of Americans identified themselves with either party (compared with 75% in 1964) and only 24% claimed to be "strong" identifiers (compared with 37% in 1964). During the 1970s and early 1980s, the number of independent identifiers outnumbered Republican identifiers. Identification with the Democratic party has continued to decline and about 30% of electors continue to identify themselves as independents.[40] Ticket splitting also has increased, as has the degree of negative voting. According to survey data, in the 1988 presidential election half of each candidate's supporters voted more to stop the other ticket than because they genuinely approved of their choice.[41]

Both countries, then, have witnessed two-party decline. The decline and the comparison should not be pushed too far. Of those who do vote, three out of four in the United Kingdom, and usually nine out of ten in the United States, vote for one of the two main parties. In the United Kingdom, two-party voting appears to have reached its low point in the 1970s and improved since. The decline is not identical in the two countries. Consequently, explanations for that decline differ. In the United Kingdom, the explanations of decline correlate closely with the partisan preferences of those who advance them. We have considered already (chapter 5) explanations of changes in voting behavior in Britain. Those explanations focused upon the decline of the class-party nexus and what may have replaced the influence of class. However, though these factors may help explain greater electoral volatility, they do not necessarily explain the *decline* in two-party voting. The fact that the two parties may not be able to rely on a core base of class support as in the past does not necessitate voters defecting from those parties. Geographical analyses may help us understand a realignment in party voting but again do not necessarily provide an explanation of two-party decline. Similarly, why should issue voting necessarily produce a decline in support for *both* main parties? Essentially, the changes identified help facilitate a decline in the two-party vote but they do not explain why it has declined. The principal explanations for two-party decline may be subsumed under the headings of *structural dealignment* and *policy orientation.* The structural analysis tends to be advanced by members of center parties and by a few within each of the main parties. The policy-orientation thesis is advanced predominantly by protagonists *within* the two main parties.

Structural Dealignment

The structural thesis is one we have touched upon already (chapters 3 and 5). The contention is that the decline in support for the two main parties is the product of the structure of the two-party system. The two parties dominate the political agenda, taking positions that are not congruent with the wishes of most electors. Such a stance is dictated by the electoral system, forcing the parties to compete for the all-or-nothing spoils of electoral victory and, in so doing, to compete vigorously with one another in an adversary relationship. Once in office, a party often must modify or abandon its program when it discovers the resources do not exist to meet the more extravagant of its promises (made in order to outbid its opponent party). There is thus a poor fit between what electors want and what the parties actually provide. Britain, in short, has a dysfunctional party system.[42] As the economic resources to meet manifesto promises have declined, in inverse relationship to the growth of such promises, so voter disenchantment with the two parties—one in government, the other forming the alternative government—has grown. Such voters then have the option of voting for a third party or, given that the electoral system works against third parties, of staying at home on election day. That, on this argument, is what they have been doing for the past 20 years.

Given that the party system cannot be separated from the workings of the nation's electoral arrangements, it is not surprising that proponents of this thesis advance reform of the electoral system as a primary means of resolving the problem. Reform of the electoral system, with the introduction of a form of proportional representation (PR), would allow voters to choose more precisely those candidates whose policies they agree with and, as no one party would (on current voting patterns) achieve an overall parliamentary majority, also produce some form of center-coalition government, allowing for a more consensual approach in policy making. Such a change, it is contended, would produce a much better fit between voters' wants and public policy as well as increase support for, and participation in, the political system.

The problem with this argument, as Nevil Johnson has observed, is that a decline in support for one or both of the two main parties does not of itself demonstrate a decline in support for the two-party system.[43] Voters may support a particular third party because they wish it to replace one of the existing major parties in a two-party framework. There are no objective data to suggest that electors wish to dispense with what supporters view as the fruits of a two-party system: a clear choice between parties, and a party government with an overall majority. Indeed, there are data that suggest the opposite. Survey data reveal broad, but not deep, support for some change in the electoral system but not for the consequences such a change would have.[44] Electors dislike the prospects of a Parliament in which no one party has an overall majority. A 1986 poll found that 50% of respondents thought the return of a Parliament without a majority party would be ''a bad thing for the country,'' compared with 28% who thought it would be a good thing.[45] A similar finding emerged in a poll conducted in the final days of the 1992 general election campaign, 56% of those questioned being opposed to a ''hung'' Parliament.[46] The final objective data are voting figures. In the 1992 general election, fewer than one in four electors went to the polls to cast a vote for a party committed to a new electoral system and a new constitution for the United Kingdom. A decline in two-party support should not be equated with a collapse in two-party support. And, as we have seen, that decline appears to have been most severe in the 1970s. In the 1992 general election, there was an increase both in voter turnout—the second highest turnout since 1959—and in the proportion voting for the two main parties.

Policy Orientation

This thesis about the two-party decline takes different forms, largely dependent upon where one stands in the political milieu. One form, which may be described as the *consensus thesis,* attributes decline in party support to the consensus policies of the 1950s and 1960s when the two parties followed similar Keynesian economic policies. This was the era of the social democratic consensus, or what Samuel Beer termed the Collectivist era.[47] For socialists within the Labour party and neoliberals within Conservative ranks, this consensus was responsible for the decline in support for their parties. It was responsible for that decline for two reasons. First, the policies themselves were deemed inadequate to meet Britain's fundamental problems. Socialists favored more state control; neoliberals wanted a free market economy. Second, the consensual stance of the parties robbed the electors of a clear choice between competing policies. The absence of a clear choice continued into the 1960s and 1970s, Labour governments pursuing orthodox economic policies and the Conservative government of Edward Heath in 1972 moving away from a noninterventionist stance.

Those advancing this thesis could point to the decline in two-party support being most marked in the 1970s. For neoliberals in the Conservative party, the pursuit of Thatcherite policies from 1979 onward ensured a clear choice and one that resulted in successive victories in four general elections. Socialists in the Labour party attributed Labour's failure in 1970 and 1979 to the absence of a socialist program and its continuing failure in the 1980s to the retrospective evaluation by electors of earlier Labour governments. Voters were continuing to vote on their evaluation of past performance rather than on an evaluation of what was being offered for the future. As Paul Whiteley expressed it, "If centrist policies fail, as they have done for the most part during Labour's tenure in office, no amount of moderation will bring electoral success."[48]

This thesis is challenged by the *extremist thesis*. This contends that a decline in support for both parties was the result of extreme policies pursued by both of the parties. The left-wing programs of Labour in the 1980s, and especially in the 1983 election, resulted in a disastrous electoral performance, resulting in the party almost being squeezed into third place by the Liberal/Social Democratic alliance. The Conservative party won three elections under Margaret Thatcher's leadership, but did so despite Thatcherism and not because of it. Electors, on balance, preferred a Conservative government to a Labour one, but they did not support, nor they did move more in the direction of supporting, Thatcherite policies.[49] The policies, particularly the economic policies, pursued by the Thatcher government alienated many voters, resulting in disaffected Conservative supporters switching their support to center parties. What support the party did retain was the result of the Falklands War and dissarray within the ranks of the opposition party. Although the Conservative party won the elections, it did so on a low share of the poll. Hence, Conservative victory over Labour masked an underlying decline in support. When both parties moved more toward the center ground, the Conservatives under the leadership of John Major and Labour— especially in the 1992 election—under Neil Kinnock's leadership, the support for the principal third party declined. A more moderate approach by the Major government, it is argued, helped keep the Conservatives in power, and a more moderate program helped Labour increase its support and make it an effective contender for power.

There is thus a basic disagreement as to the cause of two-party decline. Socialists and neoliberals blame it on the consensus politics of postwar decades. Labour and Conservative moderates ascribe the decline to the pursuit of non-consensus policies by both parties, especially in the 1980s. Consequently, prescriptions differ. For those who adhere to either of the theses of policy orientation, the solution lies in the retention or abandonment of particular policies. For those who adhere to the thesis of structural dealignment, the solution is a more fundamental and permanent one.

NOTES

1. See especially C. O. Jones, "Can Our Parties Survive Our Politics?" in N. J. Ornstein (ed.), *The Role of the Legislature in Western Democracies* (American Enterprise Institute, 1981), pp. 20–23. Despite the parties becoming relatively more organized and cohesive, especially in Congress, in recent years, the generalization remains valid.
2. See especially L. Hartz, *The Liberal Tradition in America* (Harcourt, Brace and World, 1955).
3. L. D. Epstein, "What Happened to the British Party Model?" *American Political Science Review,* 74 (1), 1980, pp. 9–22.
4. *A Bicentennial Analysis of the American Political Structure* (Committee on the Constitutional System, 1987).
5. R. H. S. Crossman, "Introduction" to W. Bagehot, *The English Constitution* (Fontana ed., 1963), p. 39.
6. See J. Vincent, *The Formation of the British Liberal Party 1857–68* (Penguin, 1972).
7. P. Norton. "The Organization of Parliamentary Parties," in S. A. Walkland (ed.), *The House of Commons in the Twentieth Century* (Oxford University Press, 1979); P. Norton, "The Parliamentary Party," in A. Seldon and S. Ball (eds.), *The Conservative Party in the Twentieth Century* (Oxford University Press, 1994).
8. R. Blake, *The Conservative Party from Peel to Churchill* (Eyre and Spottiswoode, 1970), p. 2.
9. See C. E. Bellairs, *Conservative Social and Industrial Reform,* rev. ed. (Conservative Political Centre, 1977).
10. P. Norton and A. Aughey, *Conservatives and Conservatism* (Temple Smith, 1981), ch. 2.
11. See R. Rose, "Parties, Factions and Tendencies in British Politics," *Political Studies,* 12, 1964, pp. 33–46.
12. See P. Norton, *Conservative Dissidents* (Temple Smith, 1978), ch. 4.
13. The epithet *wet* has different meanings and uncertain origins. In the present context, it derived from Mrs. Thatchers's habit of annotating papers with the word when she wished to indicate that a particular proposal or comment was indecisive, bland, and poorly argued.
14. "The Thatcher Style," *The Economist,* May 21, 1983, p. 32.
15. See H. Young, *One of Us* (Macmillan, 1989), pp. 431–458.
16. This and succeeding paragraphs are derived from P. Norton, "The Conservative Party from Thatcher to Major," in A. King (ed.), *Britain at the Polls 1992* (Chatham House, 1993), pp. 29–69.
17. Norton and Aughey, pp. 241–243.
18. "Named: The Tycoons Who Bankrolled Major," *The Sunday Times,* "Insight" Report, September 27, 1992, p. 7. See M. Pinto-Duschinsky, "Trends in British Party Funding 1983–87," *Parliamentary Affairs,* 42 (2), April 1989, p. 210.
19. "Named: The Tycoons Who Bankrolled Major," *The Sunday Times,* September 27, 1992, p. 7.

20. D. Butler and D. Kavanagh, *The British General Election of 1992* (Macmillan, 1992), p. 245.
21. "Broke Tories Owe £5m. Saatchi Bill," *The Sunday Times,* October 11, 1992, p. 1.
22. C. F. Brand, *The British Labour Party* (Stanford University Press, 1965); see also F. Williams, *Fifty Years March* (Odham, n.d.), part 1.
23. S. H. Beer, *Modern British Politics,* rev. ed. (Faber, 1969).
24. H. Pelling, *A Short History of the Labour Party,* 5th ed. (Macmillan, 1976), p. 44.
25. P. Seyd, "Labour: The Great Transformation," in A. King (ed.), *Britain at the Polls 1992* (Chatham House, 1993), p. 76.
26. I. Crewe, "Why Did Labour Lose (Yet Again)?" *Politics Review,* 2 (1), September 1992, pp. 2–11.
27. "Labour Curbs Union Power," *The Times,* October 1, 1992, p. 8. See also John Smith's speech following his election as leader. "Smith Pledges to End Reign of the Union Block Vote," *The Times,* July 20, 1992, p. 7.
28. See P. Norton, "Mixed Emotions, Ringing Oratory and Camera Angles," *The House Magazine,* 565, September 28, 1992, pp. 19–20; and P. Norton, "More Than a Rally," *The House Magazine,* 566, October 5, 1992, p. 20.
29. *NEC Report,* Labour Party Conference 1992 (Labour Party, 1992), p. 8.
30. P. Rowland, *The Last Liberal Governments* (Macmillan, 1969), p. 34.
31. See T. Wilson, *The Downfall of the Liberal Party 1914–1935* (Fontana, 1968), p. 20.
32. The Liberal National MPs became allied with and were eventually absorbed into the Conservative party.
33. See A. Michie and S. Hoggart, *The Pact* (Quartet, 1978).
34. See I. Bradley, *Breaking the Mould?* (Martin Robertson, 1981); and P. Zentner, *Social Democracy in Britain* (John Martin, 1982).
35. H. M. Drucker and G. Brown, *The Politics of Nationalism and Devolution* (Longman, 1980), p. 167.
36. See R. Taylor, *The Fifth Estate* (Pan Books, 1980), p. 325.
37. B. Sarlvik and I. Crewe, *A Decade of Dealignment* (Cambridge University Press, 1983), pp. 333–334. See also I. Crewe, B. Sarlvik, and J. Alt, "Partisan Dealignment in Britain 1964–1974," *British Journal of Political Science,* 7 (2), 1977, pp. 129–190.
38. G. Heald and R. J. Wybrow, *The Gallup Survey of Britain* (Croom Helm, 1986), p. 14.
39. P. Tether, "Recruiting Conservative Party Members: A Changing Role for Central Office," *Parliamentary Affairs,* 44 (1), 1991, pp. 20–32. See also S. Ball, "Party Organization," in A. Seldon and S. Ball (eds.), *The Conservative Party in the Twentieth Century* (Oxford University Press, 1994).
40. H. W. Stanley and R. G. Niemi, *Vital Statistics on American Politics,* 2nd ed. (CQ Press, 1990), p. 146.
41. *The Independent,* November 10, 1988.
42. See S. E. Finer, *The Changing British Party System 1945–1979* (American Enterprise Institute, 1980).
43. N. Johnson, book review, *The Times Higher Education Supplement,* July 22, 1983.
44. See P. Norton, "Does Britain Need Proportional Representation?" in R. Blackburn (ed.), *Constitutional Studies* (Mansell, 1992).
45. "The Voters Don't Care for Balance," *The Economist,* July 5, 1986, p. 19.
46. *The Times,* April 6, 1992. When given a straight choice between PR or one-party government, or between majority or coalition government, a plurality has tended to favor the existing arrangements: In an exit poll during the 1987 election, 49% were for the existing system, 46% for PR (*The Independent,* June 13, 1987), and in a MORI

poll in 1991, 38% were for majority government, 25% for coalition government (*The Independent,* April 25, 1991).

47. Beer, *Modern British Politics.*

48. P. Whiteley, ''The Decline of Labour's Local Party Membership and Electoral Base, 1945–1979,'' in D. Kavanagh (ed.), *The Politics of the Labour Party* (Allen and Unwin, 1982), p. 132. See also P. Whiteley, *The Labour Party in Crisis* (Methuen, 1983).

49. See especially I. Crewe and D. Searing, ''Ideological Change in the British Conservative Party,'' *American Political Science Review,* 82 (2), 1988; and R. Jowell, S. Witherspoon, and L. Brook, *British Social Attitudes, Fifth Report* (Gower, 1988).

CHAPTER 7

Interest Groups
Insiders or Outsiders?

Interest groups have commonly been defined as bodies that seek to influence government in the allocation of resources without themselves seeking to assume responsibility for government. This definition is usually employed to distinguish such groups from political parties, which do seek, through electoral success, to form the government. The distinction, though not watertight, is nonetheless a useful one.

Interest groups have been variously subdivided for analytic purposes. The two most common categories employed are those of *sectional* interest groups and *promotional* groups. The former, as the name implies, are formed to defend and pursue the interests of specific sections of the community, sections usually defined on an economic basis. (Indeed, to emphasize the point, some writers distinguish between economic or producer groups and promotional groups.) Promotional groups exist to promote particular causes, which may draw their support from disparate individuals and are not based on economic divisions within society. There are a number of recognizable interest groups that fall somewhere between the two categories (for example, the Automobile Association) and others that do not easily fall into either category.

Sectional interest groups are usually permanent bodies formed for a purpose other than that primarily of influencing government. Most are created to provide services of one form or another to their members: for example, negotiating on their behalf; providing legal, social, and insurance facilities; offering advice and information; and providing a forum in which matters of common interest can be discussed and policy determined. Such groups are numerous. Examples would be trade unions, the Law Society, the National Farmers Union, the Royal College of Nursing, the Police Federation, the British Medical Association, and various employers' associations. Membership in such bodies is normally exclusive, and actual membership is often close to the potential membership. In some instances, membership in a professional body is a requirement for pursuing a particular vocation. Many have their counterparts in the United States: the AFL-CIO, for example, is the rough equivalent of the Trades Union Congress in Britain, and the American Medical Association the equivalent of the British Medical Association.

Whereas sectional groups seek to promote the interests, normally the economic interests, of their membership, promotional groups seek to promote a cause or causes that are not usually of direct economic benefit to their members. The motivation for joining a sectional group is economic, and for joining a promotional group, often moral or ideological. Promotional groups may seek to promote and defend the interests of particular categories of individuals within society (for example, the Child Poverty Action Group, the National Council for One-Parent Families), of particular rights (Liberty, formerly the National Council for Civil Liberties), or of shared beliefs (the Lord's Day Observance Society). Some seek to achieve a specific objective, one often embodied in their title (for example, the Abortion Law Reform Society, the Campaign for Homosexual Equality). A number are essentially defensive groups formed to counter the campaigns mounted by reform movements: For example, the Society for the Protection of the Unborn Child (SPUC) was formed to oppose the pro-abortion lobby, and the British Field Sports Society was created to defend hunting against the activities of the League against Cruel Sports. A number of such groups, by their nature, are little concerned with public policy and rarely engage in political activity. Others, by contrast, often exist for the purpose of pursuing a public campaign to achieve a modification of public policy and the enactment of legislation.

Interest-group activity and the study of it has been more apparent in the United States than in Britain. This difference is explicable largely in terms of the different political systems. The United States has been characterized as enjoying a "multiple access" system. A group can seek to influence a particular department or bureau. If that attempt fails, it can lobby the White House. It can lobby Congress. The separation of powers and the relative weakness of political parties—in essence, depriving representatives and senators of a protective party shield to hide behind—make members of Congress worthwhile targets for group pressure. Such pressure is applied continuously on Capitol Hill; well over 20,000 lobbyists are retained by groups of some sort to lobby members of Congress. If pressure in Washington fails, a group can always turn to the state or district to try to rouse support there. Rallies may be organized. A mass mailing to Congress may be instigated. Not surprisingly, such visible activity and its apparent effect have been the subject of serious study and much academic debate. The United States has been the breeding ground of group and pluralist theory.

The position in the United Kingdom in terms of group activity has been different. For groups seeking to influence government decisions, the principal focus of activity is the executive: the ministers and officials occupying the government departments. As we shall see, for sectional groups such contact is often institutionalized. Attempts to lobby Parliament or to maintain regular contact on a scale analogous to that maintained on Capitol Hill have been notable for their rarity. Many groups maintain friendly contact with members of Parliament; as we shall see, an increasing number make use of professional lobbyists, but their number is small at present. Lobbying of MPs is an admission that attempts to influence ministers and their officials have failed. It is often an unprofitable exercise: Failure to influence ministers will frequently be replicated in a house dominated by those same ministers. Interest-group activity, certainly that of the well-entrenched sectional interest groups, is thus not as visible as it is in the United States. Only in the past 30 years has group activity become an important topic of study in British political science:[1] Even then it has often been overshadowed by the study of more conventional topics.

The relative lack of visibility of group activity and the attention accorded it by students of politics should nonetheless not be misconstrued. Group activity in Britain has been difficult to study because it has not been conducted as obviously and as openly as in the United States. And the lack of such obvious public conduct may be indicative of group influence, not weakness. Only if groups fail to influence ministers or officials do they need to go public and concentrate on Parliament and the media. For much of the postwar period, in which group pressure increased, government was able to satisfy the wants of those groups making demands of it as well as of consumers: There was little need for the more influential sectional groups to mount campaigns. In recent years, especially following the return in 1979 of a Conservative government committed to a neoliberal economic policy, important groups have become far more visible in their attempts to influence government. And as group activity has become more visible, the role played by particular groups in the political arena has become a topic of controversy, both academic and political.

GROUP TYPES

Sectional Interest Groups

Sectional groups in one form or another have existed for many years. Some existed in the fifteenth and sixteenth centuries—for example, various merchant guilds. The earliest, according to R. M. Punnett, was the fourteenth-century Convention of Royal Burghs in Scotland.[2] There was considerable group activity in the nineteenth century, but the phenomenon of a large and diverse body of permanent, well-organized sectional groups making demands of government is a relatively recent one, largely associated with the growth of government activity, especially in the years after the Second Wold War. "This surely was inevitable," wrote Robert McKenzie. "Once it had been largely agreed by all parties that the government (national and local) should collect and spend over a third of the national income, tremendous pressures were bound to be brought to bear to influence the distribution of the burdens and benefits of public spending on this scale."[3] Those pressure were channeled through and articulated by the sectional interest groups. Groups needed government in order to ensure that their members got the share of the economic cake that they desired. Conversely, government needed the groups—for advice, for information, and for cooperation. The relationship becme one of mutual dependence.

As government extended its activities into the economic and social life of the nation, and especially as it began to utilize Keynesian techniques of economic management, it came to depend on information on which it could base both particular and macroeconomic policies. Such information often could be supplied only by sectional interest groups. The groups were also in a position to offer advise. The nearer the actual membership of a group came to its potential membership (all solicitors are members of the Law Society, for example, and 75% of full-time farmers are members of the National Farmers Union of England and Wales), the closer the group came to enjoying a monopoly of the expertise and understanding peculiar to that section of society. "If doctors are powerful," writes one observer, "it is not just because of their characteristics as a pressure group but because of their functional monopoly of expertise."[4] Government also became dependent on such groups for cooperation in the implementation of policies. If groups are ill-disposed toward a government proposal that affects them, they have the sanction of withdrawing their support in the carrying out of that proposal. A policy of noncooperation may cause grave and sometimes insurmountable difficulties for government. The 1971 Industrial Relations Act, for example, failed largely because of the refusal of trade unions both to register under its provisions and to recognize the National Industrial Relations Court it created. The act was subsequently repealed. Such instances of noncooperation are rare, a sign not of group weakness but of political strength. Anticipation of opposition from affected groups will frequently induce government to refrain from pursuing a particular policy or, more likely, to seek some modification acceptable to the groups concerned; in 1989, for example, the Conservative government modified proposals for reform of legal services following opposition from the legal profession.

The growing interdependence of government and groups led some observers to view sectional groups as central to policy making. They saw the ideological gap between the parties as having narrowed, with government acting primarily as arbiter between competing group demands, seeking to meet the demands of groups while meeting the expectations of consumers. It was seen as the age of what Beer referred to as the "new group politics."[5] Whereas the electoral contest between parties may appear to emphasize an adversary relationship, the relationship between government and groups was perceived as a consensual one. To proceed with a given policy, government and the affected groups had to reach some measure of accord: One had to influence the other. In the formulation of public policy, government and groups could be seen increasingly as being inseparable.

As the relationship between government and sectional groups developed, political scientists formulated and applied various models to further understanding of that relationship. The three most important are the pluralist, the rational action, and the corporatist. These I shall discuss in looking at the current debate. As a preliminary to study of that debate, two important features of sectional groups and of their relationship with government need to be drawn out. One is the diversity of the groups themselves, and the other is the extent of the institutionalization of their relationship with government.

Diversity. There are at least several thousand bodies in Britain that constitute sectional interest groups. It is common to look at such groups under the three sectoral headings of labor, business, and agriculture. Although the business and labor sectors have "peak," or umbrella, organizations, they are notable for the number of groups that exist within them.

Labor.   The groups within the labor sector comprise primarily trade unions. There are just over 300 of these. Some are extremely small and specialized, whereas others are large and not confined to a particular industry or trade. Almost 40% of unions have memberships of under 500. The eight largest unions account for more than half of all union membership. Within the union movement, the older unions representing manual workers (such as miners) have suffered a dramatic decline in membership, and those representing white-collar workers (scientists, teachers, technicians, and other professional employees) have grown rapidly in recent years. The growth of white-collar unions appears to have helped slow a dramatic decline in union membership. Total union membership in 1993 stood at just over 7.3 million, following a continuous decline from over 12 million in 1979.

The income of each union comes primarily from membership subscriptions and from interest on invested capital. (Union pension funds are among the major investors in Britain.) Annual subscriptions vary from union to union, ranging from a few pounds a year to £20 or £40 (about $30 to $60). In return, unions provide a variety of services to members, such as insurance schemes, benevolent funds, discounts on purchases at certain stores, help with house purchases, strike funds, wage negotiations with employers, and the compiling and publishing of information useful to members. More than two-thirds of union expenditure is on working expenses (paying the salaries of full-time officials, rent, and running of headquarters), and most of the remaining one-third is spent on providing various benefits to members.

The "peak" organization for trade unions is the Trades Union Congress (TUC). In 1992, 72 unions were affiliated with it (see Figure 7.1). Although a majority of trade unions are not affiliated, it is a far more inclusive body in terms of the large and important unions than is its equivalent in the United States, the AFL-CIO (the American Federation of Labor-Congress of Industrial Organizations). A number of the largest unions in the United States, such as the auto workers, are not affiliated with the U.S. body. In Britain, the largest unions are in the TUC. Indeed, the 72 affiliated unions represent more than three-quarters of all trade unionists.

The TUC coordinates the activities of its members and represents them in dealings with government. It has a number of specialist departments on topics such as employment, economic matters, social matters, and education; these departments research and compile data and help various specialist committees of the TUC formulate policy. It provides a service of trade union education and it provides members to serve on various advisory and quasigovernmental bodies. It has an executive body, the General Council, which, following a 1989 rule change, has 53 elected members and a general secretary. Membership used to be based on industrial groupings, such as railways and mining; this arrangement, which had favored the old trades unions, was changed in 1983 following pressure from white-collar unions that considered themselves underrepresented. Council membership since then has been determined by the size of union membership.

TRADES UNION CONGRESS
Congress House, Great Russell Street, London,
WC1B 3LS
071-636 4030   *Fax:* 071-636 0632

The Trades Union Congress is a voluntary association of independent unions. At the beginning of 1992 it consisted of 72 unions representing 7,757,000 workers. Its governing body is the annual Congress consisting of 900 delegates. Between Congresses, a General Council of 50 members meets monthly. The main job of the TUC is to encourage unions to work together. It prepares common policies on matters of importance to people at work and has representatives on a number of public bodies. It maintains close links with trade union movements overseas and runs a substantial education service for union officers on issues such as employment law. There is also an extensive regional network.

General Secretary   Norman Willis
Deputy General Secretary   John Monks
Assistant General Secretary   David Lea
Press Officer   Mike Smith

CONFEDERATION OF BRITISH INDUSTRY
Centre Point, 103 New Oxford Street,
London, WC1A 1DU
071-379 7400, *Telex* 21332

The Confederation of British Industry, CBI, is an independent non party-political body financed entirely by industry and commerce. It exists primarily to ensure that Governments of all political complexions understand the intentions, needs and problems of British business. It is the acknowledged spokesman for business and is consulted as such by Governments.

President   Sir Michael Angus
Director-General   Howard Davies
Deputy Director-General and Secretary   Maurice Hunt
Deputy Director-General   Richard Price
Deputy Director-General   Mark Radcliffe
Chief Economic Adviser   Prof. D. McWilliams
Directors:
   Company Affairs   Graham Mason, OBE
   Economic Affairs   Dr Andrew Sentence
   Education and Training   Tony Webb
   Employment Affairs   Robbie Gilbert
   Environmental Affairs   John Cridland
   Public Affairs   John Dunkley
   International Affairs   John Scates
Manufacturing Industries   Andy Scott
Membership   Mrs Elizabeth Ames
Head of Parliamentary Office   John Warburton

FIGURE 7.1   The TUC and the CBI

SOURCE: Entries in *Dod's Parliamentary Companion 1993.*

Three pertinent points can be made about trade unions. First, they are largely decentralized. The TUC conference represents at best a federal body. Individual unions are largely autonomous and often have difficulty in asserting their wishes over local branches. Most industrial stoppages, for example, are unofficial, which means they take place without the official sanction of the union. (Since the relevant statistics on strikes began to be collected in 1960, unofficial strikes have accounted for more than 90% of strikes.) However, in terms of the number of strikes and days lost through such stoppages, Britain is not unusual in international comparison. It is in the remaining two features that unions are unusual. Politically, the trade unions have a close relationship with the Labour party, much closer than is the case between any union and party in the United States or most other European countries.[6] As we have seen (chapter 6), the trade unions were the largest sponsoring element when the Labour party was formed, and they continue to be its main provider in both income and affiliated membership. This relationship may in part help explain the third feature. Although unions may and do seek to influence government policy on such issues as employment and the economy, union militancy and strikes are used to pursue wage claims rather than political ends. Overtly political strikes or "days of action" are rare; unions rather look to the Labour party to achieve their political goals.

Business.   In the business sector, sectional groups are equally if not more diverse. Although there is a well-known peak body for firms in industry, the Confederation of British Industry, it is far from all-encompassing. According to Wyn Grant and David Marsh, "There is . . . a large and complex system of associations which look after the interests of individual industries or, in some cases, the interests of manufacturers of particular products, and many large firms deal directly with government."[7] Finance and the retail sector have their own structures and arrangements with government that are separate from those of the industry sector. "The City," the name given to the interests and institutions that inhabit the square mile of the City of London (Bank of England, the Stock Exchange, the Discount Market, the London Bankers' Clearing House, the commodity markets, insurance companies, and the like), is essentially a separate interest with its own structures and concerns, the latter not always compatible with those of business organizations. There are chambers of commerce throughout the country, though they tend to be most active and effective at regional and local levels rather than on a national scale.[8] In addition, there is a host of trade associations, important ones being bodies such as the Society of Motor Manufacturers.

These examples give some flavor of the diversity of business organizations. The most important body, that which receives most academic and media attention, is the Confederation of British Industry (the CBI). It was formed in 1965 as a result of the amalgamation of the Federation of British Industries (known, confusingly to Americans, as the FBI), the British Employers' Confederation, and the National Association of British Manufacturers. It sought to bring together the resources of the amalgamated bodies to form a more efficient servicing body and a more effective representative of industry's needs in discussions with government. Indeed, its functions are not dissimilar to those of unions: It provides various services to its members and it seeks—its primary and explicit aim (see Figure 7.1)—to represent them in negotiations with government departments and with government generally. It provides advice and assistance on industrial problems; it provides information on such things as technical translation services, and conditions in foreign countries; it produces its own economic reports; and, in practice, it provides a medium through which firms and associations can make new and useful contacts. It seeks to act as a voice for the needs of industry, not only through making representations directly to government and through appointing representatives to various advisory bodies, but also now through its own annual conference, a relatively recent innovation. (The TUC, by contrast, has been holding annual conferences since the nineteenth century.) A survey by Grant and Marsh found that the smaller firms in the CBI joined particularly because of the services it offered, whereas the larger industrial giants tended to join because of its position as a lobbying body on behalf of industry.[9]

Membership in the confederation is broad, though industrial companies are predominant. In 1989 more than 250,000 public and private companies, and more than 200 trade associations, employer organizations, and commercial associations were members. Of the company members, approximately half had fewer than 200 employees. Most small firms, though, are not members; the smaller the firm, the less likely it is to be a member. (The Smaller Businesses Association claims to speak for such firms.) The biggest companies are more strongly represented, with about 80 of the top 100 companies in the United Kingdom being members. More than half of the CBI's income comes from the companies with more than 1,000 members (subscriptions being based on a company's salary bill and its U.K. turnover), and more than three-quarters comes from industrial companies. In 1988 the confederation had an income of almost £13 million (just over $21m.), used primarily to finance its staff of just over 300, headquarters in London's Centre Point, 13 regional offices, and an office in Brussels.[10] The organization has an increasingly active seminar and conference program, which in 1988 generated more than £2 million.

The main body within the CBI is its council, a large body comprising up to 400 members nominated by the trade associations, CBI Regional Councils, and the CBI General Purposes Committee. The council meets several times a year but most of the work is conducted through a variety of committees, particularly the formulation of policy on industrial and economic questions. Within the council, the two most prominent and influential figures are the president, usually an industrialist drawn from one of the major companies, and the director-general, the full-time chief executive, usually drawn from a senior position in industry.

Politically, the CBI has no formal link with any political party but it is closely associated with the Conservatve party and tends to be sympathetic to its policies. In 1981, when the director-general of the CBI, Sir Terence Beckett, made some critical comments about Conservative government policy, a number of firms withdrew or suspended their membership; there has been no similar gaffe since. Although the CBI itself makes no contribution to Conservative party funds, a number of its members are contributors to party funds and, as we have seen (chapter 6), a significant proportion of Conservative party income nationally derives from business donations.

Agriculture.   Although not an inclusive peak organization, the CBI nonetheless is more extensive than any similar body in the United States. Similarly, in the agriculture sector the National Farmers Union of England and Wales (NFU) is the predominant body; in the United States there are more obviously competing bodies in the form of the Farmers' Union, the National Grange, and the American Farm Bureau Federation. The NFU in 1990 had a membership of 110,000, constituting approximately three-quarters of all full-time farmers in England and Wales. (There are separate NFUs in Scotland and Northern Ireland.) It is by no means the only body seeking to represent farming interests. The Farmers' Union of Wales, for example, is now recognized by the Ministry of Agriculture as a representative body for the purposes of discussions on the annual farm price review. There are also bodies representing more specialized interests within the broad sector of agriculture, such as dairy producers.

Like its union and business counterparts, the NFU provides various services to members (notably advice and information) and also represents the interests of members in discussions with government. Unlike the two other sectors, the agriculture sector is covered primarily by one government department, the Ministry of Agriculture, Fisheries and Food, and so the relationship with government is more concentrated and, in many respects, more structured and discreet than is the case with the TUC and the CBI. The ministry and the NFU discuss on a regular basis the annual review of farm prices, and the union is represented on a host of advisory bodies.

Rather like the CBI, the union has a large national council, with the most influential members being the president and the general secretary. Below national level, the main unit of organization is the county branch, an often active and well-organized body, particularly in the large agricultural counties. Although farmers are traditionally strong supporters of the Conservative party, the union nationally as well as at county level tends to adopt a strict political neutrality, though this is essentially of postwar origin. Before 1945 (the union was founded in 1908), it was more closely associated with the Conservative party, despite formal assertions of nonpartisanship.[11]

Institutionalization.   As its responsibilities expanded, government came to have greater need of what groups could offer, and the groups, in turn, looked to government for the satisfaction of their demands. This relationship often necessitated frequent contact and increasingly became institutionalized. Groups not only were asked for advice on an informal or nonroutine basis, but also they became drawn into the processes of government by being invited to appoint representatives to serve on advisory bodies, tribunals, and committees of different sorts. This in itself is not a recent phenomenon. The National Health Insurance Act of 1924 provided for the functional representation of specific interests, such as the medical profession, on various committees appointed to administer the system of social insurance. Analogous provisions had appeared in the Trade Board acts of 1909 and 1918. By the late 1950s, more than 100 advisory bodies existed under statutory provision. The 1960s and 1970s witnessed the growth of bodies that comprised representatives of the peak organizations of the CBI and the TUC as well as representatves of government. Examples of such bodies were the National Economic Development Council (the NEDC, known as ''Neddy''), created in 1961 to provide a forum in which representatives of the three could meet to discuss the economy; the Manpower Services Commission (since disbanded), to promote training and job creation schemes; the Health and Safety Commission, to help regulate and supervise safety and health at work; and the Advisory, Conciliation and Arbitration Service (known as ACAS), to help resolve industrial disputes. At the same time, various bodies at a lower level proliferated in number, to consider more specialized topics and to bring together representatives of the various core (as opposed to peak) groups. Between 1974 and 1978, for example, 11 new governmental bodies were created in the sector covered by the Department of the Environment: These included an advisory group on commercial property development and an advisory board of construction experts.[12] A report on such bodies in 1978 identified more than 1,560 advisory bodies and nearly 500 similar bodies with executive powers (to issue regulations, dispense funds, and carry out similar functions), such as the Manpower Services Commission.[13] Methods of appointment to these disparate bodies have varied. In some cases there are statutory requirements to include representatives of particular groups, and in other cases the power is vested with the relevant minister, who may appoint people in a representative capacity (on behalf of a group) or in an individual capacity (drawn from but not officially representing a particular group). What is significant for our purposes is the number of such bodies and the extent to which they are staffed by, and indeed would be unable to function without, members of affected interest groups.

It is important to remember that such bodies constitute the formal, institutional embodiment of the close relationship between groups and government departments. Over and above these, there is regular contact between groups and departments through formal and informal meetings, sometimes through formal or informal social gatherings. At the level of regular contact, for example, the National Farmers Union and the Ministry of Agriculture follow fairly well established procedures each year in discussing the annual price review. Throughout the year the two are in constant touch with one another, "almost hourly contact," according to one study.[14] There is similar contact between other departments and groups within their sphere of responsibility.

What emerges from even this brief review of the institutionalization of group-departmental relationships is its range and diversity, which should not be surprising. Groups, as we have seen, are remarkably diverse, with peak organizations being at best federal or confederal bodies. Government departments are not dissimilar in diversity. Usually a department is divided into a number of functional units. The relevant outside groups will discuss a proposal with the relevant unit—comprising civil servants—and if agreement is reached, the proposal is then "sold" to the department itself before, if necessary, it is put forward for approval at a higher level. Only major policy decisions percolate up to the Cabinet for discussion and approval. Most policy is made at departmental and subdepartmental levels. There are functional and legal, as well as cultural, reasons encouraging this practice. The range and extent of government policy making is such that the Cabinet is able to deal with only a fraction of it. Formally, legal powers are vested in individual ministers (not the Cabinet), and for a proposal to be authoritative and enacted, it is often sufficient for a minister to give it formal approval. Furthermore, the political culture favors consensus within these small policy communities of officials and group representatives. Disputes are neither sought nor encouraged. It is to the advantage of both group and civil servants to avoid dissent. Each needs the other, and disputes could jeopardize their relationship as well as pass the problem on for others to resolve. A desire to decide the issue for themselves impels civil servants and the groups to seek agreement. One of the characteristics of the British policy style, according to Jordan and Richardson, is that of "bureaucratic accommodation."[15]

A combination of this diversity and institutionalization has important implications for the nature of policy making in Britain, for it favors incrementalism. Policy has been—and largely remains—subject to minor or at least not fundamental change. This situation creates problems for any government seeking to impose a comprehensive new policy on both its own departments and affected groups. Departments or their various units often become so closely associated with the groups with which they deal that they tend to represent the interests of the groups to the government rather than (or in addition to) representing the interests of government to the groups. This position, sometimes referred to as a form of "clientelism," results in departments speaking on behalf of different interests and often competing among themselves where those interests are not compatible. Thus, a government determined to cut public expenditure has the task of imposing cuts upon departments that are keen to resist them and that come up with plausible arguments for their own exemption, arguments that have the backing of the department's clientele groups. For example, cuts in the defense budget are likely to be resisted by officials, sometimes the minister (if persuaded by department officials), as well as by the armed services and the various industries that help manufacture and maintain military hardware and equipment. This is precisely what has happened on more than one occasion under the present Conservative government, most recently in 1992 and 1993 in response to defense cuts made as part of the "peace dividend." Similarly, cuts in other departments would be resisted on analogous grounds, ministers competing to defend their own departmental budgets. For government to impose a comprehensive policy, it has to persuade a variety of policy communities to agree to that policy. Although a party manifesto might provide a government with its plan of action, achieving that plan is a task for which neither the manifesto nor control of a party majority in the House of Commons may be sufficient.

Promotional Groups

Promotional groups generally lack the political clout enjoyed by sectional interest groups. They rarely have a monopoly of information and expertise, certainly not information and expertise that is needed by government. A feature of promotional groups is that normally anyone sympathetic to their aims is welcome to join them. There is no exclusive membership. Their potential membership, technically, constitutes the entire population. They have few if any sanctions that they can employ against government if it proves unresponsive to their overtures. In short, they are without the attributes enjoyed by the sectional interest groups in achieving leverage in their relationship with government. Because departments are not dependent on promotional groups for advice, information, or cooperation, they will not usually maintain regular or institutionalized contact with such groups. Indeed, given the causes promoted by some groups, a government may be keen to keep some of them at arm's length. To achieve their goals, promotional groups often find themselves compelled to seek support outside the corridors of government departments.

basis—and in part based on ad hoc gatherings as occasion demanded. Indeed, the nature and frequency of meetings at 10 Downing Street involving union representatives became popularized in the term "beer and sandwich" meetings, implying talks while beer and sandwiches were brought in to sustain the participants. Union as well as business leaders became used to being consulted by government.

The Conservative government elected in 1979 was opposed to anything that smacked of corporatism. However, corporatist tendencies in the form of tripartism had failed before Mrs. Thatcher entered No. 10. Though tripartism was highly visible and, in the eyes of critics, too strong an influence on public policy, it failed because of its intrinsic weakness. This is where the rational action model is useful in helping us understand what happened. The TUC and CBI were, and remain, loose umbrella organizations, lacking the power to enforce discipline on their members. Not all unions were affiliated with the TUC, and those that were put the interests of members first and the interests of the TUC second. In the autumn and winter of 1978, wage claims were pressed for the benefit of members; a wave of strikes in the public sector followed. Far from being able to exert pressure from the top, TUC leaders were forced by pressure from activists below to repudiate renewal of a national pay policy. Though public opinion was clearly hostile to the industrial action that occurred, individual unions pursued their claims. According to Robert Taylor, workers were striving "through fragmented and localised bargaining, to hold their position relative to workers in other workplaces and other industries," seeking at most "to climb a rung or two above those whose pay they traditionally compare with their own."[30] The result was "the Winter of Discontent" and the return of a Conservative government.

Exclusion: Thatcher to Major

Under the Conservative government of Margaret Thatcher, there was a radical departure from past practice. The divorce from the past was not total. A number of tripartite bodies remained—and remain—intact, such as ACAS, as well as bodies such as the Equal Opportunities Commission and the Commission for Racial Equality. And at the lower levels of policy formulation or, more often, policy adjustment, the relationship between civil servants and group representatives has largely retained the features of pre-1979 days. Relations remain close and institutionalized: Groups are still consulted about secondary legislation and incremental policy changes. It is at the level of high and medium policy making that changes have been significant.

To achieve its neoliberal economic policy, the government began to disengage itself from anything that smacked of corporatist relationships. The goal of a free-market economy was nonnegotiable and corporatism distorted market forces. The government sought autonomy in policy making and, at the same time, wished to restrict bodies seen as employing restrictive practices. The trade unions were seen as a particular target. They moved from the status of insiders to that of outsiders. The government introduced a number of legislative measures to reform the unions, limiting their capacity to strike and to impose closed shops, as well as attempting to break up monopolistic practices in other sectors. "Beer and sandwich" meetings at No. 10 came to an abrupt end.

By withdrawing from bipartite and tripartite relationships, the government removed an obstacle to the realization of goals by other groups. However, by virtue of its free-market orientation, it also became less responsive to demands made by those groups. A pluralist analysis thus appeared more relevant, but only partially so. On the one hand, a growing number of groups competed to influence government, the latter being in a more autonomous position than before. On the other hand, government did not assume a position as independent arbiter, and certainly not at the level of economic policy making. In terms of economic policy, policy making was formulated by government and then imposed.

Groups thus faced the problem of how to make their voice heard by government in the making of public policy. They were still heard at the lower levels, but the more important the level the less input they had. The answer for many groups has been to engage in more extensive, more open, and more professional lobbying—that is, directly and on their own initiative extolling their cases to decision makers. The years since 1979 have seen the emergence of the lobbyist.[31]

Lobbying Government.   Ministers and civil servants are the principal targets of group lobbying. Groups that are consulted but have not found their views accepted, and groups—often promotional groups—that are not consulted at all, will utilize in-house or professional lobbyists to make their case to the relevant minister or official. Many large companies now have their own in-house parliamentary or public affairs divisions, responsible for relations with government departments and Parliament. Others employ the services of independent political lobbyists, known formally as political consultants. Before 1979, there were hardly any firms of political consultants. By the beginning of the 1990s, there were about 40 such firms, the largest with about 30 or 40 employees, supplemented by a three-figure number of freelance consultants.

A 1985 survey of 180 sizable U.K. companies found that 41% of them used political consultancies and 28% used public relations firms for work involving government.[32] The practice of hiring consultants is not confined to commercial organizations. Lobbying firms are also used by sectional bodies such as the Bar as well as by a host of promotional groups, ranging from animal welfare organizations to bodies promoting the social sciences. The work of lobbyists has been supplemented by the appearance of a number of guides on lobbying; among those producing such a guide is the CBI. The result has been a more crowded and proactive field of groups seeking to make their existence and their needs known to targeted ministers and officials. The task is facilitated by the fact that political consultancy firms frequently recruit staff from former civil servants and, in some cases, former ministers.

Lobbying Parliament.   Lobbying government has added a new dimension to the relationship between groups and government departments. However, much more dramatic has been the growth in parliamentary lobbying. Parliament has always been a target of groups seeking some change in the law, but for much of the twentieth century it has not been regarded as the principal target of those seeking change. Promotional groups have variously used it, sometimes to effect (as with the social reform measures of the 1960s on issues such as divorce and homosexuality) but usually to no effect. Recognition of the limitations of lobbying Parliament resulted in many sectional groups not even bothering. They had their links with departments: in seeking to achieve some change in policy, those links were necessary and sufficient. The past 15 years have seen a change in the perceptions, and consequently the practice, of such groups. They have made far greater use of Parliament than ever before.

A survey in 1986 of more than 250 organized groups, ranging from the CBI to small charities, found that one-fifth of them hired political consultants and, more significantly, three-quarters of them had regular or frequent contact with one or more MPs.[33] It is now common for groups to circulate briefing material to MPs and to have officers or lobbyists present during the committee proceedings on a bill. During the passage of one particular bill, more than 80 references were made by MPs on the committee to representations made by outside groups.[34] The MP's daily mailbag now bulges with material from pressure groups.[35] Though ministers and civil servants remain the principal focus of group activity, Parliament constitutes an important and growing target for such activity as well.

There are a number of reasons for this change in group behavior toward Parliament.[36] One is that, finding government less responsive, groups have looked elsewhere for other channels for getting their views heard by ministers and civil servants. However, Parliament itself also has variously added to its own attractiveness. Greater behavioral independence has meant that MPs—and peers—may not only be willing but also more able than before to influence public policy (see chapter 11). The creation of a series of departmental select committees also has provided a focus for group lobbying. Previously, groups had to rely on finding and using a few sympathetic MPs, and hope that they may be able to pursue their cause on the floor of the Commons. The opportunities were rare and usually fruitless. Government controlled the parliamentary timetable. Select committees determine their own agenda and, by concentrating on particular departments, act as magnets for groups seeking to influence those departments. The televising of proceedings has further added to the attractiveness of the institution for pressure groups seeking to put their case before government and the wider public.

There has thus been a virtual explosion in lobbying since 1979. For larger groups, especially well-entrenched sectional groups, such lobbying serves as a supplement rather than a substitute for their existing, institutionalized relationship with government departments. The basic institutionalized relationship, sketched earlier in this chapter, remains largely intact, particularly for discussions of policy detail. If such contact fails to elicit a desired response, then the groups have the option of lobbying potentially sympathetic MPs (and, indeed, peers, as the House of Lords also serves as a magnet for lobbying activity). Such groups often will be consulted when a bill is being drawn up but will not know its precise contents until it is published: It is after publication of the bill that they will swing into action to achieve amendments to the bill that they favor. That lobbying will encompass the department as well as Parliament.

For small promotional groups, the availability of lobbyists has added a new dimension to their work. Despite limited resources, a number now employ political consultancy firms or, more likely, freelance consultants or in-house lobbyists. Such activity serves to reinforce the pluralist model, giving a greater number of groups access to the political system. Through the use of lobbyists, small groups can target potentially sympathetic parliamentarians. Doing this may be sufficient to initiate parliamentary action. Group influence often derives not from the scale of group resources but from the force of the argument being made. Animal welfare organizations have very limited resources, but some of them are very effective in mobilizing support in the House of Commons for particular measures they favor.

Lobbying is more extensive and visible—and has resulted in some notable instances of policy modification or even withdrawal. The extent of this influence is not amenable to precise quantification: Causal linkages between group lobbying and government action cannot usually be proved. Nonetheless, there have been some significant, and observable, examples of effective group pressure. In the 1980s, the most significant instance was the defeat of the Shops bill, introduced to liberalize the law on Sunday trading. Pressure groups were active in lobbying both for and against the bill. A coalition of trade unions and religious groups, including the Church of England, lobbied against the bill and employed the services of a lobbying firm. Their campaign was stunningly effective: 72 Conservative MPs voted with Labour MPs against the bill, producing a notable defeat for the government.[37] Other instances are on a less dramatic scale, but encompass changes to bills and to government policy—on issues as diverse as the regulation of financial services, the sale of alcohol at football grounds,[38] and broadcasting.[39]

Through lobbying, a great number of groups have achieved some access to the political process. There is thus a positive side to such activity. However, it also has come in for criticism. The use of lobbyists has been regarded by some critics as, in effect, "buying influence." Groups that can afford lobbyists can achieve a degree of access to the political process that is likely to be denied to those without such resources. This criticism has been fueled by the fact that many MPs are themselves political consultants, or are hired to advise consultants, and that many civil servants are lured away to work for consultants (the Ministry of Defence, in particular, having a reputation as a "revolving door"),[40] thus ensuring that "insider" knowledge is available to clients who retain the consultants. These developments, according to *The Observer,* constitute "worryingly corrosive influences."[41] As a result of such criticism, the activities of lobbyists have been twice investigated by the House of Commons Select Committee on Members' Interests. Various reforms have been introduced to ensure that the interests of MPs, their research assistants, and journalists are recorded,[42] and in 1991 the Select Committee on Members' Interests recommended in favor of establishing a register of professional lobbyists.[43] However, perceptions of undue influence persist.

The criticisms, though, are probably excessive. MPs and civil servants are well able to recognize, and to resist, lobbying. MPs, as we have noted, have the protective cloak of party. In recent years, MPs have shown increasing signs of being bored with overly lavish and overt forms of lobbying (such as expensive dinners and receptions) and of being increasingly selective in reading material sent by groups; a well-argued letter tends to take precedence over a glossy brochure. If there is a problem, it lies with what a colleague and I have elsewhere termed consumer accountability: It is the client, not the politician, who may be in need of protection from an amateurish and overpaid lobbyist.[44] For a group wanting to influence government, choosing a good firm of lobbyists may prove a difficult task.

On balance, lobbyists tend to facilitate rather than impede greater pluralism in the system. A group with a good case to make needs to get that case heard by government: Lobbying makes that possible. The more lobbyists at work, the more crowded the field and the less easy it is for a single group to dominate. The growing availability of freelance lobbyists serves to enhance the pluralist ideal through allowing more and more groups to achieve some greater degree of access to officials and politicians. Groups may not achieve what they want, but they have at least made their voice heard.

Lobbying by groups will nonetheless remain a point of controversy. Part of the problem derives from the activity being only partially observable; part derives from the fact that payment takes place for such activity. Given continuing criticism, some regulation of lobbyists may take place. However, lobbying is certain to continue as a growth industry. Whatever the ethics of lobbying, groups are not likely to want to be left behind in the rush to influence government.

CONCLUSION

Pressure groups in Britain are numerous and diverse. Many, especially sectional interest groups, enjoy a frequent and fairly well institutionalized relationship with government departments. For peak organizations, the relationship with government became especially close, and structured, in the 1960s and 1970s, when tripartism became a feature, or at least a partial feature, of policy making. Since 1979, government has pursued an economic policy largely independent of group pressure and negotiation. Increasingly, in order to influence policy, groups have resorted to lobbying both government and Parliament. The features of government-group relations established earlier remain largely in place, especially for discussion of policy detail, but an extra dimension has been added. By Capitol Hill standards, the development is an extremely modest one, but it is growing and is likely to continue to do so. It offers the prospect of a more, rather than a less, pluralistic system of policy making.

NOTES

1. The first pioneering study was W. J. Mackenzie, "Pressure Groups in British Government," *British Journal of Sociology,* 6 (2), 1955, pp. 133–148, followed by several other studies in the following decade.

2. R. M. Punnett, *British Government and Politics* (Heinemann, 1970 ed.), p. 134.
3. R. T. McKenzie, "Parties, Pressure Groups and the British Political Process," *Political Quarterly,* 29 (1), 1958.
4. R. Klein, "Policy Making in the National Health Service," *Political Studies,* 22 (1), 1974, p. 6.
5. S. H. Beer, *Modern British Politics,* rev. ed. (Faber, 1969), p. 326.
6. See C. Crouch, "The Peculiar Relationship: The Party and the Unions," in D. Kavanagh (ed.), *The Politics of the Labour Party* (Allen & Unwin, 1982), pp. 175–177.
7. W. Grant and D. Marsh, *The CBI* (Hodder & Stoughton, 1977), p. 55.
8. In 1967 an attempt was made to create a peak organization for the retail trade with the formation of a Retail Consortium, a loose confederation of the Multiple Shops Federation, the National Chamber of Trade, the Retail Distributors' Association, and the Cooperative Union. Only gradually did it establish itself as an influential body in its relations with government. See Grant and Marsh, pp. 61–68.
9. Ibid., pp. 44–50.
10. *CBI: Annual Review and Report for 1988* (CBI, 1989); other material is drawn from *CBI: Britain's Business Voice* (CBI, 1989).
11. P. Self and H. Storing, "The Farmer and the State," in R. Kimber and J. Richardson (eds.), *Pressure Groups in Britain* (Dent, 1974), pp. 58–59.
12. J. Richardson and G. Jordan, *Governing under Pressure* (Martin Robertson, 1979), p. 61.
13. *Report on Non-Departmental Public Bodies,* Cmnd. 7797 (Her Majesty's Stationery Office, 1980), p. 5.
14. G. K. Wilson, *Special Interests and Policy Making* (Wiley, 1977), quoted in Richardson and Jordan, p. 114.
15. G. Jordan and J. Richardson, "The British Style or the Logic of Negotiation?" in J. Richardson (ed.), *Policy Styles in Western Europe* (Allen & Unwin, 1982), p. 81.
16. See especially P. G. Richards, *Parliament and Conscience* (Allen & Unwin, 1970). For more recent examples, see P. Norton, *Does Parliament Matter?* (Harvester Wheatsheaf, 1993), ch. 4.
17. The main works on pluralism are American, most notably those of Dahl and Truman. See especially R. A. Dahl, *A Preface to Democratic Theory* (Chicago University Press, 1956); and R. A. Dahl, *Who Governs?* (Yale University Press, 1961). See also D. Truman, *The Governmental Process* (Knopf, 1962).
18. For a Marxist analysis, see R. Miliband, *The State in Capitalist Society* (Quartet, 1973). The classic U.S. elite study is that of C. Wright Mills, *The Power Elite* (Oxford University Press, 1956).
19. R. J. Harrison, *Pluralism and Corporatism* (Allen & Unwin, 1980), ch. 5.
20. R. Rose, *Do Parties Make a Difference?* 2nd ed. (Macmillan, 1984). See also A. King, "What Do Elections Decide?" in H. Penniman (ed.), *Democracy at the Polls* (American Enterprise Institute, 1980), pp. 304–308.
21. See R. I. Hofferbert and I. Budge, "The Party Mandate and the Westminster Model: Election Programmes and Government Spending in Britain, 1945–85," *British Journal of Political Science,* 22 (2), 1992, pp. 151–182.
22. M. Olson, *The Logic of Collective Action* (Schocken, 1968); see also, by the same author, *The Rise and Decline of Nations* (Yale University Press, 1982).
23. Grant and Marsh, pp. 50–52.
24. See A. Cawson, "Pluralism, Corporatism and the Role of the State," *Government and Opposition,* Spring 1978, p. 197.

25. P. C. Schmitter, "Still the Century of Corporatism?" *The Review of Politics,* 36 (1), 1974, pp. 85–131. See also R. Pahl and J. Winkler, "The Coming Corporatism," *New Society,* October 10, 1974, pp. 72–76.

26. Quoted in Richardson and Jordan, *Governing under Pressure,* p. 50.

27. See P. Norton, *The Constitution in Flux* (Martin Robertson, 1982), pp. 2, 179, 275, 282.

28. See A. Cox, "Corporatism and the Corporate State in Britain," in L. Robins (ed.), *Topics in British Politics* (Politics Association, 1982), p. 128.

29. Norton, *The Constitution in Flux,* pp. 272–275.

30. Quoted in S. H. Beer, *Britain Against Itself* (Faber, 1982), p. 57.

31. There are now various works on lobbying and lobbyists. See especially C. Grantham and C. Seymour-Ure, "Political Consultants," in M. Rush (ed.), *Parliament and Pressure Politics* (Oxford University Press, 1990); C. Miller, *Lobbying,* 2nd ed. (Basil Blackwell, 1990); and G. Jordan (ed.), *Commercial Lobbyists* (Aberdeen University Press, 1991).

32. "Need Seen for Westminster Advisers," *The Financial Times,* December 23, 1985.

33. M. Rush (ed.), *Parliament and Pressure Politics* (Oxford University Press, 1990).

34. P. Norton, "Public Legislation," in M. Rush (ed.), *Parliament and Pressure Politics* (Oxford University Press, 1990).

35. See especially P. Norton, *Does Parliament Matter?*

36. See P. Norton, "The Changing Face of Parliament: Lobbying and Its Consequences," in P. Norton (ed.), *New Directions in British Politics?* (Edward Elgar, 1991); and P. Norton, "Interest Representation in the House of Commons," in G. Copeland and S. Patterson (eds.), *Parliaments in the Modern World* (University of Michigan Press, 1994).

37. See P. Regan, "The 1986 Shops Bill," *Parliamentary Affairs,* 41 (2), 1988; and F. A. C. S. Bown, "The Shops Bill," in M. Rush (ed.), *Parliament and Pressure Politics* (Oxford University Press, 1990).

38. See C. Grantham, "Parliament and Political Consultants," *Parliamentary Affairs,* 42 (4), 1989; and Grantham and Seymour-Ure, "Political Consultants."

39. "The Broadcasting Act 1990: A Case Study," in *Making the Law: The Report of the Hansard Society Commission on the Legislative Process* (Hansard Society, 1993), pp. 372–387.

40. S. Berry, "Lobbyists: Techniques of the Political 'Insiders'," *Parliamentary Affairs,* 45 (2), 1992, p. 229.

41. *The Observer,* April 9, 1989.

42. Research assistants and journalists are required to register outside interests in a register maintained by the House of Commons Registrar of Members' Interests. MPs also register their interests in an annual register maintained by the registrar, though those who act as consultants are not required to list the names of clients. The Register of Members' Interests is published; the register of research assistants and journalists' interests is not.

43. *Third Report from the Select Committee on Members' Interests,* Session 1990–91, HC 586 (Her Majesty's Stationery Office, 1991).

44. P. Norton and C. Grantham, "The Hyphen in British Politics? Parliament and Professional Lobbying," *British Politics Group Newsletter* (USA), 45, 1986, pp. 4–8.

PART III

Governmental Decision Making

CHAPTER **8**

The Executive
Government at the Center

The formal process of determining public policy in Britain is dominated by the executive. Once the executive has agreed on a measure, the assent of Parliament can usually be ensured. Parliament is essentially a policy-ratifying rather than a policy-making body. Once the measure is enacted in legislative form, it will be enforced by the courts: It cannot be struck down on grounds of being contrary to the provisions of the Constitution. In the United States, by contrast, the executive enjoys no such dominance. The president cannot proceed on the basis that any proposals he makes can be ensured the assent of Congress. Once enacted, legislative measures can be and occasionally are struck down by the courts as contrary to the provisions of the Constitution. The U.S. political system has been described as a "multiple access" one. It also may be characterized as a "multiple check" system. A proposal emanating from one branch of government can be checked—that is, negated—by another. Congress has negating powers that it is prepared to and not infrequently does use; Parliament has negating powers that it can but hardly ever does use. The executive in Britain can make assumptions about legislative support that few U.S. presidents would dare to make.

Viewed in terms of the Constitution and the relationships governed by conventions, the policy-making process in Britain may appear clear and effective. An executive is formed and proceeds to implement a party program with the support of a parliamentary majority. That has been a popular perception, in Britain itself as well as elsewhere. In practice, the process has proved to be more complex and constrained than this picture suggests. An executive has to work within an increasingly intricate political environment shaped by public expectations, group pressures, party commitments, limited resources, the global economy, and an often volatile milieu of international relations. The international constraints have become more pronounced as a consequence of membership in the European Community. Domestically, Parliament has become a more active scrutineer of executive actions. Within Parliament, the executive continues to face a critical body unknown in U.S. politics: the alternative government. The second largest party in the House of Commons forms the official opposition and in recent decades its leaders have formed a "Shadow Cabinet." For every cabinet minister sitting on the government front bench, there is usually a "shadow" minister on the opposition front bench. The executive in Britain may achieve the legislative enactments it wants, but those measures may be the product of external pressures and, in being passed, are subject to a process of more organized criticism than exists in the United States.

THE STRUCTURE

It is not only the environment external to the executive that is complex and not always (if ever) harmonious. The same may be said of the executive itself. It comprises an entangled web of bodies, powers, and relationships that, in practice, are not easy to discern and that confuse any attempt to delineate clearly how policy is formulated and where power lies within government. At the apex of government stands the Cabinet, headed by the prime minister, and below that the individual government departments headed by ministers and staffed by civil servants. But even within the Cabinet there exist a complex infrastructure and sometimes shifting relationships. As government has grown, it not only has become more complex but also has experienced problems of political accountability. Over the course of the twentieth century, the civil service has variously grown. Recent years have seen the growth of semi-autonomous agencies within departments. At the edges of government, there are many nondepartmental public bodies. For the Cabinet, maintaining control of the government body itself has become an awesome task.

In terms of the structure of the executive and the lines of responsibility to Parliament, the formal position is outlined in Figure 8.1. For the purposes of analysis, it is necessary to identify the essential features of the different elements of the executive. The main elements may be subsumed under the headings of the prime minister, the Cabinet, ministers, departments, agencies, civil servants, and nondepartmental public bodies, known popularly as "quangos." The powers, structure, and composition of each element and the relationships among them have become increasingly a matter of controversy.

The Prime Minister

The prime minister stands at the apex of government. The position is a powerful and highly visible one. In the 1960s, there was a largely academic debate as to whether or not Britain had "prime ministerial government." The debate widened in the 1970s and reached new heights in the 11.5 years (1979–90) that Margaret Thatcher occupied No. 10 Downing Street (the prime minister's official residence). The debate was not stilled when she was succeeded in November 1990 by the less strident figure of John Major.

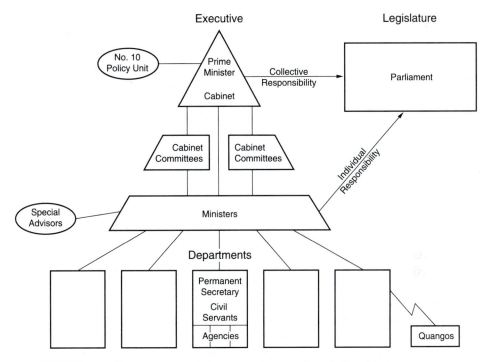

FIGURE 8.1   The structure of the executive and its relationship to the legislature

In the sixteenth and seventeenth centuries, monarchs were often dependent on particular ministers. However, it was not until the eighteenth century that a recognizable first, or "prime," minister began to emerge. George I, the first of the Hanoverian kings, had little interest in British politics, spoke little or no English, and spent six months of each year on the Continent. He left the conduct of affairs entirely to the Cabinet, his chosen group of ministers. "This," as Arthur Berriedale Keith observed, "led inevitably to the development of the office of Prime Minister; for, once the King was removed from the cabinet, the natural tendency was for some minister to take his place as a unifying influence."[1] The first minister to be considered—at least by historians—as prime minister was Sir Robert Walpole, from 1721 to 1742. The term itself had been used before and Walpole himself disclaimed it. It came eventually into colloquial but not formal use. Not until the twentieth century was the position to be referred to in a statute. The official position held by most "prime" ministers was that the first lord of the treasury, a position that is still retained by holders of the office. Over time, however, the position of prime minister grew in recognition and in powers. The growth of party government acted as a particular spur to the growth of prime ministerial power. The nineteenth century, as we have seen (chapter 3), witnessed a transfer of power from the monarch and later from Parliament to the Cabinet, a Cabinet headed—and chosen—by the prime minister.

The powers that inhere in the office of prime minister are considerable. They are also remarkable for the fact that they exist by convention and not by statute or common law. Prerogative powers, such as the appointment of ministers, reside in the monarch. Statutory powers are vested in individual ministers. The most powerful person in government is the one who wields no legal powers at all.

There are several powers that coalesce to make the prime minister the most powerful figure in government. They are summarized in the list below.

Prime Ministerial Powers
1. Appoints, moves, and dismisses ministers
2. Dispenses patronage (honors—such as peerages and knighthoods— and various appointments to public office)
3. Chairs the Cabinet
4. Determines the Cabinet agenda
5. Appoints senior members of the civil service
6. Determines the date of general elections
7. Enjoys the mandate of an election victory
8. Represents the nation at international summits
9. Is party leader
10. Is a focus of media attention
11. Occupies an office once held by Pitt, Palmerston, Gladstone, Disraeli, Lloyd George, and Churchill[2]

The best known as well as the most important of these are those of appointment and dismissal. The monarch formally appoints ministers, but by convention she does so on the advice of her prime minister. The reality of who does the choosing is well recognized. Announcements of ministerial appointments are made direct from Downing Street. The prime minister not only chooses who the ministers will be, he or she can also decide when they are no longer to be ministers. Ministerial reshuffles are used by prime ministers to make changes and bring new blood into the Cabinet, or the ranks of non-Cabinet ministers, and are sometimes controversial, as in July 1962 when Harold Macmillan dismissed one-third of his Cabinet and in July 1989 when Margaret Thatcher moved a very unwilling Sir Geoffrey Howe from the Foreign Office to the position of lord president of the council and leader of the House of Commons. The extent of prime ministerial patronage is considerable: There are now more than 100 ministers and all owe their positions to the prime minister. Nor does the patronage end with ministers. The prime minister in effect chooses new members of the House of Lords, decides other honors (such as the award of knighthoods), and can appoint individuals to a range of public positions. He even has the final say, should he choose to exercise it, over the appointments of archbishops and bishops in the established church, the Church of England.

The power to appoint ministers is not unfettered. By convention, ministers must normally be drawn from Parliament and, by convention, predominantly from the House of Commons. (There is no legal requirement that ministers be MPs or peers, and occasionally one post in particular—that of the solicitor general for Scotland—is filled by a lawyer outside Parliament.) Partisanship dictates that the ministers will be drawn from the prime minister's own party. It is also deemed politically prudent to ensure a reasonable balance of ministers, in terms of both geography—drawing ministers from different constituencies across the country— and the different wings of the party. There are also likely to be senior figures with considerable support among MPs whom the prime minister would find it difficult to exclude, not least because they could become dangerous critics from the back benches. Nonetheless, the extent of the balance is sometimes a little skewed—Edward Heath in particular was accused of selecting a personally loyal Cabinet—and few are willing to challenge the prime minister's judgments. The appointing—and dismissal—power wielded by the prime minister serves to ensure loyalty on the part of ministers and of those MPs who would like to be ministers.

The power to choose ministers is important not only in ensuring ministerial loyalty to the prime minister; it is also a major tool in influencing the direction of public policy. As Maurice Kogan has observed, the authority to appoint, transfer, or dismiss enables the prime minister to allocate values and thus change or confirm an individual minister's policies.[3] For example, when Margaret Thatcher was prime minister, she ensured that supporters of her neoliberal economic policy occupied the key economic ministries. Her replacement of Nicholas Ridley as environment secretary by Chris Patten in 1989 was interpreted as a significant policy shift, a minister sensitive to green issues taking over from one seen as more friendly to industry and developers.

Power to determine the direction of policy is not confined to the blunt weapon of appointment and dismissal. It derives also from the prime minister's position as chairman of the Cabinet. In the nineteenth century John Morley described the prime minister as *primus inter pares* (first among equals) in the Cabinet. In practice, the premier's position has always been much more than that. The prime minister (PM) determines when the Cabinet will meet and what it will discuss. She or he also sums up discussion. Very few prime ministers have resorted to taking votes in Cabinet. The PM's summing up is therefore crucial. It is that which will determine what is recorded in the minutes. As chairman of the Cabinet, the prime minister also determines the extent and composition of Cabinet committees, appointed to save Cabinet time by discussing and resolving issues before they go to full Cabinet. As we shall see, the range of such committees is extensive.

The prime minister's control is not confined to the Cabinet. It extends to the rest of Whitehall. The prime minister is minister for the civil service. The permanent head of the service reports directly to the PM. Power over the appointment of senior civil servants—primarily the permanent secretaries, the civil service heads of each department—rests with the prime minister, not the ministers in whose departments they serve. If a minister wants to have a senior civil servant moved, as occasionally happens, the support of the PM is essential. It is also a potentially risky business: The prime minister might refuse and take the side of the civil servant.[4] Some premiers have taken an active interest in civil service appointments. Margaret Thatcher in particular intervened to ensure that a number of vacancies were filled by high-flying officials rather than by the person second in seniority.

The prime minister can also determine the date of the general election and, if he leads his party to victory, has the added authority that derives from that victory. Credit tends to accrue to the person at the head of the winning campaign. Edward Heath was often seen as having won the 1970 general election for the Conservatives almost single-handedly, having led his party to an unexpected victory. A similar view was taken of Margaret Thatcher in her three consecutive election victories and of John Major in leading his party to an unexpected victory in April 1992.

As head of government, the prime minister represents the nation at major international summits, the foreign secretary acting essentially in a supporting role. The more frequent such summits—and the number has increased substantially as result of frequent meetings of the European Council, comprising the heads of government of the member states of the European Community—the greater the visibility of the PM on the international stage. As head of government, the PM also has considerable media visibility at home. He or she is a natural focus of media attention. The PM is a powerful political power—usually the most powerful political figure—and one who occupies an office once held by such towering figures as William Pitt (the elder, and the younger), Palmerston, Gladstone, Disraeli, Lloyd George, and Winston Churchill. An aura attaches to the office, one now reinforced by security considerations: The PM has to be kept some distance from ordinary public contact. He or she travels with an escort—a very modest escort by U.S. standards, but an escort nonetheless.

The PM is thus a powerful political figure. However, there is one essential component of that power that has not yet been mentioned. The PM is also leader of his or her party. It is that leadership that is a necessary but not sufficient condition for becoming prime minister. (Electoral success provides the sufficient condition.) In office, the fact of being party leader gives the PM the capacity to call on party loyalty and also to utilize the machinery of the party organization. That is particularly important on the Conservative side (see chapter 6), with all party bodies being advisory to the leader and the leader appointing all the senior officers of the party. The confluence of party leadership and the premiership thus makes the PM a tremendously powerful figure. However, it does not render the PM all-powerful. The fact of being party leader is a double-edged weapon. The party, or that part of it that selects the leader, can withdraw its support, as Margaret Thatcher found to her cost in November 1990. Having lost the leadership of the Conservative party, she resigned the premiership.

The prime minister wields the powers of the office with relatively limited institutional support. There is no Prime Minister's Department as such. The size of the staff in Downing Street is small.[5] However, as chairman of the Cabinet, the PM is serviced by the secretary to the Cabinet (who is also usually head of the civil service) and the Cabinet secretariat, which records and monitors Cabinet decisions. She or he also has the support of a number of advisors. Before the 1970s, prime ministers appointed a number of advisors on an ad hoc basis. In 1970 the Central Policy Review Staff (CPRS), more popularly known as the "think tank," was established. Comprising a small number of political appointees and seconded civil servants, it provided wide-ranging policy advice to the Cabinet and the prime minister. However, it was gradually overshadowed by a small body of advisors established to advise the prime minister—the No. 10 Policy Unit—and in 1983 the CPRS was disbanded.[6] The No. 10 Policy Unit consists of about seven or eight experts on particular subjects (the number varies), usually politically committed individuals seconded from outside bodies, and it offers party-oriented advice working directly to the PM. John Major chose as head of the policy unit Sarah Hogg, an economics journalist. Along with the PM and the party chairman, she was a key figure in drawing up the 1992 Conservative election manifesto.

The prime minister thus has a small but important body of his or her own to offer advice independent of that coming from ministers and civil servants. It reinforces the PM's capacity to lead within government. The extent to which the prime minister chooses to lead, though, depends very much upon the occupant of the office.

Britain has had 19 prime ministers since 1900 (see Table 8.1). Their approach to the office has varied considerably. Some have been forceful wielders of power,

TABLE 8.1   Prime ministers since 1900

Took Office	Prime Minister	Party
June 25, 1895	The marquess of Salisbury	Unionist (Conservative)
July 12, 1902	Arthur James Balfour	Unionist (Conservative)
December 5, 1905	Sir Henry Campbell-Bannerman	Liberal
April 8, 1908	Herbert Henry Asquith	Liberal[a]
December 7, 1916	David Lloyd George	Liberal[b]
October 23, 1922	Andrew Bonar Law	Unionist (Conservative)
May 22, 1923	Stanley Baldwin	Unionist (Conservative)
January 22, 1924	J. Ramsay MacDonald	Labour
November 4, 1924	Stanley Baldwin	Conservative
June 5, 1929	J. Ramsay MacDonald	Labour
August 24, 1931	J. Ramsay MacDonald	National Labour[c]
June 7, 1935	Stanley Baldwin	Conservative[c]
May 28, 1937	Neville Chamberlain	Conservative[c]
May 10, 1940	Winston S. Churchill	Conservative[d]
May 23, 1945	Clement Attlee	Labour
October 26, 1951	Sir Winston Churchill	Conservative
April 6, 1955	Sir Anthony Eden	Conservative
January 10, 1957	Harold Macmillan	Conservative
October 19, 1963	Sir Alec Douglas-Home	Conservative
October 16, 1964	Harold Wilson	Labour
June 19, 1970	Edward Heath	Conservative
March 4, 1974	Harold Wilson	Labour
April 5, 1976	L. James Callaghan	Labour
May 4, 1979	Margaret Thatcher	Conservative
November 28, 1990	John Major	Conservative

[a] Coalition from May 1915
[b] Coalition government
[c] National government
[d] Coalition government May 1940–May 1945; national government May–July 1945

others more emollient occupiers of the office. Some have been driven by a powerful ideological world view, others by the need to satisfy their egos. One useful way to analyze the 19 people who have occupied No. 10 in the twentieth century is to look at their purpose in seeking office. Utilizing this approach, it is possible to identify four prime ministerial types:

Innovators. They seek power in order to achieve a future goal of their own creation and are prepared, if necessary, to bring their party kicking and screaming in their wake in order to achieve that goal.

Reformers. They seek power in order to achieve the implementation of a particular program, but one drawn up by the party rather than by the premier.

Egoists. They seek power for the sake of power; they are concerned with enjoying the here and now of office rather than with future goals, and they fight to keep power.

Balancers. They fall into two categories: those who seek power in order to achieve balance, within society and within party, and those who share the same goal but, rather than seeking power, have it thrust upon them, usually as compromise choices for leader; the latter may be described as conscripts in the office.

These four are ideal types. Some premiers have straddled categories. Others have changed over time: Winston Churchill was essentially an innovator as wartime prime minister but a balancer in peacetime. Nonetheless, the categories are useful for assessing and distinguishing prime ministers. Table 8.2 categorizes

TABLE 8.2   Typology of prime ministers

Innovators	Reformers	
Churchill (wartime)	Campbell-Bannerman	
Heath?	Asquith	
Thatcher	Chamberlain	
	Attlee	

	Balancers	
Egoists	*Power-Seeking*	*Conscripts*
Lloyd George?	Salisbury	Bonar Law
MacDonald?	Balfour?	Douglas-Home
Eden	Baldwin	
Wilson	Churchill (peacetime)	
Heath?	Macmillan	
	Callaghan	
	Major	

SOURCE: Developed from P. Norton, "Prime Ministerial Power," *Social Studies Review,* 3 (3), 1988, p. 110.

the twentieth-century premiers. The past 30 years have seen power-seeking balancers (Macmillan, Callaghan, Major), a conscript balancer (Douglas-Home), an egoist (Wilson), an obvious innovator (Thatcher), and a premier who straddled the categories of innovator and egoist (Heath).[7] The quest to occupy the office thus draws many different politicians. Which one actually reaches the top of what Disraeli described as "the greasy pole" will affect significantly how the powers of the office are used. Had Michael Heseltine (an egoist-innovator) won the Conservative party leadership—and hence the premiership—in 1990, he would almost certainly have utilized the powers of the office in a very different way from John Major. Had the Labour party won the 1992 general election, Neil Kinnock (an egoist) would have acted very differently from his two immediate predecessors. Practices between premiers have varied considerably. Margaret Thatcher used to hector the Cabinet and was reputed to sum up discussions at the beginning! John Major has allowed the Cabinet to operate more as a relaxed seminar, with ministers questioning other ministers.

A particularly determined occupant of No. 10 is likely to achieve more, at least in the short term, than a less determined individual. Nonetheless, however determined the individual might be, wielding the powers of the office will not necessarily achieve the desired result. Prime ministerial power depends in part upon the skills of the individual in the office. He or she has to engage in "impression management." As Barbara Kellerman put it in the U.S. context, "the president must seem presidential":[8] so the prime minister must appear prime ministerial. She or he must not only look fit for the office, but also has to have a feel for it, or in other words an intuitive grasp of how to deploy, or not deploy, the powers of the office. Some prime ministers have managed to mold a united Cabinet, some have been able to judge what is or is not politically acceptable (a particular skill of Mrs. Thatcher's until it deserted her in 1989 and 1990), some have been able to judge the parliamentary and the public mood and to capitalize on it, and some have proved good manipulators of other actors in the political system (the principal skill attributed to Mr. Major). Few have managed to combine all such skills.

How the skills of the individual are deployed will help determine the extent to which the PM can influence the immediate political environment, encompassing not just the Cabinet but also the rest of the executive, the legislature, and other proximate actors. In seeking to influence that immediate environment, the prime minister enjoys a position of superiority but not one of hegemony. The prime minister's time and resources are limited. Neither the PM nor his or her staff at No. 10 can oversee and control all aspects of government. The Cabinet, individual ministers, civil servants, and Parliament itself are not lacking in powers of their own to influence public policy in the United Kingdom.

Success also depends in part, and sometimes crucially, upon external circumstances over which the prime minister can have little or no control. Crop failure, a recession in the United States, ethic conflict in the former Yugoslavia, a reunified Germany, a refusal of the German Bundesbank to lower interest rates, or the uncertain intentions of the president of Iraq can and do have major implications for the United Kingdom. The future of the British prime minister may depend upon events well beyond Britain's shores and hence beyond her or his immediate political reach.

The Cabinet

The Cabinet is the collective decision-making body of British government. It usually comprises just over 20 members (see Table 8.3), constituting the ministerial heads of all the principal government departments as well as a number of ministers without departmental responsibilities (such as the lord president of the council and the lord privy seal, titles usually given to the ministers who serve as managerial leaders in the two houses of Parliament). By convention, as we have seen, its members are drawn from, and remain within, Parliament. A minimum of two peers (the lord chancellor and the leader of the House of Lords), and rarely more than four, are appointed to the Cabinet. Most members have served a parliamentary apprenticeship, having moved up from the back benches to junior ministerial office and then to minister of state level before being considered for Cabinet appointment. It is rare for Cabinet ministers to be appointed from the ranks of backbenchers or from people outside the Commons. There have been rare exceptions: In the Second World War, for example, union leader Ernest

TABLE 8.3   The Cabinet, July 1993

Prime Minister, First Lord of the Treasury and Minister for the Civil Service—The Rt. Hon. John Major, MP

Lord Chancellor—The Rt. Hon. The Lord Mackay of Clashfern

Secretary of State for Foreign and Commonwealth Affairs—The Rt. Hon. Douglas Hurd, CBE, MP

Chancellor of the Exchequer—The Rt. Hon. Kenneth Clarke, QC, MP

Secretary of State for the Home Department—The Rt. Hon. Michael Howard, QC, MP

President of the Board of Trade (Secretary of State for Trade and Industry)—The Rt. Hon. Michael Heseltine, MP

Secretary of State for Transport—The Rt. Hon. John MacGregor, OBE, MP

Secretary of State for Defence—The Rt. Hon. Malcolm Rifkind, QC, MP

Lord Privy Seal and Leader of the House of Lords—The Rt. Hon. The Lord Wakeham

Lord President of the Council and Leader of the House of Commons—The Rt. Hon. Tony Newton, OBE, MP

Secretary of State for the Environment—The Rt. Hon. John Gummer, MP

Secretary of State for National Heritage—The Rt. Hon. Peter Brooke, CH, MP

Secretary of State for Employment—The Rt. Hon. David Hunt, MBE, MP

Secretary of State for Social Security—The Rt. Hon. Peter Lilley, MP

Chancellor of the Duchy of Lancaster—The Rt. Hon. William Waldegrave, MP

Secretary of State for Scotland—The Rt. Hon. Ian Lang, MP

Secretary of State for Northern Ireland—The Rt. Hon. Sir Patrick Mayhew, QC, MP

Secretary of State for Education—The Rt. Hon. John Patten, MP

Secretary of State for Health—The Rt. Hon. Virginia Bottomley, MP

Minister of Agriculture, Fisheries and Food—The Rt. Hon. Gillian Shephard, MP

Chief Secretary to the Treasury—The Rt. Hon. Michael Portillo, MP

Secretary of State for Wales—The Rt. Hon. John Redwood, MP

Bevin was brought straight into government. In such cases, the normal practice is for the new minister to be created a peer or to be found a safe seat to win in a by-election.

The Cabinet, like the position of prime minister, developed in importance during the eighteenth and nineteenth centuries. However, as the monarch's principal body of advisors, it was not particularly efficient. It often had little to do, decisions were frequently leaked by waiters (it met for dinner at the home of one of its members), members sometimes slept during meetings, and there was no agenda. In the twentieth century, as the demands on the Cabinet grew—public policy becoming both more extensive and more complex—it developed in terms of its political significance and its organization.

The second decade of the twentieth century witnessed a particular improvement in organization as well as an authoritative clarification of what its role was. In 1916 the Cabinet Secretariat came into being, responsible for circulating agenda, papers, and minutes and for monitoring the implementation of Cabinet decisions; previously, implementation had been very much dependent on the memories of ministers, some of whom forgot what had been decided. In 1918 the Machinery of Government Committee delineated the functions of the Cabinet to be (1) the final determination of the policy to be submitted to Parliament, (2) the supreme control of the national executive in accordance with the policy prescribed by Parliament, and (3) the continuous coordination and delimitation of the authorities of the several departments of state. This delineation remains extant. It has not been superseded but what has changed has been the Cabinet's mode of fulfilling its functions. As the functions became more onerous for a single body meeting once or twice a week, it developed a complex infrastructure. Consequently, there are two vehicles through which the Cabinet now operates: Cabinet committees and the full Cabinet.

Cabinet committees have burgeoned, particularly since 1945. They are formed from the ministers relevant to the area covered by the committee as well as some ministers free of departmental responsibilities. The committees' creation, membership, and chairmanship are determined by the prime minister. They are serviced by the Cabinet Secretariat, which, among other things, provides briefing papers for the chairmen.

Until the premiership of Margaret Thatcher, the committees were shrouded in secrecy. No details were given about them: Officially, they did not exist. Mrs. Thatcher broke with tradition to admit their existence and named four standing committees. Her successor, John Major, took the revelations one step further and authorized the publication of the names, membership, and terms of reference of all Cabinet committees. In 1993, there were 19 committees and 7 subcommittees (see Table 8.4). Each is usually referred to by coded initials. The committees are supplemented by various and, indeed, numerous committees appointed on an ad hoc basis, and known by the code MISC or GEN. In the first six years of her premiership, for example, Margaret Thatcher appointed about 150 ad hoc committees—a large number but fewer than the number created by her predecessors, and less than half the number formed by Clement Attlee during his six-year premiership.[9]

TABLE 8.4   Cabinet committees, 1993

Name and Coded Initials	Chairman
Committees	
Economic and Domestic Policy (EDP)	PM
Defence and Overseas Policy (OPD)	PM
The Gulf	PM
Nuclear Defence Policy (OPDN)	PM
European Security (OPDSE)	PM
Hong Kong and Other Dependent Territories (OPDK)	PM
Northern Ireland (NI)	PM
Science and Technology (EDS)	PM
Intelligence Service (IS)	PM
Industrial, Commercial and Consumer Affairs (EDI)	LPS
Environment (EDE)	LPS
Home and Social Affairs (EDH)	LPS
Local Government (EDL)	LPS
The Queen's Speech and Future Legislation (FLG)	LPC
Legislation (LG)	LPC
Civil Service Pay (EDC)	LPC
Subcommittees	
Health Strategy (EDH(H))	LPC
Public Sector Pay (EDI(P))	LPS
European questions (OPD(E))	Foreign Sec.
Eastern Europe (OPD(AE))	Foreign Sec.
Terrorism (OPD(T))	Home Sec.
London (EDL(L))	Environment Sec.
Drug Misuse (EDH(D))	LPC
Co-ordination of Urban Policy (EDH(U))	Environment Sec.
Alcohol Misuse (EDH(A))	CDL
Women's Issues (EDH(W))	Employment Sec.

PM = prime minister; LPS = lord privy seal; LPC = lord president of the council;
CDL = chancellor of the duchy of Lancaster.

Committee membership ranges in number from 4 (the committees on the Gulf, nuclear defense policy, and European security) to 18 (the committee on home and social affairs).[10] The standing committees comprise solely senior ministers. The first nine committees listed in Table 8.4 are chaired by the prime minister. The other committees are chaired by a senior nondepartmental minister, either the lord privy seal or the lord president of the council. Subcommittees are not confined to Cabinet ministers and, with the exception of the subcommittee on terrorism, comprise senior and junior ministers. The subcommittee on alcohol abuse, for example, comprises one Cabinet minister, three ministers of state, and eight junior ministers.

Decisions emanating from the committees have the same authority as full Cabinet decisions, and since 1967, disputes within committees can be referred to the full Cabinet only with the approval of the committee chairman. When important issues are under discussion, it is usual for the designated members to attend, though on other occasions senior ministers can and do replace themselves with their junior ministers.[11] Richard Crossman, subsequently a Cabinet minister himself, took the view that the committees detracted from the power of the Cabinet,[12] though the more general view is that they serve as a useful complement to the Cabinet, lightening its workload, clarifying issues for it, and allowing it to concentrate on the more central and general matters of government.

The full Cabinet usually meets every Thursday morning in the Cabinet Room at 10 Downing Street. In addition to the Cabinet ministers, the government chief whip attends the meetings. He (never yet she) is the minister responsible for ensuring the support of the parliamentary party in parliamentary votes and he acts as a channel or communication between the Cabinet and its parliamentary supporters. He advises on likely parliamentary reaction to proposed measures. The Cabinet secretary attends and sits on the prime minister's right. Meetings usually last for one to three hours, with additional meetings, if necessary, on Tuesdays and sometimes other days as necessary.

The Cabinet remains important as the central forum for the resolution of disputes between departments, particularly in the allocation of public expenditure. Ministers usually defend their particular department, often supported on a reciprocal basis by ministers representing other spending departments. Much depends on the personalities involved, not least that of the PM. Some PMs tend to involve themselves in a wide range of items being brought forward by ministers, whereas other content themselves with concentrating on central issues of the economy and foreign affairs, leaving other departmental ministers to get on with their jobs unhindered. The process by which a Cabinet determines policy thus varies from PM to PM and, depending on changing political circumstance, may vary during the tenure of office of one PM. The Cabinet remains the forum for the resolution of most major issues of public policy, but a number of those issues may effectively be resolved elsewhere, either in Cabinet committee or by a meeting of senior ministers. Less central issues usually do not reach the Cabinet at all.

As with the position of prime minister, no formal powers are vested in the Cabinet: It exists and operates by convention. The most important convention, one that in part governs its behavior as well as its relationship to Parliament, is that of collective responsibility. This convention, which developed during the eighteenth and nineteenth centuries, prescribes that members of the Cabinet accept responsibility collectively for decisions made by it. Ministers may argue in Cabinet session, but once a decision has been made they are required to support that decision publicly. Any minister failing to support a Cabinet decision in public once it had been announced would be expected to resign: Failure to do so would result in the PM requesting that minister's resignation.

The convention is deemed also to dictate the necessity for secrecy to attach to Cabinet discussions. The authority of the Cabinet and of particular ministers could be undermined if Cabinet disputes were made public. Ministers publicly defending decisions with which they are known to have disagreed in Cabinet session would weaken the Cabinet in trying to ensure implementation of those decisions. A minister's authority and influence could be undermined if it were known that he or she was implementing a policy against which he or she had fought in the Cabinet. Nonetheless, recent years have witnessed a weakening of this aspect of the convention, with ministers engaging in semipublic and, for all intents and purposes, public leaks and disagreements, and with some ex-ministers recording Cabinet discussions in their memoirs. On two occasions in the Labour government of 1974–1979 the convention was actually suspended in order to allow ministers to vote against government policy in the House of Commons. Both occasions concerned the issue of British membership in the European Community, on which Cabinet members were bitterly divided. To avoid the possibility of resignations or the Cabinet falling apart, the PM (Harold Wilson in 1975, James Callaghan in 1977) decided to suspend the convention. Although the convention remains extant, it is becoming a difficult one for PMs to enforce.

One other condition dictated by the convention of collective responsibility continues to be followed. A government defeat in the House of Commons on the motion "that this House has no confidence in Her Majesty's Government" necessitates the government's resigning or requesting a dissolution. On March 28, 1979, when the minority Labour government was defeated on a vote of confidence, the PM immediately went to Buckingham Palace to request a dissolution. This requirement stipulated by the convention is one of the few about which it remains possible to generalize with confidence.

The Cabinet remains at the heart of British government, but its capacity to make the final determination of government policy is limited. In some sectors, power has passed upward to the prime minister (sometimes in conjunction with senior ministers) and to the institutions of the European Community. Because of the sheer workload, power over much nonessential policy has passed downward to individual ministers. The departmental responsibility of ministers makes it difficult for the Cabinet to act as a truly collective decision-making body; most ministers are concerned with fighting for their departments and, where matters do not affect their departments, they take no interest. Yet despite this limitation, the Cabinet remains a powerful body. No prime minister, however hard he or she may try, can ignore it. The Cabinet can constitute an important constraining influence. On occasion it may actually go against the wishes of the PM. Even Churchill at the height of his wartime powers could not always get the Cabinet to agree to what he wanted. The same was true of Thatcher. Though it has little opportunity to be proactive in the policy-making process—the initiative for policy comes from below or above—the Cabinet nonetheless forms a sig-nificant reactive body. Despite being hand-picked by the prime minister, the Cabinet is not always predictable in its actions.

Ministers

When a PM forms an administration, he or she is called on to select not only the senior ministers to head the various departments of state, as well as senior ministers without portfolio, but also a host of junior ministers. In addition to a ministerial head, who is usually of secretary of state rank, each department normally has one and sometimes more ministers of state and one or more undersecretaries of state. The PM also appoints a chief whip and 12 or 13 other whips in the Commons as well as a chief whip and 5 or 6 others whips in the House of Lords. In total, a little more than 100 ministerial appointments are now made (see Table 8.5). Despite the demands made of government, the increase

TABLE 8.5 Number of government ministers, March 1993

Rank	House of Commons	House of Lords	Total
Cabinet ministers (including PM)	20	2	22
Ministers of state[a]	23	5	28
Law officers	2	1	4[b]
Undersecretaries of state	24	8	32
Whips (including chief whips)	14	7	21
TOTAL	83	23	107[b]

[a] Includes the financial and economic secretaries to the treasury. Excludes the patronage secretary to the treasury (chief whip), who is listed with the whips.
[b] Includes the solicitor general for Scotland, Thomas Dawson, who is not a member of either house.

in the number of ministers during the course of the twentieth century has been a modest one.

Of the ministers appointed, the most important are, as one would expect, those appointed to head the various departments (see Table 8.6). The significance of junior ministers tends to vary. In past decades, many parliamentary undersecretaries had little to do and often were regarded as constituting something of an insignificant life form within the departments. To some extent, that remains the case today for a number of undersecretaries, known in Whitehall circles under the acronym PUSS (parliamentary undersecretaries of state). The influence of junior ministers within departments tends to depend on the ministerial head. There is a growing tendency for ministers to assign greater responsibility for certain functions to their ministers of state and undersecretaries; when junior ministers attend Cabinet committees, they gain some knowledge of the workings of the higher echelons of government. Nonetheless, disputes between junior ministers and the chief civil servant, the permanent secretary, in a department can be resolved only by the ministerial head, and there remains a tendency for interested bodies to try to influence the senior minister even on matters delegated to junior ministers.

The heads of departments have tended to become even more important decision makers than they were hitherto. Indeed, there is a case for arguing that, far from having prime ministerial or Cabinet government, Britain has a form of ministerial government. As demands on government have increased, only the most important matters have percolated up to the Cabinet for resolution. Most important decisions affecting a department are taken by the minister. The relationship between a minister and the House of Commons and between the minister and his or her department is governed by the convention of individual ministerial responsibility. The convention is important not only for determining who is responsible to whom (civil servants to minister, minister to Parliament), but also for determining who is responsible for what. The Cabinet as a body has no legal powers; powers are vested in ministers. When government takes on new responsibilities by statute, powers to fulfill those responsibilities are granted to a minister. "The Secretary of State shall have power to . . . " According to Nevil

TABLE 8.6 The principal government departments headed by ministers in 1993

Department	Responsibilities
Agriculture, Fisheries and Food	Agriculture, horticulture, fishing, food
Defense	Defense policy, control and administration of armed services
Education	Education
Employment	Staffing policy, unemployment benefits
Environment	Wide range of responsibilities covering the physical environment, including housing, construction, land use, regional planning, countryside, and local government structure and finance
Foreign and Commonwealth Office	International relations, protecting British interests abroad, certain administrative responsibilities in dependent territories
Health	Administration of National Health Service (NHS) in England; certain aspects of public health
Home Office	Domestic functions not assigned to other departments, including administration of justice, police, immigration, public safety and morals, and prisons
Law Officers' Department	Law officers are the chief legal advisors to the government and appear on behalf of the Crown in major court cases; the attorney general has ultimate responsibility for enforcing the criminal law
Lord Advocate's Department	Equivalent in Scotland to the Law Officers' Department in England
Lord Chancellor's Department	Assists the lord chancellor in the administration of the courts and the law
National Heritage	Broadcasting, film, the arts, sport, tourism, and heritage
Northern Ireland	Exercises executive powers in Northern Ireland on behalf of the U.K. government; encompasses agriculture, commerce, education, community relations, finance, environment, health and social services, housing, and staffing
Privy Council Office	Minor functions (e.g., for arranging Royal Proclamations); office usually occupied by minister responsible for government's legislative program in the Commons or Lords

TABLE 8.6   (continued)

Department	Responsibilities
Public Service and Science	Day-to-day responsibilities for management of the civil service, Citizens' Charter, executive agencies, civil science and technology, research councils (headed by the chancellor of the duchy of Lancaster)
Scottish Office	Government functions in Scotland, including agriculture, education, economic planning, home affairs, health, and development
Social Security	Social security, disablement, benefits, pensions
Trade and Industry	National and regional industrial policy, aerospace policy, overseas trade policy, information technology, competition policy, consumer affairs, and (since 1992) energy
Transport	General transport policy, railways, ports, freight movements, road safety, inland waterways
Treasury	Economic strategy, public expenditure, fiscal policy, foreign currency reserves, international monetary policy
Welsh Office	Within Wales, agriculture (jointly with Ministry of Agriculture), primary and secondary education, town and country planning, water, roads, tourism, new towns, forestry, urban grants

Note: There are a number of other bodies classed officially as departments but not headed directly by a minister. These include the Board of Customs and Excise and the Board of Inland Revenue, parliamentary responsibility for which is exercised by Treasury ministers.

Johnson, "the enduring effect of the doctrine of ministerial responsibility has been over the past century or so that powers have been vested in ministers and on a relentlessly increasing scale."[13]

Ministers, then, are very much at the heart of the government process. Major issues are resolved in Cabinet session as is the battle for departmental budgets. Other issues are usually but not always resolved at the departmental level. And when issues go to Cabinet, it is the minister who is responsible for the document or proposal. Major changes in policy are usually announced through the publication of a white paper. Such policy documents have to go through the Cabinet (discussed in Cabinet committee and then presented to the full Cabinet), but they are drawn up within departments on the minister's instructions. Indeed, the education secretary, John Patten, personally wrote part of his 1992 education white paper.

staff terms are the Treasury (excluding the Inland Revenue) and the Department for Education. Small staff numbers, though, do not necessarily mean either limited influence or simple internal structures. The Foreign and Commonwealth Office, for example, has a relatively small number of civil servants—fewer than 10,000—but great political clout and a complex departmental infrastructure.

Each department is normally divided into functional areas. Each functional unit, the division is headed by a civil servant of assistant undersecretary of state rank. Above the units are deputy undersecretaries and, above them, the civil servant responsible for running the department, the permanent undersecretary of state (known as the permanent secretary). He (rarely she) is in effect the chief executive officer of the department and answers directly to the minister. Figure 8.2 shows the organization within a relatively small department, the Department for Education, chosen because it provides a manageable and not too complex diagram. Many other departments have far more functional units: The Foreign and Commonwealth Office, for instance, has more than 50.

Despite a basic similarity in structure, departments vary considerably in size and functional organization. They are complex organizations. That complexity is now greater as a result of the creation of executive agencies.

Agencies

In 1988, following a report from an efficiency unit set up by the prime minister, the government decided that to the greatest extent possible the executive functions of departments (as distinct from the function of advising ministers) should be carried out by operationally distinct agencies, each with clearly defined tasks and managerial responsibility for carrying out those tasks.

Various sections within departments were identified as suitable for agency status. The initial list was a modest one, both in terms of numbers and responsibilities. The first agency created was the Vehicles Inspectorate, followed by bodies such as Her Majesty's Stationery Office. By early 1990, only 12 agencies, employing just over 10,000 staff, had been created. However, the program then gathered pace and by the middle of 1991 there were 48 agencies employing 220,000 civil servants: A year later, there were 75 agencies, with a staff exceeding 300,000—more than half the total number of civil servants. Most departments now have some agencies. They range form the Social Security Benefits Agency, employing 68,000 civil servants, to the small Forensic Science Service, employing fewer than 600.

The agencies are essentially semi-autonomous bodies within government. Each has a tailor-made framework document, setting out its aims and objectives, relationships with ministers and Parliament, and the regimes under which it will work. Performance targets are published. One of the targets for the Driver and Vehicle Licensing Agency in 1990–1991, for example, was to reduce the average waiting time for a driving test from eight to nine weeks to six weeks.

Each agency is headed by a chief executive, who is also the accounting officer. In other words, the chief executive—not the permanent secretary in the department—is accountable for how money is spent. A majority of chief

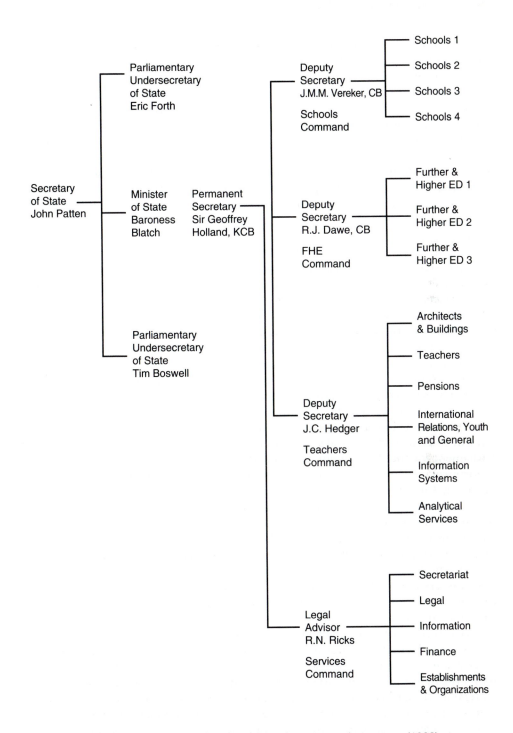

FIGURE 8.2 Department for education: departmental structure (1993)

SOURCE: Department for Education.

of the principal reasons for the government's decision in 1988 to create executive agencies was to improve management within the civil service, creating a new team of identifiable managers separate from the permanent secretary, who previously was the general manager of a whole department.

Senior civil servants nonetheless remain essentially generalists drawn from a particular social background. The similarity in social and educational background has produced a body of public servants that is relatively homogeneous. There is regular contact between senior officials, not only in an official capacity—the various interdepartmental committees and the meetings necessary to prepare material for ministers—but also socially: Senior civil servants are often members of the same London clubs and will variously dine or wine together. This homogeneity, and their permanence in office, is often seen as giving civil servants a common and a relatively long-term perspective on policy—relative, that is, to politicians—geared to what one permanent secretary referred to as "the common ground."[24] Civil servants carry out the wishes of their ministers but will be influenced by civil service and departmental norms and, as we shall see, their perceptions of that common ground.

Quangos

The term *quango* is used to denote what in U.S. terminology would be referred to as an offline governmental agency (for example, the Environmental Protection Agency). It is an acronym for quasi-autonomous nongovernmental agencies, though it has confusingly been assumed to stand for quasi-autonomous national government organizations. An inquiry into their activities in 1980 concluded that the term *nondepartmental public bodies* was more appropriate.[25]

Quangos comprise public bodies set up either by administrative act or by statute to carry out various executive actions or to operate in an advisory capacity on a particular subject. Advisory bodies are usually formed to provide government with advice that it cannot get from within its own ranks. Such bodies will normally comprise representatives or appointees of interested groups (see chapter 7). Bodies with executive powers are often formed in order to establish an arm's-length relationship between government and a particular concern.

Such bodies differ from executive agencies in two important respects. First, agencies remain part of the structure of government. Their creation forms a hiving off of functions *within* a department, not *from* a department. Quangos may be associated with a particular department but are not part of that department. Second, executive agencies have been in favor with government since 1988. Quangos, as a species of institution, are out of favor.

A number of quangos—nondepartmental public bodies—are long-standing and not confined to the twentieth century.[26] The number increased considerably in the twentieth century and in two periods in particular: in the decades after the Second World War and again after 1968. The growth of government and the welfare state after 1945 spurred the creation of a wide range of nondepartmental public bodies. A report in 1968—the Report of the Fulton Committee on the Civil Service—raised the possibility of adding to their number through the hiving off of autonomous units from departments. The concept of hiving off functions found favor with the then Labour government and with the governments—first Conservative, then Labour—of the 1970s. Despite party differences, successive administrations were influenced by a prevailing managerialism—that services could be more efficiently provided through a managerial restructuring of government.

Among major nondepartmental public bodies created in the 1970s were the Manpower Services Commission; the Health and Safety Commission; and the Advisory, Conciliation and Arbitration Service (ACAS). A report in 1980 identified the existence of more than 2,000 such bodies: 489 executive bodies and 1,561 advisory bodies. The former were responsible for spending almost £5,800 million (about $9,000m.) in 1978 and had a staff of about 217,000.

Support for quangos came to an end with the return of a Conservative government under Margaret Thatcher in 1979. They were seen as unaccountable, interventionist, a drain on the public purse, and—when acting in a quasi-judicial capacity—a threat to the rule of law. The government initiated a "quango cull" and within three years more than 440 nondepartmental public bodies had been abolished, with more than 100 scheduled for extinction. As far as possible, remaining quangos were put under the aegis of a particular department, with ministers having responsibility for their efficient and effective operation.

Quangos still remain a significant feature of public activity. The number in existence remains a four-figure one, and ministers continue to announce the setting up of such bodies. Recent creations have included a body to monitor broadcasting standards and a unified body—replacing previously separate bodies—to disperse funds to higher education. However, such bodies are created on an "as and when" basis rather than as part of a conscious, and favored, strategy.

THE CURRENT DEBATE

The bodies that form the executive in the United Kingdom are thus several—and greater in number than before—and the relationships among them, and between each of them and the citizen, complex. The range and complexity of those bodies have important implications for public policy. Institutions are not neutral in their effect. That fact is not lost on defenders and critics of the existing institutional arrangements. For defenders, the existing structures and relationship facilitate coherent and effective policy making. For critics concerned with Britain's economic performance, those structures and relationships are part of the problem, not part of the solution.

Debate has been wide ranging, but can be considered under three broad heads: those of elective dictatorship, an unelected dictatorship, and the structure of government.

Elective Dictatorship

This thesis contends that power is concentrated at the center, with few if any significant checks on that power. As we have seen (chapter 3), this constitutes one of the political explanations offered for Britain's poor economic performance.

Power is seen as overly centralized, with a prime minister and Cabinet armed with an evergrowing array of formal powers, with no other body—be it the civil service, Parliament, or the courts—able to stop a determined government from carrying out whatever policy it wishes; policy that is imposed on a population that is increasingly detached from the process of policy making and one that, because of the adversarial nature of British politics, is not easily mobilized in support of particular measures of public policy. The result is both poor decision making and an inability to raise resources to meet the nation's demands.

It is also argued that the degree of centralization has become more acute in recent years. Power has become more concentrated in the hands of government and, within government itself, in the hands of the prime minister. A number of writers have claimed that Britain now has a form of "prime ministerial government." The concentration of power in the hands of the PM, according to Labour MP Tony Benn, has gone too far "and amounts to a system of personal rule in the very heart of our parliamentary democracy."[27] This charge was leveled against successive prime ministers in the 1970s but has gained especial prominence in the years since 1979.

Longevity in office, large parliamentary majorities, and a radical program of public policy derived from the prime minister's particular philosophy combined, in the eyes of many critics, to provide Britain's most extreme example of prime ministerial government. They claimed that Margaret Thatcher ensured that supporters of her neoliberal economic philosophy occupied the key economic ministries; kept Cabinet discussion on economic policy—indeed, on policy generally—to a minimum; used bullying tactics in Cabinet—described by one Cabinet minister as "Stalinist"—in order to get her way; and used her powers to "handbag" any institution, including the civil service, that got in her way. (The concept of "handbagging" derives from the observation of one Conservative MP that Mrs. Thatcher could not see an institution "without hitting it with her handbag".)[28] "Her conduct of meetings," recalled one senior minister, "became increasingly authoritarian. . . . Margaret, . . . when there was an issue on which she had already formed a firm view, would start with an unashamedly tendentious introduction of her own, before inviting the responsible and sometimes cowed Minister to have his say."[29] The prime minister, in short, "summed up" at the beginning.

In the wake of her third election victory in 1987, Mrs. Thatcher was seen by many, including some within her own party, as politically invulnerable, capable of achieving what amounted to a system of one-woman rule. Texts analyzing the creation of "the strong state" grew in number, claiming that traditional safeguards were being eroded as more and more power became concentrated in the Thatcher government.[30] In a lecture in 1976, former Conservative Cabinet minister Lord Hailsham identified the emergence of what he termed an "elective dictatorship."[31] The term referred to government; a decade later it was more frequently applied to one particular part of government: the office of prime minister.

The argument that Britain was experiencing prime ministerial government was lessened but not stilled following Thatcher's replacement as prime minister in 1990 by John Major. Mr. Major continued to exercise the powers of the office. As party leader, he determined the content of the party's 1992 election manifesto and was credited by many within the party for leading the party to electoral success in the election itself. Central policy decisions were taken, and continue to be taken, by the prime minister in consultation with a few senior ministers. When early in 1993 the prime minister and chancellor of the exchequer decided to reduce interest rates, one senior Cabinet minister was unaware of the decision until some hours after it had been publicly announced.

Proponents of this thesis of prime-ministerial government argue the case for a return to Cabinet government and for greater systemic restraints on prime ministerial power. There have been demands for a greater dispersal of power to Parliament—including a reformed and more powerful upper house—and to the courts and, as we shall see, for a new, semi-autonomous level of regional government. Tony Benn has argued for a package of reforms, including making public appointments subject to parliamentary confirmation, making the internal operations of government more open to the public gaze and, when Labour is in office, for members of the Cabinet to be elected by Labour MPs.

Calls for radical reform of the political system have tended to come from the center and left of the political spectrum. Calls for a return to Cabinet government have been more broadly dispersed. During Margaret Thatcher's tenure in Downing Street, various Conservative MPs—including ministers, speaking semipublicly—endorsed the need for a greater degree of collective decision making by the Cabinet. As we have seen in chapter 6, dissatisfaction with Mrs. Thatcher's style of prime ministerial leadership, and in particular her practice of making decisions unilaterally, became pronounced in 1989 and 1990.

This thesis, though, does not go unchallenged. It is countered by the claim that the charges leveled at the prime ministership are exaggerated and that the position of the prime minister relative to the Cabinet and, most important of all, relative to the wider political environment has not changed as significantly as critics claim over the course of the twentieth century. The prime minister has always been powerful, but that power has not been exclusive or constant.

The Cabinet, meeting once or twice a week, is not a body geared to extensive debate and reflection. Much has been left to the PM and individual minister. It was ever thus.[32] Instances of strong prime ministerial leadership are to be found as much in the nineteenth century as in the twentieth. Being powerful, though, is not the same as being all powerful. The Cabinet acts as a deterrent, a brake on prime ministers, however strong they may appear or want to be. Margaret Thatcher failed to get some of her favored issues through Cabinet. The government's reform of trade unions never went as far as she wanted. Her own position was thrown into question when she could not rally a Cabinet majority to resolve the Westland crisis in 1986. When she could not muster support for her views, "she could then become unbelievably discursive . . . generally going round in circles and getting nowhere. . . . Broadcasting and education were two cases in point."[33] Indeed, her tactics in Cabinet were essentially evidence of prime ministerial weakness, not strength. Ministers had to be browbeaten because their support could not be taken for granted. Most of her predecessors—even Churchill in wartime—had faced similar difficulties.

The demands on the prime minister's time are extensive. An increasing amount of time has to be spent abroad, not least at European Community summits.[34] As we have seen, the resources at the PM's disposal in No. 10 are limited. As a result, much—especially at the level of medium and micro-policy making—has to be left to individual ministers.

Furthermore, the prime minister has a wider political environment to cope with. There are the party, Parliament, and the people.[35] In recent decades, that environment has become far more pluralist. There has been a fragmentation of power.[36] Interests are more organized than before. Policy-making competence in various sectors has passed to the institutions of the European Community. Some of the established institutions—including courts and Parliament—have become more active. Prime ministers have had to use more extensively the weapons in their prime ministerial armory to keep pace with the changes in the wider environment.[37]

Margaret Thatcher's 11.5-year premiership demonstrated above all that prime ministerial power is variable, not constant. There were times when she was clearly dominant—as in the wake of election victories and following the military retaking of the Falkland Islands in 1982. At other times, she was in a vulnerable position (see chapter 6): in 1981 with the government split over economic policy, in April 1982 when the Argentineans invaded the Falkands, in 1986 over the Westland crisis, and from 1988 onward on a range of issues. She was at the peak of her power in the wake of the 1987 general election. Three years and five months later, she was in tears when reading a statement to the Cabinet announcing her intention to stand down.[38] Her power base—the parliamentary party—had failed to sustain her in the party leadership. Her final words in Cabinet reflected not so much prime ministerial hegemony but rather the vagaries of political life: "It's a funny old world."

The Unelective Dictatorship

For some critics, the problem of government is not to be found with the prime minister and ministers generally. They are, after all, the leaders of a party elected to office. Rather, the problem is seen as being with the nonelected part of the executive: the civil service.

Senior civil servants are seen by critics as having the means to ensure the outcomes they want. Furthermore, those outcomes are criticized for contributing to Britain's poor economic performance. The background of civil servants has produced a body of generalists, with no particular knowledge or understanding of the problems faced by British industry and commerce. Rather, they are guided by some amorphous notion of "common ground"—which, for critics, means the common interest of senior civil servants.

Ministers come and go, but senior officials remain in place. Battles lost by civil servants under one minister can be fought again under another. A new government provides particular scope to refight old battles. By tradition, incoming ministers do not see the papers of their predecessors. This provides senior civil servants with an almost clean ministerial canvass on which to try their persuasive brushwork. During a minister's tenure, officials have various means for influencing outcomes. Ministers look to their permanent secretaries for knowledge of how their departments work. They look to officials for advice and briefing documents. They look to the civil servants in their private offices to control the flow of paperwork that reaches their desks, and also to control their diaries.

Officials thus have the opportunity, should they choose to exercise it, to skew advice in favor of a particular course of action. They can swamp a minister with an excess of paperwork to obscure the importance of a particular document. They can submit important documents at the last minute to prevent time for reflection and outside advice. They can schedule so many meetings that the minister has little time to devote to particular issues. And, if these techniques fail to work, they can brief their counterparts in other departments, engage in some degree of misinterpretation of the minister's wishes, or simply stall until a new minister takes over. "Oh, he won't be here in another year or so" is a phrase that has been heard from the lips of civil servants, including in the hearing of this writer. And adding to their influence in recent years has been British membership in the European Community. Not only has membership entailed increased demands on ministers' time, especially in attending meetings of the Council of Ministers, but it also has given a greater role to bureaucrats. Most of the documents discussed by the council are prepared by officials: Contact between civil servants in the member states and officials in the European Commission is extensive. The dispersal of power also makes it increasingly difficult for government to monitor the implementation of policy, especially that which is carried out through EC officials in Brussels.[39]

For ministers, there is thus the problem of ensuring that they have control of their departments. A capable and determined minister will normally enjoy mastery of the department. Even so, that mastery will usually extend only to important issues drawn to the minister's attention or to specific policy goals set by the minister. Other matters, of necessity, will be dealt with at lower levels. If there is a problem with senior officials—"some ministers," as Pyper notes, "operate in an atmosphere of almost continuous tension and conflict with their officials"[40]—then, as we have seen, the minister lacks the power to remove those officials. The matter has to be resolved by the prime minister and it may not necessarily be resolved in the minister's favor. Less forceful, energetic, or intelligent ministers may find themselves guided by the papers and recommendations put before them by officials. In the days before he became a minister, Sir Ian (now Lord) Gilmour estimated that "only about one Minister in three runs his department."[41] When quizzed about this estimate after he had served as a Cabinet minister, he said that "on reflection, I think it was probably an overestimate."

Compounding the problem is the homogeneity of senior officials. Insofar as they seek to influence decisions, they do so in support of what they see as the national interest—or "common ground"—but which critics claim as more the common interests of senior civil servants, the "national interest" often being synonymous with departmental or general civil service interests. The shared background and continuing social contact of officials reinforces both their shared perception of what is needed to maintain the common ground and their influence in order to effect the desired outcome. For critics, outcomes are as bad as the means by which they are arrived at, reflecting the self-assured but limited views of a social elite that has no experience of life beyond public school, Oxford, and the corridors of Whitehall.

Such criticisms have been voiced frequently on the Left. For many Labour MPs, such as Tony Benn and ex–civil servant Brian Sedgemore, the senior civil service stands as an impediment to a Labour government ever being able to implement radical policies.[42] As a Labour Cabinet minister from 1974 to 1979, Benn had various clashes with his civil servants—from which he did not always emerge the victor. He, along with many of his supporters, favors not only a reformed civil service but also a more open one, stripped of the secrecy that allows officials to work behind a screen of anonymity. Secrecy, according to Benn, works only in the interests of weak ministers and strong civil servants.

In recent years, parallel criticisms have come from the Right, a civil service committed to established practices being seen as standing in the way of the achievement of a free-market economy. The civil service, enjoying close—and sometimes closed—links with attentive interest groups, was viewed as part of the corporatist structure and as enjoying the ethos of that culture (see chapter 7). Margaret Thatcher brought to the premiership a strong animosity toward the civil service, born of her neoliberal philosophy and of her own ministerial experience in the early 1970s: She had experienced poor relations with officials when she was education secretary. As one permanent secretary told Peter Hennessy, "She doesn't think clever chaps like us should be here at all. We should be outside, making profits."[43]

These critical attitudes have generated demands for reform. These encompass the relationship with ministers and recruitment to the service. To strengthen ministers' control over officials, various critics have recommended that ministers have power to dismiss officials. "We need to ensure that ministers are able to secure compliance with the policies they were elected to implement," wrote Benn. "Proposals to this end have been widely discussed and would certainly involve making the most senior officials in each department more responsible to the ministers which they serve."[44] Others have argued that ministers should be provided with more extensive sources of advice. Sir John Hoskyns, a former head of the No. 10 Policy Unit under Mrs. Thatcher, has advocated the creation of advisory bodies similar to the French *cabinets,* allowing ministers to bring together a small group of hand-picked specialists—thus offering the twin benefits of expert knowledge and independence of the civil service.[45]

The Thatcher period did witness some changes. Various senior officials were retired. A number of high-flying officials were promoted above their superiors to the posts of permanent secretaries. The Civil Service Department created following the 1968 Fulton Report was disbanded and various techniques were introduced—such as the Financial Management Initiative—designed to increase efficiency and better management.[46] The number of special advisors was increased. At the more personal level, perceived failures by a department to achieve what was expected of it resulted in the relevant civil servants being called to No. 10 for a prime ministerial harangue.

There also were various calls for, and some attempts to achieve, greater openness in recruitment. Attempts at reform following the 1968 Fulton Report were largely nullified by the civil service, with civil servants dominating the final selection procedure. Candidates tend to be selected in the image of those doing the selecting. The creation of executive agencies has resulted in some outsiders being drawn in but the senior civil service still remains largely the preserve of, and continues to admit to its ranks, Oxbridge-educated generalists. The chances of an Oxbridge generalist being successful are about 1 in 8; the chances of a non-Oxbridge graduate about 1 in 75.[47] Demands are variously made for more outsiders to be recruited to the service and for those who leave the service to be able to return at a higher grade than they left it.[48] The inherent unlikelihood of achieving any major reform, though, was well summarized by one member of the Fulton committee. "The real difficulty," he said, "is that you are trying to solve a problem with people who are themselves part of the problem."[49]

The charge of government by the civil service—like that of prime ministerial government—does not go unchallenged. The civil service, it is pointed out, is not quite the monolithic entity it is sometimes made out to be. Departmental ethos and attitudes differ. The Environment Department, for example, has a reputation for being a fairly open one, whereas the Home Office has a reputation for excessive secrecy. Insofar as there is a civil service ethos, it is one that compels compliance with ministers' wishes. The relationship between ministers and officials is often more congenial and collegial than it is conflictual. Civil servants may argue a point in preliminary discussions, but once ministers have decided they then carry out whatever has been decided.[50]

"In my view," recorded one member of Margaret Thatcher's Cabinet, "a good cabinet minister can always get what he or she wants out of the Civil Service."[51] Obstructive civil servants, he noted, could always be moved. Though there were problems with moving officials in the 1970s—largely because the prime minister did not trust the minister involved—a number have been moved in recent years, most notably in 1992.[52] Such occasions, though, are rare. Civil servants may not always like the substance of what a minister decides, but—as Headey found—they do like ministers capable of making decisions. And, once the decision is made, they implement it. One energetic junior minister recalled the occasion when she summoned officials to discuss a big event she was organizing to promote health education. "I realized then just how disciplined some civil servants are when faced with a pesky minister with 'ideas.' It must have taken a lot of effort for the one who had to run the thing to keep saying 'Yes, Minister,' but bless her cotton socks, she did it."[53]

The proposal to give ministers power to sack and select their own officials is opposed on the grounds that it would politicize the civil service, with civil servants becoming too identified with a particular minister and the policies of that minister. It is also considered an unlikely change, given that a prime minister is not likely to give up the power to make the ultimate choice. Making the actions of civil servants more open is challenged on the grounds that this would undermine their usefulness to ministers. If the advice of officials was made public, it would inhibit those officials from providing wide-ranging advice. In terms of defending and explaining decisions once taken, then officials are more open than ever before, not least as a result of appearances before the departmental select committees of the House of Commons.

The thesis of "civil service government," like that of prime ministerial government, is difficult to sustain. Civil servants are powerful actors in the policy cycle, but they do not determine the content of the principal measures of public policy. Their influence is greater the lower the level of policy making.

Processes and Structure

Some critics have directed their attention not at ministers and civil servants but rather at the processes and structure of government, which have been seen largely as inefficient. These criticisms have variously been taken on board by governments over the past 30 years. The most important change, in terms of procedures, has been in determining public expenditure. The most important change in terms of structures has been in departments.

Before the 1960s, each item of public expenditure had been determined by government on its merits and not considered in terms of the government's overall priorities or of the long-term consequences. This was changed with the introduction of the public expenditure survey exercise. This was an exercise to assess proposed departmental expenditure in terms of the government's priorities, with the final decision being made by the Cabinet. Variously modified since it was first introduced, it is now a central part of government. As we shall see, it involves the Cabinet determining the overall target for public spending, subsequent negotiations between spending ministers and the relevant Treasury minister, the resolution of disputes through a Cabinet committee, and final agreement by the Cabinet—a process lasting from July to November each year.

Improvements in the process of determining public expenditure have delivered a more coherent process. However, criticisms were frequently voiced—including by the Treasury and Civil Service Committee of the House of Commons in the early 1980s—that the announcement of government spending plans was divorced from the annual budget, which dealt with taxation and revenue raising. The government responded in 1992, the chancellor of the exchequer announcing that in future years, expenditure and revenue would be considered together, the budget announcement being merged with the autumn statement on expenditure. In 1993, there was therefore the usual spring budget—the last of its kind—followed in the autumn by the first "unified budget."

The changes in the structure of departments, as we have seen, have been various. The emphasis in the 1950s, 1960s, and 1970s was on creating large departments. In the 1960s and 1970s, the emphasis on managerial efficiency resulted in the hiving off of various bodies from departments. In the 1980s and 1990s, the emphasis has shifted to a hiving off within departments, with service-delivering units being crafted into executive agencies.

Pressure remains for further structural change. Exponents of executive agencies want to see the process taken further, until virtually all units of government exist as agencies, with only those senior civil servants who give policy advice to ministers remaining outside the agency framework. This is seen as the logic of the 1988 report that recommended the creation of agencies. It had noted that 95% of civil servants delivered services or carried out decisions. The central civil service—those advising ministers and running departments—should constitute a small core.

This emphasis on efficiency drawn from the private sector—with identifiable and responsible units working to meet specified targets—has not gone unchallenged. There remains the problem of accountability, to ministers and to Parliament. Civil service unions are worried that the greater the autonomy given to chief executives, the greater the threat to maintaining comparable pay and conditions among agencies. They also suspect that agency status may be the first step toward the agencies being transferred to the private sector.[54]

Pressure for structural change is not confined to those pressing for an expansion of the agency program. Various calls have been made for a further reorganization of government departments. Some critics of the Ministry of Agriculture, Fisheries and Food, for example, have claimed that it is too much of a clientele department, representing the interests of farmers to government rather than the other way around, and that it should be abolished and its functions dispersed to other departments—Environment (taking over fisheries and agriculture) and Health (taking over food). Others have directed their fire at the Cabinet, arguing that a body of more than 20 is too large and unwieldy for operating as an executive body. As a former chancellor of the exchequer Nigel Lawson recorded, ''twenty-two people attending a two-and-a-half hour meeting can speak for just six and a half minutes each on average. If there are three items of business—and there are usually far more—the ration of time just exceeds two minutes, if everyone is determined to have his say. Small wonder then that most ministers keep silent on most issues or confine themselves to brief but pointed questions or observations.''[55] A smaller Cabinet, it is believed, would allow for more detailed deliberation, a view taken by former prime minister Sir Edward Heath and one reportedly shared by the present prime minister, John Major.[56]

There are also demands for a more radical reform of the structure of government. The reform of departments and departmental structures in the 1970s was designed not only to improve managerial efficiency but also to strengthen links between government and the citizen by identifying clear ministerial responsibility for particular functions. Critics have claimed that this intention was never fully realized and that what is needed is a new tier of government, with some executive powers being devolved to new elected regional governments. This, it is contended, would bring government closer to the people as well as relieve an excessive burden currently carried by central government. Opponents claim it would add a burdensome layer of government, would be expensive, and would likely result in conflict between regional and national governments, and exacerbate economic disparity among the regions.

Pressure for the devolution of powers to elected assemblies in Scotland and Wales—which will be considered in greater detail in chapter 9—built up in the 1970s but failed in the face of parliamentary opposition and the results of referendums in the two countries. It has built up again in recent years, with all political parties—except for the party in government, the Conservative party—advocating some form of devolution.

CONCLUSION

Two conclusions can be drawn about the executive in Britain. The first is that it is misleading to refer to "the executive" as a monolithic body. It consists of a sophisticated and complex infrastructure, with relationships that are neither static nor easy to discern. There is no one part of the executive that can be identified clearly and unambiguously as the body for the making of public policy.

In so far as generalization is possible, one can identify a continuous and significant flow of advice and policy recommendations between officials and ministers, with the policy-making process resembling—insofar as a coherent shape can be ascribed to it—a pyramid, as shown in Figure 8.1. Policy is formulated and agreed at different levels. What may be termed high policy (such as economic policy) is usually made at the level of prime minister and Cabinet; medium-level policy (a new initiative on transport safety or school examinations, for example) at the ministerial level within departments; and low level, or day-to-day incremental, policy at the civil service level, often in consultation with those representatives of outside groups who, together, form policy communities (chapter 7). This last category probably accounts for the bulk of public policy or, perhaps more accurately, policy adjustments.[57]

Even this three-fold delineation must be treated with caution. The boundaries are far from clear-cut. Contact between ministers and officials is extensive and continuous and few decisions are taken in isolation. The more important, and the more extensive, the policy the greater the involvement of all elements of government. This is well illustrated by the annual public expenditure round, a process involving civil servants, departmental ministers, treasury ministers, a Cabinet committee, the prime minister, and the full Cabinet. Box 8.1 identifies the various stages and actors in the process. On other occasions, important issues may, for reasons of time or security, have to be decided quickly or secretly by a few ministers. Minor issues may suddenly achieve public prominence and move up the decision-making ladder. Some decisions may, in effect, move down the ladder as a consequence of a lazy or not overly bright minister deferring to officials. The extent to which this happens, given the secrecy that still attaches to the process of government, is difficult to determine. All that one can say with confidence is that the process may resemble a pyramid, but that pyramid may be variously misshapen.

The second conclusion is that the structure and processes of government are not static. Not only are they variously modified—sometimes radically—but also they remain the subject of demands for further change. As we have seen (chapter 3), some of the explanations offered for Britain's poor economic performance are political—most notably, in the context of this chapter, the concentration of power in central government and, within that government, in

BOX 8.1   **The Annual Public Expenditure**
Round—The Essential Stages

July Cabinet

The chief secretary to the treasury—the treasury minister with responsibility for public expenditure and a member of the Cabinet—presents a paper giving current expenditure trends and recommends the cash limit for the coming year for total public spending. The chancellor of the exchequer explains the general economic context and the tax consequences of alternative spending decisions, and recommends acceptance of the chief secretary's recommendations. The Cabinet agrees to the recommendations.

Bi-lateral Negotiations

The chief secretary discusses with individual ministers from spending departments the "bids" from their departments. The bids are drawn up in each department, involving considerable effort and discussion by ministers and their senior civil servants. For some ministers, it constitutes "a matter of virility . . . egged on by their officials, to put in bids well above anything remotely consistent with the overall envelope agreed by Cabinet." Two or three meetings may be necessary to agree on a compromise between the bid of the department and the figure on which the chief secretary is working. These bilateral meetings are extensive, beginning shortly after the July Cabinet, and—after the summer break—extending to early October and, if necessary, the party conference. Bilateral discussions are known to take place in the chief secretary's conference hotel room.

Resolving Conflicts

If agreement cannot be reached with a spending minister, then the minister may be seen privately by the chancellor of the exchequer or, if major spending issues are involved, by the prime minister, chancellor and chief secretary. Otherwise, an ad hoc Cabinet committee is employed. For most of the 1980s and first two years of the 1990s, this committee—known as the "Star Chamber"—comprised four or five ministers under the chairmanship of a senior minister who did not head a spending department. In 1992, the practice was changed, with the Star Chamber being replaced by a committee headed by the chancellor, reverting in effect to an earlier practice.

The committee is usually chosen in such a way as to favor the position taken originally in the July Cabinet. (The chairmanship of the chancellor reinforces this bias enormously.) It is employed when a number of ministers fail to reach agreement with the chief secretary; it is rare for an individual minister to risk incurring the opprobrium of Cabinet colleagues by being

BOX 8.1 *(continued)*

the only one to hold out for adjudication by the committee and in recent years it has rarely been necessary for it to meet.

Back to the Cabinet

In the autumn, the Cabinet completes the process. The outcomes of the negotiations are reported to it. If any minister has still not agreed to his departmental expenditure, the matter is decided in Cabinet, but it is very rare for a minister to hold out until full Cabinet. Ministers are invited to contribute to discussion, in an order determined by the prime minister (usually in conjunction with the chancellor). The chancellor outlines the extent to which the agreed figures match the July guidelines (usually fairly close) and the Expenditure Statement he will make to the House of Commons. Cabinet agrees to a brief statement—drafted in advance by the chancellor, and approved by the prime minister—summarizing what has been agreed. This is then released to the press.

SOURCE: Adapted from N. Lawson, *The View from No. 11* (Bantam, 1992), pp. 287–295, 1016.

the hands of the prime minister. Others have identified problems within that central government in terms of the civil service and the processes employed for determining public policy. The nub of the argument, which will form the basis of our concluding chapter, can be simply put. For critics of the existing political system, that system has not served the country well. For defenders, it constitutes a system that is, despite its complexity, both coherent and accountable.

NOTES

1. A. B. Keith, *The British Cabinet System,* 2nd ed. by N. H. Gibbs (Stevens & Sons, 1952), p. 14.
2. Derived from B. Donoughue, *Prime Minister* (Jonathan Cape, 1987); and A. King, "The British Prime Ministership in the Age of the Career Politician," in G. W. Jones (ed.), *West European Prime Ministers* (Frank Cass, 1991).
3. M. Kogan, *The Politics of Education* (Penguin, 1971), p. 35.
4. Labour ministers Barbara Castle and Tony Benn both encountered problems in trying to get prime ministerial support in battles with senior officials in their departments (Castle when transport minister, 1965–1968, and Benn as industry secretary, 1974–1975, and energy secretary, 1975–1979). Ministers under the premiership of John Major have had more success: See below, note 52.
5. See especially G. W. Jones, "The Prime Minister's Aides," in A. King (ed.), *The British Prime Minister,* 2nd ed. (Macmillan, 1985), pp. 72–95. At present, the number of No. 10 staff is approximately 70.
6. See T. Blackstone and W. Plowden, *Inside the Think Tank* (Heinemann, 1988).
7. P. Norton, "Prime Ministerial Power," *Social Studies Review,* 3 (3), 1988, p. 110; see also P. Norton, "Prime Ministerial Power: A Framework for Analysis," *Teaching Politics,* 16 (3), 1987, pp. 325–345.

8. B. Kellerman, *The Political Presidency* (Oxford University Press, 1984), p. 37.

9. P. Madgwick, *British Government: The Central Executive Territory* (Philip Allan, 1991), pp. 73–74.

10. The membership and terms of reference may be found in *Dod's Parliamentary Companion 1993* (Etchingham, East Sussex: Dod's Parliamentary Companion, 1993), pp. 816–827.

11. J. Barnett, *Inside the Treasury* (Andre Deutsch, 1982), p. 27.

12. R. Crossman, "Introduction" to W. Bagehot, *The English Constitution* (Fontana, 1963 ed.).

13. N. Johnson, *In Search of the Constitution* (Methuen, 1980), p. 84.

14. "The Typhoon Hits Hong Kong," *Sunday Times Magazine,* August 30, 1992, p. 21.

15. P. Hennessy, *Whitehall* (Secker & Warburg, 1989), p. 380.

16. See Sir R. Clarke, "The Machinery of Government," in W. Thornhill (ed.), *The Modernization of British Government* (Pitman, 1975), p. 65.

17. T. Butcher, "Improving Civil Service Management: The Next Steps Programme," *Talking Politics,* 3 (3), 1991, pp. 110–15; and P. Norton, "Getting the Balance Right," *The House Magazine,* 18 (585), March 8, 1993, p. 16.

18. B. Headey, "Cabinet Ministers and Senior Civil Servants: Mutual Requirements and Expectations," in V. Herman and J. Alt (eds.), *Cabinet Studies* (Macmillan, 1975), pp. 131–135.

19. See R. Pyper, *The Evolving Civil Service* (Longman, 1991), pp. 33–37.

20. See Pyper, p. 98; and G. Drewry and T. Butcher, *The Civil Service Today* (Blackwell, 1988), pp. 71–72.

21. Drewry and Butcher, Table 3.9, p. 71.

22. See Hennessy; and J. Garrett, *Managing the Civil Service* (Heinemann, 1980).

23. Quoted in Butcher, p. 111.

24. Sir Anthony Part, speaking on an Independent Television program, "World in Action," January 7, 1980.

25. *Report on Non-Departmental Public Bodies,* Cmnd. 7797 (Her Majesty's Stationery Office, 1980), pp. 3–4.

26. See P. Holland, *The Governance of Quangos* (Adam Smith Institute, 1981), pp. 10–12.

27. T. Benn, "The Case for a Constitutional Premiership," *Parliamentary Affairs,* 33 (1), 1980, p. 7.

28. J. Critchley, *Westminster Blues* (Futura, 1986), p. 126.

29. N. Lawson, *The View from No. 11* (Bantam, 1992), p. 128.

30. As, for example, A. Gamble, *The Free Economy and the Strong State* (Macmillan, 1988); C. Graham and T. Prosser (eds.), *Waiving the Rules* (Open University Press, 1988); and P. McAuslan and M. J. McEldowney (eds.), *Law, Legitimacy and the Constitution* (Sweet & Maxwell, 1985).

31. Lord Hailsham, *Elective Dictatorship* (BBC, 1976).

32. Norton, "Prime Ministerial Power," p. 114.

33. Lawson, p. 128.

34. P. Madgwick, *British Government: The Central Executive Territory* (Philip Allan, 1991), p. 142.

35. Madgwick, pp. 170-180.

36. J. Greenaway, S. Smith, and J. Street, *Deciding Factors in British Politics* (Routledge, 1992), pp. 236–238; and P. Norton, "In Defence of the Constitution," in P. Norton (ed.), *New Directions in British Politics?* (Edward Elgar, 1991), pp. 153–160.

37. Norton, "Prime Ministerial Power," pp. 113-114.

38. P. Norton, "The Conservative Party from Thatcher to Major," in A. King (ed.), *Britain at the Polls* (Chatham House, 1993), p. 29.

39. Greenaway, Smith, and Street, p. 237.

40. Pyper, p. 34.

41. I. Gilmour, *The Body Politic,* rev. ed. (Hutchinson, 1971), p. 201.

42. T. Benn, *Arguments for Democracy* (Penguin, 1982), ch. 3; and B. Sedgemore, *The Secret Constitution* (Hodder & Stoughton, 1980).

43. Hennessy, p. 592.

44. Benn, *Arguments for Democracy,* p. 66.

45. *Reskilling Government* (Institute of Directors, 1986).

46. See Greenaway, Smith, and Street, pp. 151-159.

47. 1985 figures calculated from Drewry and Butcher, Table 3.9, p. 71.

48. Hennessy, ch. 17.

49. Quoted in B. Page and I. Hilton, "The 'Reformers' Who Made Sure Nothing Changed," *Daily Express,* April 6, 1977, p. 11.

50. See H. Young and A. Sloman, *But, Chancellor* (BBC, 1984), pp. 36–42.

51. N. Ridley, *"My Style of Government"* (Fontana, 1992), p. 41.

52. In 1992, the permanent secretary at the Office of Public Service and Science, Peter Kemp, was retired and some senior officials moved from the Department for Education. On Kemp's departure, see "Brave New Broom of Whitehall Who Was Swept Away," *The Sunday Times,* July 26, 1992, p. 11.

53. E. Currie, *Life Lines* (Sidgwick & Jackson, 1989), p. 161.

54. Butcher, p. 114.

55. Lawson, p. 126.

56. "Heath Leads Call for Reform," *The Times,* March 22, 1993, p. 4.

57. See especially Greenaway, Smith, and Street, especially ch. 10.

CHAPTER 9

Subnational Government
Government below the Center

The United States is a federal nation. As such, autonomous powers are vested in both federal and state government. Article 1, section 8, of the Constitution enumerates the powers of Congress. The Tenth amendment stipulates that powers not delegated to the United States by the Constitution, nor prohibited by it to the states, ''are reserved to the States respectively, or to the people.'' The Constitution thus prescribes and protects two layers of government. Below those two levels there is a third: local government.

The position in the United Kingdon stands in stark contrast to that in the United States. The United Kingdom is a unitary state. State power is not divided. It resides at the center. The only units of government that exist below the national level are those created by an act of Parliament. They can be changed and removed by an act of Parliament. What units of government that have been created by an act of Parliament have been at the level of county or below. There is no intermediate tier of elected regional government.

Subnational government within the United Kingdom can be discussed under two headings: actual and proposed (see Table 9.1). The first of these, existing subnational government, comprises local government, regional organization of some public bodies, and administrative devolution in Scotland, Northern Ireland, and Wales. Only the first of these (local government) is an elected tier of government. The second, proposed subnational government, encompasses demands for elected assemblies in Scotland, Wales, and the English regions, and for constitutional change in Northern Ireland. Demands for change have been on the political agenda for some time. Those affecting Northern Ireland, with no agreement on what form change should take, have proved especially contentious.

TABLE 9.1 Subnational government in the United Kingdom

Level	Existing Governmental Bodies	Proposed Governmental Bodies
Territorial		
England	No specific countrywide English bodies	
Scotland	Scottish Office (United Kingdom government department)	Elected assembly with legislative/executive powers
Northern Ireland	Northern Ireland Office (United Kingdom government department)	Elected assembly with executive powers; power sharing
Wales	Welsh Office (United Kingdom government department)	Elected assembly with limited executive powers
Regional	Regional offices of government departments Disparate public bodies, e.g., regional health authorities	Elected regional assemblies
Local (counties and towns)	Elected councils	Some modification to existing structure; single-tier authorities

ACTUAL: LOCAL GOVERNMENT, REGIONAL ADMINISTRATION, AND ADMINISTRATIVE DEVOLUTION

Local Government

Structure.   For the first six decades of the twentieth century, the structure of local government in England and Wales remained largely unchanged. The system, created in the nineteenth century, was a two-tier one. The first tier consisted of county boroughs, exercising control over all local government services within their boundaries, and county councils, each exercising control over certain local government services within the county (other than in county boroughs within their borders). Below the county councils was the second tier: municipal boroughs, urban districts, and rural districts, each exercising limited functions. Within rural districts, there was an additional layer of local government in the form of parish councils, each exercising very limited functions.

As demands on government grew and the responsibilities of local government expanded, the structure of local government appeared increasingly appropriate. Allowing county boroughs to exercise functions that seemed more suitable to a larger authority (such as control of planning and roads) came in for criticism, and many municipal boroughs exacerbated the problem by applying for county borough status. Reform came on the political agenda. After a period of little change, local government witnessed a period of significant change, and continues to do so. The changes have produced three different patterns of local government in a period of 20 years.

1963–1986. There were two waves of reform during this period. The first was the reform of local government in Greater London, the second the reform of local government in England (outside London), Wales, and Scotland.

Local government in Greater London was reorganized under the provisions of the 1963 London Government Act. The act created a Greater London Council (GLC) with responsibility for planning, roads, traffic, overspill housing, and other needs affecting the whole of the Greater London area. Responsibility for education in the area covered by the old London County Council was vested in an Inner London Education Authority (ILEA). However, responsibility for personal health services (except ambulances) and for most local authority housing was retained by the 32 borough councils within the GLC area.

Local government in the rest of England, and in Wales, was reorganized in 1974. The 1972 Local Government Act, which took effect on April 1, 1974, created a new two-tier system. It established 47 county councils, each with responsibility for education, transport, highways (except motorways and unclassified roads), planning housing, personal social services, libraries, police, fire service, garbage disposal, and consumer protection. Below them a second tier of more than 300 district councils was created, each with responsibility for town planning, environmental health, building and housing management, and various registration and licensing functions. The act also created 6 separate metropolitan counties. Each metropolitan county council was given the same functions as the other county councils with the exception of education, personal social services, and libraries. Below the metropolitan counties was created a second tier of 36 metropolitan districts that, because of their population density and some reluctance by central government to give metropolitan counties too much power, were given control of education, personal social services, and libraries, as well as the other functions given to district councils. In addition, the metropolitan counties and districts were to share responsibility for certain amenities, such as parks, museums, and airports. Below the two tiers, provision for parish councils was retained.

The local government map of England and Wales following these reforms is given in Map 9.1. In Scotland, under the provisions of the 1973 Local Government (Scotland) Act, a two-tier division was also created, between regional and district councils. Nine regional councils were established but because of the concentration of population in the western lowlands of Scotland, one region—Strathclyde—contained more than half of the country's population.

The reforms did not prove lasting, at least not in their entirety. The aim of the reorganization had been to achieve a more rational system of local government. The emphasis was on an efficient managerial approach. Whereas the chief permanent officials of the old borough councils had been titled town clerks, the chief appointed officials of most of the new authorities were titled chief executives and the approach to administration was that of corporate management. The chief executive was seen as a coordinating head, advised and supported by a team of management officers. Councils continued to exercise their functions largely through committees (in marked contrast to the form of government at national level), though each council was given greater latitude than before in deciding

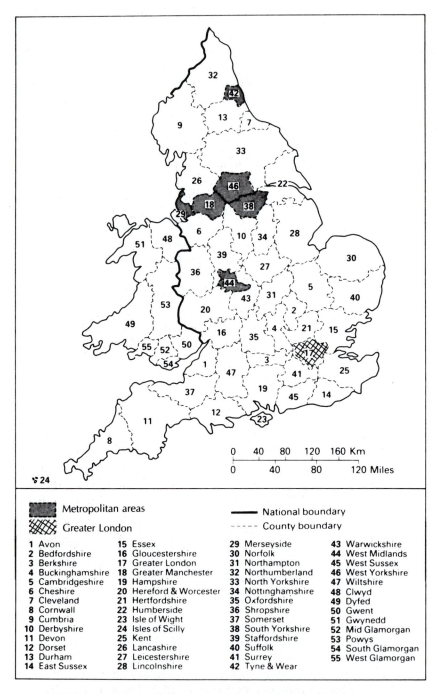

MAP 9.1 England and Wales: Metropolitan and nonmetropolitan counties

The map legend and county index:

Metropolitan areas
Greater London
National boundary
County boundary

1 Avon
2 Bedfordshire
3 Berkshire
4 Buckinghamshire
5 Cambridgeshire
6 Cheshire
7 Cleveland
8 Cornwall
9 Cumbria
10 Derbyshire
11 Devon
12 Dorset
13 Durham
14 East Sussex
15 Essex
16 Gloucestershire
17 Greater London
18 Greater Manchester
19 Hampshire
20 Hereford & Worcester
21 Hertfordshire
22 Humberside
23 Isle of Wight
24 Isles of Scilly
25 Kent
26 Lancashire
27 Leicestershire
28 Lincolnshire
29 Merseyside
30 Norfolk
31 Northampton
32 Northumberland
33 North Yorkshire
34 Nottinghamshire
35 Oxfordshire
36 Shropshire
37 Somerset
38 South Yorkshire
39 Staffordshire
40 Suffolk
41 Surrey
42 Tyne & Wear
43 Warwickshire
44 West Midlands
45 West Sussex
46 West Yorkshire
47 Wiltshire
48 Clwyd
49 Dyfed
50 Gwent
51 Gwynedd
52 Mid Glamorgan
53 Powys
54 South Glamorgan
55 West Glamorgan

what committees they wished to establish. (Certain committees were and remain mandatory, principally police, education, and social services committees.) Especially popular was the creation of a policy committee to establish priorities and monitor resources and policy implementation. By the end of the decade, though, the corporate approach had not proved as worthwhile as many councils had hoped it would, and a number reverted to the more traditional approach, thereby doing away with the concept of the chief executive and redrawing committee responsibilities based on established services rather than based on expenditure functions.

The reorganization also proved costly and did little to enhance consent for government: There was little apparent increase in citizens' awareness of local authority responsibilities. As Anthony King observed, "things are not working out quite as expected."[1] Certain features of the reorganization created resentment. Inhabitants of counties that had been dismembered or abolished were often vehement in their vocal opposition to the changes. So too were former councillors and other citizens in the boroughs that were reduced to parish council status. Within some of the new counties, a number of boroughs resented and continue to resent the dominance of larger conurbations. Dissatisfaction with the new structure found expression in the Labour party manifesto in 1979, which committed the party to restoring to the larger district councils in England the responsibility for education, personal services, planning, and libraries. The party repeated the commitment in 1983.

However, of greater significance was the attitude toward local government adopted by the Conservative government returned in 1979. It clashed with many local authorities, especially the Labour-controlled GLC and metropolitan counties. The government wanted to limit public spending, and local government spending was one of the major features of public spending that exceeded government targets. In 1983–1984, for example, GLC spending exceeded grant-related expenditure (the amount government considered it should spend) by 81%. The need to limit public spending was accorded priority over the commitment to the principle of local autonomy, and various measures were introduced to limit the spending of local councils. However, the GLC and many other Labour-controlled councils also constituted an additional thorn in the government's flesh as a result of campaigns that they waged on particular political issues. The GLC, under its leader Ken Livingstone, supported campaigns on a wide range of issues—usually opposed to government policy—and funded organizations (such as feminist and gay groups) that the government regarded as inappropriate recipients of public funds. By 1983, because of the government's annoyance at such activities, it promised to introduce a bill to abolish the GLC and the six metropolitan councils. The commitment was embodied in the party's 1983 election manifesto and was carried through two years later in the 1985 Local Government Act.

1986–1994.   The GLC and the metropolitan councils ceased to exist on March 31, 1986. The functions of the metropolitan councils were dispersed to metropolitan boroughs and to joint authorities to run police, fire, and passenger transport services. The functions of the GLC were given to the 32 London boroughs.

The resulting structure of local government in England and Wales is given in Figure 9.1. The structure of local government in what are termed the "shire counties" (those with county councils) remained that established by the 1972 act (county councils, district councils, parish councils—all elected). The metropolitan areas had elected metropolitan district councils, with more extensive functions than those given by the 1972 act, and in addition had a number of joint authorities (made up of representatives from the councils) to administer certain countywide functions; as in shire counties, parish councils also remained, though serving little purpose.

This structure, though, did not become a settled one. The absence of an authority to cover the whole of London proved unpopular with opposition parties and with many London residents. The bifurcation of responsibilities between county and district councils created by the 1972 act continued to cause resentment and some confusion. Some of the new counties created by the 1972 act remained unpopular with residents. A number of cities resented having no more than district council status. This sense of dissatisfaction influenced the political parties. Both the Conservative and Labour parties committed themselves to a further reform of local government and in 1992 the Conservative government achieved passage of a new Local Government Act. The act created a new local government commission to review local government structures and boundaries.

1994–.   The local government boundary commission established by the 1992 act began work in the autumn of 1992. It adopted a peripatetic approach, visiting different parts of the country and conducting inquiries to discover local opinion. The minister responsible for the 1972 act, Michael Heseltine, had envisaged a radical reform, favoring the establishment of a single tier of local government.

FIGURE 9.1   Local government structure in England and Wales since 1986. (Principal local government authorities in capital letters.)

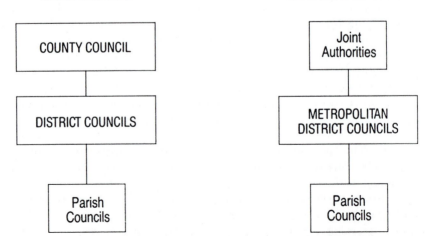

His successor as environment secretary, Michael Howard, expressed a less rigid view, and intimated that the commission would be free to recommend whatever structure of local government appeared best suited to the particular area. It was thus open to the commission to recommend one or two tiers and, if one tier, whether that should be at the level of county, district, or somewhere in between. The commission began to issue recommendations in 1993, with implementation of those recommendations scheduled to begin in 1994.

Election and Members.   Local government, as we have had cause to note already, differs significantly from government at the national level. Not only is local government subordinate to national government, its approach to administration (committee based, emphasis on professional administrators) is essentially the opposite of that adopted at the national level (not committee based, emphasis on the generalist). It differs also in that elections to local councils take place, as in the United States, on a fixed-term basis; elections to the House of Commons, in contrast, take place on a flexible basis.

Councillors are elected for four-year terms, with no limit on the number of terms one can serve. All county councils, London borough councils, and about one-third of district councils are elected in their entirety every four years. In the remaining districts, and in all the metropolitan districts, one-third of the councillors are elected in each of the three years between county council elections.

The franchise to vote in local elections is essentially the same as that for national elections; citizens age 18 or over who are resident in the area on the qualifying date. (Members of the House of Lords, who cannot vote in elections to the House of Commons, can vote in local elections.) Candidates in local elections must be citizens age 21 or over and be resident in the local authority area or have resided in premises in the area for the preceding 12 months or, in that 12 months, have had their principal place of work in that area. No one may be elected to a council of which he or she is an employee. This prohibition was extended in 1988 by an act prohibiting senior council officials from being elected as councillors in any authority.

Election procedure is essentially the same as that for national elections. (In May 1979 the two actually coincided, a general election taking place the same day as local elections.) Although elections are fought ostensibly on local issues, candidates at other than parish council level now usually stand under a party label, a tendency that increased in postwar years and was given added impetus by the reorganization of the 1970s. Large authorities are now such significant bodies of public expenditure and policy making that the national parties cannot afford to ignore them. Party has become the most important variable influencing the voting behavior of those electors who bother to cast a vote (turnout, as in local elections in the United States, is low, rarely reaching 40% of eligible voters); local elections are viewed as an annual opportunity to pass judgment on the incumbent national government. The governing party is expected to lose council seats during the midterm of a Parliament; a net gain of seats would be hailed as a considerable victory.

Although councillors are elected on party labels and usually operate within coherent party groupings, with elected officers and whips, they behave differently depending on local circumstances. Given that the needs and demands of communities vary, local parties temper their responses accordingly. The councillors themselves tend to be disproportionately male and drawn from nonmanual occupations. The likelihood is greater now than it was prior to the mid-1970s that they will have university educations. In the opinion of two observers, "The rise in the proportion of councillors with higher educational qualifications suggests that local-authority service is attracting its fair share of the best-educated sections of society—although a fall in the number of manual workers elected might make some voters feel that local authorities might be remote from them and so unresponsive in their needs."[2] One innovation introduced in 1972 to increase the attractiveness of local government service to able and economically inactive citizens (many councillors were retired persons) was attendance allowances for councillors. The introduction of such allowances also may have been encouraged by the desire to lessen the incentives for corruption, an occasional unfortunate feature of local government life not usually witnessed at a national level.[3] To consider cases of alleged maladministration, a number of local government ombudsmen (known as local commissioners) were established under the Local Government Act of 1974.

Once elected, councillors devote much time to casework and also tend to specialize in their committee work. Very few appear interested in helping formulate authoritywide policy.[4] What motivates individuals to seek election to local councils is not at all clear. Some appear to see it as a stepping-stone to higher things (a number are subsequently selected as parliamentary candidates); some do it out of a desire to further the aims of their party; some do it out of a sense of civic responsibility (to be found also in the performance of a wide range of other local activities, such as serving on the local magistrates' bench and doing voluntary social work); some do it to enhance their status in the community; and some, possibly a majority, do it for the simple reason that they were inveigled into running by friends or local party activists. One writer with several years' council experience summarized the position succinctly: "Most of us stand in the first instance by accident or because we are bullied into it but then we discover that Council work is interesting and worthwhile, although hard, so many councillors stay in local government for a lifetime."[5] Because of the number of councillors to be elected and the level of public indifference toward local government, local parties sometimes have difficulty recruiting candidates to contest elections. In some areas, it might be described as a seller's rather than a buyer's market.

Powers and Finance.   Local councils enjoy no constitutionally protected autonomous powers and can exercise only those powers vested in them by law. Their scope for branching out into areas of activity for which they have no specific statutory authority is limited: Under the 1972 Local Government Act, they could levy up to a 2p rate for generally whatever purpose they wished; under the 1988 Local Government and Housing Act, this amount was replaced by a per-adult limit (£5 per adult, for example, in the case of London borough and metropolitan district councils). In addition to having to work within statutorily defined limits, councils are also constrained within the confines of powers held and policies pursued by national government. Ministers have various statutory powers to make orders as well as to issue circulars to local authorities giving guidance on the implementation of government policy. The limitations upon local government are considerable and in recent years these have grown.

Local authorities are nonetheless major spenders and employers. Almost 2.5 million people are employed by councils in England and Wales.[6] In 1989–1990, gross expenditure by those councils was almost £56 billion (nearly $87b.). Of this figure, just over half (55%) was spent on two services: education and housing. Local environmental services accounted for a further 17% and personal social services 8%.[7] Local authorities thus constitute significant economic units.

Local authorities derive their revenue from three principal sources: a central government grant, known as the rate support grant; income from services provided by the authority; and a local tax. The income from services constitutes the smallest of the three sources. The central government grant has traditionally been the largest element, but has declined significantly from 1979. In 1979, it accounted for about 60% of income, but now accounts for well under a half. The local tax has grown in importance. Until 1990, it took the form of an annual tax on real estate, based on a notional property value; each house had a rateable value and the local authority determined how much to levy each year. Known as "the rates," the system was replaced at the end of the 1980s, and has had two successors.

The Conservative government returned in 1979 took the view that the rating system was inherently unfair; a single person in a house paid the same rate as did a large family living next door, the former helping subsidize the services consumed by the latter. It decided to replace the rates with a community charge, immediately dubbed the "poll tax," levied on individuals rather than on property. Because everyone (with very few exceptions) would pay all or part of the new tax, the government argued that it would increase local accountability—because everyone would have a vested interest in how the council spent their money. The new tax was brought in first in Scotland in 1989, and in England and Wales the following year. It was accompanied by a uniform business rate (UBR), set centrally by government, replacing the business rate that had been set by councils and that had varied significantly from one authority to another.

The new tax proved extraordinarily unpopular, its introduction sparking mass demonstrations and London's worst riot in recent decades. It was one of the contributory factors to Margaret Thatcher's loss of the leadership of the Conservative party (chapter 6): She had seen it as the flagship of her legislative program and was not prepared to contemplate its demise.[8] She was replaced by a leader who was willing to let it die, and in 1992 a new measure was approved by Parliament, replacing the poll tax with a "council tax." This new tax was based on actual property values, but with a reduction for people living alone. It came into effect on April 1, 1993.

These changes in local government finance constituted part of a wider body of reforms introduced by the Conservative government. Since 1979, more than 50 acts affecting local government have been passed by Parliament. In the Parliaments from 1979 to 1987, the government was concerned especially to acquire powers to limit the spending and the spending powers of local councils. In 1981 the block grant given to councils that exceeded the government's spending targets was reduced. In 1982, the power of councils to raise supplementary rates (that is, additional rates levied after the rate for the year had been set) was abolished; and, after the government was returned for a second term in 1983, power was also taken to impose a maximum limit on the rates that could be levied by big-spending authorities.

The government has used its powers rigorously to penalize councils exceeding spending limits. It has also, since 1987, placed an emphasis on making local government services more competitive, the aim being to increase efficiency and get greater value for money. Competitive bidding has been encouraged. Under this system, local government services are put out to bid and private firms are able to compete for the contract. Under the provisions of the 1988 Local Government Act local authorities are required to submit six services to competitive bidding, including street cleaning and ground maintainance. In line with European Community rules, large contracts have been open to EC-wide bidding. In at least one authority, the contract for street cleaning has been won by a French firm.

The purpose of these various changes has been to end the role of councils as "universal providers." According to one Conservative party publication in 1989, councils will "increasingly become regulators not suppliers, guarantors not participants, enablers not providers."[9] The extent to which this goal has been achieved is a matter of considerable debate. Opposition parties accuse the Conservative government of having set out deliberately to emasculate local government. Other critics do not necessarily believe that the government's measures have been consciously crafted to destroy local government, but nonetheless consider that the result has been a "policy mess."[10] In the view of the government, the changes have introduced greater efficiency and restrained excessive spending. What is clear is that in the years since 1979 there has been a major change in the role, powers, and (in 1986 and 1994) structure of local government in Britain. It remains a major spender and employer, but one operating under greater statutory and central control than before.

Regional Government

In Britain, there are no directly elected governmental bodies between the local and the national level. There are, though, a number of governmental or quasi-governmental bodies that operate at a regional level. They are significant not only for being nonelected but also for being disparate, not integrated with one another, and decreasing rather than increasing in number. Nonetheless, they constitute an important level of government in Britain.

Various factors have contributed to governmental functions being fulfilled at a regional level. Among the more important pressures have been administrative convenience, the need to involve more local authorities, technical advantages, the desire to dissociate central government from certain decision-making activities, and pressure from groups and professional bodies seeking some degree of regional autonomy in their sphere of activity.[11] The reason the number of government or public bodies operating at such a level has decreased in recent years has been the knock-on consequence of the Conservative government's privatization policy. Various public utilities, which previously had an extensive regional organization (the Regional Water Authorities being the most extensive), are no longer in the public sector.

Among public bodies with some regional organization are the British Broadcasting Corporation (BBC) and British Railways. Eight government departments have some organization at the regional level, either as an integral part of the department or as part of a service for which the department is responsible. The Prison Department in the Home Office, for example, has a regional organization. Within the Lord Chancellor's Department, courts are organized on a circuit— that is, regional—basis (see chapter 13). Both the Department of the Environment and the Department of Trade and Industry have regional offices, each under a director. The regional offices in the DTI have responsibility for administering the department's regional development policy and act as significant conduits for the disbursal of funds to firms in areas designated as Assisted or Development Areas. However, the most extensive regional organization is that of the Regional Health Authorities in the Department of Health.

The Regional Health Authorities (RHAs) were established under the National Health Service Reorganization Act of 1973, replacing regional hospital boards. The act also created a second tier of 90 Area Health Authorities. Below them were the main operational units, the District Management Teams. The structure did not prove a success—it was seen as too costly and the Regional and Area Health Authorities achieved a degree of autonomy that put them almost beyond ministerial control—and in 1982 the Area Health Authorities were abolished, and District Management Teams replaced by District Health Authorities.

The National Health Service is thus administered now at essentially two levels: at the local level, with District Management Teams (though these now have a reduced role, with a number of hospitals having taken the power, recently conferred, to opt out of the existing management structure and acquire self-governing trust status), and at the regional level, where the RHAs have responsibility for regional planning, resource allocation, major capital building work, and certain specialized hospital services that are more appropriately administered on a regional basis. Regional organization thus continues to constitute a central feature of the National Health Service, though its future is not certain. The cost and bureaucracy of the regional structure are coming under government scrutiny.

There is thus a layer of government operating at a regional level in Britain. However, that layer is not a prominent one and, as we have seen, is diminishing. (British Rail is the next public body scheduled for privatization.) Furthermore, the regional structures that do exist vary in size and authority. Part of the problem stems from the spatial disparity in population and resources but it is also attributable to the absence of clearly acknowledged regions in England. The boundaries of the regions vary, depending on which government department, public body, or political organization is responsible for defining them.[12] Map 9.2 shows the 14 Regional Health Authorities in England. Other public bodies organized on a regional basis would not usually have a separate Mersey region or divide the southeast into Thames regions. The creation of Oxford and, to some

MAP 9.2 Regional health authorities

extent, Wessex regions is not a common practice. There is an RHA for East Anglia. The Department of Trade and Industry has an eastern region. The Department of the Environment has neither. This lack of standardization not only provides a muddled picture in any discussion of regional government, but it also points to an important problem in any attempt to create a new tier of elected regional government: the absence of any clear picture of what the regions actually are.

Administrative Devolution

The principal functions of government are exercised in England by a number of functionally differentiated departments (agriculture, education, environment, and so on). Those functions are exercised in Scotland by a single department. The same is true of Northern Ireland and, to a much lesser extent, Wales. This concentration of functions in territorially defined departments has been given a number of labels, the most common and the most appropriate being that of administrative devolution. Instead of being governed by London-based departments, Scotland and Northern Ireland are governed in effect by single departments based in Edinburgh and Belfast, respectively.

The Scottish Office (SO) is a government department that has existed for some time. The first secretary for Scotland was appointed in 1885. However, not until 1939 did the department absorb many important functions affecting Scotland that previously had been carried out by other bodies. At the same time, the bulk of the department was moved from London to St. Andrews's House in Edinburgh.[13] Since then, the department has expanded and acquired new responsibilities. In the immediate postwar period it was given responsibility in Scotland for the National Health Service, assistance to agriculture, and town and country planning. More recently it has acquired responsibility for economic development.

The SO is divided into functional units known as departments. There are currently five principal departments (see Table 9.2), plus a central services unit, which is in effect a sixth department and is responsible for personnel and finance, and four smaller departments (the Scottish Record Office, Scottish Courts Administration, General Register Office for Scotland, and the Department of Registers for Scotland). At the political apex stands the secretary of state for Scotland, assisted by four ministers, one drawn usually from the House of Lords. Because the number of departments in the SO exceeds the number of junior ministers, one minister will often be given responsibility for more than one department. Below the ministers, at the civil service level, there is a management group made up of departmental heads, with a secretariat and regular meetings.

Despite this concentration of functions in one department and the attempt at coordination, the heads of each department retain considerable autonomy and, as two observers write, "departmental interaction resembles the independence of Whitehall ministers."[14] The individual departments in conjunction with outside interest groups would appear to form the policy communities within the SO. Which outside group raises an issue will normally determine which department will deal with it, and apparently groups rarely refer to the Scottish Office as such,

TABLE 9.2   Scottish Office departments

Department	Responsibilities
Agriculture and Fisheries	Most agricultural and fisheries matters
Environment	Housing, local government, roads, land-use planning, environmental protection and the countryside, historic buildings, certain transport functions
Industry	Industrial and regional economic development, energy, tourism, urban regeneration, new towns
Education	Education outside the universities, libraries, social work services, the arts, sport, museums
Home and Health	Police, criminal justice, legal aid, NHS, prisons, fire service, home defense

talking instead of individual departments.[15] Once a policy has been agreed on by the SO, Cabinet or Cabinet committee discussion and agreement are often influenced by the nature of the issue. Where a proposal falls clearly within the scope of the SO and affects Scotland solely, it is often approved without debate.[16] A proposal that has wider U.K. implications is considered in the same way as proposals emanating from other government departments.

The picture that emerges is thus one of a government department that operates in a particular territory almost as a minigovernment. It is a government department and yet in many respects is more than a government department. The same is true of the Northern Ireland office. It is of more recent origin than is the SO. For the 50 years prior to 1972, Northern Ireland had its own Parliament, granted to it by the U.K. Parliament. It was organized on the model of the U.K. government, with departments and ministers, and with members elected to it known as members of Parliament. For reasons to be discussed shortly, it was suspended in 1972 and replaced with direct rule from the U.K. government. This entailed the creation of the Northern Ireland Office, which was formed as a government department under a secretary of state and a number of junior ministers. Its civil service staff was drawn largely from the Northern Ireland civil service, and the bulk of the department was based at Stormont, just outside Belfast, the home of the old Northern Ireland Parliament.

The department is similar to the SO in the scope of its responsibilities and the functional separation of its responsibilities into departments. These departments encompass health and social services, finance, environment, education, economic development, agriculture, and Northern Ireland Office responsibilities specific to the province. As with the SO, the number of departments exceeds the number of junior ministers and so one minister may be given responsibility for more than one department. At the moment, the secretary of state is assisted by two ministers of state and two parliamentary undersecretaries. In addition, he has an executive committee, comprising these ministers and the civil service heads of department. It serves as a coordinating committee and has been likened by one minister to a cabinet.[17]

The department is unlike the Scottish Office in that the ministers do not sit for seats in the province. Also, though it is usually very successful in obtaining money from the Treasury, it is less of a lobbying department for its territory in London. Rather, it is more concerned with the task of administration and with carrying out U.K. government policy in the province.[18] Much of its time has been taken up with bringing the law in the province in line with that of the rest of the United Kingdom. For the secretary of state, the task is one of heading an administrative department while at the same time seeking a political solution to the problems peculiar to the province. It places him in a unique position. When first introduced, direct rule in Northern Ireland was intended as a temporary expedient. So far, it has survived the various attempts to introduce new forms of government for the province.

The Welsh Office constitutes something of a hybrid department. It is much smaller than the Scottish Office and the Northern Ireland Office—with a secretary of state, one minister of state, and one parliamentary undersecretary—and it does not enjoy quite the same degree of autonomy. Nonetheless, it has mutifunctional responsibilities. Within Wales, it has responsibility for health, primary and secondary education, town and country planning, housing, local government, new towns, roads, water, forestry, tourism, national parks, and historic buildings. It shares with the Ministry of Agriculture responsibility for agriculture in the principality. It also has a general duty to supervise the carrying out of government policy in Wales. Like its other territorial counterparts, it is based mainly in the territory itself, with its headquarters in Cardiff. It maintains only a small office in London.

To reiterate, the government of the United Kingdom fulfills various functions. In England these are carried out by different, functionally based departments, whereas in Scotland, Northern Ireland, and, to a lesser extent, Wales they are carried out by single, territorially defined departments that operate largely as minigovernments. However, such an arrangement has not met with the overwhelming approval of the inhabitants of the territories concerned. Direct rule in Northern Ireland, as I have noted, was intended as a temporary expedient. In Scotland and Wales, government by nonelected and, despite their location, U.K. government departments has generated calls for change. In recent years, proposals for reform have been on the agenda of political debate.

PROPOSED: DEVOLUTION

Of reforms proposed in subnational government in recent years, the most prominent have been those for the devolution of executive and legislative powers to some form of elected assemblies in Scotland and Wales, and, in a somewhat different format, Northern Ireland. Various schemes have been proposed and received parliamentary approval but none has yet proved successful.

Scotland and Wales

The proposal for devolving some executive and legislative powers to national assemblies in Scotland and Wales is not new. The Liberal party advocated the somewhat more radical proposal of federalism during most of its history,[19] and the Scottish National party favors complete independence for Scotland, though it is prepared to accept some form of devolved government in the interim. Only in the past 20 years, however, has devolution become a significant issue of political debate.

Some form of home rule for Scotland and Wales has been advocated by the Scottish National (SNP) and Plaid Cymru (PC) parties, respectively, since their formation earlier in the twentieth century, but the main achievement of the two parties prior to the 1960s was simply to have survived. This situation was to change in the 1960s, when each party won one seat at a by-election and also made gains in local elections. The apparent growing strength of nationalist sentiment was sufficient to encourage the Labour government to establish a Royal Commission on the Constitution; announced in 1968, it was appointed in 1969 and reported in 1973. The nationalist parties had not done well in the 1970 general election, with the SNP winning only one seat. Four years later the picture had changed significantly: The Royal Commission had reported in favor of some form of devolved government and there had emerged what A. H. Birch has referred to as the "eruptive factor,"[20] North Sea oil. The SNP was able to play on the argument that the location of the offshore oil fields meant the oil was Scotland's as much as anyone's and that revenue from it would be sufficient to make a Scottish government viable. By playing on the expectation of a rising middle class in Scotland, whose expectations had been left unfulfilled by the Westminster government, the SNP began to make electoral inroads into the strength of both main parties. By playing on the cultural fears of the Welsh people, the PC had some impact in Wales. In the February 1974 general election, the SNP won 7 of the 71 Scottish seats and the PC won 2 of the 36 Welsh seats. In the October general election, the SNP increased the number of seats won to 11 and the PC to 3. Of the SNP's 11 seats, 9 were won from the Conservatives but the party had come second in 35 out of 41 Labour-held seats. In total number of votes received, it was the second largest party in Scotland.

The Labour government that was returned to office in 1974 saw the prospect of the SNP developing into the dominant party in Scotland and, in so doing, ruining Labour's chances of winning future elections (both Scotland and Wales constitute important electoral bases for the party; see chapter 5). To respond to the nationalist challenge, the government put forward proposals for a form of devolved government in both Scotland and Wales and in 1976 introduced a Scotland and Wales bill. The bill provided for an elected assembly in each of the two countries, each with a fixed term of four years, with responsibility for countrywide concerns such as health, land use, and tourism, though with Scotland having more devolved power than Wales. Neither assembly was to have powers of taxation; money was to be provided by means of a block grant voted by Parliament as well as through local authority taxation and borrowing by local authorities and public corporations.

The bill ran into serious parliamentary opposition. The Conservative opposition did not like the provisions and decided to vote against it. Many Labour members also found it unpalatable. A number were opposed to devolution, seeing it as a step on the road to eventual independence. Some MPs from the north of England disliked it because they felt it would effectively discriminate against regions that were not to have similar assemblies. To facilitate the bill's passage, the government announced its agreement to the devolution proposals being submitted to referendums in Scotland and Wales. The bill achieved a second reading but ran into sustained opposition from both sides of the House in committee (taken on the floor of the House), and the government decided to introduce a motion to limit debate (a guillotine motion). The vote on the guillotine maximized the opposition to the measure and, with 22 Labour MPs voting with the opposition (a further 21 abstained from voting), the government suffered an embarrassing defeat.

The government decided not to proceed with the bill as it stood. Instead, it introduced two new bills, the Scotland bill and the Wales bill. The Scotland bill largely retained the proposals incorporated in the original bill, whereas the Wales bill provided only for a very limited form of devolution to the principality. On this occasion the government achieved passage of both bills, though only after a number of amendments had been carried against the government's wishes. The most important of these stipulated that if 40% of eligible voters did not cast a "yes" vote in the referendum in Scotland, the government was to bring forward a motion for the repeal of the act. A similar provision was inserted in the Wales bill. In this way, MPs created an important and unprecedented hurdle to the achievement of devolved government.

The referendums in Scotland and Wales were held on March 1, 1979, and were preceded by vigorous campaigns in the two countries. In Wales, it appeared that the prospect of devolved government aroused suspicion among non-Welsh-speaking inhabitants—the majority—and was not gaining overwhelming support. In Scotland, the debate was keenly fought between pro- and antidevolutionists. Some opponents feared devolution would constitute the thin end of the wedge, leading to an eventual breakup of the United Kingdom; supporters argued that it was necessary in order to maintain the unity of the kingdom. On March 1, 950,330 voters in Wales voted "no" to the devolution proposals: Only 243,048 voted "yes." In Scotland, the result was a close one: 1,230,937 people voted "yes," and 1,153,502 voted "no." Although a slight majority of those who voted had opted for the devolution proposals, the number voting "yes" did not constitute 40% of all eligible voters. As a consequence, the Cabinet decided not to proceed with devolution, a decision that precipitated Nationalist MPs withdrawing their support from the government. This loss of Nationalist support deprived the government of a majority in a vote of confidence on March 28, 1979. The result was a general election and the return of a Conservative government. In the new Parliament, the government introduced the relevant motions for the repeal of the two acts and both motions were carried.

In the wake of the 1979 general election, it looked as though devolution was no longer an important issue on the political agenda. The SNP won only two seats in the election, as did Plaid Cymru. The new government was not keen to pursue the issue—Prime Minister Margaret Thatcher being a notable opponent of devolution—and other issues came to the fore. However, from the early 1980s onward, the subject began to reemerge as a feature of debate. Initially, much of the running was made by the Liberal party and then the newly formed SDP. In alliance, the two parties pressed for elected assemblies in Scotland, Wales, and the English regions. This commitment was reiterated in 1988, when the two parties merged to form the Liberal Democratic party. The Labour party, which had maintained a commitment to some form of devolution throughout the decade, also committed itself—following its policy review of 1987–1989—to support ten regional assemblies in England as well as assemblies in Scotland and Wales. There was also some pressure within Conservative ranks for some devolution of power to a Scottish assembly. Calls for such a policy became more pronounced from Scottish Conservatives following the party's disastrous showing in the 1987 general election, when it won only 10 of the 72 seats. The marginal improvement in the party's position in 1992—winning 11 seats—did not still calls for some form of elected assembly. However, the official Conservative policy remains opposed to devolution, Prime Minister John Major being just as firm an opponent as his predecessor. The government has emphasized the importance of the union and has pursued a limited political initiative in the context of that union: In 1993, it strengthened the position of the Scottish Office and a number of parliamentary bodies responsible for Scottish affairs.

The Conservative party remains the only party in Parliament opposed to devolution. All the other parties represented favor some form of devolution or, in the case of the SNP, independence for Scotland within the European Community.

The arguments advanced in favor of devolution have centered on both consent and effectiveness. Decisions taken in Scotland and Wales by elected government, it is argued, would be more efficient and effective because of a better appreciation of the area—its needs as well as its resources—and additionally, would enhance consent by being closer to the people. Devolving governmental responsibilities would also serve to reduce pressure on central government and on Parliament. Both government and people, it was felt, would benefit. Against this, Conservatives, as well as some Labour MPs, have expressed the fear that devolution could lead to a breakup of the United Kingdom. They have also opposed it on the grounds that it would introduce another expensive and unnecessary layer of government (people being more interested in their individual needs being met by government—any government—than in being able to elect another body of government) and that it would exacerbate economic inequality between the regions. Economically, it is argued, wealthy regions will wish to retain as much of their wealth as possible. Among the poorer parts of the United Kingdom to suffer would be Scotland; its small population and limited resources make it economically dependent on the rest of the United Kingdom. The argument, in short, is that more government is not necessarily better government.

In terms of popular attitudes, supporters draw attention to the electoral support given to prodevolution parties in Scotland and Wales and to opinion polls showing overwhelming support for some form of devolution or even independence. When European Community leaders met for a summit in Edinburgh in December 1992, more than 25,000 people marched through the streets to demonstrate in support of Scottish home rule. Opponents point out that devolution nonetheless is not a priority as far as the Scots and the Welsh are concerned. At the 1992 general election, 36% of Scots questioned rated devolution as the most important issue facing Scotland. By the end of the year the figure was down to 15%, on a par with those considering the National Health Service and the economic situation the most important issues. Seventy-five percent rated unemployment as the most important issue.[21]

The activity of the prodevolutionists in Scotland, organized now on a cross-party basis under the banner of "Scotland Now," and the stance of the Labour party ensure that devolution remains on the political agenda. At a practical level, there is no likelihood of devolution being introduced under the Conservative government of John Major. In the event of the Labour party being returned to office with an overall majority or, even more so, if it depends for holding power on the support of the Liberal Democrats (committed to widespread constitutional reform), then the constitutional framework of the United Kingdom is likely to undergo a major reformulation. The principle of the unitary state would be retained, but with major powers devolved to elected assemblies throughout Great Britain.

Northern Ireland

The problems of Northern Ireland and its form of government are particular to the province. Those problems arouse perplexity, incredulity, and misunderstanding in other parts of the United Kingdom as well as abroad. (Indeed, the failure of some Americans to comprehend the problems of the province has been a bone of contention both within Northern Ireland and in government circles.) Whereas in Britain there is a consensus favoring a cetain norm of political behavior—abiding by the rules of the constitutional game even if one favors a change of the rules (or even a new game)—there is no such consensus in Northern Ireland. There never has been. To Britons reared on solving or avoiding disputes by talk and compromise, the vehement and often violent pursuit by opposing communities of mutually exclusive goals is a vexing and near-incomprehensible phenomenon.

The history of Ireland has been a depressing and troubled one extending over many centuries and marked by bitter conflict between the English and the Irish and, within Ireland, between indigenous Catholic Irish and Prostestant Scottish Presbyterian settlers. The Irish uprising in 1916 forced the U.K. government to recognize Irish demands for self-determination. In 1920 the Westminster Parliament passed the Government of Ireland Act, which provided for home rule in the country and created two Parliaments: one for the 6 northern counties, part of the region of Ulster, and one for the remaining 26 counties. The provisions for the southern counties were stillborn. The continuing troubles in the country resulted in the Treaty of Ireland of 1922, which realized the Irish Free State. Ireland was partitioned and the provisions of the 1920 act applied in the new province of Northern Ireland. A bicameral Parliament was established at Stormont, from which an executive was drawn. The new government of the province exercised a number of devolved powers and, in exercising those powers, was not much hindered by the Westminster government. British politicians were not keen to be drawn again into the infructuous bog of Irish politics.

The province of Northern Ireland was created at the forceful behest of the Protestant community of the North. Largely derived from Scottish Presbyterian stock, it had no wish to be engulfed within a Catholic Irish state. Within the new province, it was dominant. It was not, though, the only community within the province: One-third of the population was Catholic. The religious divide between the two communities was reinforced by social, economic, and educational differences as well as by centuries of ingrained animosity. Catholic children were educated in Catholic schools, were taught Irish history, played Gaelic games, and lived in Catholic communities. Protestant children were taught British history, played non-Gaelic games, lived in Protestant communities, and were taught to look down on Catholics as being lazy and threatening to the existence of the province. Catholics, in turn, looked on Protestants as being gravely in error. The divisions ran deep. The Protestants continued proudly to celebrate the victory of Protestant William of Orange in the Battle of the Boyne in 1690. Indeed, in the new province the anniversary of the victory was made a public holiday.

Northern Ireland after 1922 became for all intents and purposes a one-party province. The Unionists party, representing the Protestants, regularly won two-thirds of the seats at Stormont (there was little alternation of seats from one party to the other) and formed the government, enjoying uninterrupted power. Despite occasional violence by the self-styled Irish Republican Army (the IRA), which wanted a united Ireland and was prepared to engage in terrorist activities to achieve it, the Stormont government enjoyed sufficient coercive powers to impose its will and did so in a manner that favored the Protestants. Catholics were discriminated against in the allocation of houses and jobs and were forced to live in an environment where they felt themselves to be second-class citizens. There was little they could do about the situation within the existing political structure, a position analogous to that faced by blacks in the deep south of the United States.

The position in the province was to change in the latter half of the 1960s. A new, relatively liberal Unionist prime minister, Terence O'Neill, sought better relations with the Republic of Ireland, a move that caused consternation in the more traditional ranks of his party. On the Catholic side, the steps taken by the O'Neill government were seen as being too little and too late. A civil rights movement sprang up in the province, inspired by the experience of the United States. The Civil Rights Association was formed in 1967 and was joined the following year by a more revolutionary organization, the People's Democracy. The two groups engaged in tactics designed to provoke a violent response in the hope that this would draw attention to the plight of the Catholic minority in the province. They organized demonstrations and marches. These resulted in a vigorous reaction from the police force, the Royal Ulster Constabulary, as well as from various Protestant groups. Clashes between protesters and their opponents erupted into civil disorder that the police and their auxiliary forces, the so-called B-Specials (despised in the Catholic community), were unable to contain. In August 1969, at the request of the Northern Ireland Cabinet, the Westminster government sent troops to the province to maintain order. In return for such action, the government insisted on phasing out the B-Specials and the introduction of full civil rights for Roman Catholics. Ensuring that the latter demand was complied with was another matter.

The arrival of troops was initially welcomed by Catholics in the province. However, the use of troops to support the civil authorities—in other words, the Protestant government and the police—and the search of Catholic areas for arms produced a rapid dissipation of that support. A "shooting war" broke out between the IRA and the British Army in February 1971. In August the British government decided to intern without trial suspected IRA leaders. Instead of lessening the violence, the action appeared to exacerbate it: Internment aroused greater sympathy for the IRA cause among the Catholic community, and the interned leaders were replaced by more extreme followers. At the same time, tension increased between the Stormont and Westminster government, the former contending that the latter was not doing enough to counter the activities of the IRA. The Stormont government even made a request for troops in the province to be put under its control. The request was denied.

Violence in the province became more marked toward the end of 1971, with more than 100 explosions a month. In the first two months of 1972, 49 people were killed and another 257 injured as a result of gunshots and bombings. In an attempt to break the deadlock in the province, the Conservative government at

Westminster decided to pursue some form of political initiative: Pressure for such action had been building up for some weeks, both abroad and at home, including pressure from the Labour opposition. The government's proposals included periodic plebiscites on the issue of the border, a start to the phasing out of internment, and the transfer of responsibility for law and order from Stormont to London. The last proposal proved unacceptable to the Northern Ireland Cabinet, which made clear that it would resign if the proposal was implemented. In consequence, Prime Minister Edward Heath informed the House of Commons on March 24, 1972, that the British government was left with no alternative but to assume full and direct responsibility for the administration of Northern Ireland until such time as a political solution to the problem of the province could be achieved. To give effect to the government's decision, the Northern Ireland (Temporary Provisions) bill was quickly passed by Parliament, enjoying the support of the Labour opposition as well as of the Liberals. The new act suspended the Stormont Parliament and transferred its powers to the Westminster government. A new Northern Ireland Office was established under a secretary of state.

The task of succeeding Northern Ireland secretaries has been twofold: to try to maintain security within the province, doing so in a way that will not alienate either community (the Protestant community by not doing enough, the Catholic by doing too much), while at the same time seeking a political solution that is acceptable to both. Various political initiatives have been attempted since 1972, each failing to mobilize the cross-community support necessary to sustain it.

The first secretary of state, William Whitelaw, proposed and then established a power-sharing elected assembly, as well as a consultative council of Ireland to provide what was commonly referred to as "the Irish dimension." Elections were held and agreement reached on the formation of a multiparty executive. However, the executive and the council of Ireland aroused massive opposition within the Protestant community. In the February 1974 general election, 11 of the 12 Northern Ireland seats were won by Unionists opposed to power sharing. A provincewide strike organized by the Protestant Ulster Workers Council effectively brought the province to a standstill. The new Labour government in London was unwilling to use its coercive powers to try to break the strike. The executive resigned. It had lasted four months.

The Labour government then proposed an elected constitutional convention to act as a medium for political leaders in the province to reach agreement on the way forward. In the elections to the convention, held in May 1975, Unionists opposed to power sharing won 46 of the 78 seats. The convention issued a report favoring a Stormont-type cabinet government—that is, a reversion to government by the majority party, unhindered by any form of power sharing—which was rejected by the government. The government asked the convention to reconvene, which it did, but it failed to reach any new agreement. It was dissolved on March 6, 1976.

For the next three years, the government pursued the approach of trying to maintain order in the province while encouraging its people and their leaders to reach agreement among themselves. Some modest proposals for a nonlegislative assembly were made, only to be rejected by the parties in Northern Ireland.

Various attempts by the Conservative secretary of state appointed in 1979, Humphrey Atkins, to find some acceptable compromise among the parties failed. A conference he convened at the beginning of 1980 was boycotted by the Ulster Unionist party. The parties that did attend disagreed on the form of government they favored for the province. A proposal by Mr. Atkins to create an advisory council of elected officials drawn from the province, to fulfill advisory and reporting functions until such time as a more durable settlement could be reached, was stillborn. It was overshadowed by hunger strikes of IRA prisoners in the Maze prison (demanding various concessions, including the reintroduction of "political status") and by a recommendation from former prime minister James Callaghan that the province develop into a "broadly independent State."[22]

The problem of Northern Ireland remained intractable. The refusal of the government to give in to the demands of the IRA hunger strikers forced an end to the strike, but the strikers had aroused sympathy for the IRA cause among a large section of the Catholic community. One hunger striker, Bobby Sands, was elected MP in a by-election in Fermanagh and South Tyrone. He died a month later. Protestants for their part were extremely suspicious and dismayed by meetings between Mrs. Thatcher and her opposite number in the Irish Republic, meetings that resulted in the agreement on the formation of an Anglo-Irish intergovernmental council. The council was to involve regular meetings at ministerial and official levels to discuss matters of common concern between the two governments. Protestants were also highly critical of the government's security policy in the province, considering it to be inadequate. In November 1981 a Unionist MP, Robert Bradford, was assassinated. The leader of the Democratic Unionist party, Ian Paisley, accused the prime minister of being a traitor to Northern Ireland. He also threatened to make the province "ungovernable." For the government, the problem appeared to be getting worse rather than better.

The government continued to emphasize the need for achieving a political solution and since 1982 it has undertaken three major initiatives. The first, that of "rolling devolution," was initiated in 1982. The second took the form of negotiations with the government of the Irish Republic and resulted in the Anglo-Irish Agreement, signed in November 1985. The third has been a new round of talks with interested parties, started by the Northern Ireland secretary, Peter Brooke, in 1991 and resumed by his successor, Sir Patrick Mayhew, in 1992.

Rolling Devolution

The first of the three initiatives involved the election of a 78-member assembly under a system of proportional representation. It differed from previous such assemblies by virtue of its internal organization: It was to have a committee system, each committee paralleling a government department. The committees were to have salaried chairmen and deputy chairmen, chosen to reflect the party composition in the assembly, and were to have powers to make reports to the assembly and to the secretary of state. The concept of "rolling devolution" allowed the assembly to propose at any time the transfer of executive responsibilities for any particular department to its own jurisdiction. The ultimate objective was full devolution, but to be achieved at a pace made possible by the assembly itself. In practice, the assembly proved short-lived. The elections to it, in October 1982, provided a publicity coup for Sinn Fein, the political wing of the Provisional IRA: It garnered one-tenth of the first-preference votes cast and saw five of its candidates elected. SDLP as well as Sinn Fein candidates elected to the assembly boycotted its sittings. Only Unionists attended. In March 1986 they decided not to fulfill the assembly's statutory functions in protest of the Anglo-Irish Agreement. Three months later the government decided to disband the assembly; like its predecessors, it had fallen foul of the lack of consensus it was designed to counter.

The Anglo-Irish Agreement

The Anglo-Irish Agreement was the product of the discussions that had taken place under the aegis of the Anglo-Irish intergovernmental council. Signed at Hillsborough Castle in Northern Ireland on November 15, 1985, by the British prime minister, Mrs. Thatcher, and the *Taoiseach* (prime minister) of the Irish Republic, Dr. Garret Fitzgerald, the agreement had three essential elements. Under Article 1, both governments recognized that "any change in the status of Northern Ireland would only come about with the consent of the majority of the people of Northern Ireland." This was the first time the Irish government had given legal recognition to Northern Ireland's right to self-determination. The British government hoped this part of the agreement would help make the whole document acceptable to the Unionists. The second element was embodied in Articles 2 to 8, which established the Intergovernmental Conference, chaired by the secretary of state for Northern Ireland and the foreign minister of the republic. Through the conference, the republic was enabled to raise issues on the administration of the province that were of particular concern to the minority community. The committee was an advisory one, with a small secretariat. It became a particular target for Unionist opposition. The third element, covered by Articles 6, 7, and 9, provided for greater cross-border cooperation on security matters, and security became a subject regularly discussed at meetings of the conference. The agreement also dealt with a number of other topics, including the creation of an Anglo-Irish parliamentary body, and this came into being in February 1989.

The first and third elements of the agreement proved insufficient to make it acceptable to the Unionist parties. To them, the Intergovernmental Conference allowed a foreign government the opportunity to interfere in the affairs of the province and constituted a "thin end of the wedge," the first step toward forcing the province into a united Ireland. In protest, all 15 Unionist MPs in the province resigned their seats in December 1985, fighting by-elections as a means of demonstrating popular opposition to the agreement. The move was partial success: One Unionist failed to achieve reelection; the rest were returned, including Enoch Powell in the highly marginal seat of Down South (he lost the seat in the 1987 general election). Their next step, as we have seen, was to refuse to fulfill the statutory functions of the Northern Ireland Assembly, in effect signing the assembly's death warrant. Their actions failed to dent the government's resolve to persist with the agreement.

Five years after the signing of the agreement, the British government could point to a notable increase in cross-border coordination on security matters. It was also able to claim that the number of deaths and injuries each year attributable to the security position in the province was running well below that of the 1970s. Unionists could point to the fact that the biggest decline predated the agreement taking effect. (The annual figures for the period from 1969 to 1991 are shown in Table 9.3.) There was greater contact between the British and Irish governments, with the Irish government agreeing to make some changes to its extradition policy, a contentious issue on which the British government had been pressing for reform for some years. On the British side, various measures had been introduced to meet some of the fears and demands of the nationalist community: an independent commission for complaints against the police, a Fair Employment Act, the extension of the franchise for council elections, and the removal of special protection for the Union flag. Relative to the previous initiatives, the agreement—in terms of substance and longevity—constitutes the most successful initiative taken by the British government since the imposition of direct rule.

The Brooke/Mayhew Talks

Despite the Anglo-Irish Agreement—or, in the view of some of its opponents, because of it—the situation in the province remained tense. Ninety-three people were killed in 1988, the same number as in the previous year. The

TABLE 9.3 Northern Ireland: Deaths due to the security situation, 1969–1991[a]

Year	Number of deaths	Year	Number of deaths
1969	13	1981	101
1970	25	1982	97
1971	174	1983	77
1972	467	1984	64
1973	250	1985	54
1974	216	1986	61
1975	247	1987	93
1976	297	1988	93
1977	112	1989	62
1978	81	1990	76
1979	113	1991	94
1980	76		

[a] Of those killed, just over half—about 55%—have been civilians, almost one-third have been members of the security forces, and the remainder—about 14%—members of republican or loyalist paramilitary groups.
SOURCE: "Soldier's Death Sabotages Ulster Peace Rally," *The Guardian*, August 29, 1992, p. 3.

government sought to go beyond, and build on, the agreement in order to reach a political solution.

On March 26, 1991, Northern Ireland Secretary Peter Brooke announced to the House of Commons that the basis for formal talks involving all the constitutional parties in the province had been established—the first such talks since the collapse of the convention in 1976. The parties accepted that the talks should concentrate on the establishment of new institutions for governing the province, the relationship between those institutions and the Republic of Ireland, and the relationship between the British and Irish governments.

Bilateral meetings between the secretary of state and the various parties began in April 1991, followed—after various delays—by a full meeting in June. Delays and disagreement hampered the talks and in July they were brought to a conclusion. Mr. Brooke told the House of Commons that, despite the ending of the talks, the plenary sessions had demonstrated that there were grounds for resuming the talks later. The resumption took place—under his successor, Sir Patrick Mayhew—in April 1992, when discussions were held on the first of the three elements: the institutions of government in the province. In July, the talks moved on to intergovernmental relationships.[23]

The talks took place on the basis that "nothing will be agreed until everything is agreed." By 1993, no agreement had been reached. Unionists remained suspicious of the role to be played by the Irish government and some ministers in the Irish government took the view that the legislation that had led to the partition of Ireland in 1922 should be up for discussion. The secretary of state continued—and continues—to seek a political solution through the talks. He has had to operate against a backdrop of IRA activity on the British mainland—involving bombings in different parts of the country and the shooting of a number of police officers—and an escalation of retaliatory killings of Catholics in the province by outlawed Protestant paramilitary groups.

Constitutional Conundrum

At the heart of the attempts to find a solution is a perplexing conundrum, one to which there is no obvious answer. At least nine different constitutional options have been proposed. The problem is that each one is unacceptable to one or more interested parties.

Direct rule has little attraction to any party as a permanent solution. For the British government it is an onerous responsibility, one that it would prefer not to shoulder. It denies parties within the province a role in government and conveys the impression of a form of colonial rule.[24] This form of government from London is recognized for what it is: a temporary expedient. *Self-government* within the United Kingdom, akin to the pre-1972 position, remains the "emotional favorite" for many, probably most, Unionists[25]—especially the Democratic Unionists (see chapter 6)—but finds no favor with Catholics in the province, the British and Irish governments, or, for that matter, the Clinton administration in the United States. *Integration* within the United Kingdom, analogous to the position of Scotland and Wales, finds favor among many Unionists, especially Ulster Unionists, but is unacceptable to a majority of Catholics as well as to people in Britain: "neither elites nor masses show any wish to become more closely involved with Northern Ireland."[26] The problems peculiar to the province are thought to require a constitutional framework distinct from that of the rest of the United Kingdom.

A *power-sharing assembly* is supported by the British government but opposed by a significant proportion of the Unionists in the province. They object to sharing power with a minority that is not committed to the maintenance of the union with Britain. It is also unacceptable to the predominantly Catholic Social Democratic and Labour party (SDLP) unless achieved within the context of an "Irish dimension." *Unification*—the province becoming part of a united Ireland—is sought by the Irish government, by most Catholics in the north, and is the long-term goal of the Labour party, subject to the agreement of the people of Northern Ireland. It is totally opposed by the Protestant majority. An absolute majority in the province voted in a plebiscite in 1973 to retain the border: 99% of those who voted, representing 58% of the total electorate, voted for retention. It is an option that also fails to carry majority support in Britain itself: Only one in five people questioned in Gallup polls express a preference for it (Table 9.4).

A *federal Ireland,* advocated by some Catholics and by Michael Sheane in *Ulster and the German Solution,*[27] is unacceptable to the majority of Protestants, as it is to the IRA: The Protestants consider that it goes too far, the IRA that it does not go far enough. A *redrawing of the boundary* between Northern Ireland and the republic has been proposed by some writers but is unacceptable to a majority of both Protestants and Catholics. A redrawing of the boundary would solve little and would create new problems, including the potential for some to flee from their existing homes. (Many Protestants probably would not wish to remain in Fermanagh if it became part of the republic.) The creation of an *independent Northern Ireland* has been advocated by some politicians, notably former prime minister James (now Lord) Callaghan, but finds little favor among Catholics, Protestants, the British and Irish governments, or other countries.[28] As Table 9.4 shows, it attracts minority support within Britain, albeit it a sizable minority. It is generally believed that the province would not be able to sustain itself as an independent entity.

TABLE 9.4   The future of Northern Ireland

	July 1992	January 1988	May 1986
Q: What would you prefer to happen:			
Northern Ireland to:			
remain part of the United Kingdom	28%	26%	26%
become part of the Republic of Ireland	20%	21%	24%
become independent from both the United Kingdom and the republic	36%	36%	35%
don't know/don't care	16%	16%	15%

SOURCE: Gallup Political and Economic Index, Report 363, July 1992.

The other solution that has been put forward, though it does not constitute a "constitutional" resolution to the problem, is *the withdrawal of British troops,* thus allowing competing forces within Northern Ireland to sort out, or rather fight over, the future of the province. It has a certain appeal to opinion within Britain, polls showing just over half of those questioned preferring a withdrawal at some stage. However, as Table 9.5 reveals, there is no agreement as to what stage it should be. It is not an option acceptable to the British government. Successive governments have accepted responsibility for the province, admitting the need to maintain order and to create a framework for a solution, while maintaining the union as long as a majority of the people in Northern Ireland wish to maintain it. There is also the realization that to withdraw troops could precipitate a bloodbath within the province, with the conflict spreading into the republic and onto the British mainland as well. As much as Britain's government would like to be rid of the problem, it accepts that it cannot just wash its hands of it.

In summary, then, Britain is faced with a problem that appears to have no obvious or easy solution. It has tended to proceed on the basis of a settlement premised on traditional British assumptions, and for that very reason its efforts have tended to be unsuccessful: It is faced with a very non-British problem. It is a problem that annually takes more lives within the province and sometimes, in quite horrific attacks of violence, on the mainland as well. It is a problem that Britain would like to be free of but one that it is committed to resolve without giving in to violence. The one thing that prevents the IRA from achieving its goal of a united Ireland is the very violence it pursues in order to achieve it. The problem of Northern Ireland is one riddled with paradox.

TABLE 9.5 Attitudes toward withdrawal of British troops from Northern Ireland: Gallup Poll, July 1992

Which of these statements comes closest to the way you, yourself, feel about the presence of British troops in Northern Ireland?

	Today	January 1988	August 1981	Mid-September 1979	Early September 1979
We should withdraw our troops immediately	29	24	34	44	43
We should withdraw our troops within 5 years	22	20	17	15	12
British troops should remain in Northern Ireland till a settlement is reached	37	42	33	27	27
We should not withdraw our troops	6	7	7	7	9
Don't know	6	7	6	7	8

SOURCE: Gallup Political and Economic Index, Report 383, July 1992.

CONCLUSION

Below the level of national government in Britain, the picture is a complex one. Scotland, Northern Ireland, and Wales each has a multifunctional government department largely responsible for the administration of the territory. At a regional level (which usually means regions within England, plus Scotland, Wales, and Northern Ireland), there are disparate and discrete public bodies, such as the Regional Health Authorities, whereas at the level of counties and towns there are elected councils.

Despite this complexity, these bodies have one thing in common. They are subordinate units of government. What powers they enjoy are granted at the discretion of Parliament, which means in practice (or largely so) that of the government. As resources have diminished, central government has proved increasingly willing to rein in some of the activities of these subordinate units. Squeezed between the demands and expectations of local electors and those of central government, local government is not in an enviable position.

In terms of political authority, local government can be seen to be encountering problems in raising resources to meet its commitments to the local community, hemmed in by the demands of local citizens and the limitations imposed by central government, and to be having difficulty in maintaining the consent of citizens. Attempts to maintain political authority by the creation of national or regional assemblies, bringing some decision making closer to the people, have not come to fruition, or else, in the unique case of Northern Ireland, have failed. There is no consensus among political leaders as to what the next step should be.

NOTES

1. A. King, "The Problem of Overload," in A. King (ed.), *Why Is Britain Becoming Harder to Govern?* (BBC, 1976), p. 9.
2. M. Beloff and G. Peele, *The Government of the United Kingdom* (Weidenfeld & Nicolson, 1980), p. 267.
3. The functions and proximity of local councils make certain officials and committee chairmen more likely targets for attempts at corruption by bodies seeking preferential treatment than is the case at the more distant levels of central government; the problem has been exacerbated by the fact that some local authorities are dominated, more or less permanently, by one party.
4. See R. E. Jennings, "The Councillor as a Point of Access to Local Government," paper presented at the annual conference of the American Political Science Association, Washington, DC, 1980; and G. W. Jones, "The Functions and Organization of Councillors," *Public Administration,* 1973, pp. 140–141.
5. Professor Howard Elcock to author, July 18, 1989.
6. The figure was almost 3 million by the end of the 1980s but was reduced by the abolition of the GLC and metropolitan county councils and by the transfer of certain functions out of local government responsibility.
7. *Local Government Financial Statistics, England,* No. 3, 1991 (Her Majesty's Stationery Office, 1991), p 17.

8. See P. Norton, "The Conservative Party from Thatcher to Major," in A. King (ed.), *Britain at the Polls 1992* (Chatham House, 1993), pp. 43–45.

9. Conservative Research Department, *The Campaign Guide 1989* (Conservative Central Office, 1989), p. 414.

10. See R. A. W. Rhodes, "Now Nobody Understands the System: The Changing Face of Local Government," in P. Norton (ed.), *New Directions in British Politics?* (Edward Elgar, 1991), pp. 83–112.

11. See B. W. Hogwood, "Introduction," in B. W. Hogwood and M. Keating (eds.), *Regional Government in England* (Oxford University Press, 1982), pp. 10–12.

12. See B. W. Hogwood and P. D. Lindley, "Variations in Regional Boundaries," in B. W. Hogwood and M. Keating (eds.), *Regional Government in England* (Oxford University Press, 1982), pp. 21–49.

13. M. Keating and A. Midwinter, *The Government of Scotland* (Mainstream Publishing, 1983), p. 14.

14. Ibid. See also P. Hennessy, *Whitehall* (Secker & Warburg, 1989), pp. 460–465.

15. Keating and Midwinter, p. 17.

16. Ibid.

17. D. Birrell and A. Murie, *Policy and Government in Northern Ireland* (Gill and Macmillan, 1980), p. 84.

18. See J. Loughlin, "Administering Policy in Northern Ireland," in B. Hadfield (ed.), *Northern Ireland: Politics and the Constitution* (Open University Press, 1992), pp. 70–71.

19. David Steel refers to the commitment to such a policy as stemming from Gladstone's pamphlet of 1886 that argued for a reform of government consistent with the aspirations of the individual nations in Great Britain. D. Steel, "Federalism," in N. MacCormick (ed.), *The Scottish Debate* (Oxford University Press, 1970), p. 81.

20. A. H. Birch, *Integration and Disintegration in the British Isles* (Allen & Unwin, 1977).

21. *British Public Opinion,* 15 (10), December 1992 (Market & Opinion Research International, 1992), p. 4. See also "For Auld Lang's Syne," *The Economist,* March 5, 1993, p. 31.

22. *House of Commons Debates (Hansard),* sixth series, Vol. 7, col. 1050.

23. See especially "Talks May Answer Ulster Question," *Financial Times,* July 3, 1992, p. 10.

24. See P. Norton, *The Constitution in Flux* (Blackwell, 1982), p. 200. See also R. Rose, *Northern Ireland: A Time of Choice* (American Enterprise Institute, 1976), p. 154.

25. *The Sunday Times,* June 28, 1981.

26. J. Whyte, "Why Is the Northern Ireland Problem So Intractable?" *Parliamentary Affairs,* 34 (4), 1981, p. 432.

27. M. Sheane, *Ulster and the German Solution* (Highfield, 1978).

28. See Norton, *The Constitution in Flux,* p. 207.

CHAPTER 10

The European Community
Government beyond the Center

Prior to the 1970s, the United Kingdom had entered into various treaty obligations with other nations. It was a founding member of the United Nations Organization. It had joined the North Atlantic Treaty Organization (NATO). It signed, though did not incorporate into domestic law, the European Convention on Human Rights. At no time, though, did it hand over to a supranational body the power to formulate regulations that were to have domestic application within the United Kingdom and be enforceable as law.

This situation was to change on January 1, 1973. On that date the United Kingdom became a member of the European Community. Forty-two volumes of legislation promulgated by institutions of the European Community were incorporated into British law and, under the provisions of the 1972 European Communities Act, future legislation emanating from the Community was to be incorporated as well. The United Kingdom entered into a relationship for which the United States has no parallel.

THE EUROPEAN COMMUNITY

The European Community comprises the European Steel and Coal Community, the European Atomic Energy Community (Euratom), and the better known European Economic Community (the EEC). The Steel and Coal Community, formed in 1951 under the Treaty of Paris, placed iron, steel, and coal production in member countries under a common authority. Euratom and the EEC were created under the Treaty of Rome and came into being on January 1, 1958. Euratom was designed to help create a civil nuclear industry in Europe. The EEC formed a common market for goods within the community of member states.

The three bodies were merged in 1967 to form the European Communities, known now by the singular term, the European Community (the EC).

Britain declined to join the individual bodies when they were first formed. The Labour government in 1951 found the supranational control of the Steel and Coal Community to be unacceptable. The succeeding Conservative government was not initially attracted by the concept of the EEC. The economic and political arguments for joining, which weighed heavily with the member states, did not carry great weight with British politicians. Britain was still seen as a world power. It was enjoying a period of prosperity. It had strong political and trading links with the Commonwealth. It had a "special relationship" with the United States. It had stood alone successfully during the Second World War. Lacking the experience of German occupation and the need to re-create a polity, Britain was not subject to the psychological appeal of a united Europe, so strong on the continental mainland.[1] Neither main political party was strongly attracted to the idea of a union with such an essentially foreign body. The Conservatives still hankered after the idea of empire, something that had died as a result of the war (Britain could no longer afford to maintain an empire and the principle of self-determination had taken root) and something for which the Commonwealth now served as something of a substitute. Labour politicians viewed with distrust the creation of a body that they saw as inherently antisocialist, designed to shore up the capitalist edifice of Western Europe and frustrate any future socialist policies that a Labour government in Britain would seek to implement. It was one of the few issues on which the leader of the Labour party, Hugh Gaitskell, found himself in agreement with left-wingers within his own party.

The attitude of the British government toward the EEC, at both a ministerial and official level, was to undergo significant change in 1960. Britain's economic problems had become more apparent. Growth rates compared poorly with those of the six member states of the EEC (i.e., France, Germany, Italy, and the Benelux countries). There was a growing realization that having lost an empire, Britain had gained a Commonwealth. That Commonwealth, however, was not proving as amenable to British leadership as many Conservatives had hoped, nor was it proving to be the source of trade and materials that had been expected. Even the special relationship with the United States was undergoing a period of strain. The "special" appeared to be seeping out of the relationship. Some anti-Americanism lingered in Conservative ranks following the insistence of the White House that Britain abort its operation to occupy the Suez Canal zone in 1956, a distrust still not wholly dispelled. The sudden cancellation by the U.S. administration in 1960 of the Blue Streak, a missile that Britain had ordered and intended to employ as the major element of its nuclear defense policy, awakened British politicians to the fact that in the Atlantic partnership, Britain was very much the junior partner. The U.S. administration itself began to pay more attention to the EEC, and President John F. Kennedy made clear to his friend and distant relative, Prime Minister Harold Macmillan, "that a British decision to join the Six would be welcome."[2] The option became one that had an increasing attraction to Britain.

Politically, the EEC was seen as a vehicle through which Britain could once again play a leading role on the world stage. Economically, it would provide a tariff-free market of 180 million people, it would provide the advantages of economy of scale, and it was assumed that it would encourage greater efficiency in British industry through more vigorous competition. Political and economic advantages were seen as inextricably linked. Economic strength was necessary to underpin the maintenance of political authority.[3] "If we are to meet the challenge of Communism, . . . " Macmillan wrote to Kennedy, "[we must show] that our modern society—the new form of capitalism—can run in a way that makes the fullest use of our resources and results in a steady expansion of our economic strength."[4] On July 31, 1961, he announced to the House of Commons that Britain was applying for membership.

The first application for membership was vetoed in January 1963 by the French president, General de Gaulle. He viewed British motives with suspicion, believing that Britain could serve as a vehicle for the United States to establish its dominance within the EEC. A second application was lodged in 1967, this time by the Labour government of Harold Wilson.[5] Agreement to open negotiations was reached eventually in 1969. Negotiations began under the newly returned Conservative government of Edward Heath in 1970. Relations between the British and French governments on the issue were now more amicable, de Gaulle having resigned the presidency in 1969, and no French veto was imposed. Negotiations were completed in 1971, and the British government recommended entry on the terms achieved. On October 28, 1971, following a six-day debate, the House of Commons gave its approval to the principle of membership on the terms negotiated. The vote was 356 in favor, 244 against.[6] Both parties were badly divided. Of Labour members, 69 voted with the Conservative government in favor of entry and a further 20 abstained from voting. Of Conservatives, 39 voted with the Labour opposition against entry, and 2 abstained.[7] It was the most divisive vote of the Parliament.

At the beginning of 1972, the Treaty of Accession was signed, and the European Communities bill, to give legal effect to British membership, was given a second reading on February 17. To ensure its passage, Prime Minister Heath made the vote one of confidence. Despite that, the majority for the bill was a slim one of only 8, because opposition MPs had largely united against the measure.[8] The bill faced sustained opposition from Labour members and a number of dissident Conservatives, but it completed its remaining stages without amendment and was given a third reading on July 13.[9] The United Kingdom became a member of the European Community on January 1, 1973.

Britain's membership in the EC has been anything but uneventful. Following the return of a Labour government in 1974, the terms of membership were renegotiated and the renegotiated terms put to—and approved by—the electorate in Britain's first nationwide referendum in 1975. After the return of a Conservative government in 1979, Prime Minister Margaret Thatcher argued that Britain's financial contribution to the EC was too high and pressed for a reduction. After several heated meetings with other EC heads of government, agreement was reached in 1984, with the United Kingdom receiving refunds on previous years' payments and with a new system to operate in the future. Mrs. Thatcher caused further controversy in 1988 when she made clear her opposition to full monetary union within the Community and defined a role for the EC that was at odds with that envisaged by leaders of other member states. She was committed to achieving a single market but opposed to any moves designed to create a supranational government that could impose its will on member states. Her "so far and no further" stance left her often in a minority of one at EC summits and badly split the Conservative party. Her unwillingness to modify her negative stance was a contributory factor in her loss of the party leadership in 1990 (see chapter 6).[10] Her successor, John Major, adopted a more emollient approach and had some success in negotiations on a new Community treaty, the Maastricht Treaty, in 1991. However, the rejection of the treaty in a referendum in Denmark acted as a spur to British opponents of further European union—Margaret Thatcher now constituting the spiritual leader of Conservative opponents—and the government ran into trouble in trying to get the bill, necessary to give legal effect to the treaty, through the House of Commons.

January 1, 1993, marked the twentieth anniversary of British membership of the European Community. Throughout most of those 20 years, the issue of "Europe" had been a contentious, and perplexing, one. As the country entered its twenty-first year of membership, the issue was becoming, if anything, more rather than less divisive.

Economic Implications

The economic attractions for joining the EC were, as we have seen, a major influence in Britain's applying for membership. The Community offered, in trading terms, a "common market" (the popular name for the EEC), one which has assumed increasing significance for the British economy.

In the first nine years of membership, British exports to EC countries increased by 27% a year, compared with a 19% average annual growth in the country's exports to the rest of the world. After 20 years of membership, British dependence on the EC was well established. In 1973, 36% of British exports went to EC countries: By 1993, it was 57%, with exports to Germany alone equalling those to Japan and the United States combined. The country also has attracted significant inward investment. By the end of 1991, the United Kingdom had received 41% of total Japanese investment in the EC and 36% of U.S. investment.

Britain also receives money from what are known as the Community's "structural funds": those administered by the European Social Fund (ESF), the European Regional Development Fund, and the European Agricultural Guidance and Guarantee Fund. The Social Fund was established to assist with the training and retraining of workers. Since 1973 it has been used to help agricultural workers who are leaving the land, workers obliged to leave textile and other industries, migrant workers requiring language or vocational training, handicapped workers, and those who are unemployed or in need of some form of training. Since 1983, Britain has received either the highest or second highest allocation from the fund; in 1990 the amount totaled more than £350 million (over $540m.), about 16% of the money available from the fund.[11] The Regional Development Fund came into being in 1975 to promote economic activity and the development of the infrastructure in the poorer regions of the Community. The fund can be used to contribute up to 50% of national expenditure on a given scheme if it is for the relief of agricultural poverty, for industrial change, or for the provision of infrastructure. Since 1985, it has adopted a more Community-wide focus. The United Kingdom receives more than 10% of the fund (1990 figures), particularly for building the infrastructure in the north of England, Scotland, Wales, and Northern Ireland. The fund has been used to assist with building a reservoir, improving roads, building a new airport runway, and constructing new buildings, such as an enterprise center, in Northern Ireland. The Agricultural Fund has been more contentious. The guarantee part of the fund supports the Common Agricultural Policy (the CAP) for which the United Kingdom has sought, and achieved, various reforms. Britain has a highly efficient agricultural sector, especially in comparison with other member states. The CAP has favored price supports rather than cheap food, thus working to the benefit of countries with large farming communities, such as France. The guidance part of the fund, forming part of the structural funds, is designed to help finance the modernization of farming and to provide income support in rural areas.

The EC also administers a number of other funds and programs, such as one to provide assistance with energy research and development, and it also encompasses the European Investment Bank. Created under the Treaty of Rome, the bank operates on a nonprofit basis to grant loans and guarantees that facilitate the financing of new investment and projects concerned with modernization. By 1988, the bank had provided more funds than did the combined structural funds, lending almost £7 billion (more than $11 billion). In 1991, the amount of finance provided by the bank in different forms (but mostly individual loans) to the United Kingdom was just under £1.5 billion (more than $2.2 billion), about 15% of the total amount of finance provided by the bank within the Community. Only Italy and Spain received greater amounts.[12]

However, the principal benefits to the United Kingdom is in terms of trading opportunities, rather than in terms of support from EC funds. Despite the income from the structural funds, the United Kingdom—along with Germany and France—remains a net contributor to EC funds.[13]

It is in terms of trade that Britain faces now its greatest challenge and its greatest opportunity. Though the EEC was formed to create a common market for goods, services, and labor, various barriers to achieving that market remained in place. To help achieve a single European market (SEM), the Single European Act (the SEA) was implemented in 1987, designed to speed up the decision-making process within the EC, allowing a majority within the Council of Ministers to pass a measure despite the objections of one or two member states. In 1985, the EC Commission identified approximately 300 measures that were necessary for achieving the SEM. December 31, 1992 was agreed upon as the deadline for completing these measures. Many of the measures were approved quickly—almost half by the end of 1988, three-quarters by early 1992. Not all, though, had been approved by the end of 1992. "1992" came to be seen as a concept rather than a precise date. Nonetheless, there was a notable change on January 1, 1993, with checks for customs duties at the borders between member states wholly or largely disappearing.

For member states, the SEM constitutes a major challenge. The free flow of goods and services is expected to provide major benefits. An EC Commission report on the economic benefits of the SEM (the Cecchinin Report), though now recognized as being excessively optimistic, estimated that the total economic gain would be £120 billion ($186 billion) at 1988 prices, with several million jobs being created in the short and long term. However, what is not clear is how the benefits will fall. Many firms have a national base and orientation and are not geared to operate in a wider market. (Indeed, some U.S. firms that operate on a European rather than a country-specific basis, such as Ford, are better placed to exploit that wider market.) Competition at an international level, with no protection afforded by national government, will force the demise of inefficient and unprepared companies. Though the British government and the Confederation of British Industry initiated campaigns prior to the SEA to ensure that businesses in the United Kingdom were aware of the SEA and its implications,[14] it will be some years before the effects of the SEA are apparent in the United Kingdom and the other member states.

Political Implications

British membership in the Community has had political implications in terms of U.K. domestic politics. It remains a contentious issue. However, it has wider political implications—that is, in terms of the member states acting together as a political power bloc. That, as we have seen, was one of the motivations for Britain joining the Community. For Britain, the prospect of EC member states acting together looked increasingly attractive as other avenues for maintaining a world status (the Commonwealth, the "special relationship" with the United States) receded in significance.

The Community already had taken steps toward achieving some degree of political cooperation before Britain became a member. In 1970, EC foreign ministers approved the Luxembourg Report, which established the basic procedures for some form of cooperation on foreign policy. As a member, Britain has supported the development and formalization of this cooperation, as long as it has not affected the capacity of the United Kingdom to determine its own priorities in foreign policy. The government supported both the process of European Political Cooperation (EPC) being put on a formal treaty basis under the provisions of the Single European Act and the development of a Common Foreign and Security Policy (CFSP) under the Maastricht Treaty.

European Political Cooperation is "the process of information, consultation and common action" among the member states in the field of foreign policy.[15] It entails regular meetings of the foreign ministers of member states (at least two per EC presidency); at least one meeting of heads of government per presidency (the presidency rotates among countries on a six-month basis) to discuss Community and EPC subjects; and monthly meetings of the Political Committee, which comprises senior officials drawn from the foreign ministries and having responsibility for the day-to-day business of EPC. There also exists the Group of European Correspondents, made up of one official from each country's foreign ministry, to monitor the functioning of EPC, and there are 15 to 20 Working Groups, drawing on experts, with each group meeting at least two or three times per presidency. The country holding the EC presidency is in charge of EPC and responsible for setting the agenda and drafting common statements.

The EPC process produced some common positions, as on South Africa and Iraq—as well as helping develop links with other international organizations, such as the Gulf Cooperation Council, the Arab League, and the United Nations—and in 1991 heads of government agreed in the Maastricht Treaty to "define and implement a common foreign and security policy.

That common policy is to be achieved through intergovernmental cooperation: that is, the process continues to lie outside the existing EC institutions and outside the provisions of the Treaty of Rome. In reaching a common policy, unanimity will remain the rule. Any majority voting will have to be authorized first by unanimous vote. Britain was especially keen on the provision for unanimity in order to ensure that nation states could continue to determine their own foreign policy priorities.

The motivation for the government supporting the move toward a CFSP, and doing so through the medium of intergovernmental cooperation, was well expressed in one Conservative publication in 1992: "A Common Foreign and Security Policy," it declared, "will . . . present Britain with a real opportunity to lead European foreign policy-making, given the world-wide resources at our disposal, our historical links with Eastern Europe and our leading role in most of the key international organisations. Crucially, the CFSP will be conducted on an *intergovernmental* basis, with no Community competence."[16] Britain, in short, would be able to lead—one of the motivations for joining—without jeopardizing its national interest.

Constitutional Implications

As we have already had cause to note (chapter 4), membership in the EC added a new dimension to the British Constitution. Under the provisions of the European Communities Act, existing EC law was to have general and binding applicability in the United Kingdom, as was all subsequent law promulgated by the Communities. Section 2(1) of the act gives the force of law in the United Kingdom to "rights, powers, liabilities, obligations and restrictions from time to time created or arising by or under the Treaties." Section 2(4) provides that directly applicable EC law should prevail over conflicting provisions of domestic legislation. The net effect of membership and the provisions of the act was to introduce two new decision-making bodies into the ambit of the British polity (the Council of Ministers and the European Communities Commission), to restrict the role and influence of Parliament in matters that came within the competence of the Communities, to inject a new judicial dimension to the Constitution (disputes concerning the treaties or legislation made under them to be treated by the British courts as a matter of law, with provision for their referral to the European court for a ruling), and to allow for British representation in the European Parliament, albeit until 1987 a body with very limited powers.

The constitutional implications were a matter of controversy at the time Britain joined the EC. Equally controversial were the implications of the Single European Act. Implemented in 1987, it was agreed upon by the United Kingdom under the provisions of the 1986 European Communities (Amendment) Act. The effect of the SEA, as we earlier observed, was to effect a shift in power relationships *within* the institutions of the EC as well as *between* the institutions of the EC and the member states. Under the SEA, the European Parliament not only was designated as a Parliament (its formal title previously was that of Assembly) but also was given a more powerful role in the EC lawmaking process. To allow for the approval of the measures necessary to achieve the single European market, provision for the Council of Ministers to determine issues by weighted majority voting also was extended, thus making it possible for measures to be passed despite the opposition of a small number of member states. By the end of the decade, British ministers had variously found themselves outvoted under this procedure.

British accession to membership of the EC in 1973 and the implementation of the Single European Act in 1987 had the effect of shifting power from the U.K. government to the institutions of the EC. The effect of the Maastricht Treaty negotiated in 1991 was less clear-cut. The treaty established a "European Union" and established economic and monetary union as an objective of the Community. It also enhanced, though not greatly, the powers of the European Parliament. However, it also acknowledged the importance of decisions being taken at the lowest level possible—the principle of "subsidiarity"—and, in a protocol, encouraged "greater involvement" by national parliaments in the activities of the European Union. The U.K. government also negotiated an opt-out clause on a single European currency (allowing the U.K. Parliament to decide whether the United Kingdom should participate or not) and achieved deletion of any reference to a "federal" Europe, a term implying in the view of the United Kingdom more centralization.

The effects of the treaty have yet to be seen, especially in terms of the principle of subsidiarity. What the treaty left unclear was who was to decide at what levels decisions should be taken, and hence it appeared to constitute an invitation to struggle between the EC Commission and national governments.

INSTITUTIONS OF THE COMMUNITY

Within the EC, the main bodies are the European Council, the Council of Ministers, the EC Commission, the European Parliament, and the Committee of Permanent Representatives. In addition, there is the European Court of Justice, which ensures that EC law is observed in the interpretation and application of the treaties, and this court can itself interpret EC law. Its judgments are binding on member states and enforceable through the national courts. Under the SEA, the Council of Ministers may now attach to the court a new Court of First Instance, to help reduce the burden on the court in a limited number of areas.

The European Council, more commonly known as the "European Summit," comprises the heads of government of the member states. Though already a regular feature of the EC, it was not until the passage of the SEA that it was given treaty status. The SEA provides that the council shall meet at least twice a year. However, though it is of central political importance, the body has no legislative powers. For its wishes to be enacted, action has to be taken by the Council of Ministers.

The Council of Ministers comprises the ministers from the member states whose portfolios cover the subject under discussion. Thus a proposal on agriculture will be considered by the council comprising agriculture ministers. (In practice, it would be more appropriate to refer to *councils* of ministers.) The demands made of the council vary according to the subject. The Council of Foreign Ministers and the Council of Finance Ministers meet more often than do the others. The council seeks to proceed on the basis of consensus and tacit agreement. Even before passage of the SEA, many matters could, under the EC treaties, be resolved by weighted majority voting. (Under this procedure, each of the larger countries—the United Kingdom, Germany, France, and Italy—has 10 votes; Spain has 8; Belgium, Greece, the Netherlands, and Portugal each have 5; Denmark and Ireland each have 3; and Luxembourg has 1. For a measure to be adopted, 54 votes are required.) Provision for such voting was extended by the SEA. Other issues are subject to simple majority voting (at least 7 members voting in favor, each country having 1 vote) or to unanimity (or rather, "nobody against," as abstention is not sufficient to prevent adoption). Under the so-called Luxembourg Compromise of 1966, a country may veto legislation if "very important interests" are involved. However, this is a highly contentious provision, with no clear agreement on what is actually entailed. The British government takes the view that the compromise is unaffected by the SEA. Others, including the House of Commons Select Committee on Foreign Affairs, have taken a more skeptical view.[17]

The EC Commission constitutes the bureaucracy of the EC. It is headed by a College of Commissioners. The 17 commissioners are drawn from the member states (2 each from the United Kingdom, Germany, France, and Italy; 1 from each of the smaller countries), though each takes an oath not to seek to represent national interests. Each is appointed for a four-year term, though under the Maastricht Treaty this is to be extended to five years from 1995. (Britain's two commissioners—first appointed in 1989 and re-appointed in 1993—are Sir Leon Brittan, a former Conservative MP and Cabinet minister, and Bruce Millan, a former Labour MP and Cabinet minister, both nominated by the prime minister.) From their number, the commissioners choose a president, who serves a two-year, renewable term. The commissioners head a sizable bureaucracy with a highly developed infrastructure. There are 23 Directorates-General, each responsible for different aspects of EC work (e.g., DGIV deals with competition, DGVI with agriculture, and DGXVI with regional policy), plus a number of specialized services. Commissioners formulate proposals within their area of responsibility aimed at implementing the treaties. The commissioners as a body then discuss the proposals and decide on the final form the proposals shall take. Decisions are taken by simple majority vote.

Until the passage of the SEA, the European Parliament was an advisory body in dealing with EC legislation. It did have two formal, but rather blunt powers: One was to reject the budget, a power it did employ, and the other was to force the resignation of the EC Commission *en bloc,* a power it did not use. In the legislative process, it was called upon to offer an opinion on a proposal emanating from the commission. That opinion was then passed on to the European Council to consider along with the actual proposal. Under the SEA, there now exists a "cooperation procedure." After a proposal has gone through the traditional procedure (from commission to council, with an opinion offered by the Parliament), the council adopts a "common position." This then goes to the Parliament, which may reject or amend it by majority vote. The commission then reexamines and resubmits its proposal, taking account of the Parliament's views. The council can then adopt the resubmitted proposal by a qualified majority but can only amend it or reinstate a proposal rejected by the Parliament by unanimity. The Parliament works primarily through committees, and the effect of the SEA has been to enhance the significance of both the Parliament as a whole and its committees.[18]

Under the Maastricht Treaty, the powers of the Parliament are further enhanced, with power to block measures on a number of issues. If the council and Parliament cannot agree after each giving a measure two readings, they have to form a "conciliation committee"; if no agreement is reached, the council version prevails unless the Parliament votes it down. Parliamentary approval is also required for most international treaties. The EP is also empowered to ask the commission to propose laws. However, the Parliament remains limited as a legislature. It has no power of its own to propose measures and is limited, in practice, by the poor attendance of members. Many have other responsibilities elsewhere—as members of national parliaments or even governments—and getting an absolute majority present to carry amendments is difficult.

The Parliament, nonetheless, has greater powers now than before, powers that it has variously proved willing to employ. Early in 1992, for example, it threw out EC aid packages to Morocco and Syria on human-rights grounds and forced the council to accept an environmental fund in the 1992 budget. It also blocked a measure to open up Europe's nonlife assurance market until the member states agreed to more EC-wide rules on social protection.[19] It has also been careful to ensure that greater coordination on EC affairs among the parliaments of the member states is under its own umbrella.

The other principal body in the process is the Committee of Permanent Representatives (known as COREPER), which has responsibility for preparing the work of the Council of Ministers and for carrying out tasks assigned to the council. As the name implies, COREPER comprises official representatives (classified often as ambassadors) from the member states, each assisted by a staff of diplomats and officials seconded (released from regular duty and temporarily assigned elsewhere) from the national civil service. COREPER studies a proposal on behalf of the council, isolating any problems associated with it. If the committee reaches agreement, it is usual for the council to adopt the proposal without further discussion.

These bodies are supplemented by a number of advisory bodies with members drawn from different organizations within the member states. The Economic and Social Committee, based in Brussels, has 189 members (24 of them from the

United Kingdom) made up of representatives of employers, trade unions, and consumers, and it has to be consulted on proposals relating to economic and social matters. Under the Maastricht Treaty, a new Committee of the Regions is established, with representatives drawn from regional and local authorities, also to operate in an advisory capacity. Members are appointed by national governments for a four-year term.

There is thus a major decision-making process within the EC, taking place essentially at one remove from national government. Following the Single European Act in 1987 and the negotiation of the Maastricht Treaty in 1991, there is considerable debate as to the future role of national institutions in policy making within the Community. There are many within the Community who wish to consolidate and extend the powers of Community institutions in order to realize the objective of European union. There are others, especially in the United Kingdom and Denmark, who harbor no such wish.

ELECTIONS TO THE EUROPEAN PARLIAMENT

With the passage of the SEA, elections to the European Parliament have taken on a new significance. Until 1979, members of the Parliament were drawn from the national parliaments of the member states. Since 1979, they have been elected. The argument for election is that it enhances the legitimacy of the institution. In the British case, it also provides a more direct link between electors and the Parliament, members being elected—via the plurality, first-past-the-post method—for constituencies. However, one criticism leveled at the change was that it ended a useful linkage between the EP Parliament and the member parliaments. The linkage that now exists between members of the EP Parliament and the Westminster Parliament is largely informal and tenuous.

Each Parliament sits for a fixed term of five years. There have thus been three elections to the Parliament: in 1979, 1984, and 1989. In the first two elections in Britain the Conservative party did especially well, benefiting in large measure from the fact that these were periods when the Conservative government was doing well in the opinion polls. In 1989 the party's fortunes were reversed: It lost 13 of its 45 seats to Labour candidates (see Table 10.1). The Scottish National party held onto its one seat and the Green party polled unexpectedly well, largely at the expense of the Social and Liberal Democrats. Turnout, as in the previous two elections and in the 1975 referendum, was low. For every elector who went to the polls, approximately two stayed at home. Though low, the turnout was not exceptional. Within the EC as a whole, 100 million out of 240 million stayed at home. Though support for the Community appears to be broad, the results suggest it is not deep. European election campaigns have yet to attract attention on the same scale as national elections. For anyone traveling across Europe at the height of the European election campaign early in June 1989 (as I was), it was difficult to detect that there was an election taking place.

Within the Parliament, the British Labour members (MEPs) are members of the Socialist group, which has enjoyed increased influence since the 1989

TABLE 10.1 Elections to the European Parliament, 1989

Party	Number of Seats Won (Change from 1984 in parentheses)	% of Votes Won
Conservative	32 (− 13)	34.7
Labour	45 (+ 13)	40.1
SLD	0	6.2
Greens	0	14.9
SNP	1	3.4[a]
Total (Britain)[b]	78	99.3

[a] Includes votes of Plaid Cymru. The SNP won 25.6% of the votes in Scotland, Plaid Cymru 12.9% of the votes in Wales.
[b] Northern Ireland elected three members by a system of proportional representation, returning, as in 1984, one Ulster Unionist, one Democratic Unionist, and one Social and Democratic Labour member.

elections; the effect of the elections was to transform a small Center-Right majority into a small Center-Left majority. Prior to the elections, the Conservative MEPs, along with 17 Spanish and 4 Danish MEPs, formed a European Democratic Group. Following the elections, the Spaniards withdrew from the group (disagreeing with the Conservative stance on European integration) and the Conservatives were too small in number to have much impact as a separate group. Following the more emollient attitude taken toward European union by the U.K. government, they subsequently were able to join the Christian Democrats (supporters of European union) in the Parliament, thus becoming part of the European People's party, the second largest political group in the Parliament (see Table 10.2). Each political group within the Parliament sits as a group and has its own staff.

THE CURRENT DEBATE

In the first half of the 1970s, debate on the European Community centered on whether or not Britain should be a member. After it became a member, various groups were formed to campaign for British withdrawal. The results of the 1975 referendum were taken as confirming that Britain was committed to remaining in the Community, and much of the debate had died down by the end of the decade. In the latter half of the 1980s, the issue of the EC returned. This time it was not so much a question of continued membership (though a number, especially on the left of the Labour party and the right of the Conservative party, remained opposed to membership), but rather what form the EC was to take in the future.

Toward the end of the 1980s the implications of the Single European Act began to be more clearly discerned. The 1986 European Communities (Amendment) Act had been motivated by economic considerations: the need to achieve the single European market. Constitutional considerations were seen as largely secondary or at least not entailing major changes to the existing constitutional

TABLE 10.2 Political groups in the European Parliament, as of January 1, 1993

Group	Number of Members
Socialist	179
European People's party	162
Liberal and Democratic Reformist Group	45
Green Group	28
European Unitarian Left	28
European Democratic Alliance	21
Rainbow	15
European Right	14
Left Unity	13
Independents	11

constitutional arrangements. When it was apparent that the constitutional implications were significant, a public and—for the Conservative party—divisive debate erupted. From being if not a largely moribund debate at least a secondary one, it came to occupy a central place in political debate. The debate was largely precipitated by a speech given by Prime Minister Margaret Thatcher in 1988 and it achieved a particular intensity following the negotiation of the Maastricht Treaty in December 1991 by Thatcher's successor in Downing Street, John Major.

At the heart of the debate was the question of how the EC was going to develop, and it embodied three approaches. One approach was taken by what were dubbed "Euro skeptics." Another, diametrically opposite, approach was that taken by "Euro fanatics." The third approach, falling between the other two, was that taken by "Euro pragmatists."

The Euro skeptics took their lead from Margaret Thatcher. To her, the EC constituted a collection of sovereign states cooperating in order to achieve a single market. That process should not entail each member state losing its particular culture and identity, nor should it entail the creation of a new layer of decision-making bureaucracy. "To try to suppress nationhood and concentrate power at the centre of a European conglomerate," declared Mrs. Thatcher in her seminal 1988 speech in Bruges, "would be highly damaging and would jeopardize the objectives we seek to achieve."[20] The objectives, as far as she was concerned, were to achieve a free trade in goods, in services, and in capital. It was a means of reducing barriers, not creating new ones. She made clear that she was totally opposed to the creation of a supranational government capable of imposing its will upon member states. "We have not successfully rolled back the frontiers of the state in Britain," she declared, "only to see them reimposed at a European level, with a European super-state exercising a new dominance from Brussels."[21]

To Mrs. Thatcher and the Euro skeptics, the Single European Act constituted a Trojan horse through which European integrationists would seek to achieve a new layer of European government. This recognition came too late to do anything about the Single Act itself, but it spurred opposition to any attempt to take the Community any further in the direction of European integration. This stance—in effect "so far and no further"—resulted in Mrs. Thatcher taking a hard and negative line in European summits, often being outvoted by her fellow heads of government. It was a stance that split the Conservative party. Euro fanatics within the party were opposed in principle to her stance. Euro pragmatists were increasingly worried that it was leaving Britain isolated within the Community as well as damaging the party at home. As we have noted already, Thatcher's refusal to modify her position contributed to her loss of the party leadership in November 1990.[22]

For Euro fanatics, European union constituted an opportunity and not a threat. European union was viewed as necessary and desirable. It would ensure a united block of nations, powerful in world affairs, able to ensure a greater degree of economic and political stability. Each nation within the EC would retain its own identity—in the same way, for example, that Scotland had retained its very distinctive culture and legal and educational systems within the United Kingdom—and the concept of a "federal" Europe was one in which the member states retained some degree of autonomy, hence federal rather than unitary.

For the Euro fanatics, European union was desirable—and inevitable. EC Commission President Jacques Delors—the *bête noire* of the Euro skeptics—described the process toward EC control of economic and social development as part of an "irretrievable process."[23] Monsieur Delors was responsible for the report on European economic and monetary union, commissioned by the European Council in 1988. The report envisaged a three-stage process toward achieving such a union. Stage I envisaged realization of the single market, liberalization of capital movements, freedom from exchange rate controls, and membership by all member states of the Exchange Rate Mechanism (ERM). Stage II envisaged the creation of a European System of Central Banks (ESCB). Stage III would entail the achievement of, especially, monetary union, plus controls on fiscal policy, with members setting "binding limits" on each other's fiscal deficits.[24] For Margaret Thatcher, Stage I was acceptable, other than for membership of the ERM. (She was eventually persuaded to accept membership in 1990, though the United Kingdom withdrew from it in September 1992 at the height of a pound sterling crisis.) The remaining stages were anathema to her. To Euro fanatics, they were essential. When the Maastricht Treaty was negotiated in 1991, it was seen as part of the "irretrievable" process. To Euro skeptics, it sounded the death knell of nation states, handing over power to determine economic policy to a supranational authority over which an individual state would have no control. On the Maastricht Treaty, there was thus no meeting of minds between Euro skeptics and Euro fanatics. They adopted mutually exclusive positions.

For Euro pragmatists within the Conservative party, the concept of European union had to be treated with some caution. They harbored some of the doubts of the Euro skeptics about centralization of power in Brussels. At the same time, they recognized that consistent opposition to moves toward European integration—especially when unaccompanied by alternative proposals—was leaving the United Kingdom isolated in EC decision making, and to no purpose: The other member states were reaching agreement and moving forward. They therefore sought a middle path, allowing Britain to have some influence in discus on the future shape of the Community but without committing the United Kingdom to a "federal" system—seen, with Euro skeptics, as implying centralization of power.

Margaret Thatcher was succeeded as leader of the Conservative party by a Euro pragmatist. John Major moved quickly to meet fellow heads of government and to convey a new mood on the part of British government. In the 1991 negotiations on the Maastricht Treaty, he largely achieved his objectives. As we have noted already, he negotiated an opt-out clause for the United Kingdom on monetary union and, among other objectives, achieved recognition of the principle of subsidiarity.[25] The government was able to claim that the treaty represented a great success for Mr. Major's negotiating skills, and when the bill to give legal effect in the United Kingdom to the treaty's provisions came before the House of Commons, it achieved a second reading by 336 votes to 92.[26] The Labour party proposed an amendment regretting the failure of the government to sign the social chapter on employer-employee relations, but when that amendment was rejected by 360 votes to 261, the party abstained on the vote to give the bill a second reading. The MPs voting against comprised Euro skeptics of both parties: 61 Labour MPs and 22 Conservatives, the remaining dissenters being from the Northern Ireland Unionists.

The bill was given its second reading on May 21, 1992. It looked set to complete its remaining stages by the summer. However, on June 2, the Danes rejected the treaty in a referendum. The British government decided to wait until the legal and practical implications of the referendum result were clear before proceeding with the bill. The referendum also had another effect. It galvanized the Euro skeptics, many of whom had voted reluctantly for the second reading of the bill. They now realized that the ratification of the treaty was not certain. Sixty-nine of them immediately put their signatures to a motion calling for "a fresh start with the future development of the EEC," with an emphasis on extending the borders of the Community and creating a fully competitive common market. The withdrawal of Britain from the Exchange Rate Mechanism in September gave the skeptics a further boost. "It seems irrefutable," declared a former Conservative Cabinet minister (a member of the Cabinet when the treaty had been negotiated), "that last week [the withdrawal from the ERM] tore a gaping hole in the Maastricht treaty . . . . The Danes have given us an opportunity to think again about the next step forward."[27]

The Euro skeptics grew both in number and confidence in the latter half of 1992. On November 4, the Commons debated a motion reaffirming Britain's commitment to Europe and inviting the government to proceed with the bill. The Labour opposition tabled an amendment calling for consideration of the bill to be postponed until after a forthcoming European summit in Edinburgh. It was widely reported that the prime minister would resign if the government failed to carry the motion. The amendment was defeated by 319 votes to 313, and the motion then carried by a wafer-thin majority of 3 votes: 319 votes to 316. Labour MPs were united in their voting behavior, but 26 Conservatives voted with Unionists and Nationalists in the opposition lobby.[28] The government was saved by the votes of 19 Liberal Democrats, representing a party totally committed to European integration.

The bill's passage in 1993 was equally fraught, with the government being defeated on an amendment covering the new EC Committee of the Regions.[29] The gruelling parliamentary debates took up valuable time and served to call attention to the rifts within the ranks especially of the Conservative party. The Labour party was also divided, but—as the party of opposition—received less attention. Conservative party members loyal to the prime minister, both in Parliament and the local parties, were keen to take some action against the more vocal Euro skeptics; the more they pressed for action, the greater the rift within the party. Euro skeptics maintained their opposition and made repeated demands for a referendum on the issue.

The activity of the Euro skeptics served to tap a continuing doubt about European union among many Britons and to again raise doubts in the rest of the Community about Britain's commitment to the Community. Since entry in 1973, popular attitudes in the United Kingdom have varied considerably, but Britons have generally been dubbed "reluctant Europeans." This has been borne out by survey data. A *Eurobarometer* survey in late 1991 found that, though most Britons questioned thought EC membership a "good thing," the proportion saying it was a "bad thing"—15%—was surpassed only by 20% of Danes giving a similar response.[30] More tellingly, the same survey also found that more Britons were against a European government than were for it (40% against, 35% for), whereas in all other member states, except for Denmark, a clear majority were in favor of a European government. (In Denmark, there was a large majority against—60% to 25%.)[31] Gallup polls in 1992 also found a population divided on how they would vote if there was a referendum on the Maastricht Treaty (Table 10.3) but less divided on how they would react if told that the European Community had been scrapped (Table 10.4): Most would be indifferent or relieved. The consolation for supporters of European union was that the proportion giving a negative response was lower than in previous years.

The ambivalence of many MPs and citizens in the United Kingdom toward the Maastricht Treaty renewed doubts on the part of Community leaders about Britain's commitment to European union. Britain, to them, appeared to have resumed its position as a half-hearted partner. Criticisms were leveled at Britain's delay in ratifying the treaty and its refusal to sign the social chapter. The louder the criticisms, the louder, too, became the voices of the Euro skeptics. Prime

TABLE 10.3   Attitudes toward the Maastricht Treaty: Gallup Poll, June 1992

Q: If there was a referendum in this country on whether or not the British Government should ratify the Maastricht Treaty, would you vote "yes" or "no"?

Would vote "yes"	38%
Would vote "no"	35%
Would not vote	3%
Don't know	24%

SOURCE: Gallup Political and Economic Index, Report 382, June 1992.

TABLE 10.4 Attitudes toward scrapping of the EC: Gallup Poll, July 1992

Q: *If you were told tomorrow that the European Community (Common Market) had been scrapped, would you be very sorry about it, indifferent, or relieved?*

	July 1992	July 1987	January 1985	March 1984
Very sorry	26%	18%	23%	19%
Indifferent	41%	42%	35%	37%
Relieved	27%	36%	36%	40%
Don't know	6%	5%	6%	4%

SOURCE: Gallup Political and Economic Index, Report 383, July 1992.

Minister John Major was the son of a trapeze artist. He tried to emulate his father in walking a difficult tightrope.

CONCLUSION

The United Kingdom has been a member of the European Community for more than two decades. Membership has had major economic, political, and constitutional implications. After initial doubts, there is now acceptance at both elite and mass levels that the United Kingdom is a permanent member of the Community. However, there remains uncertainty as to the direction the Community should take. Of the U.K. political parties, only the Liberal Democrats have been committed to the concept of European union on a consistent basis. The others have expressed reservations—the Labour party, at various times, outright opposition— reflecting some measure of public uncertainty and ambivalence. The United Kingdom may now be married to the Community, but the state of that marriage has fluctuated considerably: It has never reached the plane of being blissful.

NOTES

1. See A. King, *Britain Says Yes* (American Enterprise Institute, 1977), pp. 2–7.
2. M. Camps, *Britain and the European Community 1955–1963* (Oxford University Press, 1964), p. 336.
3. See the comments of E. Heath, *Our Community* (Conservative Political Centre, 1977), p. 4.
4. H. Macmillan, *Pointing the Way* (Macmillan, 1972), p. 310.
5. On the first two applications, see R. J. Lieber, *British Politics and European Unity* (University of California Press, 1970); and U. Kitzinger, *The Second Try* (Pergamon, 1968).
6. *House of Commons Debates (Hansard),* Vol. 823, cols. 2211–2218.

7. See P. Norton, *Dissension in the House of Commons 1945–1974* (Macmillan, 1975), pp. 395–398; and U. Kitzinger, *Diplomacy and Persuasion* (Thames and Hudson, 1973), ch. 13 and appendix 1.

8. *House of Commons Debates (Hansard),* Vol. 831, cols. 753–758.

9. See P. Norton, *Conservative Dissidents* (Temple Smith, 1978), pp. 64–82.

10. P. Norton, "The Conservative Party from Thatcher to Major," in A. King (ed.), *Britain at the Polls 1992* (Chatham House, 1993).

11. "The Structural Funds in 1990," European Parliament *EP News,* June 8–12, 1992.

12. European Investment Bank, *Annual Report 1991,* p. 25.

13. Given that, the United Kingdom is reluctant to see a large increase in the EC budget, especially given the share of the existing budget devoted to the Common Agricultural Policy. About 60% of EC spending goes on the CAP—that is, 60% of a budget that in 1993 totalled £47 billion (almost $73 billion).

14. The campaign appeared to have achieved its desired goal: By the end of 1988, 90% of British businessmen were aware of the coming of the single European market. *The Campaign Guide 1989* (Conservative Central Office, 1989), p. 532.

15. *European Political Cooperation* (EPC) (Office for Official Publications of the European Communities, 1988), p. 5.

16. *The Campaign Guide 1992* (Conservative Central Office, 1992), p. 315.

17. See *The Single European Act: Third Report from the Select Committee on Foreign Affairs,* Session 1985/66, HC 442 (Her Majesty's Stationery Office, 1986), and the Government's Response (Cmnd. 9858). The House of Lords Committee on the European Communities also took a skeptical view.

18. From July 1987 to March 1989 inclusively, the commission accepted 67% and the council adopted 50% of the amendments proposed by the Parliament on first reading (i.e., when giving its first opinion). The figures for second reading (amendments made under the cooperation procedure) were 60% and 25%. D. Millar, "The European Parliament," *Study of Parliament Group Newsletter,* 5, Spring 1989, p. 11.

19. "Talking-shop Becomes Hyper-market," *The Economist,* February 1, 1992, p. 56.

20. M. Thatcher, *Britain and Europe* (Conservative Political Centre, 1988), p. 4. The pamphlet constitutes the text of Mrs. Thatcher's speech.

21. Ibid.

22. See chapter 6, and, above, n. 10.

23. Speaking to the TUC Congress. Quoted in House of Commons Library, *Brussels, Westminster and the Single European Act,* Background Paper No. 220 (House of Commons Library, 1988), pp. 21–22.

24. For a discussion of the report, and the position of the British government, see *The Delors Report: Fourth Report from the Treasury and Civil Service Select Committee,* Session 1988/89, HC 341 (Her Majesty's Stationery Office, 1989).

25. Among other provisions sought successfully by the U.K. government was recognition of the primacy of NATO in European defense, deletion (as we have already noted) of any reference to a "federal" Europe, and agreement to move forward in a number of areas—as in foreign policy—on the basis of intergovernmental agreement.

26. *House of Commons Debates (Hansard),* Vol. 208, cols. 597–600.

27. Former home secretary, Kenneth Baker. *House of Commons Debates (Hansard),* Vol. 212, col. 57.

28. P. Norton, "Parliament," in P. Catterall (ed.), *Contemporary Britain: An Annual Review 1993* (Blackwell, 1993).

29. The amendment concerned whether U.K. representatives should be elected or appointed by government. The defeat of the government was important more for

30. *Eurobarometer 36,* December 1991, Figure 1.6, p. 14.
31. *Eurobarometer 36,* December 1991, Figure 4.6, p. 56.

PART **IV**

Scrutiny and Legitimation

CHAPTER **11**

Parliament
Commmons and Lords

The United States has a bicameral legislature. In legislative matters, each house is the equal of the other.[1] Both houses are chosen by popular vote, albeit by differently defined constituencies. They are elected separately from the executive, and members of the two houses are precluded by the Constitution from holding any civil office under the authority of the United States. There is a formal separation between the executive and the legislative branches not only in personnel but also of powers. Congress displays the characteristics of what Michael Mezey has aptly termed an "active" legislature: Its policy-making power is strong and it enjoys popular support as a legitimate political institution.[2] Each house is master of its own timetable and proceedings.

In their behavior, not least in their voting behavior, senators and members of the House of Representatives are influenced by party, more so than is sometimes popularly supposed.[3] Nonetheless, though party is an important influence, it is not an exclusive one. Members of Congress are responsive to other influences. The political landscape bears the bodies of senators and representatives who, regardless of party, fell to the wrath of their electors because of their neglect of their constituencies or because of their stance on a particular issue. Although the initiative in policy making has passed largely to the executive, Congress remains an important part of the policy-making process. As Professor Mezey writes, "Even though a decline in the power and authority of the Congress has been announced on several different occasions, it remains today one of the few legislative institutions in the world able and capable of saying no to a popularly elected president and making it stick."[4]

The United Kingdom has also a bicameral legislature, but there the similarity ends. Of the two houses, only one—the House of Commons—is popularly elected. Members of the upper house, the House of Lords, serve by virtue of birth, by appointment for life, or because of the positions they hold. The two houses are no longer equal: The House of Commons as the elected chamber enjoys preeminence and can enforce its legislative will over the upper house under the provisions of the 1911 and 1949 Parliament Acts (see chapter 3). The executive, or rather the political apex of the executive (i.e., ministers), is drawn from Parliament—there is no separate election—and its members remain within Parliament. The executive dominates both the business program (deciding what will be debated and when) and the voting of Parliament, party serving as the means of that domination. Party cohesion is a feature of voting in the House of Commons. (The same is largely true of the House of Lords, though fewer votes take place there.) Party is the determining influence in an MP's election and it is normally the determining influence in his or her parliamentary behavior. Parliament exhibits the features of what Mezey has termed a "reactive" legislature: It enjoys popular support as a legitimate political institution but enjoys only modest power, if that, in policy making. Discussion of "the decline of Parliament" has been a characteristic feature of political discourse in Britain in recent years. MPs have on occassion been known to look with envy across the Atlantic at the power and influence of their U.S. counterparts.

The reasons for executive dominance of the legislature in Britain have been sketched already (chapter 3). For part of the nineteenth century, Parliament exhibited the characteristics of an "active" legislature. The 1832 Reform Act helped lessen the grip of the aristocracy and of the ministry on the House of Commons (seats were less easy to buy, given the size of the new electorate), allowing MPs greater freedom in their parliamentary behavior. Debates in the House could influence opinion and the outcome of votes was not a foregone conclusion. This period was short-lived. The 1867 Reform Act and later acts created a much larger and more demanding electorate. With the passage of the 1884 Representation of the People Act, a majority of working men were enfranchised. Electors were now too numerous to be bribed, at least by individual candidates. The result was that "organized corruption was gradually replaced by party organization,"[5] as one observer puts it, and both main existing parties were developed from small cadre parties to form mass-membership and complex organizations. Party organization made possible contact with the electors. To stimulate voting, candidates had to promise something to electors, and electoral promises could be met only if parties displayed sufficient cohesion in parliamentary organization to ensure their enactment.

Institutional and environmental factors combined to ensure that the pressures generated by the changed electoral conditions resulted in a House of Commons with low policy influence. Competition for the all-or-nothing spoils of a general election victory, the single-member constituency with a plurality method of election, and a relatively homogeneous population (relative to many other countries) would appear to have encouraged, if not always produced, a basic two-party as opposed to a multiparty system. One party was normally returned with an overall parliamentary majority. Given that the government was drawn from and remained within Parliament, the electoral fortunes of MPs depended primarily on the success or failure of that government. Government was dependent on the voting support of its parliamentary majority both for the passage of its promised measures and for its own continuance in office. Failure of government supporters to vote against a motion expressing "no confidence" in the government or, conversely, not to vote for an important measure that the government declared a "matter of confidence" would result in a dissolution. Within the House of Commons, party cohesion quickly became the norm.

Internal party pressures also encouraged MPs' willingness to defer to government. A member was chosen as a party candidate by the local party and was dependent on it for renomination as well as for campaign support. Assuming local party loyalty to the party leadership (an assumption that usually but not always could be made), local parties were unlikely to take kindly to any consistent dissent from "their" members. The norms of the constitution and of party structures also encouraged acquiescence. There were no career channels in Parliament alternative to those of government office, and a place in government was dependent on the prime minister, the *party* leader. Achieving a leadership position in the House meant, in effect, becoming a minister.

The nature of government decision making as well as the increasing responsibilities assumed by government also had the effect of moving policy making further from the floor of the House. The conventions of collective and individual ministerial responsibility helped provide a protective cloak for decision making within the Cabinet and within departments. Only the conclusions of discussions could be revealed. Furthermore, as government responsibilities expanded and became more dependent on the cooperation of outside groups (see chapter 7), government measures came increasingly to be the product of negotiation between departments and interest groups, who then presented those measures to Parliament as packages already agreed on. As the demands on government grew, these "packages" increased in extent and complexity. The House of Commons was called on primarily to approve measures drawn up elsewhere and for which it had neither adequate time nor resources to submit to sustained and informed debate.

Parliament thus came to occupy what was recognized as a back seat in policy making. This is not to say that it ceased to be an important political body. The government remained dependent on Parliament for its support, and both houses continued to provide significant forums of debate and scrutiny. In an important article in 1975, Nelson Polsby distinguished between transformative legislatures (enjoying an independent capacity, frequently exercised, to mold and transform proposals into law) and arena legislatures (providing a formal arena in which significant political forces could express themselves).[6] The British Parliament can most appropriately be described as having moved from being a transformative legislative in the second third of the nineteenth century to an arena legislature in the twentieth. The U.S. Congress, by contrast, has remained a transformative legislature.

THE HOUSE OF COMMONS

The events of the nineteenth century that served to transfer power from Parliament to the executive served also to ensure the dominance of the House of Commons within the triumvirate of monarch, Lords, and Commons. The Commons constitutes the only body of the three that is popularly elected. Indeed, its dominance has become such that there is a tendency for many to treat "House of Commons" and "Parliament" as almost synonymous terms. The attention accorded it by the media and outside observers is far more extensive than that accorded the House of Lords. It has a greater "working" membership and more importance is attached to the functions it is expected to fulfill.

Members

The House of Commons has a much larger membership than its U.S. equivalent. It has 651 members, each elected to serve a particular constituency (see chapter 5). The size of the House has varied, ranging from a twentieth-century high of 707 members (from 1918 to 1922, subsequently reduced because of the loss of most Irish seats) to a low of 615 (from 1922 to 1945). Since 1945, the size of the House has increased gradually as a result of the recommendations of the Boundary Commissions.

There is no formal limit on the number of terms an MP can serve. It is not uncommon for MPs representing safe seats to sit in the House for 20 or 30 years, sometimes longer. Of MPs returned at the 1992 general election, 12 had been first elected to the House before 1960. The MP with the longest continuous service in the House is given the courtesy title of "father of the House." Following the return of the new Parliament in 1992, the title fell to former prime minister Sir Edward Heath, an MP since 1950.

The House elects one of its members as speaker. The speaker is normally drawn from the majority party in the House, though once in office may serve in succeeding Parliaments despite a change of government. The House departed from this practice in 1992. Indeed, it broke from tradition in two ways. Although a Conservative government was returned to office, the House elected a Labour MP to the speakership. (The previous speaker had retired at the end of the preceding Parliament.) Furthermore, that Labour MP was a woman (Betty Boothroyd), the first female speaker in the history of Parliament. The speaker, once elected, disclaims any party affiliation and serves as an independent presiding officer. Though she or he enjoys important powers of discipline and some business management, much of the speaker's activity is governed by precedent, most of it embodied in the handbook of parliamentary practice, known as *Erskine May* (after the clerk in the nineteenth century responsible for its initial compilation); the speaker is also advised by the clerks, the full-time officers of the House of Commons. Three other members of the House are appointed to serve as deputy speakers.

Since 1945, MPs have become notably more middle class. Before the Second World War, and for a little time thereafter, the Parliamentary Labour party (the PLP) boasted a significant proportion of MPs from working-class backgrounds, often miners; the Conservative ranks were swelled by members of aristocratic families and very wealthy industrialists. As parliamentary work has become more demanding, and as salaries and resources have improved, more members drawn from the professions and from academia have entered the House. Today most MPs have university degrees and enter the House after a spell in business or the professions. Tables 11.1 and 11.2 show the backgrounds of members returned to the House in 1992. An increasing number are drawn from careers in the political world, either as party researchers or as representatives of groups making demands of government. Critics contend that such MPs have little knowledge of the world outside the political domain; their defenders point out that they enter the House well versed in the ways of government and hence are in a good position to influence government on behalf of their constituents.

MPs are more numerous than members of the U.S. House of Representatives. There is also another notable difference. MPs, compared with their U.S. (and indeed most Western) counterparts, are underpaid and under-resourced. The payment of salaries to MPs is a twentieth-century phenonomen—first introduced in 1912, when the princely sum of £400 ($620) was paid annually—and has generally lagged behind legislative salaries elsewhere and behind salaries of middle-level managers in the United Kingdom. Even in 1964 an MP enjoyed a salary of only £3,250 (just over $5,000)—and little else. Most MPs had no offices (they had to make do with lockers) and for research and information were dependent on the facilities of the Commons' Library, a body with limited staff. There were no secretarial or research allowances. A number of MPs could not afford to hire secretaries and some replied to constituents' letters in longhand.

Conditions have variously improved since then. Every MP now has desk space. Acquisition and conversion of various buildings close to the Palace of

TABLE 11.1 The educational background of MPs, 1992

Type of Education	Conservative	Labour	Liberal Democrat
Elementary	—	2	—
Elementary +	—	7	—
Secondary	19	34	2
Secondary + poly/college	28	61	2
Secondary + university	81	127	6
Public school	28	—	—
Pub sch + poly/college	16	2	1
Pub sch + university	164	38	9
Total	336	271	20
Oxford	83	28	4
Cambridge	68	16	2
Other universities	94	122	9
All universities	245	166	15
Eton	34	2	—
Harrow	7	—	—
Winchester	3	1	—
Other public schools	164	37	10
All public schools	208	40	10

SOURCE: Derived from B. Criddle, "MPs and Candidates," in D. Butler and D. Kavanagh (eds.), *The British General Election of 1992* (Macmillan, 1992), Table 10.3, p. 224.

TABLE 11.2 The occupational background of MPs, 1992

Occupation	Conservative	Labour	Liberal Democrat
Professions			
Barrister	39	9	5
Solicitor	21	8	1
Doctor/dentist	4	2	—
Architect/surveyor	3	—	—
Civil/chartered engineer	3	—	—
Accountant	12	2	—
Civil servant/local govt.	10	16	—
Armed services	14	—	1
Teachers			
University	4	14	1
Polytechnic/college	2	24	—
School	16	38	3
Other consultants	2	—	1
Scientific/research	1	2	—
Total	131	115	12
	(39%)	(42%)	(60%)
Business			
Company director	37	1	—
Company executive	75	8	2
Commerce/insurance	9	1	—
Management/clerical	4	11	—
General business	3	1	—
Total	128	22	2
	(38%)	(8%)	(10%)
Miscellaneous			
Miscellaneous white collar	9	36	1
Politician/pol. organizer	20	24	2
Publisher/journalist	28	13	3
Farmer	10	2	—
Housewife	6	—	—
Student	—	—	—
Total	73	75	6
	(22%)	(28%)	(30%)
Manual workers			
Miner	1	12	—
Skilled worker	3	43	—
Semi/unskilled worker	—	4	—
Total	4	59	0
	(1%)	(22%)	(—)
Grand Total	336	271	20

SOURCE: Derived from B. Criddle, "MPs and Candidates," in D. Butler and D. Kavanagh (eds.), *The British General Election of 1992* (Macmillan, 1992), Table 10.4, p. 226.

Westminster has meant an increasing number of members have their own offices. By the end of the 1990s every MP should have an office. (Though the MP's office will not necessarily be the same as the office occupied by the MP's secretary. The latter is allocated by the Serjeant at Arm's office—an administrative office of the Commons—and the former is allocated by the party whip's office—a political office. Consequently MPs can be several buildings away from their secretaries.) A secretarial allowance—of £500 ($775)—was introduced in 1969 and has since been increased to cover research as well as secretarial support: It is now known as the office cost allowance. Allowances have also been introduced to cover the cost of living away from one's main residence; for MPs representing seats in the capital there is a London supplement. Members have travel passes, with some provision made for spouses. Library facilities have also been expanded, in terms of personnel and resources. There is a computer retrieval system known as POLIS (parliamentary online information system) and greater space provision through the use of outlying parliamentary buildings. The office cost allowance now proves sufficient to hire additional secretarial help (an increasing number of MPs have a constituency-based secretary in addition to a Westminster-based secretary, though both are not necessarily full-time) and some research assistance. MPs voted, against the advice of government, to increase the office cost allowance by 50% in 1986 and by 40% in 1992. As a result of the latter vote, the allowance became £39,960 ($62,000), allowing—as a rough generalization—an MP to have a staff of two-and-a-half. An MP's annual salary is £30,854 (roughly $48,000). In terms of pay and resources, many MPs look with some envy (others, believing in frugality, with some distaste) at the position across the Atlantic—in Canada as well as the United States—as well as, in some instances, across the English Channel to bodies such as the German Bundestag.

The limited pay and resources almost certainly stimulate the ambition of MPs to become ministers. Ministers are paid separate ministerial salaries, enjoy the trappings of office (chauffeur-driven car, ministerial office and staff) and, as MPs, receive part of the parliamentary salary and remain eligible for the office cost allowance. In 1993, Cabinet ministers sitting in the House of Commons received £63,047 ($98,000), a figure including their parliamentary salaries (the prime minister and lord chancellor received more; Cabinet ministers in the House of Lords, other than the lord chancellor, received less); ministers of state received £51,402 ($80,000) and junior ministers £44,611 ($70,000), again with ministers in the Lords—and thus with no constituency responsibilities—receiving less.

Functions

The Commons, like other legislatures, is a multifunctional body: That is, it fulfills a variety of tasks in addition to the defining task of legislatures (that of giving assent). The most important twentieth-century functions of the Commons are those of providing the personnel of government, of legitimation, of debate, and of scrutinizing and influencing government. The list is not exhaustive, nor are the functions mutually exclusive.

Parliament provides the personnel of government—that is, ministers; by convention, most ministers, including the prime minister, are drawn from the Commons. This function is largely a passive one in that the House itself does not do the choosing. The outcome of a general election determines which party will form the government, and the prime minister chooses who will fill which ministerial posts. The House, nonetheless, exerts some influence. Ministers remain within the House. They have to cope with the demands of a sometimes rowdy

chamber and of supporters who may be less than happy with ministers' performances at the Commons' despatch box. A poor performance may hamper, on rare
occasions even destroy, a ministerial career.[7]

Legitimation is fundamental to the existence of Parliament. It constitutes the
core defining function of the institution and is the oldest function of the House
of Commons. Government requires the formal assent of Parliament both for the
passage of legislation and for the grant of money. Given the government's control
of a parliamentary majority, such assent is normally forthcoming. The giving of
this assent, however much it may be taken for granted, fulfills an important
symbolic role. It constitutes the elected assembly giving the seal of approval on
behalf of the citizenry. Furthermore, it is important because the House retains
the power to deny that assent. It may hardly ever use the power, but the option
to do so remains.

The function that is the most obvious manifestation of an arena legislature
is that of debate. Parliamentary debate forms a central mechanism for scrutinizing
and attempting to influence government, but serves also as an important safety
valve. The House provides an authoritative forum in which different and often
conflicting views in society can be given expression. The most structured
expression is through political parties, but MPs can also use the chamber to raise
the concerns of other groups in society and to express the specific views of
constituents. Debate takes place in public session and with ministers present to
hear what is said.

The House itself is not the government but government is drawn from it and
remains answerable to it. The House is thus uniquely placed to subject government
to scrutiny, and to seek to influence it, on behalf of the citizenry. The means
of scrutiny and influence are varied. They can be divided into those used for
legislation and those employed for executive actions.

Legislation

Legislation is subject to a well-defined procedure once it has been submitted for
parliamentary approval (see Table 11.3). First reading constitutes the formal
introduction of a bill. At this stage, it is not debated. Indeed, it does not even
exist in printed form. Once formally introduced, it is printed and set down for
its second reading. Compared with the analogous procedure in the U.S. Congress,
the second reading is distinct in two significant respects. First, it is the government
that determines when the debate will take place. (With the exception of 20
"opposition days," 3 estimates days, and a number of days—usually Fridays—
and certain specified debates given over to private members' bills and motions,
the government has control of the parliamentary timetable.) The Cabinet approves
legislation to be placed before Parliament and a Cabinet committee (the Queen's
Speech and Future Legislation Committee—see chapter 8) decides the program
for the forthcoming session. Second, the debate in plenary session precedes the
committee stage. On second reading, the principle of the bill is debated and
approved. Only after it has received its second reading is it referred to a committee
for consideration of its specific provisions.

TABLE 11.3 Legislative stages in Parliament

Stage	Where Taken	Comments
First reading	On the floor of the house	Formal introduction; no debate
Second reading	On the floor of the house*	Debate on the principle
[Money resolution: Commons]	On the floor of the house	
Committee	In standing committee in the Commons unless house votes otherwise (certain bills taken on the floor of the house); almost invariably on the floor of the house in the Lords	Considered clause by clause; amendments may be made
Report	On the floor of the house**	Bill reported back to house; amendments may be made
Third reading	On the floor of the house	Final approval; no amendments possible in the Commons
Lords (or Commons) amendments	On the floor of the house	Consideration of amendments made by other house

*In the Commons, noncontentious bills may be referred to a committee.
** If a bill is taken in committee of the whole House and no amendments are made, there is no report stage.
SOURCE: P. Norton, *Does Parliament Matter?* (Harvester Wheatsheaf, 1993), p. 73.

At committee stage, bills are considered by standing committees. The name is a misnomer: They are appointed on an ad hoc basis. A committee will be appointed to consider a specific bill and then, having completed its deliberations, ceases to exist in that form. (Committees are known by letters of the alphabet, such as Standing Committee A, and once a committee with the letter A has finished its deliberations, a new Standing Committee A will be appointed to consider another bill—but the members of the committee will be different.) Each committee has a membership of between 16 and 50 members, usually now 18 members for all but the largest and most contentious bills. They meet to discuss bills clause by clause. In practice, their ability to amend and influence the content of measures is circumscribed. Once the house has approved the principle of the measure, a committee cannot make any changes that run counter to the principle embodied in the bill. The greatest constraints, however, are political. The format adopted at committee meetings is an adversarial one: Government MPs sit on one side, opposition MPs on the other. Debate is usually along party lines, as is voting. The result is that the amendments that are carried are almost always those introduced by ministers.[8] (One or more ministers from the relevant department are always appointed to the committee.) Because most bills discussed by standing committees are introduced by the government, the main purpose of introducing government amendments is to correct drafting errors, improve the wording, or, more substantially, to meet points made by outside groups or meet points made by MPs that the government finds acceptable.

Standing committees thus differ considerably from their U.S. counterparts. They have no power to summon witnesses or evidence,[9] they are presided over by an impartial chairman (an MP drawn from a body of MPs appointed for their ability to chair such meetings), and they are confined in their deliberations solely to the content of bills. They have no power to undertake inquiries or to discuss anything other than the bill before them. The government's majority on a standing committee is in proportion to its majority in the house as a whole. Hence, as long as it has a majority in the house, it is ensured a majority on such committees. The result is that bills usually emerge from committees relatively unscathed. Unlike U.S. congressional committees, standing committees are not a burial ground for bills. Rather, they serve as temporary transit points in their passage.

Once a standing committee has completed its deliberations, a bill is then returned to the house for the report stage, during which the house may make further amendments. This stage is not dissimilar to the committee stage and the government may use it to introduce amendments that it had not been able to introduce in committee (for example, to meet points raised in committee but for which it had not had time to formulate a precise amendment). The outcome of votes on amendments is the same as in committee. Government amendments are normally carried. Amendments introduced by private members are usually defeated, unless they find favor with the government. The acceptance rate is similar to that in committee.[10]

All bills considered in standing committee go through a report stage. Certain important bills, such as those introducing constitutional change (for example, reform of the House of Lords), have their committee stage on the floor of the house. If they emerge from this stage without amendment, there is no report stage. In 1972, for example, the European Communities bill was taken on the floor of the house and was not amended. It thus proceeded directly to the final stage, that of third reading. At third reading, the house gives its final approval to a measure. Debate at this stage is usually shorter than on second reading, and it must be confined to the content of the bill. Suggestions for amendments are out of order.

Once the House has approved third reading, the bill is sent to the House of Lords. (The exceptions, of course, are any bills that originate in the Lords.) If the Lords make any amendments, these are then sent to the Commons. The house debates these amendments, usually on a motion to agree or disagree with them. If the House disagrees with a Lords amendment, this fact—along with the reasons for the disagreement—is communicated to the upper house. The House of Lords then usually concurs with the Commons and does not press its amendment. Once a bill has passed both houses, it proceeds for the Royal Assent.

Government bills dominate the legislative timetable. This is hardly surprising given the onus placed on government to initiate measures and the fact that the government controls the timetable. Up to 50 government bills are introduced and passed each year (see Table 11.4). Opportunities for private members to introduce bills of their own are limited. Certain Fridays each session (usually 10) are set aside to discuss private members' bills. So limited is the time available and so great the number of members wishing to introduce bills that a ballot is held each parliamentary session (that is, each year), and the resulting 20 top members have priority in introducing bills. In practice, only about the first 6 whose names are drawn out will stand much chance of getting their bills discussed,

TABLE 11.4 1987–1992 Parliament: Bills introduced

Session	Bills Introduced				
	Government			Private Members'*	
	Passed	Failed		Passed	Failed
1987–1988	49	0		13	109
1988–1989	37	0		9	136
1989–1990	34	2		11	120
1990–1991	49	3		19	103
1991–1992	33	6**		13	51
Total	202	11		65	519

* The number of private members' bills includes bills introduced in the House of Lords but never brought to the Commons.
** The high number of government bills failing in this session is because the session was cut short by the calling of the general election.
SOURCE: P. Norton, *Does Parliament Matter?* (Harvester Wheatsheaf, 1993), p. 55.

and even then there is no guarantee of the bills being passed. The opportunities available for a substantial or contested bill to get through all its stages during private members' time on Fridays are small. Such a bill will normally need more time than is available and will be dependent on government's finding time in its own timetable. The government is thus in a position to determine the fate of most private members' bills. It can deny such bills the necessary time to complete the required legislative stages or it can persuade its supporters to defeat them in a parliamentary vote. As a result, most private members' bills cover matters that are not politically contentious and are unlikely to arouse the opposition of government. (A fairly high number of such uncontentious bills are passed; 68 in the 1983–1987 Parliament and 65 in the 1987–1992 Parliament; see Table 11.4.)[11] A further important constraint is that such bills cannot make a charge on the public revenue: Only ministers can introduce bills that make such a charge.

Hence, the scope for legislative initiative by private members is limited but not nonexistent. Occasionally, a private member may introduce a bill on an important issue toward which the government is sympathetic and for which it is prepared to find time. This was the case especially in the 1960s, when a number of major social measures—reforming the law on abortion, divorce, homosexuality, and the death penalty—were enacted through private members' legislation.[12] The government left it up to the House, providing time where necessary in order for members to reach decisions. There has been no occasion since then of so many major measures being passed in a single Parliament. On occasion, though, an important bill does get through or prompts the government to introduce a measure of its own.[13]

The number of days the House spends in session each year is shown, for the 1987–1992 Parliament, in Table 11.5. About one-third of its time is taken up with debate on government bills. Less than 5% of its time is spent discussing private members' bills. Most of the rest of the time is given over to scrutinizing, in one form or another, the actions of government.

TABLE 11.5 The House of Commons: Sittings and parliamentary questions, 1987–1992

	Parliamentary Session				
	1987–1988[a]	*1988–1989*	*1989–1990*	*1990–1991*	*1991–1992[b]*
Number of days sitting	218	176	167	160	83
Number of hours sitting	1,978	1,581	1,468	1,373	695
Average length of sitting day	9 hrs.	9 hrs. 4 min.	8 hrs. 48 min.	8 hrs. 35 min.	8 hrs. 23 min.
Parliamentary questions:					
Oral[c]	24,940	23,932	24,687	5,811[d]	2,383[d]
Written	47,726	39,540	41,358	32,843	16,050

[a] Long session (spring 1987 to fall 1988).
[b] Short session because of the dissolution of Parliament in March 1992.
[c] Oral questions appearing on the Order Paper: Most receive a written answer.
[d] Following a change in procedure in 1990, only the top 30 or so questions tabled for oral answer appear on the Order Paper instead of—as previously—every question so tabled.
SOURCE: Figures derived from House of Commons, *Sessional Information Digest,* for each session.

Executive Actions

Ministers and civil servants spend most of their time pursuing and administering policies and programs for which legislative authority has already been given or for which authority is not necessary (for example, policies pursued under prerogative powers). Hence, the formal approval of Parliament is not required. Nonetheless, the House of Commons subjects such actions to scrutiny. Various devices are employed for this purpose, principally parliamentary questions, debates, select committees, early day motions, and—outside the formal procedures—correspondence and private party meetings.

Parliamentary Questions. Question Time is a feature of the House of Commons for which there is no parallel in the Congress of the United States. It has its origins in the eighteenth century and it entails the regular appearance of ministers, including the head of government, in the House to answer questions submitted by backbench MPs. (The rough equivalent in the U.S. Congress would be for Cabinet secretaries and the president to appear regularly on the floor of the House or Senate to answer questions, such sessions taking place several times a week.) Question Time in the House of Commons takes place each parliamentary sitting day, Monday to Thursday. (There is no Question Time when the House sits on a Friday.) Though sometimes referred to as "Question Hour," it lasts between 45 and 55 minutes. The house meets at 2:30 P.M., and Question Time begins following prayers and certain items of formal business. It finishes at 3:30 P.M. It is subject to well-defined procedures.[14] Ministers answer questions on a rota basis, each principal minister coming up on the rota every four weeks.

The prime minister has a regular twice-weekly slot, answering questions for 15 minutes from 3:15 to 3:30 on Tuesdays and Thursdays.

Each MP is restricted in the number of questions that can be submitted (eight in any ten sitting days and no more than two on any given day), though the number submitted remains substantial, averaging now more than 20,000 a session. As time only exists for about 20 questions to be dealt with in one Question Time, the questions are selected by a random "shuffle." All the questions submitted—sometimes numbering in the hundreds for a single day—used to be printed but now usually only the top 30 are published in the daily Order Paper (see Figure 11.1).

At Question Time, the MP whose question has come to the top in the shuffle rises and says, "Number One, Madam Speaker." The minister then rises to answer the question. Questions are submitted two weeks in advance, so ministers come armed with relevant information or responses compiled by their civil servants or special advisors and normally give prepared answers. Once the answer has been given, the speaker will then call on the MP who asked the question to put a supplementary, or follow-up, question. It is at the speaker's discretion as to how many supplementaries are allowed. If a member of the opposition front bench rises to put a supplementary, he or she enjoys priority over backbenchers. Having allowed one or more supplementaries—and rarely more than three or four—the speaker then calls the MP in whose name the second question stands. The MP rises, says, "Number Two, Madam Speaker," and the process is repeated. Questions that appear on the Order Paper but are not reached receive instead written answers that appear in *Hansard,* the official report of proceedings.

MPs also have the option of submitting questions for written answer. These are more numerous than questions tabled for an oral answer at Question Time: In some sessions, more than 40,000 are tabled. The answers, along with the questions, are published in *Hansard.* Written questions are popular as a means of eliciting statistics and other material that cannot easily be given in oral form. Oral questions, by contrast, are used to elicit statements and comments on government policy and matters that MPs thing might embarrass (or, if the MP is on the government side, help) government or generate favorable attention back in the constituencies.[15] Prime minister's Question Time has become a particular vehicle for the partisan clash between the parties, and especially between the prime minister and the leader of the opposition.

Debates. Various types of debate are held on the floor of the House of Commons. The most important can be classified as general debates, held to discuss particular government policies. These are usually of just over three or seven hours' duration. They start once any business after Question Time, such as ministerial statements, is concluded. A half-day debate lasts usually until 7:00 P.M. and a full day's debate until 10:00. Such debates take place on motions tabled by the government (for example, on motions to approve particular policies or to take note of particular documents) or, on 20 "opposition days," by opposition parties (the official opposition decides the topic on 17 days, the third largest party—presently the Liberal Democrats—on the other 3 days). General debates

ORDER PAPER

PRIVATE BUSINESS AFTER PRAYERS

CONSIDERATION OF LORDS AMENDMENTS

BILL WITH AMENDMENTS

Dawat-e-Hadiyah Bill.

[*Copies of the Amendments may be obtained by Members from the Vote Office or inspected in the Private Bill Office.*]

★ *Indicates a Question for Oral Answer*

QUESTIONS FOR ORAL ANSWER

★1 **Mr Neil Gerrard** (Walthamstow):   To ask the President of the Board of Trade, what assessment he has made of the impact of local government reform on the work of trading standards officers.

★2 **Mr Peter Mandelson** (Hartlepool):   To ask the President of the Board of Trade, what plans he has to strengthen the manufacturing base of the North East.

★3 **Estelle Morris** (Birmingham, Yardley):   To ask the President of the Board of Trade, when he expects to make a statement on the future of the Post Office.

★4 **Mr David Clelland** (Tyne Bridge):   To ask the President of the Board of Trade, what plans his Department now has to ask the European Commission for access to the intervention funds for British war shipyards; and if he will make a statement.

★5 **Mr Geoffrey Dickens** (Littleborough and Saddleworth):   To ask the President of the Board of Trade, if he will make a statement on recent trends in (a) exports and (b) imports; and if he will make a statement.

★6 **Mr William McKelvey** (Kilmarnock and Loudoun):   To ask the President of the Board of Trade, if he will give the date on which he received the last representations on consumer guarantees; and when he expects to announce the results of his consultation.

★7 **Mrs Ann Winterton** (Congleton):   To ask the President of the Board of Trade, what steps he is taking to remove unnecessary administrative and regulatory burdens upon businesses.

★8 **Mr Nicholas Winterton** (Macclesfield):   To ask the President of the Board of Trade, what steps he is taking to prevent the erosion of the United Kingdom's manufacturing base.

★9 **Mr Robert N. Wareing** (Liverpool, West Derby):   To ask the President of the Board of Trade, what representations he has received alleging abuses of monopoly power within the brewery industry; what his response has been; and if he will make a statement.

★10 **Mr Bill Etherington** (Sunderland North):   To ask the President of the Board of Trade, how many requests he has received from British Coal for a portion of the subsidy for expanding the coal market.

★11 **Mr Edward O'Hara** (Knowsley South):   To ask the President of the Board of Trade, if he will make a statement about recent discussions between his Department and the administrators of Polly Peck.

FIGURE 11.1   Questions on the House of Commons Order Paper, June 23, 1993. Questions continue on subsequent pages of the Order Paper. (Copyright 1993 by the Crown. Reprinted by permission of the Controller of Her Majesty's Stationery Office.)

are also held at the beginning of the parliamentary session on the Debate on the Address. Following the Queen's Speech opening the new session, in which government policy for the year is announced, a five-day debate is held. Formally, it takes place on an address to the queen, thanking her for her gracious speech, but in practice it covers particular government policies: One day, for example, is normally given over to a discussion of foreign affairs.

The other main type of debate is the adjournment debate. In practice, there are two forms of adjournment debate. One is the same essentially as a general debate; the only difference is that no substantive motion is before the house. Instead, a motion to adjourn is put down as a way of allowing debate to range freely on a topic for which the government has no specific policy or action that it wishes to be approved. In short, it is a useful means of sounding out the opinion of the House. At the end of such debates, the motion to adjourn is generally negatived without a vote. The other type of adjournment debate is known as the half-hour adjournment debate and is held at the end of each day's sitting, usually from 10:00 to 10:30 P.M., on Mondays through Thursdays (2:00 to 2:30 P.M. on Fridays). These debates allow an MP, chosen usually after a ballot, to raise an issue, usually of constituency interest, for about 15 minutes, and allow the relevant minister (traditionally a junior minister) about 15 minutes to respond to the points made. After exactly 30 minutes have elapsed, the House is automatically adjourned. These short debates take up little time but are extremely popular with backbench MPs, allowing them to raise constituency problems or important but nonparty issues (for example, problems such as gambling, drug misuse, or the transferability of pensions). MPs raising the issues normally give ministers advance information of the points they intend to raise, thus allowing for a full reply to be prepared.

There are one or two other forms of debate, the most important but rarely employed being that of the emergency debate. A member can ask leave to move the adjournment of the House "for the purpose of discussing a specific and important matter that should have urgent consideration." If the MP can convince the speaker that the matter (1) deserves urgent attention, (2) falls within the responsibility of government, and (3) cannot be raised quickly by another procedure, then the debate may be granted. If the debate is granted, it takes place the next day (or the following Monday if granted on a Thursday) or, if the speaker considers that the urgency of the matter justifies it, that same evening at 7:00 P.M. In practice, the speaker tends to dislike the interruptions to scheduled business caused by such debates, and few are granted: on average, only about four a session. They nonetheless constitute a useful safety valve function, allowing members to discuss an important topic on occasion that the government had not proposed to have discussed.

Of these various types of debate, general debates take up the most time. About 10% of the House's time is taken up with debates on government motions. The format of such debates is similar to that of second reading debates. A government minister moves the motion; an opposition front-bench spokesman speaks (each probably for half an hour or more, the minister in particular reading from a prepared brief); then backbench MPs speak, called alternately from each side of the House; then an opposition front-bench spokesman winds up for the opposition and a minister concludes for the government. Ministers and opposition front-bench spokesmen tend to dominate not only in terms of the time they take but also in the audience they attract. Few MPs remain to listen to the speeches of backbench MPs. Instead, they tend to leave the chamber, returning when the final front-bench speeches are being made and in time for the vote (if there is to be one). In practice, any debate thus takes place among very few members. Indeed, it is a misnomer to refer to "debates." Most speeches are delivered from prepared notes and often have little relevance to the speeches that have preceded them. Nonetheless, any member wishing to have a speech appear in *Hansard* has to be present, catch the speaker's eye, and deliver it. There is no procedure in debate analogous to the U.S. practice that allows for material to be inserted in the official record without it having been presented verbally in the chamber.

Select Committees.   Away from the floor of the House, the most important device employed for the scrutiny of the executive is that of select committees. These committees have responsibility for maintaining scrutiny of particular departments or sectors of government responsibility, though they have no responsibility for the formal scrutiny and approval of legislation (that is the function of the separate standing committees, unlike the procedure in the United States, where the two responsibilities are combined in congressional standing committees). Select committees have been variously utilized in past centuries[16] but not on any consistent or comprehensive basis. Only two such committees have existed as important committees for any length of time. One is the Public Accounts Committee, first appointed in 1861 to ensure that public expenditure was properly incurred for the purpose for which it had been voted. Over time the committee has interpreted more widely its terms of references, conducting value-for-money exercises and investigating possible negligence. The committee has developed a reputation as a thorough and authoritative body, its recommendations resulting in government action to implement them or to provide a reasoned response to them. Traditionally, the committee is chaired by an opposition MP. The other important committee was the Estimates Committee: Unlike the Public Accounts Committee, it no longer exists. It was first appointed in 1912 and, after being suspended from 1914 to 1921, existed until 1971. It was appointed to look at the annual estimates and to consider ways in which policies could be carried out more cost-efficiently. It was not supposed to consider the merits of policies but after 1945 began to venture into areas that could not be described as solely administrative. However, it was hampered by limited resources both in staff and in terms of the information presented to it by government. In 1971 it was replaced by a larger committee, the Expenditure Committee, itself divided into functional subcommittees. This committee disappeared in 1979, when a new system of committees was introduced.

The Select Committee on Nationalized Industries was formed in 1955 and a number of similar committees formed in the latter half of the 1960s. These later committees were disparate in the range of areas covered and vulnerable to government displeasure: One—a committee on agriculture—was wound up after encountering Foreign Office opposition to an inquiry it wanted to carry out in Brussels. In 1978, a Commons procedure committee recommended that if Commons scrutiny of the executive was to be effective, a new committee system was necessary, created on a systematic and permanent basis. Pressure for the creation of such a committee system built up within the house, and in 1979 the new Conservative leader of the house, Norman St. John-Stevas, brought forward motions for the appointment of the recommended committees. By 248 votes to 12, the House approved the creation of a such committees to "examine the expenditure, administration, and policy of the principal Government Departments . . . and associated public bodies." Twelve committees were agreed upon, though a further two—covering Scottish and Welsh affairs—were added shortly afterward. There have been some variations in numbers since.[17] Following the 1992 general election, a total of 16 committees were appointed. The committees are listed in Table 11.6. They are generally referred to as departmental select committees, thus distinguishing them from the other select committees of the House, including "domestic" select committees covering such matters as procedure, privileges, catering, and administration.

The committees have faced a number of problems. Each committee now has 11 members and usually meets once a week for about 90 minutes. Of necessity, each has to be selective in its choice of topics for investigation and in deciding whether to opt for short- or long-term studies, and whether to focus on policy,

TABLE 11.6   House of Commons: Departmental select committees, appointed July 1992

Committee	Chairman
Agriculture	Jerry Wiggin (Con.)
Defence	Sir Nicholas Bonsor (Con.)
Education	Sir Malcolm Thornton (Con.)
Employment	Ron Leighton (Lab.)
Environment	Robert Jones (Con.)
Foreign Affairs	David Howell (Con.)
Health	Marion Roe (Con.)
Home Affairs	Sir Ivan Lawrence (Con.)
National Heritage*	Gerald Kaufman (Lab.)
Science and Technology*	Sir Giles Shaw (Con.)
Scottish Affairs**	William McKelvey (Lab.)
Social Security	Frank Field (Lab.)
Trade and Industry	Richard Caborn (Lab.)
Transport	Robert Adley (Con.)
Treasury and Civil Service	John Watts (Con.)
Welsh Affairs	Gareth Wardell (Lab.)

Con. = Conservative, Lab. = Labour
* New committees established in July 1992. At the same time, the Energy Committee was abolished.
** Re-appointed after being in abeyance in the 1987–1992 Parliament.

estimates, or administration (few have opted for estimates).[18] They have limited resources: usually one full-time clerk each, secretarial support, and, in some cases, one or two specialist assistants, with some specialist advisors drawn from outside institutions and paid on a per diem basis. They have the formal power to "send for persons, papers and records," but that is of limited use in ensuring the attendance of ministers and other parliamentarians. (An order to attend, if ignored, can be enforced only by a resolution of the House, which is unlikely to be forthcoming against the wishes of government.) Civil servants attend on behalf of their ministers and cannot express personal opinions or reveal any internal advice given to ministers. The relationship of the committees to the floor of the house is limited. The three estimates days each year are used to discuss committee reports, but that allows for less than 2% of reports to be debated. Other reports may be mentioned ("tagged") on the Order Paper when a relevant debate occurs and occasionally there may be a special debate on a particular report, but there is no automatic procedure under which a committee can ensure its report is considered by the House. And, ultimately, the government may choose to ignore the recommendations of the committees. Though the government is committed to publishing a response to each report, it is not committed to taking any further action on them.

Yet, despite these limitations, the committees have proved to be major improvements on their predecessors. They have proved to be more extensive and thorough in their scrutiny, have operated as identifiable and often cohesive units, and have attracted the enthusiasm of members: They are usually well attended and—unlike most standing committees—there is demand to join them. They have proved to be prolific: In the first three Parliaments of their existence (that is, from 1979 to 1992) they issued just over 900 substantive reports. (Examples of committee reports are shown in Table 11.7.) They have attracted

TABLE 11.7 Select committee reports, session 1991–1992: Defence, Health, and Home Affairs Committees

Committee	Substantive Reports
Defence	Anglo-French defense cooperation
	Procurement of advanced air-to-air missiles
	Options for change: Army
	Options for change: Reserve forces
	Progress of the Trident program
	European fighter aircraft
Health	Financing of private residential and nursing home fees
	Maternity services
	European Community and health policy
Home Affairs	Fire safety and policing of the Channel Tunnel
	Annual report of HM chief inspector of fire services
	Electoral counting methods
	Police complaints procedure

SOURCE: House of Commons, *Sessional Information Digest 1991–92* (Her Majesty's Stationery Office, 1992).

more extensive media attention than their predecessors and they have become significant targets for representations from outside groups, something that never happened before. By their evidence-taking—and most committee sessions are used to take evidence from ministers, civil servants, or representatives of outside bodies (see Table 11.8)—they have served to obtain information that otherwise would not be on the public record and also have served to inform debate. By taking evidence from outside bodies, they have provided the House with advice additional, or as an alternative, to that offered by government. They also have provided groups with an authoritative forum in which to make their views known and get them on the public record. They also have variously served to have some influence on public policy. That impact has varied from committee to committee and is not amenable to precise quantification (government will not always give committees credit for a particular proposal) but there is some evidence of influence. The Foreign Affairs Committee, for example, influenced both British and Canadian governments on the patriation of the Canadian Constitution, the Energy Committee influenced the fiscal regime on North Sea oil, and the Home Affairs Committee got the government to repeal a particular criminal offense.[19] When the government did attempt to quantify the number of committee recommendations it had accepted in a single year, the number totalled 150.[20] It has to be recorded, though, that the recommendations accepted were not on matters of high policy.

Early Day Motions.   Early day motions (EDMs) are put down by members, technically for debate ''on an early day.'' In practice, there is no time available to debate them. Rather, given that they are published, they serve as a means of expressing a written opinion. Members can and do add their signatures to such motions and the number of names a motion attracts serves as some indication of opinion within the House. A large number of signatures may occasionally influence the government to take action or may seriously embarrass it. In 1988, an EDM tabled by two former Conservative Cabinet ministers calling for the immediate abolution of the Inner London Education Authority (ILEA—see chapter 9) attracted so many signatures from Conservative MPs that the government decided to act on it. In 1992, the ''fresh start'' motion on the European Community signed by nearly 70 Conservative MPs (see chapter 10) signalled the growing disquiet about the Maastricht Treaty on the Conservative benches. Such occasions, though, are rare. The impact of EDMs is limited by the large number tabled, now more than a thousand a year, and by the range of topics covered. Some are essentially flippant or congratulatory (congratulating some prominent figure on a recent achievement, for example), whereas others express opinions on important issues of policy. Members are free to submit and to sign as many motions as they like. Some rarely do so; others have a reputation for signing every motion with which they have some sympathy. (At least one has been known to sign two motions that were mutually exclusive.) As a result, the significance of such motions is effectively diluted.

Correspondence.   Members do not rely solely on formal procedures. They can and do write to ministers, normally to elicit information and to convey the

TABLE 11.8 Select committees: Meetings in public in the period February 22–26, 1993

MONDAY, FEBRUARY 22
PUBLIC ACCOUNTS
Subject: Major projects statement 1991
Witness: Dr. M. McIntosh, Chief of Defence Procurement, Ministry of Defence

WELSH AFFAIRS
Subject: Preservation of historic buildings and ancient monuments
Witnesses: Historic Buildings Council, Royal Commission on Ancient and Historical Monuments
             in Wales

TUESDAY, FEBRUARY 23
FOREIGN AFFAIRS
Subject: Role of the United Nations
Witness: Ambassador Sahnoun, Former Special Representative of the United Nations in Somalia

WEDNESDAY, FEBRUARY 24
ENVIRONMENT
Subject: Housing Corporation
Witnesses: National Federation of Housing Association Officials

PARLIAMENTARY COMMISSIONER FOR ADMINISTRATION
Subject: Reports of the Health Service for 1991–1992
Witnesses: South West Thames Regional Health Authority; Tayside Health Board

FOREIGN AFFAIRS
Subject: Europe after Maastricht
Witness: Rt. Hon. Lord Lawson of Blaby

AGRICULTURE
Subject: Changes in the Hill Livestock Compensatory Allowances
Witnesses: U.K. Agriculture Departments

HOME AFFAIRS
Subject: Legal Aid: The lord chancellor's proposals
Witnesses: Bar Council and Law Society; Rt. Hon. Lord Mackay of Clashfern, lord chancellor

EDUCATION
Subject: Special educational needs
Witnesses: Association of Educational Psychologists; National Association for Special
             Educational Needs

EMPLOYMENT
Subject: Unemployment levels and "Workfare"
Witness: Rt. Hon. Gillian Shephard MP, secretary of state for employment

HEALTH
Subject: Community care
Witnesses: Institute of Health Services Management; Association of Directors of Social Services

PUBLIC ACCOUNTS
Subject: Police cell accommodation
Witness: Sir C. Whitmore GCB, CVO, permanent undersecretary of state, Home Office

TREASURY AND CIVIL SERVICE
Subject: European Community monetary and budgetary matters
Witnesses: Bank of England officials

SOURCE: House of Commons, *Weekly Information Bulletin,* No. 26, February 27, 1993.

284

grievances, demands, and opinions of constituents and of different interests.[21] Letter writing is an extensive activity, with between 10,000 and 20,000 letters a month being written by MPs to those of their number who are ministers. When a constituent writes to an MP, the MP will normally pass the letter on to the minister, requesting a response; there are printed cards available for the MP to use. A letter from an MP receives priority within a government department. A letter from a member of the public normally receives a reply from a civil servant. A letter from an MP must by convention be replied to by a minister. An MP's letter thus ensures that the particular issue reaches the minister's desk. In replying, ministers are not subject to the same time and partisan constraints that apply on the floor of the House. A detailed response can be and often is given, and this is then sent by the MP to the constituent.

In writing to ministers, MPs are acting as important links between citizens and ministers. More than 10% of constituents communicate with their member of Parliament.[22] Survey data also show that, in the event of a harmful measure being considered by Parliament, most contituents "would" write to their MP—the most popular course of personal action—and a plurality believe that this constitutes the "most effective" course to take.[23] Writing to ministers following receipt of constituents' letters is also a time-efficient process of communication for MPs: It is a task undertaken at a time convenient to them, or at least less inconvenient than other means—such as questions for oral answer—that require their presence at a particular place at a particular time. If a minister's reply proves unsatisfactory to the member, then these other devices may be used.

Private Party Meetings.   Both the Conservative and Labour parliamentary parties have a reasonably extensive organization. Apart from weekly plenary meetings of the party, each has a series of party committees. The Conservative committees tend to meet more regularly and be more active than Labour committees.[24] Such committees cover particular sectors—foreign affairs, finance, trade and industry, and so on—and meet to listen to invited speakers, to discuss forthcoming business, and to question ministers (or, in opposition, opposition frontbenchers). Meetings are in private, thus providing an opportunity for plain speaking between backbenchers and frontbenchers. Each Conservative committee meeting is normally attended by a whip, and if there are serious expressions of dissent on a particular issue this is reported back to the chief whip and, if the dissent is serious and on a major issue, to the Cabinet. If a Conservative minister encounters problems with the relevant backbench committee, this may cause the minister to modify or even abandon the particular policy (more likely the former) and may harm the minister's reputation and future career prospects. Any Conservative MP can attend a Conservative committee meeting, and a large attendance can often signal widespread concern or dissent. (Attendance is normally fairly low, with numbers often not reaching double figures.) When the trade and industry secretary, Michael Heseltine, announced extensive—and unpopular—closures of coal pits in 1992, his appearance before the party's back-bench trade and industry committee drew more than 150 MPs and signalled to the minister the need to modify his plans.

These, then, constitute the primary devices available to members of Parliament to debate and scrutinize the actions of government. Most such devices are long-standing ones, though used more often in recent years than they were previously. Others are of recent origin. Indeed, the House has witnessed significant developments in recent years which, in the view of some observers, have made it a more effective instrument of scrutiny and influence. Others, as we shall see, consider the changes inadequate as a means of ensuring that the House can constrain an ever-growing executive.

Recent Developments

Given the stranglehold of party throughout most of the twentieth century, the House of Commons has been an essentially closed institution. For any groups or individuals wanting to have some input, the route has been through party. If party has proved unresponsive, there has been little scope for having much, if any, impact. Recent decades have seen the emergence of a relatively more open institution. Party remains preeminent but not quite on the same scale as before.

This change is the result of several independent developments that, in combination, have had an important, in some respects dramatic, effect on the House. They can be grouped under two heads. The first is the increased demands made of the house. The second is the greater attractiveness of the House in meeting those demands.

Greater Demands.   MPs have been subject to increasing demands made by constituents and by pressure groups. The increase in constituency demands has occurred over the past three decades, but has been pronounced in the 1980s and the 1990s.[25] The main channel for such demands has been correspondence, though an increasing number of constituents—especially in London seats—use the telephone. A typical MP now receives more than 150 letters a week, receiving in one day the amount of correspondence that the MP in the 1960s used to receive in one week. Several million letters flow each year from constituents and groups to MPs, generating for members a large increase in work and constituency casework. Such correspondence is supplemented by constituency "surgeries," members making themselves available at set times at set places in their constituencies so constituents wishing to see them in person can do so. The average MP will hold at least two surgeries a month, some one or more each week. Interviews with new MPs returned in 1992 revealed that the biggest surprise to them was the volume of correspondence they received. The most used question in conversation between them, as one put it, was, "How big is your backlog?"[26]

As we have seen in chapter 7, there also has been a massive increase in parliamentary lobbying by pressure groups. Groups now inundate MPs with briefing material and requests to take action. We have recorded the findings of a 1986 survey of more than 250 organized interests that found that three-quarters maintained regular or frequent contact with MPs. Of those maintaining such contact, over 80% had asked MPs to table parliamentary questions for them, and most had asked members to table motions and amendments to bills, and arrange meetings for them at the House of Commons (see Table 11.9). As we have seen (chapter 7), the use of professional lobbyists—little known before 1979—is now common.

The explanations for the increased demand made of MPs are varied. Those that explain the increase in lobbying by pressure goups were identified in chapter 7. Since 1979, government has been seen as adopting an arm's-length relationship with interest groups. In terms of economic resources, groups have had to compete with one another for the same share of an economic cake that is not greatly expanding. They have therefore looked for new routes to have some input into, and influence on, public policy making. For constituents, the expansion of government activity and, in particular, the creation of the welfare state has brought them into more regular contact with public bodies and therefore increased the potential for some grievance against a public agency or particular public official. Increased educational opportunities and television reporting of proceedings have also increased awareness of the availability of members of Parliament; and the more members have done for constituents the more other constituents have learned about and made use of them.[27]

In terms of effect, MPs have generally achieved the response desired by constituents, who more often than not want an authoritative explanation or some other information rather than a changed decision. One 1990 survey of more than 700 constituency letters found that more than 60% wanted provision of further information or confirmation that the matter was in hand.[28] Members have been able to satisfy those demands, usually through writing to ministers. They also frequently have been able to meet the demands of pressure groups. The 1986 survey of organized interests found that more than 90% of those that maintained contact with MPs rated that contact useful or very useful, and of those

TABLE 11.9 Use made of MPs by interest groups*

	Answering "yes"	
	n	%
Q: *Have you ever asked an MP to:*		
Put down a parliamentary question?	157	83.1
Table a motion?	97	51.3
Introduce or sponsor a private member's bill?	70	37.0
Table an amendment to a bill?	117	61.9
Arrange a meeting for you or your organization at the House of Commons?	148	78.3
Arrange a dinner or reception or similar function at the House of Commons?	78	41.3
Arrange a meeting with a minister?	94	49.7
Total respondents	*189*	

* From a 1986 survey of 253 organized interests. Responses of 189 that maintained regular or frequent contact with MPs.
SOURCE: M. Rush, *Parliament and Pressure Politics* (Oxford University Press, 1990), p. 281.

that had attempted to influence legislation through MPs, an absolute majority (55%) rated their efforts as quite or very successful; less than 6% rated their efforts as unsuccessful.[29]

Greater Attractiveness.   The House has come under greater demand from constituents and pressure groups and, independent of those demands, has seen changes—essentially internal to the House—that have had the consequence of making it a more attractive institution to those seeking to influence it. The most important changes have been in terms of MPs themselves— their ambitions and their parliamentary behavior—and the structures of the House.

Members' Ambitions.   As we have seen, MPs are more middle class than before. They also are more career oriented. Recent decades have witnessed the emergence of the careerist MP—wanting to make a full-time, and a lifetime's, career in Parliament—displacing the MP who had independent means and other interests, and for whom reelection to the House was not crucial for fulfilling a lifetime's ambition.[30] For the careerist MP, reelection is essential. Given the waning of the class-party nexus (see chapter 5), the support of class supporters in safe seats cannot be taken for granted in the way that it could be in earlier decades. This would appear to motivate a greater orientation on the part of new members to constituency service. Recent years have witnessed greater constituency activity, with newly elected MPs more likely than ever before to live in their constituencies.[31] MPs, especially new MPs, thus appear responsive to constituency demands— indeed, some now seeking out constituency problems, rather than waiting for problems to be brought to them[32]—and there is some evidence of an electoral reward for such activity. First-term MPs up for reelection in the 1987 general election did consistently better than other candidates—incumbents and challengers—establishing, in effect, a ''personal vote'' that was crucial in a number of marginal seats.[33] Constituency work adds enormously to the burden of work of MPs, but brings rewards for them in the form usually of job satisfaction and possibly extra votes—and to the House in terms of enhanced legitimacy. MPs are seen to be fulfilling the task expected of them by constituents.[34]

Parliamentary Behavior.   There also has been a change in MPs' behavior in the House. They are relatively more independent of party than they were for the first seven decades of the twentieth century. Though party cohesion remains the norm, there has been some erosion since 1970. At the beginning of the 1970s, Conservative backbenchers proved more willing than ever before to vote against their own side, to do so in greater numbers, and with much more effect.[35] On six occasions, the Heath government lost votes in the Commons' division lobbies. This behavioral change extended to the Labour benches when Labour was returned to power in 1974 and continued after the return of a Conservative government in 1979.[36] Large overall majorities meant that the Conservative governments, especially those of 1983 to 1992, could absorb most instances of cross-voting by disaffected supporters, but what was remarkable— and unprecedented—during this period was that there were occasions when a large overall majority was not sufficient to stave off defeat or the threat of defeat. In 1986, the Thatcher government lost a bill—the Shops bill, to deregulate Sunday trading—when 72 Conservative MPs voted with Labour MPs to defeat it;[37] on other occasions, the government withdrew proposals to avoid defeat. The return of a Conservative government with an overall majority of 21 in 1992 made it particularly vulnerable to backbench pressure.[38]

The explanation for this behavioral change is not to be found in the "new breed" of careerist MP entering Parliament. There is no correlation between dissenting behavior and date of first election.[39] A more plausible explanation, according to my own research, is that it was initially triggered by the prime ministerial leadership style of Edward Heath. His failure to listen to his own backbenchers and to take any action to meet their disquiet led them to take the only remaining means available of making their position clear: voting against the government on the floor of the House.[40] Once triggered, there was no returning to earlier practices of unthinking loyalty; and, indeed, as the incidence of dissent increased, so it encouraged a change of attitude on the part of many MPs, discarding their old deferential attitude toward government in favor of what Samuel Beer has termed a more "participant" attitude.[41]

This change in attitude motivated MPs to press for better resources and facilities to scrutinize and influence government. It also made members more attractive to pressure groups. They were now relatively more receptive to information and advice flowing in from outside and, because of their change of behavior, more likely to be able to take some action that would result in some substantive change to a particular measure.[42] Party remains the dominant influence on MPs, overwhelmingly so, but it is no longer the exclusive influence that it once was.

Structural Change.   The change of attitude on the part of many MPs in the 1970s generated demands for better structures and resources that would permit them to do a more effective job of scrutinizing government. The result was a number of structural and procedural reforms, often carried by the House against the wishes of government. Several of these were carried in the 1979–1983 Parliament, foremost among them being the establishment of the departmental select committees. The House also passed, against the initial opposition of the government, the National Audit Act, forming a new National Audit Office to undertake efficiency audits of departments; under the comptroller and auditor general, its reports are considered by the Public Accounts Committee. The House also approved the establishment of three estimates days each year to discuss specific estimates—and now used for debates of select committee reports—and introduced provision for some bills to be referred to committees that could take evidence on them (special standing committees), though a provision used only in respect so far of five bills.[43]

The creation of the select committees has proved especially important from the perspective of interest groups. The committees, as we have seen in chapter 7, provide a clear focus of the attention for such groups. Groups can now target their resources in a way they could not do before. The departmental select committees, as we have noted, act as magnets for group attention. Of the groups questioned in the 1986 survey of organized interests, almost two-thirds (65.6%) had given evidence to select committees (approximately half had given oral evidence); of these, more than 85% thought their evidence had had "some" impact or a "significant" impact on the resulting report.[44]

The other major change coming under this head has been televised coverage of proceedings. The House of Lords admitted the television cameras in 1985. The House of Commons voted to admit them in 1988 and transmission began in November 1989. The cameras cover proceedings on the floor of the house and in committee. Committee coverage has been more extensive than parliamentarians originally expected, and viewing figures for a number of programs dedicated to parliamentary proceedings also have been higher than expected.[45] Television coverage gives MPs some political leverage in their scrutiny of government—any slip on the part of ministers will now be more visible—and makes them more visible to constituents, probably encouraging greater contact between constituents and their MPs. Televised proceedings also add to the attractiveness of the House to interest groups: If they can persuade members, or a select committee, to pursue their cause, it may attract some televised coverage.[46]

These various changes have coalesced to create a much busier, and more effective, House of Commons. However, they have not stilled pressure for more radical reform.

THE HOUSE OF LORDS

The House of Lords was gradually forced in the nineteenth and early twentieth century to accept a subordinate position in its relationship with the House of Commons. The reason for this is clear. It was well stated by the earl of Shaftesbury during debates on the 1867 Reform bill. "So long as the other House of Parliament was elected upon a restricted principle," he declared, "I can understand that it would submit to a check from a House such as this. But in the presence of this great democratic power and the advance of this great democratic wave . . . it passes my comprehension to understand how an hereditary House like this can hold its own."[47] Although not altogether swept away by this "great democratic wave," the House was at least to be swamped by it. It could not maintain a claim to equal status with the elected House, a house elected on an ever-widening franchise.

It is clear that the House of Lords cannot sustain a claim to being a representative chamber. Peers represent no one but themselves: Their writs of summons are personal. No member serves by virtue of election. A peer is a member of the upper house either by virtue of birth (hereditary peers), by virtue of appointment by the Crown on the advice of the prime minister (life peers and hereditary peers of first creation), or by virtue of position (lords of appeal in ordinary; the archbishops of Canterbury and York; the bishops of London, Durham, and Winchester; and 21 other bishops of the Church of England in order of seniority). They are divided into the Lords Temporal and the Lords Spiritual.

The Lords Temporal are the hereditary and life peers, comprising (in order of seniority) the ranks of duke, marquess, earl, viscount, and baron. There are hereditary peers of all ranks, life peers being created only as barons. The Lords Spiritual comprise the archbishops and the senior bishops representing the established Anglican Church, the only members of the House who may be deemed to sit in some albeit tenuous form of representative capacity.

There are now more than 1,200 peers (1,213 at the end of 1992), making it the largest legislative assembly in the world sitting on a regular basis. (The Russian Congress of People's Deputies is bigger but sits irregularly.) In practice, many peers do not attend, for reasons of infirmity, other commitments, lack of interest, or simply physical location; some live in distant and rural parts of the United Kingdom and a number live abroad. About 800 attend one or more sittings of the House a year, and the average daily attendance is just over 300 (see Table 11.10). As a proportion of the total, life peers are more active than hereditary peers. Life peerages were introduced under the provisions of the 1958 Life Peerages Act and made possible the introduction of new blood to the upper house, especially that drawn from the ranks of those who disliked the hereditary principle (notably Labour party supporters). Life peerages also served to prevent the inflation of membership, as the title—and eligibility to sit in the Lords—dies with the holder. There are almost 400 life peers, and elevation to the House of Lords is in practice now usually by the conferment of a life peerage. Labour Prime Minister Harold Wilson suspended the conferment of hereditary peerages in 1964, a suspension continued by his successors until 1983. Mrs. Thatcher created three hereditary peerages; her successor has not appointed any, but has not ruled out the possibility of doing so.

Given that it is not an elected body and it occupies a subordinate position in relation to the House of Commons, what functions are performed by the House?

TABLE 11.10 Increased activity of the House of Lords

	Sittings of the Lords (by calendar year)									
	1979	*1980*	*1981*	*1982*	*1983*	*1984*	*1985*	*1986*	*1987*	*1988*
Sitting days	101	159	151	151	123	149	152	159	116	158
Hours	572	1,019	960	973	798	1,084	1,038	1,160	793	1,113
Average length of sitting (hrs./mins.)	5.40	6.25	6.21	6.27	6.29	7.16	6.50	7.18	6.50	7.03
Average daily attendance	289	290	289	286	303	323	318	317	332	329
Monday sittings	14	31	28	32	25	31	33	32	26	34
Friday sittings	1	13	11	9	6	11	11	15	2	13
Late sittings (after 10:00 P.M.)	17	60	52	46	45	83	57	84	66	53

SOURCE: M. A. J. Wheeler-Booth, ''The House of Lords,'' in J. A. G. Griffith and M. Ryle (eds.), *Parliament: Functions, Practices and Procedures* (Sweet & Maxwell, 1989), p. 472.

For one thing, as we have seen, it provides some of the personnel of government. No fewer than two but usually no more than four peers are chosen to be Cabinet ministers. Up to fifteen more may be chosen as junior ministers, with six or seven also being appointed as government whips.

The other functions may be subsumed under the broad rubric of scrutiny and influence (of legislation and of executive actions), of providing a forum for public debate, and, formally, of legitimation. The House also has a unique judicial function as the highest domestic court of appeal, a function in practice now exercised by a judicial committee (see chapter 13). These may be identified as the main functions of the House. Of them, one—that of legitimation—has been circumscribed both by the provisions of the Parliaments acts and by the acceptance by peers of their politically surbordinate status.

Recognizing their undemocratic nature, as well as their one-party dominance (the House has a permanent Conservative predominance—see Table 11.11), the Lords has refrained from seeking to challenge the House of Commons. There have been occasional periods of bad feeling between the two houses, notably in the period of Labour government from 1974 to 1979, but the upper house rarely seeks to press an amendment—let alone delay a measure—when it is clear that the Commons is not prepared to support it. As a result of an agreement between the two front benches in the 1945–1950 Parliament, the official opposition in the Lords does not force a vote on the second reading of any bill promised in the government's election manifesto. A government is usually ensured of the upper house approving the principle of any measure it proposes.

Given the Lords' reluctance to challenge the government on the principle of measures, the House concentrates instead on scrutinizing the specific provisions of such measures. Bills pass through the same legislative stages as in the Commons, though committee stage is taken on the floor of the House rather than in standing committee. Consideration of a bill in the Lords allows for discussion of many provisions that may not have been debated fully in the Commons, for what may be termed technical scrutiny (ensuring that the specifics of a measure make sense

TABLE 11.11 Political affiliation of peers, 1992

Excluding peers on leave of absence or who have not taken the oath or who have not declared any political affiliation, the state of the parties in the House of Lords on December 31, 1992 was:

Conservative	478
Labour	117
Liberal Democrats	58
Social Democrats	12
Cross-benchers	275

SOURCE: Dod's Parliamentary Companion 1993 (Dod's Parliamentary Companion Ltd., 1993), p. 389.

and that they are correctly drafted), and for the introduction of further amendments. Of amendments made to bills during their passage through the House, the majority are initiated by the government. Not surprisingly, therefore, most amendments made by the Lords prove acceptable to the Commons. Of those that do not, the Lords rarely seeks to press any.

Under the rubric of scrutiny of legislation may now be included scrutiny of draft legislation emanating from the European Community (see chapter 10). It is a function shared with the House of Commons, but one that the Lords is generally credited with fulfilling most effectively. The function is fulfilled primarily through the Select Committee on the European Communities and five subcommittees. The subcommittees cover different subjects and make greater use than does the Commons of specialist advisors and outside witnesses. Peers who are not members of the subcommittees may attend to offer the benefit of their knowledge and experience in particular cases. These factors, coupled with the fact that the Lords concentrates on the legal and administrative (as opposed to the political) implications of draft proposals and can comment on their merits, has meant that the house has achieved a more formidable reputation than its Commons counterpart in scrutinizing EC legislation.[48]

Apart from scrutinizing bills introduced by government (and draft EC legislation), the House seeks also to scrutinize the actions of the executive. The procedures available to do this are similar to those employed in the Commons: debates and questions. The House spends about one-fifth of its time on general debates, though not all are confined to discussion of government actions and policy. The procedure for asking questions differs somewhat from Commons procedure. At the start of the day's business, only four oral questions may be asked, though supplementary questions are permitted. At the conclusion of a day's business, what are termed "unstarred questions" are taken (see Figure 11.2). These are questions (previously submitted, like all questions) on which a short debate may take place before a minister replies. As in the Commons, written questions may also be put down, and the answers are published in the Lords' *Hansard*. In the Lords, unlike the Commons, all questions are addressed to Her Majesty's government and not to individual ministers.

Except for its work in the sphere of EC draft legislation, the House makes little use of committees. It has a number of what may be termed domestic committees, covering the internal administration of the house and its privileges, but it has rarely employed select committees as tools of scrutiny. Nonetheless, it has made some moves in the direction of such committees. It has a sessional (i. e., permanent) committee on science and technology, notable for the expertise of its members,[49] and it has used ad hoc committees for inquiries into unemployment and into the offense of murder and life imprisonment.[50] It also has begun to experiment, very tentatively, with the use of committees for the committee stage of bills.[51]

The other main function that may be ascribed to the Lords is that of providing a forum for debate of important public issues. A similar function, of course, may be ascribed to the Commons. The difference between the two is that the Lords allows greater scope for the discussion of important topics that are not the subject

H.L. 22° Junii   2653

NOTICES AND ORDERS OF THE DAY
Items marked † are new or have been altered.

WEDNESDAY THE 23RD OF JUNE
At half-past two o'clock

*The Lord Hylton—To ask Her Majesty's Government whether they will publish the evidence given to, and the conclusions of, Sir John May's enquiry into miscarriages of justice, and if not, why not.

*The Earl Russell—To ask Her Majesty's Government whether before implementing any cuts in the social security budget they will attempt to calculate their effects on the budgets of other ministries, and therefore on the total level of public spending.

*The Lord Boyd-Carpenter—To ask Her Majesty's Government what action they are taking in the light of the reports by auditors on the operations of Lambeth Borough Council.

*The Lord Taylor of Gryfe—To ask Her Majesty's Government whether, in the light of the British Medical Association's report "The Boxing Debate", they will consider setting up an independent enquiry into the risks of brain injury associated with boxing.

†European Communities (Amendment) Bill—House to be again in Committee.
[THE BARONESS CHALKER OF WALLASEY]

The Lord Henderson of Brompton—To ask Her Majesty's Government what is their view of the report entitled "Four Years' Severe Hardship" published by Barnardo's and Youthaid, and what is their estimate of the number of young people aged 16 or 17 who are not in full-time education, employment or training.

[It is expected that the above question will be asked during the 1 hour dinner adjournment]

FIGURE 11.2   Questions on the House of Lords Order Paper, June 23, 1993. (Copyright 1993 by the Crown. Reprinted by permission of the Controller of Her Majesty's Stationery Office.

of contention between parties. The Commons concentrate on partisan issues, with little time for discussion of subjects outside the realm of party debate.

The upper house not only has the time and the inclination to debate important but essentially nonpartisan issues, but it can also claim the expertise to do so. Whereas MPs are essentially professional politicans (even though they may have expertise derived from preparliamentary employment), many peers hold—indeed are often ennobled on the basis of holding—leading positions in industry, the law, trade unions, finance, and the arts. Roughly one-fifth of peers are drawn from industry, about one-fifth from the education sector, just under a fifth from the legal profession, one-sixth from former diplomats and civil servants, a tenth from banking and insurance, and about 5% from past or present trade union officials.[52] Being a member of the House of Lords is usually a secondary pursuit to another activity.

Indeed, given that peers are paid only an expense allowance and receive no salary, there is little incentive for them to be full-time members of the house. The consequence is that there are frequently a number of peers who are experts in a particular field and who will attend debates only on those occasions when their subject of expertise is under discussion. The result, according to some observers, is informed and interesting debate. Many view favorably this perceived combination of expertise and lack of party bickering. Detractors would draw attention to the fact that Lords' expertise in certain areas is not replicated in other fields, producing superficial and often dull debate, and, more significantly, calling into question what attention is paid to Lords' debates by government and outside bodies.

Possibly the most significant role played by the House in acting as a forum of debate is as a safety valve. By avoiding replication of the party debate in the Commons, it allows for the occasional public debate on topics that might otherwise not receive an airing in an authoritative public forum. For some outside interests, making their voices heard through such a forum is all that they desire. The House of Lords has achieved a reputation for discussing on occasion important social issues and for helping ease onto the political agenda topics that might otherwise have been kept off. In recent years, for example, it has proved a valuable forum for those seeking to introduce constitutional reform.[53]

Recent Developments

Like the House of Commons, the House of Lords in recent years has witnessed something of a revitalization. In the 1950s and for much of the 1960s, the House sat at a very leisurely pace and very few peers attended; it came close to being a moribund institution. The position changed significantly in the latter half of the 1960s and even more in the years since then. Peers became more active, attending in greater number: Between 1963 and 1983 the average daily attendance doubled. More peers took part in debates and the house sat for longer: Whereas the average length of a daily sitting was less than 5 hours in 1963–1964, the average length by 1985–1986 was more than 7 hours; since the latter half of the 1980s, late-night sittings (those going beyond 10:00 P.M.) have become frequent. Peers also have shown themselves more independent in their voting behavior. The Labour government from 1974 to 1979 suffered a total of 362 defeats in the upper house. Given the Conservative preponderance in the House, the defeats were not unduly surprising; a number caused tension between the two houses, but in most cases the defeats were on noncontentious amendments and acceptable to the government. What has been surprising has been the degree of independence shown by the House during a period of Conservative government. Since 1979, the Conservative government has suffered more than 150 defeats in the Lords' division lobbies. Some of the issues have been contentious, including the 1984 bill paving the way for the abolition of the Greater London Council. The House has proved unpredictable, and Conservative MPs who dissent on particular issues in the House of Commons will often now send what amount to political signals to the Lords encouraging dissent there. Though the parties in the House have whips, there is no sanction they can employ against dissenting peers; peers come and go as they wish, and they sometimes vote as they please. Party voting predominates but, even more so than in the Commons, the government cannot take the assent of the House of Lords for granted.

The reason for this behavioral change has been attributed by Nicholas Baldwin to the convergence of two developments. One is the introduction of life peers. They have provided new blood, introducing many from political life who have an interest in remaining active in public affairs. As the number of life peers increased, so the House gained a larger body of active peers. The other reason was the failure to reform the House in 1969. Following the failure of the Parliament (No. 2) bill, of which more shortly, peers realized there was little likelihood of their chamber being reformed in the foreseeable future; hence it was a case of making the existing house work effectively.[54] The consequence has been a more active upper house.

For government, this greater activity has sometimes been troublesome. For interest groups, it has added considerably to the attractiveness of the House. Peers are answerable to no constituents: They can raise issues that may be unpopular with the general populace. They can raise issues outside the context of party politics. The opportunities for a backbench peer to initiate a debate in the House are reasonably good. Not surprisingly, therefore, lobbyists see the House of Lords as an important supplementary channel—and sometimes not so supplementary— to that of the Commons for getting an issue raised and onto the political agenda.[55] Of organized interests questioned in 1986, 70% had used the House of Lords to make representations or to influence public policy; of those using the house, four out of five had regular or frequent contact with one or more peers.[56]

The concept of the peerage, especially a hereditary peerage, causes considerable problems—as we shall see—but so long as the peers remain active, with a capacity to influence public policy, they are likely to be important targets for lobbying by outside groups—and by a government keen to get its measures passed.

THE CURRENT DEBATE

In historical perspective, debate on parliamentary reform has tended to be more intense—and to generate the introduction of more measures of reform—when focused on the House of Lords. In recent years, however, both houses have become targets of radical proposals for change.

The House of Commons

In the 1960s a number of Labour MPs and academics, notably Professor Bernard Crick, were active in pressing for parliamentary reform and especially for procedural change. The dominance of the government over Parliament, they argued, was too great. The House of Commons lacked the facilities to subject the government to sustained scrutiny; MPs were too badly paid, lacked adequate research facilities, and were constrained by archaic procedures.[57] Even as an arena assembly, the House was performing badly. What was needed, they argued, were reforms that would allow the House to engage in more effective scrutiny through investigation and debate. To such an end, they advocated the greater use of select committees, longer sittings of the House, better pay and research facilities for members, modernization of parliamentary procedure, the broadcasting of debates, and more opportunities for emergency debates. Such reforms, it was contended, would allow the House the opportunity to subject government to public scrutiny and to keep it responsive to public feeling, thus maintaining consent for the political system (the house doing the job expected of it) without jeopardizing the effectiveness of government (the government retaining its parliamentary majority). A strong government, declared Professor Crick, was compatible with a strong opposition.

In the 1970s pressure for limited internal reform of the House began to give way to calls for more radical change. A convergence of two developments may help explain why this happened. One was the failure of a number of internal reforms implemented in the latter half of the 1960s and early 1970s. The use of more select committees had little impact on government and on policy making. As an experiment, the House began to meet in the morning on two days a week. However, votes could not be held during these sittings and members, especially Conservative members (many of whom had outside interests), showed little interest in them and rarely attended. The morning sittings were abandoned. Pay for MPs was increased and more offices were made available, but the improvements were relative: MPs remained poorly paid and had little by way of research facilities. The relationship between the House and the part of it that formed the government remained essentially unchanged—hence an impetus for more far-reaching reform. This was reinforced by a second development. The 1970s witnessed greater economic and political turmoil than had existed in the previous decade. The country's economic position worsened, and the two general elections of 1974 produced governments elected with less than 40% of the votes cast and an apparent and significant shift away from the two main parties (see chapters 5 and 6). A combination of these developments fostered more rigorous and critical analyses of the House of Commons and its relationship to the country's economic and political malaise.

The radical reformers, led by academics such as S. E. Finer and S. A. Walkland, were intent on ripping away what they saw as the inaccurate and misleading gloss that previous writers had placed on the role of the House.[58] They assailed the House as having clung to nineteenth-century practices and beliefs during a period that witnessed major economic and social change (the welfare state and the managed economy), the swelling of bureaucracy, and the trend toward a corporate economy. It had failed to adapt and to keep pace with such developments. The electoral system encouraged the return of one party with a majority of seats, and party discipline within the House assured the resulting party government of a parliamentary majority for whatever it proposed. The result was a malfunctional parliamentary system. It was a system that undermined rather than reinforced political authority. The House was incapable of subjecting government to scrutiny, let alone having any tangible impact on public policy.

Such an analysis led reformers to advocate electoral reform. The basis of their argument and its implications were discussed in chapter 5. Electoral reform would produce, according to its exponents, a more representative House of Commons. On the basis of existing voting behavior, no one party would achieve an overall majority, thus forcing a coalition of the political center or a minority government responsive to other parties in the House. The House of Commons would continue to provide most of the personnel of government, to subject government to (more effective) scrutiny and influence, and to legitimate the government and its measures. The most significant difference would be that the House itself would have a greater claim to legitimacy in fulfilling those functions and would, in its behavior, be more consensual.

The ranks of the electoral reformers grew in the 1970s and 1980s. Electoral reform became one of the central planks of Charter '88—a constitutional reform movement started in 1988, and drawing support from Liberal Democrats and a growing number of politicians on the Left. The loss of a fourth consecutive general election in 1992 added to pressure within Labour's ranks to support such reform. A body set up in the 1987–1992 Parliament by Labour leader Neil Kinnock reported in 1993, recommending support for a new, but nonproportional, system of election—the Supplementary Vote—for the House of Commons (retaining single constituencies, with the votes of candidates coming bottom of the poll being redistributed) and a system of proportional representation for a reformed upper house. Despite this growing demand for a new electoral system, electoral reformers have not yet found themselves in a position to implement such a measure. The Conservative government—the beneficiary of the existing system— is opposed to change, and Labour MPs are divided on the issue, many being committed supporters of the existing system. Opponents of change contend that the existing system provides coherence—electors know what they are voting for—and a party of government, with election day constituting "Judgement day."[59] The party in government knows it can be turned out and so is responsive, in between elections, to shifts in public opinion.

Pressure for radical reform has become more prominent, but it has not totally eclipsed continuing demands for internal reform. Indeed, such demands have become more pronounced in recent years. The experience of the departmental select committees and, more recently, the televising of proceedings have been used to demonstrate the usefulness of change within the institution. There are demands for further change, including a reform of the legislative process. These demands have emanated from a number of MPs and from bodies such as the educational charity the Hansard Society, which produced a major report in 1993 advocating extensive change to the existing legislative process.[60] In the contest for the Conservative party leadership in 1990, one candidate—Douglas Hurd— made parliamentary reform a central plank of his manifesto. In 1992, a select committee of the Commons recommended a reform of the hours of sitting and the greater use of special standing committees.[61] Internal reform thus remains on the agenda.

Finally there is the approach associated with me.[62] This approach allows for the maintenance of government effectiveness, with the political process remaining executive-centered, while on the other side making possible an effective House of Commons, the house fulfilling and being seen to fulfill the function of subjecting governmental actions and measures to scrutiny and influence. The balance between executive and Commons would be maintained, and this balance could be jeopardized by the implementation of a new electoral system (see chapter 5). The approach I posit makes possible such a balance. It draws on recent experience as the basis for arguing not only what should be but also what can be.

This approach stipulates the need for an attitudinal change on the part of MPs as a prerequisite for effective procedural reform. Relying on the government to introduce effective procedural change—designed to act as possible critics of that very same government—is an inherently flawed stance, as witnessed by the failure of the modest reforms introduced before 1979. No amount of structural or procedural changes will make any significant difference unless accompanied by the political will to make such changes effective. Hence, if the House of Commons is to become a more effective scrutineer and influencer of government, it is up to MPs themselves to make it so.

Such an argument would, in the quarter-century after 1945, have been considered idealistic. The experience of the past 25 years has given it empirical credence. As we have seen, behavioral changes provided the basis for the most important parliamentary reform of this century: the introduction of the departmental select committees. MPs have shown that, by using their political muscle, they can craft the tools necessary for consistent and effective scrutiny of executive actions; by using that same muscle, they can reform the procedures for legislative scrutiny. The experience of the immediate past decades thus points the way forward. Members can ensure effective scrutiny and influence of government if they have the political will to do so. Without that will, blueprints for reform will remain precisely that. If the will exists, MPs can generate the structures and the resources necessary for fulfilling a more participant role, without jeopardizing the capacity of a government—a party government—to govern. A House of Commons in which the government can normally be assured a majority, but a majority it cannot take for granted, is the most effective way of ensuring the existence of a government that can govern but that is responsive to the elected House of Commons.

The House of Lords

Schemes of reform of the House of Lords are regularly put forward. The most important attempt at reform since the Parliament acts took place in 1968, when the Labour government introduced the Parliament (No. 2) bill, designed to phase out the hereditary element (hereditary peers were to become nonvoting peers and their successors were to be excluded from membership) and to reduce the delaying power of the Lords to six months. The bill encountered vigorous and sustained opposition, not from the House of Lords but from MPs in the Commons: Some Labour MPs, who thought the bill did not go far enough (they favored abolition of the House), combined with some Conservative MPs, who felt it went too far, to frustrate its passage. The government appeared to lose heart in the measure and, under fire from the critics on both sides of the House, withdrew it in April 1969. That experience deterred succeeding governments from tackling the issue. None has yet returned to it. However, pressure for reform has not been stilled. The House of Lords remains an issue of political debate.

Views as to the future of the upper house are varied. Indeed, approaches to the upper house can be summarized under four heads, the "four R's": retain, reform, replace, or remove altogether.

Retain.   Many who find the hereditary basis of the House of Lords unacceptable often express amazement that there are people other than hereditary peers who are prepared to defend the House as it currently exists. Yet a number of observers are prepared to make a case for the retention of the house in its current form, doing so on grounds of principle and practicality.[63] They contend that the hereditary principle provides peers who are able to render an opinion free of external pressures, because they are beholden to no party or patron, and that it provides peers with not only a wide range of experience but also a wide range of views. The House boasts not only a large number of independent peers (known as "cross-bench" peers because of the benches they occupy in the house, no such benches existing in the Commons), it also has a Communist member, Lord Milford. Members give freely of their services to ensure that the House fulfills its functions, and defenders contend that those functions are well fulfilled. In the absence of an acceptable alternative, the defenders contend, why not leave well enough alone? The house does its job and there is little public pressure for change.

Reform or Replace.   Reformers take a different view. Many Conservatives and some Labour supporters (notably a number of Labour peers) are of the opinion that if the upper house—indeed, any second chamber—is to survive, the existing house must be reformed or replaced; otherwise, it may fall victim to the onslaught of Labour abolitionists. Change is sought in order to conserve. Moderate reformers seek change based on the existing house. They favor a measure on lines similar to those of the 1969 bill. Such a measure was proposed by a working group of Labour peers in 1980. Other reformers seek to replace the existing House either with a completely new elected or appointed chamber or one that forms something of a hybrid between the existing chamber and an elected house. Two Conservative committees have recommended a house chosen mainly or wholly by election.[64] They argue that such election would enhance the legitimacy of the second chamber and, in so doing, create a chamber that had an acceptable basis to act as a safeguard against an overmighty House of Commons.

Other radical proposals for replacement have included a house based on regional representation and one based on functional representation. A house comprising representatives of the regions of the United Kingdom, a proposal popular with those who support devolution, is seen as a means of providing a countervailing force against the centralizing tendencies of government. The Labour party in 1989 came out in favor of an elected chamber, designed to "reflect the interests and aspirations of the regions and nations of Britain." A house formed of representatives of groups such as the trades unions and industry would allow for the co-option of sectional groups into the formal political process, enhancing the consent of such groups.

Remove Altogether. The most radical step—to abolish the House of Lords and not replace it at all, creating a unicameral legislature—has been advocated by some politicians for many years. One leading Labour politician, Tony Benn, has made it clear that he believes abolition should be the first task of any future Labour government. A second chamber, however composed, is seen as a potential obstacle to the passage of socialist legislation. The case for doing away with it has been most succinctly put by Labour Peer Lord Wedderburn: "Either the second chamber is less democratic than the Commons in which case it should not be able to delay legislation," he said, "or it is just as democratic, then there is no point in having two chambers."[65] The functions of the upper house, so abolitionists argue, could be transferred to a reformed House of Commons.

Although at the national level defenders of the existing House of Lords are in a minority, those who favor reform have difficulty finding a measure on which they can agree. Each reform proposal has its detractors: An appointed house would be little better than the existing house; an elected chamber would either duplicate the Commons or (if elected by a procedure different from that for the lower house) be a potential obstruction to measures emanating from it; a house based on functional representation would further enhance the position of already over-powerful groups; and the absence of a second chamber would generate too many pressures for the remaining chamber, as well as doing away altogether with a necessary constitutional safeguard. It has been such disagreement among those who favor change that has resulted in no significant change taking place. The only measures affecting the upper house that have been passed in the past 30 years have been those providing for the creation of life peers—a development that has breathed new life into the chamber—and for hereditary peers to disclaim their titles should they so choose. Although such changes are more radical than any made affecting the Commons, the House has undergone no fundamental change. Defenders of the House see this as no bad thing. Others believe that the longer it remains unreformed, the greater the pressure for it to be swept away altogether. The great democratic wave identified by Shaftesbury may yet swell and sweep it away.

CONCLUSION

Parliament continues to enjoy popular support as a legitimate political institution. Its output, by virtue of the doctrine of parliamentary sovereignty, is binding upon all and cannot be struck down by the courts. It is the institution from which the political apex of government is drawn and from which government derives its popular legitimacy. It has the characteristics of an arena assembly, seeking through debate to subject government to scrutiny and some measures of influence, and providing the broad limits within which government may govern.

Recent decades have witnessed claims that neither popular support for it as a legitimating political body nor its modest powers has been as great as was previously believed. The mode of election and the adversary relationship between two parties have been identified as undermining the claim of the House of Commons to be a representative assembly. The hereditary basis of the Lords continues to be used as sufficient reason for denying the house any claim to be considered an appropriate political institution. Party hegemony has been identified as constricting Parliament's ability to exercise even the modest powers ascribed to it. A consequence of these factors has been modestly successful pressure for change within the House in order to restore to Parliament both popular support and the political will to exercise modest powers in the making of public policy. Pressure for more radical reform has grown in recent years. What has been lacking among proponents of more radical reform has been agreement as to what form change should take. Although many may agree on ends, agreement as to means is notably absent. Electoral reformers seek to generate a parliamentary system that reflects and seeks to generate consensus. In their preference for their own scheme of reform, consensus is the one thing they lack.

NOTES

1. However, under Article I, section 7(1), of the U.S. Constitution, all revenue-raising bills must originate in the House of Representatives.
2. M. Mezey, *Comparative Legislatures* (Duke University Press, 1979), ch. 2.
3. See N. Ornstein, J. Mann, and M. Malbin, *Vital Statistics on Congress 1991–1992* (American Enterprise Institute, 1992), p. 199.
4. Mezey, p. 37.
5. R. H. S. Crossman, "Introduction," to W. Bagehot, *The English Constitution* (Fontana, 1963 ed.), p. 39.
6. N. Polsby, "Legislatures," in F. I. Greenstein and N. Polsby (eds.), *Handbook of Political Science,* Vol. 5 (Addison-Wesley, 1975). See also P. Norton (ed.), *Legislatures* (Oxford University Press, 1990), Part 3.
7. See P. Norton, *Does Parliament Matter?* (Harvester Wheatsheaf, 1993), pp. 40–42.
8. One, now dated, survey—covering three sessions at the beginning of the 1970s— found that usually less than 5% of amendments tabled by opposition MPs or government backbenchers were accepted. J. A. G. Griffith, *Parliamentary Scrutiny of Government Bills* (Allen & Unwin, 1974), p. 93. The figures increased in later years. See J. E. Schwarz, "Exploring a New Role in Policy-Making: The British House of Commons in the 1970s," *American Political Science Review,* 74 (1), 1980, pp. 23–37. See also P. Norton, "Legislation," in M. Rush (ed.), *Parliament and Pressure Politics* (Oxford University Press, 1990).
9. There is a particular, and recent, exception: Special standing committees (SSCs) may take evidence, but their use, as we shall have cause to comment later, has been rare since provision for their appointment was first introduced.
10. Griffith, p. 159. See also Norton, "Legislation," pp. 186–188.
11. See D. Marsh and M. Read, *Private Members' Bills* (Cambridge University Press, 1987). In the 1987–1992 Parliament, the success rate for bills lower down in the ballot was greater than for those drawn in the top six. N. Stace, "Private Members' Bills," undergraduate dissertation, University of Hull, Politics Department, 1993.
12. See P. G. Richards, *Parliament and Conscience* (Allen & Unwin, 1970); and S. Jeffery-Poulter, *Peers, Queers and Commons* (Routledge, 1991), pp. 72–81.

13. See Norton, *Does Parliament Matter?* p. 60.
14. See H. Irwin, A. Kennon, D. Natzler, and R. Rogers, "Evolving Rules," in M. Franklin and P. Norton (eds.), *Parliamentary Questions* (Oxford University Press, 1993), pp. 23–72.
15. See especially P. Norton, "Questions and the Role of Parliament," in M. Franklin and P. Norton, (eds.), *Parliamentary Questions* (Oxford University Press, 1993), pp. 194–207.
16. They were in use, for example, in the sixteenth and seventeenth centuries. See S. J. Downs, "The House of Commons: Structural Changes," in P. Norton (ed.), *Parliament in the 1980s* (Blackwell, 1985), pp. 53–54.
17. The Scottish Affairs Committee was in abeyance from 1987 to 1992 because of the difficulty of getting enough Conservative MPs representing Scottish seats to sit on it. When the Department of Health and Social Security was divided into two separate departments, the existing Social Services Committee was replaced by two new committees. In 1992, when the Department of Energy was abolished, the Energy Select Committee also disappeared. In 1992, two new committees were formed: See Table 11.6.
18. See, for example, D. Judge, *Parliament and Industry* (Dartmouth, 1990), pp. 176–184.
19. See *First Report from the Liaison Select Committee,* Session 1982–1983, HC 92 (Her Majesty's Stationery Office, 1982); D. Englefield, *Commons Select Committees: Catalysts for Progress?* (Longman, 1984), pp. 70–71; and G. Drewry, *The New Select Committees,* rev. ed. (Oxford University Press, 1989), ch. 20.
20. The year was March 1985 to March 1986. The information was provided by the prime minister in a parliamentary written answer.
21. See especially R. Rawlings, "The MP's Complaint Service," *Modern Law Review,* 53, 1990, pp. 22–42, 149–169; and P. Norton and D. Wood, *Back from Westminster* (University Press of Kentucky, 1993), ch. 3.
22. See P. Norton, "Parliament in the United Kingdom: Balancing Effectiveness and Consent?" in P. Norton (ed.), *Parliaments in Western Europe* (Frank Cass, 1990), p. 25.
23. R. Jowell and S. Witherspoon, *British Social Attitudes: The 1985 Report* (Gower, 1985), p. 12.
24. P. Norton, "The Organization of Parliamentary Parties," in S. A. Walkland (ed.), *The House of Commons in the Twentieth Century* (Oxford University Press, 1979), pp. 7–68; and P. Norton, "The Parliamentary Party," in A. Seldon and S. Ball (eds.), *The Conservative Party in the Twentieth Century* (Oxford University Press, 1994).
25. See Norton, *Does Parliament Matter?* ch. 9; and Norton and Wood, ch. 3.
26. One Labour MP, interviewed as part of a series of interviews conducted by the Study Group on New Members of the UK Study of Parliament Group, 1993.
27. See P. Norton, "The Changing Face of Parliament: Lobbying and Its Consequences," in P. Norton (ed.), *New Directions in British Politics?* (Edward Elgar, 1991); and Norton, *Does Parliament Matter?* ch. 9, 10.
28. See Rawlings, p. 44.
29. M. Rush (ed.), *Parliament and Pressure Politics* (Oxford University Press, 1990), p. 282 (Q 1(g)) and p. 285 (Q 7).
30. A. King, "The Rise of the Career Politician in Britain—And Its Consequences," *British Journal of Political Science,* 11, 1981, pp. 249–285.
31. Norton and Wood, ch. 3.
32. B. Cain, J. Ferejohn, and M. Fiorina, *The Personal Vote* (Harvard University Press, 1987), found 27% of members adopting a proactive approach to constituency work.

33. D. M. Wood and P. Norton, "Do Candidates Matter? Constituency-Specific Vote Changes for Incumbent MPs, 1983–1987," *Political Studies,* 50 (2), 1992, pp. 227–238.

34. See especially Norton, *Does Parliament Matter?* ch. 9.

35. P. Norton, *Dissension in the House of Commons 1945–74* (Macmillan, 1975).

36. P. Norton, *Dissension in the House of Commons 1974–1979* (Oxford University Press, 1980); P. Norton, "The House of Commons: Behavioural Changes," in P. Norton (ed.), *Parliament in the 1980s* (Blackwell, 1985); and T. Saalfeld, *Das britische Unterhaus 1965 bis 1986* (Peter Lang, 1988).

37. See P. Regan, "The 1986 Shops Bill," *Parliamentary Affairs,* 41, 1988, pp. 218–235; and F. Bown, "The Shops Bill," in M. Rush (ed.), *Parliament and Pressure Politics* (Oxford University Press, 1990), pp. 213–233.

38. P. Norton, "Parliament," in P. Catterall (ed.), *Contemporary Britain: An Annual Review 1993* (Blackwell, 1993).

39. See especially M. Franklin, A. Baxter, and M. Jordon, "Who were the Rebels? Dissent in the House of Commons 1970–74," *Legislative Studies Quarterly,* 11, 1986, pp. 143–159.

40. P. Norton, *Conservative Dissidents* (Temple Smith, 1978), ch. 9; and, P. Norton, "Dissent in the House of Commons: Rejoinder to Franklin, Baxter and Jordan," *Legislative Studies Quarterly,* 12, 1987, pp. 143–152.

41. S. H. Beer, *Britain against Itself* (Faber, 1982), p. 190.

42. See Norton, *Does Parliament Matter?* ch. 10.

43. See P. Norton, "Independence, Scrutiny and Rationalisation: A Decade of Changes in the House of Commons," *Teaching Politics,* 15, 1986, pp. 69–98.

44. Rush, pp. 282–283 (Qs 2, 3, 5).

45. See A. Hetherington, K. Weaver, and M. Ryle, *Cameras in the Commons* (Hansard Society, 1990), and Select Committee on the Televising of Proceedings of the House, *First Report: Review of the Experiment in Televising the Proceedings of the House,* Session 1989–1990, HC 265-I (Her Majesty's Stationery Office, 1990), especially annex 4.

46. See Norton, *Does Parliament Matter?,* ch. 12.

47. *Parliamentary Debates (Hansard),* Vol. 188, cols. 1925–1926 (1867).

48. See C. Grantham and C. M. Hodgson, "The House of Lords: Structural Changes," in P. Norton (ed.), *Parliament in the 1980s* (Blackwell, 1985), pp. 114–135; and Norton, *Does Parliament Matter?* ch. 7.

49. See P. D. G. Hayter, "The Parliamentary Monitoring of Science and Technology in Britain," *Government and Opposition,* 26, 1991, pp. 147–166.

50. See C. Grantham, "Select Committees," in D. R. Shell and D. R. Beamish (eds.), *The House of Lords at Work* (Oxford University Press, 1993).

51. See House of Lords, *Report from the Select Committee on the Committee Work of the House,* Session 1991–1992, HL Paper 35-I (Her Majesty's Stationery Office, 1992).

52. Calculated from N. Baldwin, "The House of Lords: Behavioural Changes," in P. Norton (ed.), *Parliament in the 1980s* (Blackwell, 1985), p. 105.

53. Peers, for example, have twice passed a Bill of Rights (which made no progress in the Commons)—see P. Norton, *The Constitution in Flux* (Blackwell, 1982), p. 246—and variously debated constitutional reform, as in March 1992, the latter debate initiated by the chancellor of Oxford University, and former leader of the Social Democratic Party, Lord Jenkins of Hillhead.

54. Baldwin, "The House of Lords: Behavioural Changes," pp. 96–113. See also Norton, *Does Parliament Matter?* pp. 28–29.

55. See N. Baldwin, "The House of Lords," in M. Rush (ed.), *Parliament and Pressure Politics* (Oxford University Press, 1990), pp. 152–177.
56. Rush, p. 289 (Qs 11, 11(a)).
57. B. Crick, *The Reform of Parliament* (Weidenfeld & Nicolson, 1964). See also P. Norton, *The Commons in Perspective* (Blackwell, 1981), pp. 203–204.
58. See especially S. E. Finer (ed.), *Adversary Politics and Electoral Reform* (Wigram, 1975); and S. A. Walkland, "Whither the Commons?" in S. A. Walkland and M. Ryle (eds.), *The Commons Today* (Fontana, 1981), ch. 12.
59. Sir K. Popper, "The Open Society and Its Enemies Revisited," *The Economist,* April 23, 1988, pp. 25–28.
60. See *Making the Law: The Report of the Hansard Society Commission on the Legislative Process, Chairman: Rt. Hon. Lord Rippon of Hexham* (Hansard Society, 1993).
61. *Report from the Select Committee on the Sittings of the House,* Session 1991–1992, HC 20-I (Her Majesty's Stationery Office, 1992).
62. See especially Norton, *The Commons in Perspective* (1981), ch. 9; P. Norton, "The Norton View," in D. Judge (ed.), *The Politics of Parliamentary Reform* (Heinemann, 1983); Norton, "The House of Commons: Behavioural Changes," in Norton, *Parliament in the 1980s* (1985); P. Norton, *Parliament in Perspective* (Hull University Press, 1987); and Norton, *Does Parliament Matter?* pp. 208–213.
63. See Norton, *The Constitution in Flux,* pp. 119–121.
64. Report of the Conservative Review Committee, *The House of Lords* (Conservative Central Office, 1978); and the Report of the Constitutional Reform Committee of Conservative Lawyers, *House of Lords Reform?* (Macmillan, 1978).
65. Quoted in H. Hebert, "The Lords under the Microscope," *The Guardian,* March 1, 1979.

CHAPTER **12**

The Monarchy
Above the Fray?

In the United States, the head of state is the president. In the United Kingdom, the head of state is the monarch. Both fulfill certain formal duties associated with the position. Beyond that there is little similarity between the two. In terms of history, determination of incumbency, powers, and current responsibilities, the U.S. presidency and the British monarchy have virtually nothing in common. The president is both head of state and political head of the administration. He operates directly and personally at the heart of the political decision-making process. The monarch, as head of state, stands above political decision making. In political terms, he or she serves not to decide but primarily to perform a symbolic role. The president serves by virtue of election; the monarch reigns by virtue of birth.

The monarchy is the oldest secular institution in Britain. It predates Parliament by some four centuries and the law courts by three centuries. The present monarch is able to trace her descent from King Egbert, who united England under his rule in A.D. 829. The continuity of the institution has been broken only once, during the period of military rule by Oliver Cromwell. There have been various interruptions in the direct line of succession, but the hereditary principle has been preserved since at least the eleventh century. The succession itself is governed by certain principles of common law and by statute. The throne descends to the eldest son or, in the absence of a son, the eldest daughter. By the Act of Settlement of 1701, affirmed by the Treaty of Union in 1707, the Crown was to descend to the heirs of the granddaughter of James I, Princess Sophia; this line has been confirmed by later acts.[1]

For several centuries, there was no separation of powers: executive, legislative, and judicial power was exercised by the king. With the growth of Parliament (and its power of the purse) as well as the courts, the direct exercise of these functions progressively declined. As we have seen (chapter 3), the conflict

However, there have been occasions when the monarchy has been the subject of controversy and critical comment. The most significant occasion in the twentieth century was in 1936 when the new king, Edward VIII, wanted to marry an American divorcée, Wallis Simpson. The marriage was opposed by the British government and by the archbishop of Canterbury. The problem was not that Mrs. Simpson was an American but that she was divorced (and had remarried). The king was the supreme governor of the Church of England and in the eyes of the church Mrs. Simpson was still married to her first husband. The king had to choose between the throne and Mrs. Simpson. He chose the latter and abdicated. The abdication crisis caused political controversy—some politicians, such as Winston Churchill (then out of office), backing the king's desire to marry and stay on the throne, others seeing Edward's actions as irresponsible and a threat to the institution of the monarchy. Support for the institution was largely restored by his brother, the duke of York, who succeeded him, becoming George VI.

The second most significant period of controversy is that of the 1990s. Both 1991 and 1992 proved particularly difficult years for the queen and her family, with questions being raised about the cost and role of the royal family. The institution of the monarchy was not itself at the heart of the debate, but the critical nature of the debate raised some doubt about the future of the institution.

The main areas of debate concerning the monarchy can be subsumed under three heads: (1) the monarch's exercise of certain political powers not clearly governed by convention, (2) the role and cost of the royal family, and (3) the future of the monarchy. The first is a continuing but not prominent one, and has been overshadowed in the 1990s by the second.

The Exercise of Political Powers

There is a continuing debate about the powers of the queen not clearly governed by convention. As we have seen, the exercise of most of the political powers vested in the monarch is governed largely by convention. In most cases, this entails the queen's acting on the advice of her ministers. However, certain important powers remain vested in the monarch that on occasion may require a choice among alternative options, a choice not clearly dictated by convention. The most obvious and important power involved here is that of choosing a prime minister.

It is a convention of the Constitution that the queen will select as prime minister that person whom she considers capable of ensuring a majority in the House of Commons. In practice, this usually creates no problems. If a party obtains an overall majority in a general election, the queen summons the leader of that party. But what happens if there is no party leader to be summoned or if no party is returned with an overall majority at a general election? The first possibility no longer faces the queen, though until recently it did. Until 1965, the Conservative party had no formal mechanism for choosing a leader. The leader was expected to "emerge" following soundings of one sort or another within the party. In the event of a Conservative prime minister's retiring with no successor immediately apparent, or with different contenders for the succession, the choice was left to the monarch. In 1957 the queen was faced with summoning someone to succeed Sir Anthony Eden as prime minister. After consulting with senior statesmen, she sent for Harold Macmillan instead of, as many assumed she would, R. A. Butler. In 1963 she was confronted with the difficult task of appointing a prime minister in succession to Macmillan. After taking the advice of her outgoing prime minister, she summoned Lord Home (or Sir Alec Douglas-Home, as he quickly became after renouncing his title in order to seek a seat in the House of Commons). The choice was a controversial one[10] and, though the decision was essentially that of Macmillan, it embroiled the Crown in political controversy. The prospect of any repetition was avoided when the Conservative party in 1964 introduced a procedure for the election of the party leader. The party was thus in a position to elect a leader and avoid the queen's having to make a selection on its behalf.

The second possibility, a party having no overall majority, is a real one. The outcomes of a number of general elections, most notably and most recently that of 1992, have been far from certain. What should the queen do in the event of no party having an overall majority? Usually the position does not entail her having to make a decision. The outgoing prime minister formally remains in office until resigning and may therefore seek to strike a deal with a third party (as Edward Heath attempted to do, unsuccessfully, with the Liberals in February 1974), but what if the prime minister is unacceptable to the third party but another leader—drawn from the same party—might be? Does the queen summon that leader or does she summon the leader of the opposition? In such a situation she would be saddled, as David Watt put it, "with a highly controversial and thankless responsibility."[11] It is one she would almost certainly prefer to do without.

One other power that has produced a similar debate is the power to dissolve Parliament. The usual practice is for the prime minister to recommend a dissolution to the queen and for Her Majesty to accede to that request. There is some doubt, though, as to whether it is a convention for the queen to accede automatically to that request. In the event of a government losing its parliamentary majority through defections or a major party split, and the prime minister's preference for a dissolution rather than forming a coalition with a third party is opposed by the Cabinet, would the queen be justified in withholding her consent to a dissolution? If the prime minister wanted a dissolution following a major defeat in the Commons, but his Cabinet colleagues did not,[12] what should the queen do? Lord Blake, a constitutional historian, has argued that in such or similar circumstances the queen would not be obliged to grant a dissolution.[13] When the Tribune Group, a left-wing body of Labour MPs, argued in 1974 that the prime minister had an absolute right to determine the date of the election, a senior minister responded, "Constitutional lawyers of the highest authority are of the clear opinion that the Sovereign is not in all circumstances bound to grant a Prime Minister's request for a dissolution."[14] The problem is one of determining the circumstances that would justify the queen's denying a dissolution, and whether, whatever the circumstances, such an action could be taken without seriously damaging the queen's reputation for being above the partisan fray. "For the monarch," wrote Kingsley Martin, "the only safe rule is always to follow the Premier's advice."[15] If that rule were accepted as a convention, it would ensure that the queen's actions were predictable, putting her beyond claims of partisanship. However, the problem presently is the absence of agreement that such a rule exists.

One alternative, advocated by Labour MP Tony Benn, is for the power of dissolution (indeed, all prerogative powers) to be transferred to the speaker of the House of Commons. This, Benn notes, would avoid the queen being drawn into the heart of political debate, transferring instead the power to someone who "knows the Commons intimately and is therefore specially qualified to reach a judgment about the appropriate moment for granting a dissolution and who is most likely to command a majority."[16] The difficulty with the proposal is that it would not solve the problem but rather transfer it. As we saw in chapter 11, the speaker is a neutral figure, and to exercise the power of dissolution would draw the speaker into "the heart of political debate." The speaker is no more keen to jeopardize her claim to being above the partisan fray than is the queen.

There thus remain certain circumstances in which the queen may be called on to exercise a choice. Such circumstances could, and almost certainly would, draw the queen into political controversy. Such circumstances are, though, exceptional.

The Role and Cost of the Royal Family

The Crown vests in the monarch and there are certain tasks that only the monarch can perform. However, many public duties of the monarch can be, and are, performed on her behalf by members of her family. Members of the royal family can be deputed to represent the queen abroad and at various state functions. They will also often be invited themselves to perform public duties, such as opening a factory or hospital or acting as patron of a charity.

The costs incurred in fulfilling public duties by the queen and most other members of the royal family have traditionally been met from the Civil List.[17] For the queen, this covers such items as staff costs, the upkeep of royal residences, the cost of state dinners and other functions, and transportation to official functions. For other members of the royal family, lesser sums have been provided to cover staff and related expenses. (The exception is the prince of Wales, whose income derives from the duchy of Cornwall.)[18] In 1990, to avoid an annual public debate on the amount to be paid through the Civil List, agreement was reached between the queen and the government that the size of the list should be set at £7.9 million a year (just over $12m.) for a decade. When other costs are included that are not covered by the Civil List but paid instead by government departments, such as the maintenance costs of royal castles (more than £25 million—$39m.—in 1990–1991) and of the royal yacht *Britannia* (£9 million—$14m.), the annual public expenditure on the monarchy exceeds £57 million ($88m.).[19] This expenditure has been criticized on a number of grounds, and the criticism reached a peak in 1992.

Three criticisms have been expressed for a number of years. The first has been that the Civil List is large in absolute terms. The 1990 settlement marked a significant increase on previous years, designed to take account of inflation in future years. Even in 1988, 40% of respondents in a Gallup poll expressed the view that the monarchy cost "too much."[20] The second was that the country did not get particularly good value for the money from certain members of the royal family, especially junior members. A 1989 MORI poll found that senior members, such as the queen, the prince of Wales (Prince Charles), and the princess royal (Princess Anne) were judged to be hard working and cost-effective. However, when asked which two or three members of the royal family represented the worst value for the money to the British taxpayer, 37% identified Sarah, duchess of York, and 23% identified her husband, Prince Andrew; they were followed by the queen's sister, Princess Margaret, and the queen's youngest son, Prince Edward.[21] Many critics tended to view such "hangers on," as they were often described, as serving no useful purpose. Third, there was criticism of the fact that the queen received money from the Civil List despite enjoying a large personal fortune—a fortune on which she paid no tax. The queen is reputed to be one of the richest women in the world. (Her wealth has been estimated by some publications, including *Fortune* magazine, as running into several billion pounds—some putting it as high as £7 billion [almost $11b.]—though this figure includes national treasures held in perpetuity on the nation's behalf by the monarch; her real personal, and disposable, wealth is believed to be closer to £100 million [$155m.]).[22] When income tax was introduced in the nineteenth century, Queen Victoria volunteered to pay tax and did so; in the twentieth century, the tax liability was whittled down and George VI reached agreement with the government to remove any tax burden from his successors. Various calls were made, especially by Labour MPs in the 1960s and 1970s, for the queen to be subject to income tax. In support of this view, 91 Labour MPs in 1975 voted against an increase in the Civil List.

These criticisms became more prominent in the latter half of the 1980s, in large part because of the antics of several younger—and newer—royals, such as the duchess of York, who was portrayed as enjoying frequent sojourns in expensive ski resorts in preference to fulfilling mundane public duties at home, and at the end of the decade because of the increases in the Civil List at a time of recession. However, they were to reach a new level of intensity—eventually invoking action by the queen—in 1992.

Criticism of the royal family became pronounced—generating intense, and often highly critical, media coverage—as a result of several independent developments. The first was the separation of the duke and duchess of York and the subsequent publication of photographs showing a topless duchess in intimate proximity to a Texan friend, described as her "financial advisor." The second was speculation about the state of the marriage of the prince and princess of Wales.

The speculation was fueled by publication of a book about the princess of Wales that portrayed her as the vulnerable wife in a difficult royal environment, not helped by a largely intolerant and distant husband.[23] The princess was variously alleged to have allowed, even encouraged, friends to talk to the author in order to put out her side of the story. Some of the prince's friends later retaliated, seeking to put out his side of the story. Media attention became intense following the release of a tape of an intercepted telephone conversation held

Imagine if at this moment, instead of the Queen, we had a gentleman in evening clothes, ill-made, probably from Moss Bros., with a white tie, going about everywhere, who had been elected by some deal made between the extreme Right and the extreme Left . . . ! Then we would all wait for the next one, another little man, who is it going to be? . . . "Give it to 'X,' you know he's been such a bad Chancellor of the Exchequer, instead of getting rid of him, let's make him the next President. . . . " Can you imagine it? I mean, it doesn't make sense, that would be the final destruction of colour and life and the sense of the past in this country, wouldn't it . . . ?[31]

Critics would respond that Macmillan's analysis has not necessarily been borne out by experience elsewhere. The response of supporters of the monarchy would doubtless be that Britain is not "elsewhere."

Defenders of the monarchy have also contended that it is efficient. By general consent, the queen is hard working and fulfills her duties well.[32] Though the cost of the institution became increasingly difficult to defend as 1992 progressed, the announcement that the queen had agreed to pay income tax—and to take most members of the royal family off the Civil List—strengthened the position of those advocating the case for the monarchy. Supporters also pointed out that many of the costs attributed to the monarchy—such as the maintenance of national monuments—were costs that would have to be borne by the public purse regardless of whether one had a monarch or not. They have also contended that, on balance, the nation makes a profit out of the monarchy. Since 1769, each monarch has surrendered income from Crown lands in return for a Civil List. In 1990–1991, income from Crown lands slightly exceeded the £57 million spent on the monarchy.[33] When this is coupled with the benefits derived from tourism and from the trade accruing from foreign tours—members of the royal family drumming up trade in a way an elected head of state could not—then the nation benefits financially from the monarch and the activity of members of the royal family.[34] Critics retort that the money from Crown lands is now effectively public money anyway, that tourists would still come to Britain (the national monuments would still exist), and that trade does not necessarily follow the Crown.[35] The

TABLE 12.2   Attitudes toward the monarchy, 1988

Q: Would you describe yourself as in favor of or against the monarchy as it exists at present, with the queen as head of state, acting on the advice of the government?

Favor	82%
Against	14%
Don't know	5%

The survey was conducted in December 1988.
SOURCE: *Gallup Political Index*, Report No. 341, January 1989, p. 10.

TABLE 12.3   Attitudes toward the monarchy,
May 1992

Q: In your view should the monarchy . . . ?	
Remain as it is	51%
Be modernized	31%
Be abolished	13%
None of these	1%
Don't know	3%

SOURCE: *Gallup Political Index,* Report 381, May 1992, p. 9.

prime minister can do a good job drumming up trade and is in a stronger position to offer government-backed incentives.

The controversy surrounding the royal family in recent years, and especially in 1992, has served to dent but not to destroy support for the continued existence of the monarchy. Critics made some headway but did not carry the majority with them. In the 1970s and 1980s, polls showed that 80% or more of those questioned favored retaining the monarchy. In a 1988 poll, 14% were against retaining the monarchy as it stood (Table 12.2). Even in mid-1992, those favoring abolition constituted only 13% of respondents, though almost a third wanted to see the monarchy modernized; only one in two of those questioned wanted to see it remain as it was (Table 12.3). The position by the end of 1992, following the announcement of the separation of the prince and princess of Wales, was more dramatic. Almost one in four of those questioned believed the monarchy should be abolished (Table 12.4).

Though support for the monarchy declined, Table 12.4 shows that the institution retains majority support. However, other polls suggest that support is not as deep as before. A MORI poll in 1977 found that 77% of those questioned thought Britain would be worse off if the monarchy was abolished. In 1989, this figure had declined to 58%, and in May 1992 it was down to 55%. "The mood toward royalty," commented *The Economist,* "is changing. . . . Even in the Commons, Mr. Major's expression of support for the royal pair [following the announcement of the separation of the prince and princess of Wales] failed to evince full-throated 'hear-hears.' Labour republicans like Dennis Skinner were not shouted down. . . . things can never be the same again for Britain's royalty."[36]

TABLE 12.4   Attitudes toward the monarchy,
December 1992

Q: Do you think the monarchy should be abolished?	
Yes	24%
No	69%
Don't know/other response	7%

SOURCE: Gallup Poll, reported in *The Sunday Telegraph,*
December 13, 1992, p. 2.

CONCLUSION

The queen fulfills the task of representing the unity of the nation as well as carrying out certain political tasks largely but not wholly governed by convention. Her role as a political actor is circumscribed, necessarily so in order for her to fulfill her unifying role, and any real choice she is called on to exercise is the product of circumstance and unclear conventions and not of any personal desire on her part. She carries out her duties assiduously and continues to maintain the support of the population. Recent years, however, have been problematic. She has not been particularly well served by her family and her exemption from paying income tax—now remedied—has proved contentious. The monarchy and, more especially, the royal family (the two are separate but the conduct of the latter affects attitudes to the former) have become more prominent in public debate in recent years, being the subject of especially critical comment in the *annus horribilis* of 1992. Survey data reveal a change in mood toward the monarchy but not a collapse of support. The challenge for the monarchy is one of adapting. Despite the problems of recent years, it is not in danger of imminent demise. The long-term prognosis will depend on how it adapts.

NOTES

1. This paragraph is based on *The Monarchy in Britain,* Central Office of Information Reference Pamphlet 118 (Her Majesty's Stationery Office, 1975), p. 1.
2. F. W. Maitland, *Constitutional History of England,* quoted in H. V. Wiseman (ed.), *Parliament and the Executive* (Routledge and Kegan Paul, 1966), p. 5.
3. W. Bagehot, *The English Constitution* (Fontana, 1963 ed.), p. 61.
4. F. Hardie, *The Political Influence of the British Monarchy 1868–1952* (Batsford, 1970), p. 67.
5. Ibid., p. 188.
6. I. Gilmour, *The Body Politic,* rev. ed. (Hutchinson, 1970), p. 317.
7. A. Horne, *Macmillan,* Vol. II: 1957–1986 (Macmillan, 1989), p. 168.
8. A Gallup poll in December 1988 found that 82% of respondents judged the queen's role as head of the Commonwealth to be very or fairly valuable. *Gallup Political Index,* Report No. 341, January 1989, p. 9.
9. Gilmour, p. 313.
10. See R. Shepherd, *The Power Brokers* (Hutchinson, 1991), pp. 149–159.
11. D. Watt, "If the Queen Has to Choose, Who Will It Be?" *The Times,* December 11, 1981.
12. The constitutional position in the event of such a scenario was raised in late 1992 after the prime minister's aides signalled that the PM might make the vote on the paving motion for the Maastricht bill in November (see chapter 10) a vote of confidence, thus necessitating a dissolution or the resignation of the government in the event of the vote being lost. This course of action was reported not to enjoy the support of his Cabinet colleagues. In the event, the vote was not made one of confidence, though it was believed the prime minister himself would resign if the vote was lost. As reported in chapter 10, the government won the vote with a majority of 3.
13. Lord Blake, *The Office of Prime Minister* (Oxford University Press, 1975), pp. 60–61.

14. E. Short, quoted in Blake, p. 60.
15. K. Martin, *The Crown and the Establishment* (Penguin, 1963).
16. *New Socialist,* August 1982, reported in *The Daily Telegraph,* August 27, 1982.
17. Private expenditure as sovereign, such as gifts to visiting dignitaries, is met from the Privy Purse (the income from the duchy of Lancaster), and personal expenditure as an individual, such as wedding or Christmas gifts, is met from the queen's personal wealth.
18. Prince Charles among other titles, is duke of Cornwall, and the duchy encompasses a number of revenue-generating estates. In 1991, income from the duchy exceeded £2 million ($3m.).
19. "Should One Pay Tax?" *The Economist,* January 25, 1992, p. 36.
20. *Gallup Political Index,* Report No. 341, January 1989, p. 10.
21. MORI, *British Public Opinion,* February 1989, p. 5.
22. P. Johnson, "Solving the Riddle of the Queen's Riches," *The Sunday Times,* November 29, 1992, p. 13.
23. A. Morton, *Diana: Her True Story* (Simon & Schuster, 1992).
24. *The Daily Mail,* November 24, 1992. For a summary of the chronology, see "Seven Days That Shook the Crown," *The Sunday Times,* November 29, 1992, p. 11.
25. *House of Commons Debates (Hansard),* Vol. 214, cols. 982–986 (November 26, 1992).
26. "Admitting the Obvious," *The Economist,* December 12, 1992, p. 25.
27. Ibid.
28. "Royal Survey." *The Sunday Telegraph,* December 13, 1992, p. 2.
29. A. King, "Two-thirds Oppose Idea of Queen Diana," *The Sunday Telegraph,* December 13, 1992, p. 2.
30. E. Wilson, *The Myth of the British Monarchy* (Journeyman/Republic, 1989), p. 178.
31. Quoted in A. Horne, *Macmillan,* Vol. II: 1957–1986 (Macmillan, 1989), pp. 170–171.
32. A poll carried out in 1983, for example, found that more than 90% of respondents thought the queen did "a good job." *The Sun,* April 24, 1983.
33. "Should One Pay Tax?" *The Economist,* January 25, 1992, p. 36.
34. See P. Norton, "The Case Against Abolition," *Social Studies Review,* 4 (3), 1989, p. 122.
35. See Wilson, *The Myth of the British Monarchy;* and "Britain," *The Economist,* January 25, 1992, p. 36.
36. "Admitting the Obvious," *The Economist,* December 12, 1992, p. 25.

PART V

Enforcement and Feedback

CHAPTER 13

Enforcement
The Courts and the Police

The U.S. Supreme Court, as one U.S. expert observed, is neither a court nor a political agency: "it is inseparably both."[1] This special status derives from the court's power of constitutional interpretation, a power effectively read into the Constitution by Chief Justice John Marshall in his opinion in *Marbury* v. *Madison* in 1803. "It is emphatically the province and duty of the judicial department," declared Marshall, "to say what the law is." The Constitution amounts to a paramount law and, in the event of the ordinary law conflicting with it, the Court must resolve the conflict: "This is of the very essence of judicial duty."[2]

The chief justice's reasoning did not go unquestioned.[3] Nonetheless, acceptance of the Court as the arbiter of constitutional disputes was underpinned by the Lockean philosophy inherent in U.S. society[4] and has been reinforced by reasons of practicality (somebody has to perform the task) and of history (the judiciary has, in effect, always performed it). When Richard Nixon's attorney, James St. Clair, sought to argue in the case of *United States* v. *Nixon* (1974) that the president should interpret his own powers under the Constitution, he was more than one and a half centuries too late in advancing such an argument. Acceptance of the Court's power of constitutional interpretation was too well established to be overthrown. The Court remains the judicial arbiter of a document that is inherently political and one that by its own declaration constitutes the supreme law of the land—hence the Court's dual and inseparable roles.

The position of the British judiciary in the political process is significantly different from that of its U.S. counterpart. There are two principal reasons for this. For one thing, there are inherent difficulties in seeking to interpret a constitution whose boundaries are not clearly delineated. For another, the judiciary labors under the self-imposed doctrine of parliamentary sovereignty. The courts have no power to declare unconstitutional an act of Parliament. If the judicial interpretation of an act conflicts with the intentions of Parliament, a new act may be passed making explicit Parliament's wishes: The courts are duty-bound to enforce the new act. The last word, in short, rests with Parliament.

These difficulties are crucial to an understanding of the U.S. and British courts. They serve to explain why the U.S. Supreme Court (indeed, the U.S. judiciary, given that any court can declare an act unconstitutional) may be deemed to form part of the political decision-making process in the United States, whereas the judiciary would not form part of that process in Britain. Nonetheless, such differences should not be overstated. A number of caveats need to be entered to the distinctions that have just been drawn.

On the U.S. side, it is important to record that the Supreme Court will decide a case on the basis of constitutional interpretation only when it cannot be resolved by statutory interpretation.[5] The Court itself seeks to avoid political questions that it deems nonjusticiable. Nor is it free of constraints imposed by other bodies. Congress can limit, and on occasion has limited, the Court's appellate jurisdiction.[6] The Court is dependent on the executive for the enforcement of its decisions. Although it may seek to give a lead to, or restrain the actions of, president or Congress, it will rarely beat a path too far ahead or too far behind what is politically acceptable. And in practice it has rarely struck down federal legislation.[7] Although the power to strike down a measure serves as "an omnipresent and potentially omnipotent check upon the legislative branches of government," it is a power that, as Henry Abraham observed, "courts are understandably loathe to invoke."[8]

On the British side, the courts retain the power of statutory—and common law—interpretation and can determine, in any case brought before them, whether the purported exercise of a power is authorized by law. As a result, the executive actions of ministers and administrative authorities can, when challenged, come within their purview. The determination of the courts in such cases can always be overridden by a new act of Parliament authorizing that which the courts have struck down, but by having to determine such cases the courts are brought into the political limelight. This relative prominence has been especially evident in recent years, with a significant increase in the number of such cases.

Furthermore, British entry into the European Community has added a new judicial dimension to the Constitution (see chapter 10). The 1972 European Communities Act provided that, in the event of a conflict between the provisions of EC law and domestic U.K. law, the former was to prevail. The act also stipulated that any disputes as to the interpretation, effect, and validity of the EC Treaties, or of any legislation made under them, was to be treated by British judges as a matter of law. Cases that reached the highest domestic court of appeal (the House of Lords) had, under the Treaty of Rome, to be referred to the Court of Justice of the European Communities for a definitive ruling, and lower courts could request that the European Court give a ruling on the meaning and interpretation of the treaties. The full implications of this new judicial dimension were not immediately clear but began to emerge in 1990, when a merchant fishing act passed by Parliament was challenged as being in breach of EC law. In a notable judgment, in *R.* v. *Secretary of State for Transport, ex parte Factortame,* the Court of Justice ruled that the courts could *suspend* an act of Parliament that appeared to breach EC law until such time as a final determination was made.[9] Though the ruling undermined the doctrine of parliamentary sovereignty, it did not destroy it. Parliament retained the power to repeal the 1972 act and legal authorities took the view that an express overriding of EC law by a U.K. act would be enforced by British courts under the doctrine. The ruling in *Factortame* nonetheless gave a new prominence to the judicial process.

Given this, the British courts clearly cannot be described as standing divorced from the political fray. Nonetheless, they remain distinct from their counterparts in the United States. The courts in the United States have the power to interpret the Constitution and strike down measures that conflict with its provisions. Consequently, major and social issues are often fought out before the U.S. Supreme Court. Though recent rulings by the EC Court of Justice provide the basis for a more powerful court system in the United Kingdom, British courts are nowhere near being on a par with those in the United States. Whereas in the United States the constitutional position of abortion may be fought out in the courts, in the United Kingdom its permissibility is resolved in Parliament. Given this difference between the two court systems, the judiciary has not figured prominently in studies of British politics.

THE JUDICIAL SYSTEM

The administration of justice is one of the prerogatives of the Crown, but it is a prerogative that has long been exercisable only through duly appointed courts and judges. The basic organizational division within the court system is that between criminal and civil. There is no such distinction in the court system of the United States. A simplified outline of the court system in England and Wales is provided in Figure 13.1. (Scotland and Northern Ireland each have different systems.) The Court of Appeal, the Crown Court, and the High Court together constitute what is known as (confusingly, from the perspective of the U.S. student) the Supreme Court. At the apex of the structure sits the House of Lords.

Criminal Cases

Minor criminal cases are tried summarily in magistrates' courts. The courts are local courts, presided over in most cases by unpaid lay magistrates, supplemented, especially in the larger cities, by legally qualified, full-time magistrates known as stipendiary magistrates. The courts have the power to levy fines and, depending on the offense, impose a prison sentence not exceeding six months. Stipendiary magistrates sit alone. Lay magistrates sit in a bench, which can be between two and seven in number but is almost always three. They are advised by a legally qualified clerk of the court. Cases dealt with by them cover such matters as driving offenses, assault charges, and public order offenses (for example, breach of the peace, causing a fray). The courts also have limited civil jurisdiction, primarily in matrimonial proceedings, and have semi-administrative functions in the licensing of public houses, betting shops, and clubs.

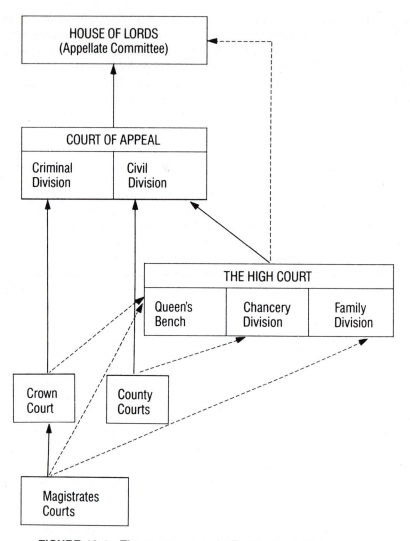

FIGURE 13.1 The court system in England and Wales

Note: Appeals are possible to higher courts as shown by arrows, usually through the immediate superior court or, in certain cases (shown by dotted lines), through another route. Tribunals and specialist courts are omitted.

For many years, magistrates' courts were linked closely with the police. Until 1952, magistrates' courts in London were known as police courts and were often attached to police stations. Until 1986, the decision whether to prosecute—and the prosecution itself—was undertaken by the police. Since October 1986, responsibility for the review and prosecution of all criminal cases instituted by police forces in England and Wales has rested, with certain exceptions, with the Crown Prosecution Service (CPS), headed by the director of public prosecutions (the DPP). (In Scotland, responsibility for prosecution rests with the Crown Office and the Procurator Fiscal Service.) Members of the CPS are lawyers, but since the inception of the service, difficulties have been experienced in recruiting a sufficient number of well-qualified staff; private practice has tended to be more lucrative. The DPP is normally a Queen's Counsel (QC), a senior barrister; in 1992, the first woman—Barbara Mills QC—was appointed to the post.

About 98% of all criminal cases are dealt with by magistrates' courts, accounting for about 2 million cases each year. Appeals from magistrates' courts are possible to the Crown Court or, in certain cases, to the High Court (to the Queen's Bench Division on points of law and the Family Division in matrimonial cases). Serious criminal cases—indictable offenses—are tried before a jury in the Crown Court. In 1991, just over 117,000 people were committed for trial in the Crown Court. The court has nearly 100 centers, divided into six court circuits. Cases are heard either by a High Court judge (who will normally preside over the most serious cases), a circuit judge, or a recorder. Circuit judges are full-time, salaried judges; recorders are part-time and salaried, and when not presiding at court pursue their normal legal practice. Judges and recorders are legally qualified and to be eligible for appointment must have practiced for at least ten years as either solicitors or barristers.

Appeals from the Crown Court may be taken on a point of law to the Queen's Bench Division of the High Court but usually are taken to the Criminal Division of the Court of Appeal. Appeals against conviction are possible on points of law (as of right) and on a question of fact (with the leave of the trial judge or Court of Appeal). The Appeal Court may quash a conviction or uphold it: It can also vary the sentence imposed by the lower court. Appeals against sentence, if not a sentence fixed by law, are also possible with the leave of the Appeal Court. Since February 1989 the power has existed (and been used) for the attorney-general to refer to the court those sentences that appear to the prosecuting authorities to be unduly lenient. The Criminal Division of the Appeal Court comprises a presiding judge, known at the lord chief justice; 27 lords justices of appeal; and a number of ex officio members. Three members of the court normally sit to hear a case.

From the Court of Appeal, an appeal to the House of Lords is possible if the court certifies that a point of law of general public importance is involved and it appears to the court or the House that the point ought to be considered by the highest court of appeal. For judicial purposes, the House of Lords does not comprise all members of the House. Instead, the task is undertaken by an appellate committee that will comprise usually five but sometimes as many as seven peers drawn from the lord chancellor, lords of appeal in ordinary (life peers appointed for the purpose of undertaking such tasks), and such peers as hold or have previously held high judicial office. The committee meets in a committee room of the House of Lords, though its judgment will still be delivered in the full chamber. In 1966 the lords of appeal in ordinary announced that they would no longer consider themselves bound by their previous decisions, and the House is thus prepared to depart from a previous decision when it appears right to do so.

Civil Cases

In civil proceedings, minor cases involving small sums of money are heard by county courts, of which there are 274; more important cases go to the High Court. The High Court comprises the Queen's Bench Division, covering mainly matters of common law; the Chancery Division, dealing mainly with equity cases; and the Family Division, for cases of divorce and custody. County courts are presided over by circuit judges. The High Court comprises the lord chief justice, who presides over the Queen's Bench Division; the lord chancellor, who is nominally president of the Chancery Court but who never sits (a vice-chancellor, in practice, presides); the president of the Family Division; and just over 80 judges who are known as puisne (pronounced *puny*) judges. In civil cases the judges normally sit alone, though a divisional court of two or more judges may be formed, especially in the Queen's Bench Division, which has important responsibilities in the issuing of writs of habeas corpus and orders of mandamus, certiorari, and prohibition. Like other senior judicial posts, puisne judges are appointed from among eminent lawyers of long standing.

Appeals in certain instances may go to the High Court. Appeals from county courts in bankruptcy cases are heard by a divisional court of the Chancery division. Appeals against the decisions of magistrates' courts in matrimonial proceedings are heard by a divisional court of the Family Division. And appeals on points of law may be taken from a magistrate's court to a divisional court of the Queen's Bench Division.

Appeals from county courts (those not going to the High Court) and from the High Court go to the Civil Division of the Court of Appeal—presided over by the master of the rolls—and from there may go to the House of Lords. In exceptional cases—on a point of law of exceptional difficulty calling for a reconsideration of a binding precedent—an appeal may go directly (with the leave of the House) from the High Court to the House of Lords. In the instance of European Community law, as we have seen, any case that reaches the House of Lords must, under the provisions of the 1972 European Communities Act, be referred to the Court of the European Communities for a definitive ruling.

The Judiciary

Concerning the judiciary itself—its recruitment, appointment, and relationship to and with the executive—a number of important points are deserving of mention. Magistrates' courts, with the exception of those presided over by stipendiary magistrates, are staffed by lay magistrates known as justices of the peace, of which there are more than 29,000. These magistrates are not legally qualified, though they do now receive some basic training; they usually are prominent local citizens and are appointed by the lord chancellor. Any citizen can recommend the name of an individual for appointment as a magistrate, though in practice recommendations tend to come from local political parties and civic bodies.

Above the level of magistrates are the legally qualified judges, who are drawn from the ranks of the legal profession. Lawyers in Britain are divided into solicitors and barristers; there is no equivalent distinction in the United States. (There are also far fewer lawyers per head of population in Britain than in the United States.)[10] A solicitor is a lawyer who undertakes ordinary legal business for clients. A barrister gives expert legal advice to solicitors and their clients and conducts cases in court. There is statutory provision as to how long one must have served as a solicitor or barrister before being eligible for appointment as a judge. Usually, judges are drawn from the ranks of barristers (occasionally a solicitor is appointed as a recorder, but none has been appointed to higher judicial office) and have generally been in legal practice for longer than the minimum period required. Those appointed are regarded as the outstanding members of their profession. The status of a judge is superior to that of a judge in the United States. Elevation to judicial office is regarded as a step up the professional ladder, something to be sought after, rather than a position one settles for if unable to establish oneself as a leading corporate lawyer.

Although judges are recruited from the ranks of well-qualified lawyers and are usually appointed or promoted on the basis of legal merit, their appointment is made by members of the executive branch. Formally, all judges are appointed by the Crown. By convention, senior judicial appointments, those above the level of puisne judges, are made by the Crown on the advice of the prime minister. Other judicial appointments are made by the Crown on the advice of the lord chancellor. In making recommendations, the prime minister will usually consult the lord chancellor. It is rare for judicial appointments to be the subject of political controversy, although that has been known to happen.[11] Such appointments are not subject to any form of parliamentary approval.

The method of appointing of judges, coupled with the unusual position of the lord chancellor and of certain senior judges, may raise doubts as to the independence of the judiciary. The lord chancellor is living proof that the separation of personnel exercised in the United States between branches of government is not rigidly adhered to in the United Kingdom. The lord chancellor is a member of the Cabinet, he presides over the House of Lords (though his position as presiding officer is not dissimilar to that of the vice-president in relation to the Senate in the United States),[12] and he is the head of the judiciary. He not only advises the Crown on the appointment of judges and magistrates, he also ranks as a senior judge, as lord chancellor. He is a member of the appellate committee of the House of Lords and, if he takes part in hearing an appeal, which sometimes he does, then he presides. Furthermore, he is not the only person in government who occupies a position in the judicial hierarchy. The positions of attorney-general and solicitor-general, as well as those of law officers for Scotland (lord advocate and solicitor-general for Scotland), are political appointments and form part of the government. Also, the lords of appeal in ordinary are life peers. As members of the House of Lords, they are free to take part in parliamentary proceedings.

Despite this overlap, and despite the ability of Parliament to overrule the courts through new legislation, the judiciary in Britain is independent. This independence is achieved in a number of ways, by statute, common law, parliamentary rules, and an acceptance by government that the rule of law requires abstention from interference with the conduct of litigation. Judges of superior courts (the High Court and above, with the exception of the lord chancellor) cannot be removed except for misbehavior in office, and their salaries are fixed by statute in order to avoid annual debate. They serve in office until they reach a statutory retiring age of 75 years. They enjoy immunity from civil proceedings for anything said or done while acting in a judicial capacity. Judges of lower courts are also immune if acting within their jurisdiction. By custom, questions are not asked in either house of Parliament about the conduct of courts in particular cases, reference may not be made in debate to matters awaiting or under adjudication before the courts (*sub judice* rules also prevent media comment on pending cases), and reflections may not be cast in debate upon the character or motives of a judge. Judges are not eligible for election to the House of Commons, and those who are members of the House of Lords, with the obvious exception of the lord chancellor, abstain from party political activities.

Two authors have suggested that another fact that promotes judicial independence is that judges "are all drawn from the bar after successful careers as barristers, a profession which tends to foster self-confidence and independence of mind."[13] Also, service as a judge is not seen as a stepping-stone to other things. One makes a career in the law, a career in which one's standing with colleagues and superiors is important and is essentially independent of partisan implications.

The degree to which judicial independence has been maintained is reflected in the fact that since judges of superior courts were accorded security of tenure under the Act of Settlement of 1701, only one judge has been removed from office—an Irish judge in 1830. He was found to have misappropriated money belonging to litigants and to have ceased to perform his judicial duties many years previously![14] In 1973, 180 Labour MPs signed a motion calling for the dismissal of the judge who presided over the new (and, in the event, short-lived) National Industrial Relations Court, a court regarded by the MPs as a political court set up to restrain the trade unions. The motion was never debated and it was very much the exception that proved the rule.

Although, as we shall see, the judiciary has not been free of criticism, the principle of judicial independence is a feature of the British Constitution and, in interpreting and applying the law, judges are generally more skilled and better regarded than their U.S. counterparts (especially those who serve in the state courts) and maintain probably a greater degree of judicial decorum in the proceedings before them. The rules and ethics of the legal profession also prevent much of the degrading touting for business by lawyers that is a feature of many U.S. courts.

Nonetheless, some of the problems experienced by the U.S. judicial system find a pale—sometimes not so pale—reflection in Britain. The use of plea bargaining generates similar problems.[15] There are delays in bringing defendants to trial. In London the average wait between committal and trial is 20 weeks. Although there are various schemes, including legal advice centers to provide advice to the less well-off and a publicly funded legal aid scheme, the cost of legal advice and various legal services is a problem for many citizens. "Top London lawyers," reported *The Sunday Times* at the end of 1992, "are the most expensive in the world"; one survey put the average hourly rate for City of London solicitors at $540, compared with $350 an hour for the top firms in the United States.[16] As legal costs have soared, eligibility for legal aid has declined. In 1992, the lord chancellor announced plans to reduce eligibility further, to those with disposable incomes of less than £2,213 ($3,430). In 1979, it was estimated that 79% of households were eligible for legal aid; by 1992, it was down to 48%.[17] For the average citizen in Britain, as in the United States, going to court is an expensive business.

THE CURRENT DEBATE

In recent decades, the judiciary on a number of occasions has entered the political limelight. It has done so because of the exercise of power already vested in the courts and because of various calls by judges and others to be vested with new powers. The powers exercised and the powers proposed have implications for the maintenance of political authority.

The courts have taken decisions that have proved controversial in both civil and criminal cases. The former concern primarily cases of judicial review and the latter miscarriages of justice. In terms of proposed powers, the debate has centered on calls for a new Bill of Rights.

Judicial Review

The courts have the power to review executive actions to determine whether they are carried out within the limits of the relevant authorizing act. If the action is deemed by the courts to be *ultra vires* (beyond the powers), it is void. A court may also declare void an action if it deems that the principles of natural justice have not been observed or if the action has entailed the abuse or unreasonable exercise of power. The power to declare an action *ultra vires* is a corollary of the principle of parliamentary sovereignty. The power to void an action for failing to observe the principles of natural justice is derived from common law. Until the 1960s, neither power was much used. In part, this may have been due to the realization that the executive dominated the legislature and could thus obtain legitimation of past or proposed actions; it may concomitantly have been due to a lack of will on the part of judges. They were, and more recently have been, accused of not being too sympathetic to the claims of the individual when those claims were pitted against the demands of government. Denied the power to question acts of Parliament and unwilling to exercise their powers over acts of the executive, few judicial decisions entered the realms of controversy.

This was to change with "the emergence of a period of judicial activism or intervention which began," according to John Griffith, "in the early 1960s and has been growing in strength ever since."[18] A number of judges, apparently concerned about the encroachment of executive power in the field of individual liberties, became more assertive in the exercise of their common-law power to review the executive actions of ministers and administrative authorities. In four important cases in the 1960s, the courts adopted an activist line in reviewing powers exercised by administrative bodies including, in two cases, by ministers.[19] The courts have maintained their activist stance since that time, succeeding governments being subject to review and to having the courts find against them. Various executive actions were the subject of review during the Labour government of 1974–1979, with ministerial actions being declared *ultra vires* in three much-publicized cases.[20] Since the return of a Conservative government in 1979, there has been a notable increase in the number of cases of judicial review. From less than 500 a year at the end of the 1970s, the number had increased to more than 1,000 a year in the latter half of the 1980s (see Figure 13.2). "Judicial review of central-government decisions has become so common," declared *The Economist* in 1989, "that all civil servants are now briefed on the dangers of falling foul of the 'judge on your shoulder' as one internal Whitehall document puts it."[21] Various ministerial actions have been struck down. In 1984, for example, the High Court quashed a decision by the environment secretary to require the Greater London Council to pay £50 million to support the newly created London Transport Authority (the decision was later reversed by legislation); the following year the High Court found that the social services secretary had failed to comply with the provisions of a 1982 act in inviting comments on regulations he had introduced under the act; and in 1990 the High Court overruled government guidelines on the administration of the Social Fund introduced in 1988.[22]

Not all cases of judicial review resulted in the action of ministers being struck down; and, indeed, not all cases involved the action of ministers. Various other authorities were subject to judicial review and a number, including—before its demise—the Greater London Council, were found to be acting *ultra vires*.[23]

FIGURE 13.2   Applications for judicial review

SOURCE: "What Checks: What Balances?" *The Economist,* November 18, 1989, p. 31.

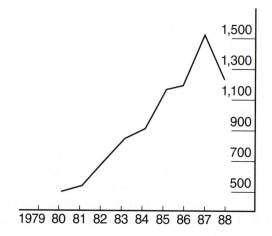

1,500
1,300
1,100
900
700
500

1979 80 81 82 83 84 85 86 87 88

This greater activism on the part of the courts has brought the courts into the political arena. It has done so not just because of the judgments made in the particular cases, but also because of the *obiter dicta* of the judges, and the interpretation given the courts' words and actions by politicians. Defenders of the courts have seen this greater activism as a protection of the individual against overpowerful public authorities. Others, not least some politicians, have seen it as an unelected—and highly conservative—body substituting its judgment for that of the people's elected representatives.[24]

Miscarriages of Justice

Confidence in the courts has been dented in recent years by a number of highly publicized cases of miscarriages of justice. The most prominent but not the only cases have involved individuals convicted of terrorist offenses: most notably the "Birmingham Six," convicted of pub bombings in Birmingham in 1974; the "Guildford Four," convicted in 1975 of bombings in Guildford; and the Maguire family, convicted of running an IRA bomb factory. In 1989 the Guildford Four were released, after spending 14 years in jail, pending an inquiry into their original conviction, the DPP having found himself unable to argue in support of the convictions. In 1990 the Maguire case was referred to the Appeal Court after the home secretary received evidence that the convictions could not be upheld. In 1991 the Birmingham Six were released, after spending 16 years in jail, when the Court of Appeal quashed their convictions. The most recent case not related to terrorist offenses involved the release in November 1991 of Winston Silcott, after the Appeal Court quashed his 1987 conviction for the murder of a police officer during a 1985 London riot.

Most of the criticism in such cases was directed at the police and the evidence they presented at the original trials, the convictions being quashed on the grounds that the evidence was unsafe or fabricated. However, the courts did not escape blame. As *The Times* editorialized, the trial judges and others involved in the trials were overreliant on the good faith of key prosecution witnesses—as was often the Court of Appeal.[25] The Appeal Court came in for particular criticism for its apparent reluctance to even consider that there may have been miscarriages of justice. As late as 1988, for example, it had refused an appeal by the Birmingham Six, doing so in terms that suggested that the home secretary should not even have referred the case to the court. Nor did the civil courts escape censure. When the Birmingham Six had brought a claim for damages, in an attempt to establish police malpractice, the then master of the rolls, Lord Denning, delivered an *obiter dictum* "to the effect that exposure of injustice in individual cases was less important than preserving a facade of infallibility," an observation that made a particularly bad impression, especially when the true facts of the case started to emerge shortly afterward.[26]

The cases also did little for the reputation of the most senior judges—notably the lord chief justice (Lord Lane) and the master of the rolls (Lord Donaldson)— who had officiated at the original trials. After the release of the Birmingham Six in March 1991, 100 Labour MPs tabled an early day motion calling for the dismissal of the lord chief justice. To "minimise as far as possible the likelihood of such events happening again," the government announced the appointment of a Royal Commission to look at the criminal justice system. The following year also saw the retirement of both the lord chief justice and the master of rolls, being replaced by judges with reputations for openness and a willingness to consider reform. The Royal Commission reported in July 1993. Among its recommendations: regular training of judges and an independent authority to consider alleged miscarriages of justice and power to refer cases to the Court of Appeal.

A Bill of Rights

Such cases brought the courts into the realms of political controversy. They have also entered the sphere of political debate as a consequence of proposals to extend their power. As we have seen, British membership in the European Community has provided a new judicial dimension to the British Constitution. Some politicians and jurists have argued for that to be extended to encompass a new bill of rights. As we have seen (chapter 3), Britain already has a bill of rights, that of 1689. That bill, which remains an extant part of British law, stipulated essentially the relationship of king to Parliament. Advocates of a new bill of rights want one that encompasses basic human rights.

Pressures for the enactment of a bill of rights, if possible with some degree of entrenchment (that is, with extraordinary provisions to limit the possibility of amendment), have built up since the latter half of the 1970s. Such a bill was initially advocated by some jurists and various Liberal and Conservative politicians, especially in the House of Lords. The case for it gained a boost in the late 1980s, when "Charter '88," a constitutional reform movement supported by some well-known figures on the Left, made a bill of rights a central feature of its manifesto.

Advocates consider that Parliament is no longer capable of resisting the encroachment of government on rights previously considered inviolate. Britain, according to Lord Hailsham, labors under an "elective dictatorship."[27] If the rights of the individual are to be protected, some new means of protection are necessary to supplement or replace those provided inadequately by Parliament. The answer is deemed to lay in a bill of rights that stipulates the rights of the individual, possibly a bill akin to that of the United States. Such a measure would then be subject to interpretation by the courts, which, if the bill enjoyed a degree of entrenchment, would be able to strike down conflicting measures as being contrary to its provisions. It is not axiomatic that the courts would enjoy such a power. Nonetheless, that is the clear intention of those who advocate the measure. They seek to put certain rights beyond the reach of government and place them into the care of the courts. Lord Scarman has imputed to society a wish for judges to defend the liberties of the individual from arbitrary acts of government.[28] "Let us keep in mind," he wrote in 1989, "that in a pluralist society many minorities have no real opportunity of acquiring political power and rely on the law's protection against oppression by the majority."[29]

Advocacy of such a bill does not go unchallenged. A number of critics, especially on the Left, oppose it because it would be handing power to judges drawn from a particular background and with a narrow view of society. According to John Griffith, judges "by their training and education and pursuit of their professions as barristers, acquired a strikingly homogeneous collection of attitudes, beliefs and principles, which to them represent the public interest."[30] The public interest is construed to favor law and order and the interests of the state (in time of perceived threat) over the rights of the individual; property rights over individual rights; and, in Griffith's view, "the promotion of certain political views normally associated with the Conservative Party."[31] The last, according to Griffith, has been notable in cases affecting, for example, trade unions. The orientation to the interests of the state has been seen in cases such as the *Ponting* case in 1985, in which the judge, Mr. Justice McCowan, interpreted the interests of the state to be whatever the government declared to be the interests of the state.

Other critics of a bill of rights have opposed it not on grounds of who the judges are and where they come from, but simply on the grounds that they are judges. "The objection is to the very fact that it is judges *qua* judges that would be empowered to determine issues that are inherently political."[32] Power would, in effect, be transferred from an elected dictatorship to a nonelected dictatorship. It would introduce into the British polity a "democratic deficit."[33]

To an American weaned on an entrenched bill of rights interpreted by independent magistrates, opposition to an entrenched bill of rights on such grounds is difficult to comprehend. Britain, however, lacks those characteristics that have underpinned the American's acceptance of constitutional interpretation by the U.S. Supreme Court. "Federalism apart," one analyst writes, "judicial review as it has worked in America would be inconceivable without the national acceptance of the Lockian creed."[34] Such a creed has not found universal assent in Britain.

Weaned on the doctrine of parliamentary sovereignty, many Britons have come to regard constitutional disputes as matters for resolution by political debate and not litigation. Whereas constitutional interpretation by the courts in the United States may serve as a support of the political system, in Britain it could serve to undermine it. "I should hate to rely upon the appointed judiciary rather than upon the elected members of a legislature for the rights of the people," declared an MP, perhaps not altogether disinterestedly.[35] If the courts are seen as not being impartial arbiters and become what Lord Joseph has termed "a party political football"—a possibility even more likely in the event of their being empowered to interpret a bill of rights whose provisions would be politically contentious—then respect for judges and the judicial process is undermined.

Whereas Americans may be largely if not wholly agreed on the provisions of the Bill of Rights, there is no such agreement in Britain as to what should be included in a British bill. It would be a politically contentious document, and anybody vested with the responsibility of its interpretation would be drawn inexorably into the political fray. Some jurists would not be averse to being drawn into that fray. Many politicians and some judges would prefer to defend the judiciary from the perils of such a course. Despite growing pressure in favor of a bill of rights, the chances of its realization in the near future are slim.

THE POLICE FORCE

The British police force has been regarded for many years as a paragon among police forces. In the past 10 to 20 years it has undergone major changes. It has also become a topic of public debate because of the problem of police accountability, accusations of corruption in certain forces, and strained relations between the police and particular elements of the community. Like police forces elsewhere, it has also been at the sharp end in tackling a rise in the recorded incidence of crime.

In the United Kingdom there are 52 police forces (43 in England and Wales, 8 in Scotland, and 1—the Royal Ulster Constabulary—in Northern Ireland), each responsible for law enforcement in its area. Outside the London metropolis each force is under the direction of a chief constable. The metropolitan police force, with its headquarters in New Scotland Yard, is under the control of a commissioner. (There is a separate City of London force.) The number of police officers has grown throughout the twentieth century and in 1992–1993 the establishment was 129,000; with civilian workers and special constables (volunteer, part-time officers), the total police strength amounted to 174,000. There is about 1 police officer for every 400 people in England and Wales, roughly the same ratio as in the United States. The police force relies for its effectiveness on the consent and the cooperation of the community. As far as possible, the police have sought to operate as a part of the local community. Police officers live in the community they serve (that is, they live in local houses rather than in barracks), they have limited but original powers, and for many years they patrolled their allotted beats on foot. Remarkable in U.S. terms is the fact that, with certain exceptions (the Diplomatic Protection Group, for example, and police in Northern Ireland), they are not armed: Police constables on beat patrol carry only a truncheon (a wooden baton). Although in some parts of the community the police have always been treated with suspicion, popular trust in the police has been a feature of recent British history, a view fostered by the police: Children have often been taught to look up with respect to the local policeman on the beat, often portrayed as a kindly figure, ready to pass the time of day with residents and obligingly telling children the time or seeing them safely across the road.

It has also been a nonpolitical force in that it has been kept largely at one remove from direct government control. (Only the Special Branch, which carries out arrests on behalf of the intelligence services, could be described as fulfilling a political role.) The fear of a national police force under government control has prevented the creation of such a force. Each force, except in London, is accountable to a Police Authority. Each authority comprises councillors and magistrates. Traditionally, two-thirds of the members have been councillors and one-third magistrates; under plans announced by the home secretary in 1993, the authorities are to be slimmed down, with councillors comprising half the members, the rest made up of magistrates, businesspeople, and others appointed by the home secretary. London has lacked such a body, the Police Authority for the metropolis being the home secretary; in 1993, the home secretary's plans for change included bringing London into line with the other police forces.

A chief constable, the head of each force, has to submit an annual report to his authority, and the authority can require him to supply a report on any topic, other than on the operational deployment of his force (or anything that could be against the public interest, as confirmed by the home secretary). The authority also appoints senior officers above the rank of chief superintendent. Funding of the police is provided by local authorities, supplemented by grants from central government. This funding provides, or could provide, both the police authorities and the home secretary with leverage in seeking to ensure police accountability. In practice, chief constables have tended to achieve autonomy in their activities, local authorities being more concerned with the provision of funds than the policies for which those funds are intended.

Pitted against the fear of centralized government control has been the desire for greater operational efficiency. Problems arising from the existence of too many autonomous police forces (such as the 40,000 police forces that exist in the United States) has encouraged the amalgamation of forces, reducing the number in England and Wales from a little under 200 in the 1920s to the present 43. There have been calls for the number to be reduced even further. In 1993, the home secretary, though not revealing plans to reduce the number, did announce that the procedure for amalgamating forces would be made simpler.

Perceptions of the police as a local, unarmed, well-trained force (all officers undergo a standard training) that is free of political direction, combined with a crime rate relatively low by international standards (especially when compared with the United States), helped produce the positive view of the police held at home and abroad, particularly in the 1950s and, to a lesser extent, the 1960s.

Since the latter half of the 1960s, the public attitude toward the police has undergone some change. In part, this is attributable to certain changes in the police force itself. From being the local constable on the beat with nothing more than a whistle to summon assistance, the police officer was transferred to driving a car (known as panda cars because of their appearance) and was equipped with a personal radio. By being in a car, able to respond more quickly to calls for assistance (the rationale for the move), the police officer had less direct contact with the local citizenry. By having a personal radio he or she was able to summon the assistance of colleagues: There was less need to appeal to local citizens or pursue a diplomatic approach in handling quarrelsome characters. There also emerged a new breed of professional chief constable, more self-assertive and imposing his (never yet her) own views on policing onto his own force.

Public attitudes toward the police force also have been affected adversely by four other developments. In combination, they have generated what has amounted to a crisis of confidence in the police, especially among certain sections of the population. Those developments are the rise in the crime rate, corruption within the police force, poor policing in certain areas, and problems of accountability.

Rising Crime Rate

By international standards, Britain is a middle-ranking country in terms of crime rates. In terms of the percentage of the population that falls victim to one or more crimes, it ranks well behind the United States, Canada, Australia, and its immediate European neighbors (see Figure 13.3). Of crimes that are reported, most are burglaries or car crimes; the bulk of the remainder are property crimes (Figure 13.4). However, what these figures mask is a notable rise in reported crime, and a decreasing clear-up rate by the police.

Before the 1920s, the police recorded fewer than 100,000 offenses each year in England and Wales. By 1950, the figure had reached 500,000 and by 1980, 2.5 million. In 1991 it was just over 4.5 million.[36] These constitute offenses reported to the police; the actual level of crime is accepted to be much higher. (Offenses such as rape are belived to be significantly underreported.) However, some of the biggest increases in 1991 were in offenses with a high level of reporting.[37] Though crime levels remain highest in urban areas, the greatest increase has taken place recently in rural areas.

As crime has increased, the percentage of offenses cleared up by the police (that is, offenses resulting in an arrest) has decreased. In 1971, 45% of indictable offenses reported to the police were classified as cleared up. In 1990, the clear-up rate—though not precisely comparable with 1971 because of some changes in accounting practices—was 32%.[38] The lowest clear-up rate was for burglary, where only one in every four reported offenses resulted in an arrest.

The low clear-up rate for burglaries also meshes with a popular perception that the police are not too interested in solving such offenses, but are more interested in major crimes. In a Gallup poll in June 1992, 59% of those questioned thought that it was fair to make such an assertion—that the police are not interested in solving minor crimes such as burglaries, but are more interested in major crimes—compared with 42% giving a similar response in 1983.[39] Though a strong case can be made for police resources to be more heavily concentrated

FIGURE 13.3 Percentage of population victim of one or more crimes: International comparison, 1988

SOURCE: *International Crime Survey*, 1988.

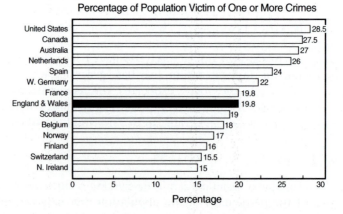

Percentage of Population Victim of One or More Crimes

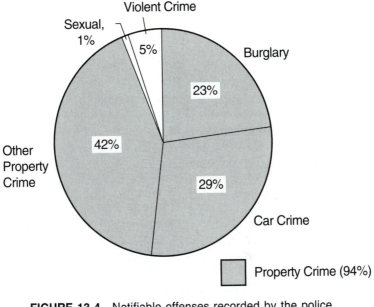

Violent Crime

Sexual,
1%

5%   Burglary

23%

Other
Property
Crime   42%

29%

Car Crime

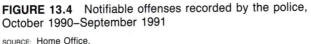 Property Crime (94%)

FIGURE 13.4 Notifiable offenses recorded by the police,
October 1990–September 1991

SOURCE: Home Office.

on serious crimes, such as those involving violence against the person, the problem for the police in terms of public perceptions is that—as Figure 13.4 reveals—burglary is more likely to affect the average citizen than an offense involving physical injury.

Furthermore, the clear-up rate has decreased as police resources—in personnel and equipment—have increased significantly. The position was summarized in 1992 by *The Economist* thus: "real spending on the police force rose by almost 70% in the 1980s—but crime continued to soar and public confidence in the police slumped."[40] The number of people believing that the police are efficient and do their job well has fallen: By mid-1992, only one in three respondents gave that response in a Gallup poll, compared with almost one in two giving that response in 1982.[41]

In an attempt to increase police efficiency and restore public trust, the government has undertaken a series of efficiency audits, opened up police performance to public scrutiny (requiring forces to publish such details as response times), and put an emphasis on returning police officers to beat patrols. Though beat patrols have little effect on crime rates, they are important for reassuring local residents. A number of police forces have also undertaken their own initiatives in an attempt to increase efficiency and public confidence, ranging from local customer surveys to transferring officers from cars to bicycles (the latter, where tried, apparently proving quite effective in silent detection and mobility). However, improving efficiency and public confidence are not always compatible goals. Some police forces have reduced the number of police stations manned on a round-the-clock basis, an action that has rarely proved popular with local citizens.

Corruption

Corruption has been a problem in the metropolitan police force for a number of years. In a five-year period in the 1970s, the commissioner removed more than 450 officers and in 1976 there was the biggest trial involving detectives seen since 1877. Cases of corruption and malpractice have continued to make the headlines since, and they have not been confined to the metropolitan police force.

The late 1980s and early 1990s witnessed a number of highly publicized cases of alleged corruption. Several cases involving officers from the West Midlands force resulted in the chief constable of the West Midlands in 1989 removing from operational duty every member of his 53-member criminal investigation department, having earlier wound up its serious crime squad following allegations of evidence having been fabricated. Various people convicted on squad evidence were released by the courts. The Guildford Four and Birmingham Six cases, described earlier, resulted in a number of officers being charged with conspiracy to pervert the course of justice (and, in the Birmingham Six case, perjury). There were also a number of less publicized cases. In 1991, the metropolitan police paid £40,000 ($62,000) in damages to a man who had alleged he had been beaten, racially abused, and framed. Four homosexuals won £30,000 ($46,500) in damages from Staffordshire police after claiming they had been maliciously prosecuted. There were a number of cases involving personal corruption for gain, most notably in November 1991 when the chairman, secretary, and treasurer of the West Midlands Police Federation Joint Branch Board were all charged with stealing funds from their members' insurance fund. There were also a number of malpractice cases involving sexual discrimination.[42]

Such cases generally, and those of the Guildford Four, Birmingham Six, and Winston Silcott in particular, led to demands for reform in order to cope with a crisis in confidence. Some change had already been instituted by the 1984 Police and Criminal Evidence Act, which required the tape recording of interviews. Most of the major cases involving fabricated evidence predated the act. However, in one case in 1989, the lord chief justice quashed a conviction after declaring that the officers in the case had shown "a lamentable attitude" to the codes of practice laid down by the act. The Bar Council (the professional body of barristers) has recommended that there should be independent corroboration of facts in a confession statement. Various calls have been made for a reform of the procedures under which complaints against the police are pursued. Disciplinary procedures are essentially internal to the force and conducted in private. There is a supervisory body, the Police Complaints Authority, which itself has recommended that minor complaints should be pursued using a lower standard of proof than that demanded in a court case and that proceedings in serious cases should be held in public.[43] As we have seen, a Royal Commission on the criminal justice system was appointed in 1991. The fact that it was the first Royal Commission appointed since the Conservative party had been returned to office in 1979 reflected the seriousness attached to the issue.

Poor Policing in Certain Areas

The police have also attracted criticism because of alleged bias or aggressiveness in dealing with certain communities. Britain experienced a number of riots in the 1980s and early 1990s in a number of urban areas. One of the reasons given for riots in some areas was the attitude taken by the police toward the local black community. There were allegations of racism on the part of some police officers and of a heavy-handed approach in dealing with black suspects. More pervasively, police officers are often seen by blacks as picking on them whenever offenses are committed and sometimes when no offense has been committed. Various other groups in society have also alleged bias against the police, including homosexuals. Various police forces, especially "the Met" (the metropolitan police force), have been criticized for targeting and harassing the gay community. In the 1980s, the police in London were criticized by gays and a number of MPs for using agents provocateurs and for singling out gays for arrest.[44] Allegations of bias continued into the 1990s.[45]

Various attempts have been made to address these problems. The 1984 Police and Criminal Evidence Act requires the police to obtain the views of local people about the policing of their area; most areas now have police-community consultative groups. The approach of the police to various communities has become more sensitive and ways of monitoring problems improved. "Bad policing can lead to riots—as in the early 1980s—and good policing can avoid them."[46] Though charges of heavy-handedness were leveled against the police in some of the violent disturbances of the early 1990s—as in Huddersfield in 1992—the causes of riots appeared to lay more with discontented youths with little to do, organized gangs, and tensions between different groups. In Blackburn, for example, "No one had any strong criticism of the police, whose misfortune seems to have been to try to make peace between the two sides."[47] The police have also attempted to recruit more black officers to their ranks, but so far with very little success. (There have been various cases of alleged discrimination within the force against black officers.)[48] Various attempts have been made to tackle discrimination against gays. In 1991 a lesbian and gay police association was formed to tackle discrimination within the force. The same year the metropolitan police responded to pressure from gay organizations and began monitoring attacks on gays in London. Allegations of bias and harassment remain but recent years have witnessed moves by the police, and a number of chief constables in particular, to address the problems that became manifest in the 1980s.

Problems of Accountability

Accountability also has become an important issue. A number of chief constables in the 1980s, such as James Anderton in Greater Manchester, adopted high profiles and variously clashed with their police authorities. (Mr. Anderton claimed to be driven by the voice of God and, among other things, called for the recriminalization of homosexual relations.) Some chief constables clashed with their authorities over the acquisition of new riot control equipment, such as plastic bullets: The chief constables wanted the equipment, the authorities were unwilling to sanction it. The Merseyside Police Authority early in the 1980s only discovered that the chief constable had acquired plastic bullets after the event. There were instances of chief constables refusing to supply particular reports to their authorities.

The lines of accountability, governed by the 1964 Police Act, are blurred, chief constables having some autonomous powers and being accountable in part to their police authorities, whereas the home secretary is vested with a number of powers that can result in the police authority being overridden. In the case of London, as we have noted, the position is different, with the home secretary alone constituting the police authority. In announcing various reforms in 1993, the home secretary—as we have already recorded—included plans for London to have its own police authority, similar to other forces. He also announced that the position of police authorities was to be clarified. These moves were generally welcomed. His announcement that the number of elected councillors on police authorities was to be reduced—and that the authorities would be chaired by people nominated by the home secretary—attracted opposition criticism that this would reduce accountability to the local community.

The Police in the 1990s

There have been various attempts by the police to address the criticisms leveled at them. However, the combination of the problems faced by them, and their extent, has undermined trust in the police force and the criminal justice system. One poll in 1959 revealed that 83% of those questioned had great respect for the police. By 1989, that figure had fallen to 43%.[49] A 1992 Gallup poll found that a growing percentage of respondents felt uneasy about the police as a result of "things that have happened recently" (Table 13.1). The problems associated with the police and the handling by the courts of cases such as the Birmingham Six appear to have contributed to a growing perception of a system of law and justice that is neither efficient nor fair to everybody. In a 1992 Gallup poll, two-thirds of respondents thought the system was not efficient, compared with just over half who thought it was not in 1985, and almost 80% thought it was not fair to everybody, up from just over 60% in 1985 (Table 13.2). There thus exists the basis for asserting a crisis of confidence in the police force and more generally in the system of justice.

TABLE 13.1   Attitudes toward the police, 1992

Q: Have any of the things that have happened recently made you feel uneasy about our police force or hasn't your attitude been affected?

Response	July 1992	April 1990	October 1989	July 1987
Attitude has been affected	44%	39%	41%	35%
Attitude hasn't been affected	56%	61%	59%	65%

SOURCE: *Gallup Political Index,* Report 383, July 1992, p. 31.

TABLE 13.2   Attitudes toward the system of law and justice, 1992

Q: Do you think our system of law and justice is or is not:

	July 1992	April 1990	October 1988	July 1987	February 1985
Efficient?					
Is	27%	32%	34%	37%	51%
Is not	66%	58%	58%	55%	45%
Don't know	8%	10%	7%	8%	4%
Fair to everybody?					
Is	15%	25%	24%	29%	34%
Is not	78%	69%	71%	66%	62%
Don't know	7%	6%	5%	5%	4%

SOURCE: *Gallup Political Index,* Report 383, July 1992, p. 31.

The crisis, though, does not amount to a total collapse of confidence. There is some countervailing evidence to that just cited. One Gallup poll in 1991 found that three-quarters of respondents had a "great deal" or "quite a lot" of trust in the police; after the armed forces, the police constituted the most trusted institution—and much more trusted than the legal system.[50] The 1990s also saw a more professional approach to policing, especially in sensitive areas. There was also widespread sympathy for unarmed police officers killed or injured while tackling violent criminals—including a special constable shot dead in 1992 after stopping a car carrying two armed IRA terrorists—and a growing recognition that the police could not be expected to tackle all the nation's growing social problems. They have, as one observer aptly noted, "been caught up in a philosophical dispute about the causes (and the politics) of crime."[51] It is difficult for the police to take action against wrongdoing when there is no consensus on what constitutes wrongdoing. "And so the police are fired at by both sides: those who seek vengeance against the disruptors of domestic peace and those who plead that the criminal is society's true victim."[52] The result for many police officers is that they themselves become victims of a system that expects almost the impossible of them.

CONCLUSION

Britain has a well-developed system of law enforcement. That system has generally worked well, enjoying popular support at home at respect abroad, but has come under pressure in recent years. The courts have been involved in a number of cases where miscarriages of justice have subsequently come to light; the number has been relatively small, though for the system to maintain its legitimacy any number constitutes too many. Reforms have been proposed both to remodel the system of criminal justice and to extend the power of the courts in protecting human rights, in order that the courts may be seen as a protector of—and not, in the eyes of some, a threat to—the rights of the individual. The police force has been subject to criticism on a number of fronts. Though remaining to many but not all citizens a broadly respected body of unarmed law enforcers, the police have had difficulty coping with a significant increase in recorded crime and in maintaining the trust of certain sections of the community. Recognition of those problems has led to various attempts to address them. The scale of the problem— encompassing the courts as well as the police—was acknowledged in 1991 with the appointment of the Royal Commission on Criminal Justice.

NOTES

1. J. J. Magee, "Constitutional Vagaries and American Judicial Review," *Hull Papers in Politics No. 10* (Hull University, Politics Department, 1979).
2. C. J. Marshall, *Marbury* v. *Madison, 1803,* 5 U.S. (1Cranch) 137 2L.Ed.60. H. W. Chase and C. R. Ducat, *Constitutional Interpretation* (West Publishing, 1974), p. 26.
3. See the cogent argument advanced by J. Gibson in his dissenting opinion in *Eakin* v. *Raub,* 1825, Supreme Court of Pennsylvania, 12 S. & R. 330. Chase and Ducat, pp. 27–33.
4. See L. Hartz, *The Liberal Tradition in America* (Harcourt, Brace & World, 1955), especially p. 9.
5. Only a minority of cases are resolved by statutory interpretation.
6. As in the nineteenth century in the case of *Ex parte McCardle.* The court's appellate jurisdiction was removed while the case was in progress.
7. From 1789 to 1987, only 120 federal laws—and just over 1,100 state and local laws— had been struck down as unconstitutional. H. W. Stanley and R. G. Niemi, *Vital Statistics on American Politics,* 2nd ed. (CQ Press, 1990), p. 284. This was out of more than 90,000 public and private laws passed.
8. H. J. Abraham, *The Judicial Process,* 5th ed. (Oxford University Press, 1986), p. 293.
9. C. Munro, "Factortame and the Constitution," *Inter Alia,* 1 (1), 1992, pp. 8–10.
10. Lawyers are more than twice as numerous, per head of population, in the United States than in the United Kingdom. Another difference is that in England barristers and solicitors (they take different examinations) are subject to one set of national standards, whereas in the United States there are variations in the standards set by the 50 state bar associations.
11. In 1982 the appointment of Lord Donaldson as master of the rolls proved controversial. The judge had presided over the short-lived National Industrial Relations Court set up under the provisions of the 1971 Industrial Relations Act and was regarded as politically suspect by the Labour party and the trade unions.
12. Like the vice-president, the lord chancellor exercises few powers as presiding officer: The Lords have minimal rules of procedure and all lords who wish to participate do so. The lord chancellor infrequently presides, the task being undertaken by one of a panel of peers appointed for the purpose. However, unlike the vice-president, the chancellor has an original but no casting vote.
13. T. C. Hartley and J. A. G. Griffith, *Government and Law,* 2nd ed. (Weidenfeld & Nicolson, 1981), p. 181.
14. Judges of inferior courts may be removed by the lord chancellor on grounds of incapacity or misbehavior, and magistrates may be dismissed by the lord chancellor as he thinks fit. Occasionally magistrates have been dismissed for failing to fulfill their

duties, and in 1977 a Scottish sheriff (a judicial, not a police position) was dismissed for engaging in political activities.

15. P. Knightley and E. Potter, "How Lawyers Bend Justice," *The Sunday Times,* July 11, 1982, p. 25.

16. J. Rozenberg, "Justice Weighed in the Pay Scales and Found Wanting," *The Sunday Times,* December 6, 1992.

17. Ibid.

18. J. A. G. Griffith, *The Politics of the Judiciary,* 2nd ed. (Fontana, 1981), p. 210.

19. See P. Norton, *The Constitution in Flux* (Blackwell, 1982), pp. 136–138.

20. Ibid., pp. 138–140.

21. "What Checks? What Balances?" *The Economist,* November 18, 1989, p. 31.

22. P. Norton, "The Judiciary," in B. Jones et al. (eds.), *Politics UK* (Harvester Wheatsheaf, 1991), pp. 490–492.

23. Norton, ibid.; and Norton, *The Constitution in Flux,* p. 141.

24. See especially the reaction to the GLC "fares' fair" case. Norton, *The Constitution in Flux,* p. 141.

25. "Sins of Confession" (editorial), *The Times,* November 26, 1991.

26. C. Harlow, "The Legal System," in P. Catterall (ed.), *Contemporary Britain: An Annual Review 1991* (Blackwell, 1991), p. 98.

27. Lord Hailsham, *Elective Dictatorship* (BBC, 1976).

28. Sir L. Scarman, *English Law—The New Dimension* (Stevens, 1974), p. 86.

29. Lord Scarman, "A Bill of Rights Could Become the Conscience of the Nation," *The Independent,* June 9, 1989.

30. Griffith, p. 193.

31. Griffith, p. 195.

32. P. Norton, "A Bill of Rights: The Case Against," *Talking Politics,* 5 (3), Summer 1993, p. 149.

33. Ibid.

34. Hartz, p. 9.

35. *House of Commons Debates (Hansard),* sixth series, Vol. 2, col. 1256.

36. *Social Trends 22* (Her Majesty's Stationery Office, 1992), p. 204.

37. "Total number of crimes could top 6 million this year," *The Independent,* March 10, 1992, p. 2.

38. *Social Trends 22* (Her Majesty's Stationery Office, 1992), p. 208.

39. *Gallup Political Index,* Report 382, June 1992, p. 40.

40. "Embattled Bobbies," *The Economist,* February 8, 1992, p. 31.

41. *Gallup Political Index,* Report 383, July 1992, p. 32.

42. R. Reiner, "Police and Public Order," in P. Catterall (ed.), *Contemporary Britain: An Annual Review 1992* (Blackwell, 1992), pp. 97–98.

43. See "Confidence in the Police" (editorial), *The Independent,* May 10, 1991; and "Sins of Confession" (editorial), *The Times,* November 26, 1991.

44. See S. Jeffery-Poulter, *Peers, Queers and Commons* (Routledge, 1991), pp. 167–173.

45. Reiner, p. 98.

46. "The Revolt of the Scrotes," *The Economist,* July 25, 1992, p. 29.

47. "Divided Community," *The Independent,* July 24, 1992, p. 3.

48. In 1991 an Asian officer in Nottinghamshire was awarded £20,000 ($31,000) following a tribunal decision that he had been refused a transfer to the Criminal Investigations Department (CID) on racial grounds. Other Asian officers also received compensation. Reiner, p. 98.

49. "Embattled Bobbies," p. 31.
50. *Gallup Political Index,* Report 368, April 1991, p. 39.
51. J. Daley, "What Are the Police For?" *The Times,* May 12, 1992.
52. Ibid.

CHAPTER **14**

Communication and Feedback
The Mass Media

Communication is an essential and integral part of any society. It is a necessary if not always well-used tool of the politician's trade. To influence others, one must communicate. With the advent of a mass electorate, politicians have had to communicate with a large audience. In the eighteenth century, when affairs of state were the concern of an aristocratic elite, communication by word of mouth or by letter was often sufficient to reach those with political influence. In the nineteenth century, the newspaper became more important as a medium of communication, especially toward the end of the century. (The only other medium of mass communication, or at least one capable of reaching a large audience, was the political pamphlet.) In the twentieth century, newspapers have remained important but have been supplemented by radio and been over-shadowed though not quite supplanted by television.

Other forms of communicating by a single medium to a large number of people have also been developed. These now include records, videocassettes, films, and books. Although some of these have served as vehicles for political communication and, more especially, influence, their impact is limited. They are rarely used to fulfill such functions and their audiences are relatively small. Book reading and cinema-going are minority interests. In Britain, as in the United States, the primary *mass* media for communicating political information remain television, radio, and newspapers. It is with these three media that this chapter is concerned.

THE PRESS AND BROADCASTING IN BRITAIN

Despite an increase in the sophistication of mass communication, the sheer size and diversity of the United States has militated against the development of "national" newspapers. The number of daily newspapers with anything other than a geographically limited readership can be counted probably on the fingers of one hand. Even the titles of most of the exceptions—*The Washington Post,* the *New York Times, The Wall Street Journal*—imply specific parochial interests; *USA Today* stands alone in its explicitly national orientation. In Britain, by contrast, factors of geography and demography have tended to encourage the development of a national daily press. The country is geographically small, with most of the population living in England, the greatest concentration living in the nation's capital. Despite some exceptions, the press in Britain is London-based and national (which often means London) in its orientation. The newspaper emerged as a medium of political information and influence at the turn of the century and has remained an important medium since. By international comparison, Britons remain great newspaper readers.

The advent of "popular" newspapers, those designed to appeal (in both content and price) to artisans and the lower middle class, took place in the 1890s, a development made possible by advances in adult literacy and in printing technology. The first such newspaper was the *Daily Mail,* founded in 1896 by Alfred Harmsworth (later Lord Northcliffe). It was followed by the *Daily Express* in 1900, the *Daily Mirror* in 1903, and the *Daily Sketch* in 1908. They built up mass readerships not enjoyed by the more sedate and serious newspapers such as *The Times,* the doyen of influential newspapers founded in 1788; the *Morning Post* (merged with the *Daily Telegraph* in 1937); or the *Manchester Guardian,* one of the few significant newspapers with a regional orientation. The mass circulation of the new popular "dailies" attracted advertisers, and income from advertising came to constitute a (and in some cases, the) main form of revenue, thus allowing the publishers to keep down the cost of their papers. Harmsworth boasted that he was able to sell a one-penny paper for half-a-penny.[1] The newspapers themselves were largely in the hands of a few wealthy individuals, known in the early decades of the century as the "press barons." The Harmsworth family was especially influential (owning the *Mail,* the *Mirror* and, from 1908 to 1922, *The Times*), as was the Canadian Max Aitken (Lord Beaverbrook), who acquired control of the *Daily Express* in 1916. Although the papers were run as essentially commercial enterprises, proprietors were not averse to using their newspapers in attempts to influence political developments. In the early 1930s the conservative leader, Stanley Baldwin, bitterly assailed the press barons for seeking to engineer his removal from the party leadership, uttering the memorable observation that they exercised "power without responsibility—the prerogative of the harlot through the ages." The attempt to oust Baldwin was one that many critics of the press would regard as the tip of a very sizable iceberg. Overt political partisanship remains a feature of British newspapers.

Newspaper circulation continued to grow in the first decades of the century. By 1945 the circulation of the main daily newspapers had reached nearly 13 million. Throughout the 1950s it exceeded 16 million, dropping to below 16 million in the 1960s and to just below 15 million in the 1970s and since. However, given that each copy of a newspaper is usually ready by more than one person (and most households order only one daily paper), the figures reveal that a majority of adults in Britain continue to read a daily newspaper. On an average day, two out of three people over the age of 15 read a national newspaper.[2] Relative to the size of population, newspaper circulation is greater in Britain than in the United States and most other developed countries.

Of the national newspapers currently available, there is in terms of numbers a relatively wide choice. There are in addition a variety of national Sunday newspapers, weekly magazines of news and current affairs (preeminent among them being *The Economist*), regional daily newspapers, and a host of local daily and weekly papers: Hardly any community is without its "local" publication. In total, there are about 130 daily newspapers, 1,700 weekly newspapers, and some 7,500 periodical publications. Table 14.1 lists the principal national newspapers, along with the names of their owners and their sales figures.

Until the 1980s, most national newspapers were edited and printed in Fleet Street, and the name of the street became synonymous with the national press. In the 1980s newspapers, taking advantage of new computer technology, began to move out, thereby weakening the influence of the traditionally powerful print unions. Led by the publications of News International, most relocated in the docklands of London. The last national newspaper left Fleet Street in 1989.

TABLE 14.1   National newspapers: Owners and circulation, 1992

Newspaper	Owner	Circulation (April 1992)
Daily newspapers		
Daily Mirror	[Mirror Group]*	2,903,000
Daily Express	United Newspapers	1,525,000
Sun	News International	3,571,000
Daily Mail	Associated Newspapers	1,675,000
Daily Star	United Newspapers	806,000
Today	News International	533,000
Daily Telegraph	Hollinger Inc.	1,038,000
Guardian	Scott Trust	429,000
The Times	News International	386,000
Independent	Newspaper Publishing	390,000
Financial Times	Pearson	290,000
Sunday newspapers		
News of the World	News International	4,716,000
Sunday Mirror	[Mirror Group]*	2,782,000
People	[Mirror Group]*	2,141,000
Sunday Mail	Associated Newspapers	1,974,000
Sunday Express	United Newspapers	1,679,000
The Sunday Times	News International	1,173,000
Sunday Telegraph	Hollinger Inc.	560,000
Observer	Lonrho International	542,000
Independent on Sunday	Newspaper Publishing	386,000

* Ownership unclear following death of the publisher Robert Maxwell and subsequent legal proceedings.
PRINCIPAL SOURCES: M. Harrop and M. Scammell, "A Tabloid War," in D. Butler and D. Kavanagh (eds.), *The British General Election of 1992* (Macmillan, 1992), pp. 181–82; and K. Newton, "Caring and Competence: The Long Campaign," in A. King (ed.), *Britain at the Polls 1992* (Chatham House, 1993), p. 153.

Although journalists may differ in their political beliefs, individual newspapers tend to adopt a particular though not always committed editorial position in support of a political party or general political persuasion. The party that benefits most from editorial preferences is the Conservative party (see Table 14.2). The *Daily Telegraph* is generally regarded as *the* Conservative newspaper and is widely read by Conservatives, as Table 14.2 reveals. *The Daily Mail, Daily Express,* and *The Sun* (originally a Labour supporter) also tend to fall firmly within the Conservative camp, though not always giving editorial support to specific Conservative policies. Of the other tabloids, both *The Star* and *Today* tend to lean toward the Conservatives, though the latter has shown leanings toward the political center and the former failed to endorse any party in the 1992 general election (though its reporting tended to be very anti-Labour). Of the serious press, both *The Times* and *The Financial Times* have a very high percentage of Conservatives among their readers and lean toward the Conservative party, though in the 1980s *The Times* showed some sympathy for the Social Democratic party and on the day of the general election in 1992 *The Financial Times* unexpectedly advised its readers to vote Labour. *The Daily Mirror* is the only mass circulation paper that has been a consistent supporter of the Labour party.[3] *The Guardian* (now national in its orientation) is a radical newspaper, its Center-Left position putting it somewhere between the Labour party and the Liberal Democrats. *The Independent* attempts to live up to its name, though with something of a campaigning, radical tinge.

Critics on the Left ascribe the Conservative bias of the press to the nature of ownership, newspapers being part and parcel of a capitalist system, with more

TABLE 14.2 National newspapers: Political profile, 1992

Newspaper	Party Leaning	Party Supported by Readers		
		Con. %	Lab. %	Lib. Dem. %
Daily Telegraph	Con.	72	11	16
Daily Express	Con.	67	15	14
Daily Mail	Con.	65	15	18
Sun	Con.	45	36	14
Star	Con.[a]	31	54	12
Today	Con.[b]	43	32	23
The Times	Con.	64	16	19
Financial Times	Con.[c]	65	17	16
Independent	Ind.	25	37	34
Guardian	Lib. Dem./Lab.	15	55	24
Mirror	Lab.	20	64	14

[a] Qualified support.
[b] Qualified support; has shown leanings to center parties.
[c] In the 1992 general election, however, advised readers "by a fine margin" to vote Labour.
SOURCES: Party support of readers from MORI, reproduced in M. Harrop and M. Scammell, "A Tabloid War," in D. Butler and D. Kavanagh, (eds.), *The British General Election of 1992* (Macmillan, 1992), p. 190; party leanings from author's own estimation.

and more newspapers coming within the control of fewer hands. Table 14.1 reveals the extent of owner concentration. Foremost among the present-day "press barons" is Rupert Murdoch, owner of News International, whose media empire includes three tabloids (*Sun, Today, News of the World*) and the quality *Times*. A similar concentration is to be found in other media, with a considerable overlap of ownership.

Whereas newspapers, being owned by private concerns, are free to express their partisan preferences (and do so), the broadcasting media are more constrained. Initially, the British Broadcasting Corporation (the BBC) enjoyed a monopoly on radio and television broadcasting. The BBC is a quasi-autonomous state corporation that came into being on January 1, 1927. (It succeeded an independent company, the British Broadcasting Company Ltd.) It was granted a license to broadcast under Royal Charter and it was and remains financed by a license fee levied originally on radio receivers (abolished in 1971) and subsequently, from 1946 onward, on television sets. The first scheduled public television service was started in 1936, though it was suspended during the Second World War. The 1950s witnessed the growth of television: More sets were purchased and more services became available.

In 1954 the BBC's monopoly was ended and the following year the first commercial independent television (ITV) channel began broadcasting. Television was well established in Britain by the 1960s: More than 10 million television licenses were issued in 1960. Succeeding decades have witnessed a massive expansion in TV and radio broadcasting. In the 1960s, a second BBC channel (BBC2) began broadcasting, catering more to minority tastes, especially in the arts and education. The BBC also began setting up local radio stations. In the 1970s independent local radio stations were authorized and began transmission. In the 1980s, a fourth television channel (Channel 4) began broadcasting, catering—like BBC2—to minority tastes, and breakfast television began. Cable television also became available (though attracting relatively few subscribers) and in 1989 the first satellite television channel—Sky television—began transmission; after a slow start, it began to attract subscribers—and, consequently, advertisers. The 1990s saw some changes in the regional ITV companies—some existing companies lost their franchises to challenging companies—and provision was made for a fifth terrestrial channel.[4] By the 1990s, the viewer or listener was thus offered what was, by British standards, a considerable choice, though the two main television channels—BBC1 and ITV (divided into regional companies)— retained the mass audience, attracting about three-quarters of the viewing public. In August 1992, BBC1 took a little under 40% of the viewing audience and ITV just over 35%.[5] Viewers also had greater choice in how to receive programs. By 1990, a majority of households owned two or more televisions and owned or rented a videorecorder.[6]

In their coverage of politics, both the BBC and the independent stations— television and radio—have a statutory obligation to be impartial. The concept of equal time has been applied to the two main parties, though the growth of third parties (and of more fringe candidates in parliamentary by-elections) has created problems in determining the allocation of time for other parties. No paid political advertisements are permitted on radio and television, though both media carry an agreed-upon number of party political broadcasts between general elections and party election broadcasts during elections. Any party fielding 50 or more candidates is entitled to a broadcast.[7] The broadcasts are scripted and presented by the parties themselves, the broadcasting media transmitting them without comment.

The BBC and the independent companies come under the control of separate semi-autonomous bodies—the BBC Board of Governors and the Independent Television Commission[8]—positioned as a cushion between the broadcasting companies and the government of the day. Although some critics see these authorities precisely as cushions—sat upon when necessary by government— the broadcasting companies generally pride themselves on their independence from government, and independence that on occasion generates tension between the two, as during the Suez crisis in 1956, over coverage of the Falklands War in 1982, and over a 1988 program on the shooting by British security forces of three IRA members in Gibraltar.

POLITICAL INFLUENCE

The mass media, by the content and method of their communicating or failing to communicate information, can exert tremendous political influence. Political evaluations and actions of politician and citizen are based on receipt of information. How that information is portrayed and transmitted can significantly affect both the evaluation and the action taken on the basis of that evaluation.

The political information transmitted by the mass media is, of necessity, limited. Newspapers do not have the space nor broadcasting media the air time to transmit comprehensive coverage of daily events (nationally or worldwide) of political significance. Nor do they have the inclination to do so. Although newspapers and the broadcasting media constitute the primary means of transmitting political information to a mass audience, they do not exist exclusively or indeed even primarily to fulfill such a function. Television and radio are essentially media of entertainment. Newspapers may make some claim, by virtue of the written word, to be more a medium of information, but the information transmitted is not usually on the subject of political behavior. Although the so-called quality newspapers (*The Times, Financial Times, Daily Telegraph, Independent,* and *Guardian*) devote a significant proportion of space to reporting and commenting on political events, the mass readership papers do not.

Indeed, the trend has been away from covering political items to what publishers consider human-interest stories. In postwar decades, news coverage in the mass-circulation dailies has decreased significantly.[9] In the case of one paper—*the Daily Herald,* which later became the *Sun*—public affairs as a proportion of editorial space was down by almost two-thirds in 1976 compared with 30 years before.[10] The tabloid newspapers have generally expanded human-interest content, entertainment features, sport, and women's articles.[11] The greater the circulation war between papers, the greater the emphasis on these human-interest features, which constitute the most consistently read part of newspapers. As the circulation war increased during and since the 1970s, the popular dailies "vied for market share with the kind of sensationalism and cheque book journalism that were the despair of quality journalists."[12] Such sensationalism was accompanied by pictures of naked or seminaked females and competitions offering huge cash prizes.

Nonetheless, the role of the mass media in transmitting political information remains of vital significance. Indeed, the significance of newspapers and television as media of communication has increased in the twentieth century not only because of the increase in the size of the audiences but also because of the increase in sophistication of communication technology. Television, in particular, is important not only for the content of what it conveys but also for the method and speed by which it conveys that content. Not only can various happenings—a bomb blast in Northern Ireland, candidates addressing meetings, politicians arguing with one another—be portrayed visually and in sound (and, nowadays, in color), but they also can be transmitted shortly after or even at the time of happening. Receiving information with such immediacy, and in such a form, can affect viewers' evaluations in a way not possible when this medium of communication did not exist. As Hedley Donovan queried once in *Time* magazine: "Could the Civil War have survived the 7 P.M. news? Could George Washington have held his command after a TV special on Valley Forge?"[13] Media coverage of the Vietnam War clearly affected the American public's perception of the wisdom, or lack of it, in such an action. In Britain, recognition of the implications of media coverage influenced the government in its actions and its control of information during the Falklands War in 1982. The government controlled the means of transmitting news from the Task Force to Britain, and facilities for the quick transmission of television pictures were not made available. To have shown on television during the conflict "pictures of the sort of realism that the Americans had during the Vietnamese war," to be seen by servicemen's families, would, in the words of one commanding officer, "have had a very serious effect" on troop morale.[14] Media coverage of particular events such as riots may extend beyond constituting an impartial recording of those events to being an alleged instigator of them. The activities of the media themselves may constitute political issues.

The way in which information is channeled, then, is not neutral in its effect. The mass media, in short, exert political influence. This influence may be primary, affecting the recipient of the communication, or it may be secondary, affecting a party independent of the communication process (e.g., a politician whose capacity to achieve a particular action is limited by public reaction to news of a certain event as, for instance, President Lyndon Johnson in the Vietnam War).[15] The influence of the media may be seen as especially important in terms of the legitimacy of the political system, the partisan support of electors, and the behavior of politicians. The influence exerted in each case may be described as that of enhancing, of reinforcing, and of constraining, respectively.

The media fulfill a function of latent legitimation of the political—as well as the social and economic—system.[16] By operating within that system and accepting its norms, newspapers and television help to maintain its popular legitimacy. When a political crisis arises, journalists and TV reporters descend upon ministers and MPs for comment, hence accepting and reinforcing the legitimacy of those questioned to comment on the matter at hand. There is regular coverage of parliamentary proceedings. What political leaders do in a public and often in a private capacity is considered newsworthy. By according this degree of status to such figures and to the institutions they occupy and represent, the media serve to reinforce the legitimacy of such bodies. Where a body does not enjoy popular legitimacy, the media probably could not create it. Where it does exist, however, they can and do reinforce it by the very nature of their activities.

At times, certain media may also fulfill the more conscious role of overt legitimation. At times of national crisis, some newspapers consider it not only their duty but also that of their readers to support the national effort, and vigorously exhort their readers to provide such support. The most recent and obvious example was that of a number of national newspapers, most notably *The Sun,* during the Falklands War in 1982. Reporting of the war was merged with vigorous, not to say crude, editorializing in support of the British effort, any critics being roundly condemned as unpatriotic. The broadcasting media, by virtue of their charters, sought to take a more detached position.

On party political preferences, the media may be seen as having primarily a reinforcing effect. This is in line with the findings of various studies of the effect of mass communication. Persuasive mass communication, according to Klapper's classic study, tends to serve far more heavily in the interests of reinforcement and of minor change than of converting opinions.[17] There is a marked tendency for the recipients of communications to indulge in a process of selective exposure, perception, and retention. This phenomenon was borne out by Butler and Stokes's study in Britain on the effects of newspaper reading.[18] Most readers chose a newspaper whose partisan stance was in line with their own stance or, for young people, with that of their parents; when the children absorbed and accepted the preferences of their parents, they continued to read the same newspaper.

The effect of reading any given partisan newspaper was characterized by Butler and Stokes as "magnetic": "Readers who are already close to their paper's party will tend to be held chose; those at some distance will tend to be pulled towards it."[19] A similar finding emerged from a study by Dunleavy and Husbands. In their analysis of media influence on voting in 1983, they found that the greater the exposure to Conservative newspapers, the greater the likelihood to vote Conservative. The relationship remained strong even when social class was controlled for. "Within all the class categories used the Conservative vote is some 30 percentage points lower among people primarily exposed to non-Tory messages than it is amongst readers of the Tory press, a high level of association that has few parallels amongst either social background or issue influences . . . . The difference is even more marked when we compare the two extreme groups, those exposed to a predominantly Tory message and those receiving a predominantly non-Tory one; the differences in Conservative support range from 36 to 58 points."[20] The relationships they established were, they concluded, too close to be attributable solely or even mainly to partisan self-selection. Hence, according to their analysis, newspaper reading can have a significant political influence. The beneficiary of such influence is the Conservative party. In successive general elections, a majority of national daily newspaper readers have been advised to vote Conservative.[21]

Media coverage also serves to have a constraining effect on politicians' behavior. To achieve their aims, politicians must be able to communicate with others, at what may be described as the horizontal level (i.e., with fellow politicians, civil servants, and other policy makers) as well as the vertical (i.e., politician to the public), and they must also at times ensure the noncommunication of material. Most politicians crave the attention of the media. Such attention enhances their legitimacy and provides them with the means to influence others. Political behavior may often be geared, in consequence, to the needs of television and newspapers. Press conferences are now *de rigueur* during election campaigns. (They are not so necessary at other times, because Parliament provides ministers with an authoritative and structured forum for communicating their views, an important facility not available to the president and Cabinet secretaries in the United States.)[22] Texts of speeches are given in advance of delivery to journalists and TV reporters. Meetings are organized so as to present a good televisual effect and also timed to meet newspaper deadlines or to get onto the early television evening news. The effect or presumed effect of the televising of particular politicians may even influence the careers of political leaders. A politician whose words in print may be persuasive may come across as hesitant and bumbling on television; he or she may physically not be photogenic. The Conservative leader in the 1964 general election, Sir Alec Douglas-Home, suffered badly from coming across as a poor performer on television; his Labour opposite, Harold Wilson, came across as a confident, dynamic young leader. (There are certain parallels with the American public's perception of the television performances of Richard Nixon and John Kennedy in the 1960 presidential election campaign.) The Labour leader Michael Foot suffered a similar fate in the 1983 general election campaign. When the television cameras entered the Commons in 1989, Margaret Thatcher was judged to come across well on the screen whereas her Labour rival, Neil Kinnock, came across as negative and hectoring. Politicians are thus constrained not only in how they behave in seeking to put across a particular message but also in how they look and how they present themselves before the television cameras.

The media may constrain a politician also in terms of what substantive actions or policies he or she may wish to pursue. Knowledge that one's activities may be observed and reported may deter a minister, for example, from engaging in a policy or particular action that is thought to be unpopular or likely to incur the wrath of one's colleagues or supporters. In both the Falklands War in 1982 and the Gulf War in 1991, policy makers were keen to achieve a quick military victory with as few casualties as possible. They were conscious that reports of heavy losses or a long-drawn-out and indecisive campaign could have an effect on public morale similar to that of media coverage of the Vietnam War. Civil servants and other public officials may decide not to pursue a particular line, albeit a secret one, for fear that details may be leaked to the press and television. The effect of media reporting may thus limit the options that policy makers believe are open to them.

Thus despite their not seeking to act primarily as channels of political information and influence, the mass media in Britain constitute an integral part of the political process. Through reading newspapers and watching television (or listening to radio), citizens receive information that helps shape and reinforce their political attitudes and that, by its presentation, reinforces the legitimacy of the political system and may at times help modify their attitudes. By similarly reading newspapers and watching news and current affairs programs, politicians are aware of the material that is being communicated to the public. Their perceptions of the likely impact of this material may influence their behavior, even if the communication does not have the impact expected.

The media also serve to communicate information to political leaders on how particular policies and programs are being received. Investigative work by journalists or television researchers may present new public evidence on a particular issue—a feature of television programs such as "World in Action" (ITV) and "Panorama" (BBC). The reporting of evidence researched by others, the coverage of demonstrations, or the publication of opinion polls commissioned by the newspaper or program serve to inform both the public and political leaders of attitudes and responses to policies and the actions of policy makers.

That the media are intrinsically significant and influential in the political process is a statement of fact. Whether the effect and influence of the media are desirable is another question and a point of current contention.

THE CURRENT DEBATE

The media serve to convey information. They also form part of contemporary political debate. This stems in part, especially in the case of national newspapers, from their own practices.

The activities of the popular press in particular in obtaining stories has proved a cause of controversy in recent years. The harassment of individuals by journalists and television crews—camping outside their homes, constantly telephoning, pursuing them down the street whenever they venture out—has been a cause of serious complaint, ranging from pursuit of aged and innocent relatives of figures in the public eye to the engulfing of certain members of the royal family and those close to them. The pursuit of the princess of Wales prior to her marriage and during her first pregnancy aroused the ire of Buckingham Palace, as did speculation about the state of her marriage following publication of a book about the princess—*Diana: Her True Story*—in 1992 (see chapter 12). The use of money to elicit exclusive stories has similarly incurred public criticism, particularly in instances when it has been employed to obtain evidence from witnesses involved in pending court cases. It has been likewise with the practice of making up "interviews" from disparate quotations already on the public record and the publication of private or intrusive photographs.

Extensive criticism has also been generated by many of the stories that have resulted, the press having considerable license to criticize and abuse. The position has been exacerbated by the limited means available to those attacked by the press to achieve a redress of grievance. The only means available are to sue for libel or to report the matter to the Press Complaints Commission. Neither is considered a particularly effective course of action. Newspapers have the resources to defend themselves against any libel actions. For individuals, the cost of pursuing a case through the courts is, in most cases, financially prohibitive. (Legal aid is not available in such cases.) Only those with personal wealth are in a position to sustain a libel action. Among those who have done so in recent years are Jeffrey Archer, the novelist and former deputy chairman of the Conservative party, who successfully sued *The Star*; Elton John, the singer, successful in a major action against *The Sun,* settled out of court for a seven-figure sum;[23] and Prime Minister John Major, who sued a weekly magazine and its distributors for carrying allegations (which the magazine accepted were false) about a relationship with a caterer. Reporting cases to the Press Complaints Commission is a course of action available to all. (Likewise with the Broadcasting Complaints Commission for television and radio.)[24] The problem here is lack of powers available to the commission. A nonstatutory body established by the newspaper industry, it came into being on January 1, 1991, replacing the Press Council. It has a smaller membership than its predecessor and a stronger code of practice, and it can investigate and adjudicate on complaints against newspapers. Of more than 1,000 complaints received each year, less than 5% are adjudicated by the full commission.[25] If it upholds a complaint, the paper concerned is committed to publishing the commission's statement. However, such reports—as with the reports of the Press Council—are not necessarily printed in a prominent position and are sometimes treated with contempt.

Public lack of confidence in the press—Gallup polls have found it the national institution in which people have least confidence[26] and one poll in 1991 found that most people questioned considered tabloid papers such as *The Sun, Mirror,* and *Star* untruthful sources of information[27]—has led to various demands for more effective means of redress. These have included providing legal aid in libel cases, strengthening the law on defamation, and providing a statutory right to reply. An official report in 1990—the Calcutt report—recommended strengthening the Press Council. It also said that if the press did not put its own house in order, then statutory restraints should be introduced. The press responded with the creation of the Press Complaints Commission and the appointment of in-house "ombudsmen" to adjudicate readers' complaints. These changes failed to satisfy many of those pressing for an effective policing mechanism. In another report in 1992, Sir David Calcutt recommended greater statutory regulation. An inquiry was undertaken by a House of Commons select committee and an attempt was made—unsuccessfully—to reform the law through the mechanism of private members' legislation.

In their political influence, the media have attracted disparate criticism. Their effect as legitimizers and as supporters or alleged supporters of the Conservative party has come in for particular complaint.

Fulfilling the function of latent legitimization has attracted criticism from left-wing bodies opposed to the existing political system. They see the media as buttressing opposition to change. Radical critics such as the Glasgow University Media Group have argued that rather than devoting space to the activities of the royal family or to interviewing MPs, television and newspapers should give greater coverage to the activities and the opinions of factory workers and the unemployed. Such criticism from the Left of the political spectrum is an enduring feature of debate, but on occasion criticism is leveled by government and other elements of the existing political system. Such criticism often stems from media coverage of bodies and activities that are opposed to the existing political order. In particular, reporting on the Irish Republican Army (IRA) in Northern Ireland, and especially the interviewing of IRA leaders and sympathizers, generates a strong reaction from political leaders in Britain. By communicating details of IRA activity, by using to some extent IRA terminology (including its name), and by showing IRA leaders and activities (the firing of guns over the coffin of a dead IRA member, for example), the media are seen as giving legitimation to an illegal organization. The response of the media, especially the broadcasting media (which are most sensitive to criticisms from government sources), is that coverage does not imply approval and that to fail to report what is going on in the province would constitute a form of censorship. Despite such criticism probably resulting in a more cautious approach to the coverage of IRA activity in the province, the government in 1988 introduced restrictions (similar to those already in existence in the Irish Republic) on the broadcast of speeches by members of the IRA and supporting organizations.

Criticism of the media function of legitimation has extended, more obviously, to its overt attempts to reinforce the legitimacy of particular institutions or of specific actions. Opponents of the monarchy decry the extent not only of coverage given the royal family by the media but also—at least prior to the 1990s—the editorializing and some degree of sycophancy in its support. Those who opposed sending the British Task Force to retake the invaded Falkland Islands in 1982 found themselves at the receiving end of intense press criticism, being characterized as unpatriotic or (if foreign) villainous. The conflict was portrayed, especially by the *Sun* newspaper, in terms of a clear contest between right and wrong, between the British and the anti-British.

And just as the media may be accused of indulging in overt attempts at legitimation, they are accused also of seeking to deny the legitimacy of certain bodies and types of activity. Among bodies or activities portrayed as being in some respect not legitimate, and hence deserving of public disapproval, are strikes (and, some critics suggest, trade unions generally), communists, homosexuals, large demonstrations by certain groups, and individuals who manage to obtain more social security payments than they are entitled to (dubbed "social security scroungers").[28] A number of Labour politicians on the Left, such as veteran Labour MP Tony Benn, also consider themselves as falling within this broad category.

On occasion, the media have also come under pressure from the government of the day for failing to indulge in more overt approval of particular actions. This has been notable at times of national crisis, especially when British troops have been in action abroad: for example, during the Suez crisis in 1956 and the Falklands War in 1982. In the latter instance, though some newspapers were enthusiastic in their support of the British action, some media—notably television—were accused of treating Argentinean news releases as being on a par with those of the British and of seeking to present in a neutral fashion both sides of the dispute.[29] The BBC came in for special condemnation from Conservative

MPs when a "Panorama" program devoted itself to a study of the Conservative critics of the action. Such programs were taken by some Conservatives as reinforcing their belief that the BBC was manned by left-wing sympathizers.

The media have also come under much criticism from Labour politicians, especially on the left wing of the party, for effectively favoring the Conservative party and, in 1981 and 1982, the Social Democrats. The partisan preference of the national daily newspapers I have recorded already. Many Labour politicians consider the broadcasting media to share a similar bias, albeit one less consciously expressed. The result is seen as a consensus among the media in support often of Conservative and certainly of conservative policies, whether introduced by a Conservative or Labour government.[30] In 1981—and here, there is some measure of agreement between Conservative and Labour politicians—the media were accused of treating the new Social Democratic party sympathetically and certainly uncritically. "The Social Democrats," declared Tony Benn, "have been the beneficiaries of the greatest display of media support ever given to any group of MPs in recent history. . . . [They] were launched upon their venture with a fanfare of publicity that rivalled the coverage accorded to the American space programme or a royal tour."[31] To many established Labour and Conservative politicians, the publicity-conscious SDP was essentially a media creation.

That newspapers do indulge in political bias has not generally been a point of contention. No one, least of all the more vociferous newspapers, has sought to deny it. Rather, the newspapers have been attacked by opponents for the views they have expressed and not for making claims to be objective. The position is somewhat different with the broadcasting media, which do make a claim to be neutral and objective. Their defense to charges of bias has tended to take the form of pointing out that they have been criticized by politicians both on the political Left and on the Right and that this fact, in some way, implies that they have pursued a neutral course. Such a defense has had little effect on their critics. Labour activists, as Mr. Benn put it, "feel that the BBC is an instrument being used by the centre against the left—and it is no answer to be told that Mrs. Thatcher does not like the BBC either."[32]

The argument that the SDP was purely a media creation cannot be proven. Although extensive media coverage facilitated the new party in getting its message conveyed to a mass audience (and the claim that much of the coverage was at first fairly uncritical may be justified), the SDP was unable to maintain a high level of support despite continuing media coverage. It is also pertinent to note the unexpected performance of the Green party in the 1988 European Parliament elections: It achieved 15% of the poll without extensive media coverage.

The failure of extensive allegedly sympathetic coverage of the SDP to maintain public support of the party is important also in responses to claims that the media, when combining on a particular issue, can determine popular attitudes on that issue. It is the case, as a number of Labour critics have noted, that the media may express the same opinion on a particular issue—for example, supporting continued British membership of the European Community in the 1975 referendum and supporting Denis Healey against Michael Foot in the contest for the Labour party leadership in 1980. However, though such support may clearly or presumably be useful to the causes in question, it does not follow that the support has been either necessary or sufficient to influence public opinion (or the opinion of the audience in question) toward supporting the line advocated. In 1980, despite media support, Denis Healey failed in his bid to become leader of the Labour party. Earlier, in the February 1974 general election, all major national newspapers but one supported the return to office of Edward Heath's Conservative government. In the event, the leader of the Labour party, Harold Wilson, was summoned to form a minority government.

Other criticisms of media influence have centered on their ability to set the agenda of political debate and on the extent to which events may be manufactured for the benefit of media coverage. The former is an important but possibly over-stated point. By selecting certain materials and events to cover, newspapers and news programs can influence the agenda of political debate. However, for that debate to be sustained, the media have to find some apparently solid base on which to pursue it and it has to be considered a salient issue by those who partici-pate in the debate. If an issue fails to elicit a response or, worse still, produces a counterproductive response (readers or viewers objecting to the line taken), then media coverage may be affected accordingly—that is, the issue may not be pursued or the editorial policy may be changed. In the case of newspapers, it is important to recall that their primary concern is to sell copies. Taking an unpopular political line that could jeopardize sales of the newspaper would be unlikely to find favor with the proprietors. Although the significance of the media in helping set the agenda of political debate is great, the preceding qualification is important. They rarely can help influence that debate by operating in a political vacuum.

Finally, the accusation that events are created for the benefit of media coverage is an important and contemporary one. Clearly, politicians and others, as we have seen, modify their actions to try to ensure media coverage. Where controversy arises is in the cases of violent demonstrations or specific acts of violence being carried out, allegedly, to attract media attention. By being present on the streets of Belfast or, during riots, in the streets of Liverpool or Brixton, television crews have been criticized for encouraging—not actively, but passively, by virtue of their presence waiting for something to happen—the stoning of troops or police by rioters. Again, it is important to stress that rioting is unlikely to take place merely for its own sake (so-called ''copycat'' riots in other parts of Britain following some of the riots of the 1980s quickly subsided), but had camera crews not been present, the incidents that occurred might not have been as extensive or as violent as they were. The problem for the media, primarily the broadcasting media, is deciding what to do in such circumstances. Once rioting has begun, they can hardly ignore it. Yet, once present at the scene, they are open to claims that their presence served to instigate continued or renewed rioting. For producers and reporters, it remains a delicate problem.

CONCLUSION

The mass media in Britain play a significant, indeed vital, role in the political process. They serve to communicate information to a mass audience. By virtue of the way in which they present that information, they can and do exert influence on attitudes toward the political system, on partisan support, on attitudes toward particular issues, and on politicians' behavior. They help set the agenda of political debate. Not only do they help communicate contemporary political debate, they are themselves in part the subject of that debate. They remain the subject of criticism, especially on grounds of political bias, from politicians on the political Left and sometimes on the Right of the political spectrum. Nonetheless, their role and influence, though great, should not be exaggerated: As we have seen, various qualifications need to be entered. Not least, it is important to record that, though constituting the primary means for communicating political information to a mass audience, the national newspapers and the broadcasting media remain first and foremost commercial concerns intent on maintaining readership and viewing figures. To achieve a large audience, they must remain media of entertainment. The most thoroughly read stories in newspapers are those dealing with tragedies and with celebrities (the celebrities attracting most consistent interest almost certainly being members of the royal family). The most watched television programs in the early 1990s—as in the late 1980s—were "Neighbours," an Australian soap opera; "Coronation Street," an ITV soap opera popular for more than two decades; and "Eastenders," the BBC's answer to "Coronation Street." Current affairs programs (as opposed to news programs, which do appear) rarely make an appearance in the TV ratings.

NOTES

1. J. Whale, *The Press and the Media* (Fontana, 1977), p. 86.
2. *Britain 1990* (Her Majesty's Stationery Office, 1990).
3. There were fears that the *Mirror* might be moving from its traditional support for Labour in 1992, following the death the previous year of the publisher Robert Maxwell—the owner of Mirror Group Newspapers—and the subsequent revelations of his financial corruption. Ownership of the group, following legal wranglings, was uncertain and the banks exercising effective control installed a former editor of *News of the World* and *Today*. In 1993 both the political editor and a leading left-wing columnist left the newspaper, alleging that it was moving away from its traditional stance. A number of those who left the *Mirror* were recruited by the *Today* newspaper, undermining the latter's already somewhat detached support for the Conservatives.
4. The only bid for the channel (Channel 5) was, though, turned down at the end of 1992. See "Channel 5 Bid Fails on Audience and Income," *The Times,* December 19, 1992, p. 5.
5. BBC2 took just over 13% and Channel 4 almost 9%. BARB figures for week ending August 9, 1992.
6. *Britain 1990.*
7. In the 1992 general election, the Conservative and Labour parties had five broadcasts each and the Liberal Democrats four. The nationalists were given a broadcast in their home countries and the minor parties meeting the 50-candidate threshold—getting a broadcast each—were the Green party, the Natural Law party, and the Liberal party (not to be confused with the Liberal Democrats—see chapter 6).
8. The Independent Television Commission (the ITC) came into being in 1991 (succeeding the Independent Broadcasting Authority), with responsibility for licensing and regulating all non-BBC television, including the proposed Channel 5 and satellite services.

9. C. Seymour-Ure, *The British Press and Broadcasting since 1945* (Blackwell, 1991), pp. 129–133; and J. Curran and J. Seaton, *Power without Responsibility: The Press and Broadcasting in Britain,* 4th ed. (Routledge, 1991), pp. 113–117.

10. Curran and Seaton, p. 116.

11. Ibid.

12. Seymour-Ure, p. 135.

13. "Fluctuations on the Presidential Exchange," *Time,* November, 9, 1981, p. 60.

14. *The Handling of Press and Public Information during the Falklands Conflict: First Report from the Select Committee on Defence,* Session 1981–1982, HC 17-I (Her Majesty's Stationery Office, 1982), p. xiv.

15. See C. Seymour-Ure, *The Political Impact of the Mass Media* (Constable, 1974), p. 22.

16. On legitimizing the social and economic system, see the comments of Curran and Seaton, p. 126.

17. J. Klapper, *The Effects of Mass Communication* (Free Press, 1960), pp. 15–18.

18. D. Butler and D. Stokes, *Political Change in Britain* (Penguin, 1971), pp. 281–300.

19. Ibid., p. 291.

20. P. Dunleavy and C. T. Husbands, "Media Influences on Voting in 1983," in J. Anderson and A. Cochrane (eds.), *A State of Crisis* (Hodder & Stoughton, 1989), pp. 291–292.

21. In the 1983 general election, 75% of readers were advised to vote Conservative, an all-time high, compared with an average of 54% in the eight postwar elections to 1970; in the 1987 election the proportion was 67%. "Political Allegiances in Step with Readers' Intentions," *UK Press Gazette,* June 22, 1987, p. 25.

22. See C. Seymour-Ure, *The American President: Power and Communication* (Macmillan, 1982), conclusion.

23. See Seymour-Ure, *The British Press and Broadcasting since 1945,* pp. 228–229; and C. Seymour-Ure, "The Media," in P. Catterall (ed.), *Contemporary Britain: An Annual Review 1991* (Blackwell, 1991), pp. 89–90.

24. The Broadcasting Complaints Commission, unlike its press equivalent, is established by statute and has the task of considering and adjudicating complaints of unjust or unfair treatment in sound or radio programs. In 1991, the commission received 1,050 complaints, only a small proportion of which fell within their jurisdiction.

25. Most complaints are deemed to involve no *prima facie* breach of the code, fall outside the remit of the commission, are submitted too late, or are insufficiently substantial. About a tenth of cases are not pursued by the complainant. 1991 figures, derived from Press Complaints Commission, *Report: No. 3* (Press Complaints Commission, 1991), p. 4.

26. *Gallup Political Index,* Report 368, April 1991, p. 39.

27. *Gallup Political Index,* Report 371, July 1991, p. 24.

28. See, e.g., S. Cohen and J. Young (eds.), *The Manufacture of News,* rev. ed. (Constable, 1981), *passim.*

29. See especially N. Tebbit, *Upwardly Mobile* (Futura, 1989), pp. 248–249.

30. This point is developed in T. Benn, *Arguments for Democracy* (Penguin, 1982), ch. 6, especially p. 115.

31. Ibid., p. 111.

32. Ibid., p. 110.

PART **VI**

Conclusion

CHAPTER 15

Flux and Strength
A Book with Two Themes

Most political science texts develop particular themes or arguments. This book is no exception. Indeed, it has two themes. What is unusual is that only one of these themes derives explicitly from what I have written in the body of the text. The other theme is drawn from what is absent from earlier pages. "Listen, Watson." "I hear nothing, Holmes." "Precisely." The first theme, clear from the preceding chapters, if that of a constitution in flux. The second, the hidden or covert, theme is that of the continuing strength of the political culture.

CONSTITUTIONAL FLUX

In terms of constitutional development, the quarter-century following the Second World War was a relatively quiet period. The Constitution was largely taken for granted. When it was mentioned it was for the purpose of commendation, even emulation, and not for critical analysis. Major reform of the Constitution was not on the agenda of political debate. Some tracts called for change, but they did not resonate at either elite or mass levels. The period since 1970 has borne little resemblance to preceding decades. The constitutional landscape of the United Kingdom has been notable for two distinctive features. One has been the degree of change that has taken place in the structures, processes, relationships, and practices of British government. The other has been the demand for further change. Since the 1970s, various approaches to constitutional change have developed. The more radical of these entail a new constitution for the United Kingdom.

The Extent of Change

The changes that have taken place since 1970 have been sketched in preceding chapters. The United Kingdom is now a member of a supranational body with legislative powers, the European Community. Membership of that body has introduced not only a new body of law to the United Kingdom but also new processes of lawmaking and legal adjudication. Both processes have developed since the 1970s, in the former case (lawmaking) as a consequence of the implementation of the Single European Act in 1987 and in the latter (legal adjudication) because of the ruling of the EC Court of Justice in the *Factortame* case in 1990 that British courts may suspend an act of Parliament, if it appears to breach EC law, until such time as a final determination is made by the courts. Membership has also introduced a new supranational deliberative assembly, one that since 1979 has been directly elected and one that since 1987 has had the formal title of a Parliament. Though 78 of the United Kingdom's 81 members of the European Parliament are elected by the plurality, first-past-the-post system employed for parliamentary elections, 3—those from Northern Ireland—are elected by a system of proportional representation.

Within the United Kingdom, the province of Northern Ireland is now governed directly by a department of the U.K. government and not by a body elected within the province itself. As we have seen in chapter 9, various constitutional innovations have been attempted within the province. Relations between the center and one province of the United Kingdom have thus changed radically. Relations between the center and local government also have changed significantly, with the structures, powers, and finances of local government being variously revised or replaced. Parliament has undergone a number of structural changes, most notably in the House of Commons with the establishment of a series of departmental select committees. The position of the monarch and the royal family has also been affected by recent pressures, especially in relation to royal finances.

The relationship of different agencies of the state to the individual has also been subject to change. Civil rights have been variously modified, extended, or restricted. To take a number of illustrative examples, the Police and Criminal Evidence Act of 1984 strengthened certain police powers while at the same time increasing protections for the suspect. An order passed by Parliament in 1981 extended the provisions of the 1967 Sexual Offences Act—legalizing homosexual relationships between consenting male adults—to Northern Ireland, whereas section 28 of the 1988 Local Government Act prohibited the "intentional promotion" of homosexuality by local authorities. The powers of trade unions have been variously extended (1974–1979) and restricted (since 1979). Recent years have witnessed the introduction by government of the Citizen's Charter, designed to clarify and stipulate what the individual has a right to expect from public bodies. Opposition parties and other critics of the government stress the restrictions on rights; the government stresses the extensions.[1]

Since 1970, various conventions of the Constitution have also undergone modification or erosion. The principle of collective responsibility has twice been suspended in order to allow ministers (in the 1974–1979 Labour government) to speak and vote against particular government policies. The principle has also been eroded by the growing practice of leaks and semipublic—and sometimes public—disputes between ministers. In the latter half of the 1970s, Tony Benn was a Cabinet minister who was in clear disagreement with government policy. Under Conservative governments since 1979, a number of ministers have distanced themselves from Cabinet colleagues—usually in coded speeches but sometimes openly, the most open disagreement being expressed by Michael Heseltine during the Westland dispute in 1986. Even Margaret Thatcher as prime minister on occasion distanced herself from her own Cabinet, as, for example, on the issue of trade union reform.[2] The application of the convention of collective responsibility to government defeats in the House of Commons was also shown not to be as restrictive as was previously thought. In the 1950s and 1960s, it was widely assumed by MPs that a government defeat on an important issue—or even on any issue—necessitated the government resigning or requesting a dissolution. In the 1970s, this was shown to be a constitutional "myth," resignation or dissolution only being required by the convention in the event of a defeat on an explicit vote of confidence.[3] The principle of individual ministerial responsibility has also been whittled away at the edges by the increasing public visibility of civil servants, especially before select committees of the House of Commons, and by the establishment, beginning in 1989, of executive agencies within departments, with semi-autonomous responsibilities.

The period, as we have seen in earlier chapters, not only underwent change but also saw various attempts at change. Most notable among them was the legislation introduced by the Labour government in the latter half of the 1970s to provide for elected assemblies in Scotland and Wales (see chapter 9), an attempt that ultimately floundered as a consequence of amendments made by a more assertive Parliament and the use of the constitutionally novel device of referendums in Scotland and Wales. As we have already mentioned—and detailed in chapter 9—various government initiatives to introduce a new constitutional framework in Northern Ireland have fallen foul of opposition from one or more parties within the province.

The past quarter-century has thus been notable, not least when compared with the preceding quarter-century, for the extent of constitutional change and the attempts at further change. It has been notable also for the demands for more change.

Approaches to Constitutional Change

As the Constitution underwent changes, so, too, did the nature of constitutional discourse. In the 1950s and 1960s, works on the Constitution flowed principally from the pens of constitutional lawyers. In the 1970s, and more especially the 1980s, constitutional law texts began to give way to works produced by political scientists or by a combination of political scientists and a new breed of (often reform-minded) law lecturers.[4] This development reflected, and in turn influenced, the nature of debate on the Constitution. The Constitution was far more at the heart of political debate, constitutional change increasingly being offered as a solution or partial solution to some of the nation's economic, social, and political ills. As it became drawn into the maelstrom of political debate, so there began to emerge a number of different approaches to constitutional change. These approaches succeeded the largely unarticulated and rather ragged consensus that had prevailed in the preceding 25 years.

In the 1980s, it was possible to discern seven separate approaches. The *High Tory* approach favored the existing constitutional framework, arguing for things to be left as they were. The *socialist* approach argued for a constitutional reformulation that would permit a strong, party-dominated central government to fulfill a party program free of external constraints. The *Marxist* approach largely rejected institutional change, regarding it as an attempt by the ruling state elite to maintain the interests of finance capital; it waited instead for the crisis of capitalism to result in a collapse of the existing political system. The *group* approach sought the more extensive incorporation of groups into the government process, and in its most radical form favored a functionalist upper house (that is, composed of representatives of the different interests in society). The *New Right* approach favored reducing the public domain, with the state withdrawing from economic activity. Under a pure type of this approach, no institution is deemed sacrosanct. One of its leading proponents argued for a "free market written constitution." The *liberal* approach (not confined to Liberals and Liberal Democrats) sought a structure that would defend the individual in society and allow for the generation of consensus-building constitutional rules. The seventh and final approach, the *traditional* approach sought limited change in order to maintain a balance between strong government and an effective Parliament, the emphasis being on the maintenance of parliamentary sovereignty and parliamentary (party) government.[5]

These approaches were not all well developed nor were they coterminous with existing political parties. Their more obvious emergence and articulation served to generate a vigorous and sometimes confused debate about the structure and the future of the British Constitution. As the debate progressed, so a number of approaches became more prominent, overshadowing others. During the 1970s and 1980s, the High Tory approach was largely overshadowed by most of the others. The socialist approach, and to a much lesser extent the Marxist, found a place in political debate, the socialist approach in particular enjoying a number of powerful advocates on the Left of the Labour party and influencing party policy in the early 1980s. The group approach found some resonance in the last years of the Heath government and during the period of Labour government of 1974 to 1979, the era of tripartism (see chapter 7). The New Right approach developed in the 1970s and emerged full-blown in the 1980s, attracting adherents in a particular section of the Conservative party as well as beyond it. (Those who adhered to the approach in its pure form were outside the party.) It largely displaced the group approach. The liberal approach developed rapidly during the latter half of the 1970s and in the 1980s, constituting the most radical of the approaches in advocating a new constitutional settlement. It favored a bill of rights, electoral reform, an elected upper house, and devolution and decentralization of power. It was pitted against the traditional approach, which remained strong in the Conservative party and retained a substantial body of adherents in the Labour party.

The configuration of support of the different approaches has changed notably since the end of the 1980s. The collapse of communist regimes in Central and Eastern Europe has served to marginalize the Marxist approach in political debate. It also had a knock-on effect for the socialist approach, itself undermined by the Labour party's attempts to restore its electoral fortunes. The loss of consecutive general elections has encouraged many on the Left to contemplate constitutional reform as a means of providing an opportunity for Labour again to have a place in government. They have begun to make common cause with adherents to the liberal approach, coming together to form the constitutional reform movement Charter '88. Founded in 1988, it advocates a charter of constitutional reforms drawn from the liberal agenda, including a bill of rights, electoral reform, a written constitution, and an elected upper chamber. It gained added strength following the return of the Conservative government in 1992, with more Labour MPs, including some leading figures on the party's front bench, looking favorably at the proposal for electoral reform. In 1993, the principal think tank of the Left, the Institute for Public Policy Research, published a book offering a new draft constitution.[6] The New Right approach, so prominent during the 1980s, lost prominence as a result of its most powerful advocate in government—Margaret Thatcher—losing the premiership. It retained its adherents within the Conservative party, and indeed within government, but its most ardent and pure advocates (of whom Mrs. Thatcher had not been one—she had been ardent but not pure)[7] were marginalized outside the party. Her departure strengthened the position of those who stuck with the traditional approach. Foremost among the traditionalists was her successor, John Major, supported strongly by those of his ministers who articulated a view on the Constitution.[8]

The 1990s thus saw debate on the Constitution become less fragmented and grouped instead around two particular approaches: the liberal and the traditional. In short, a debate between those favoring a new constitutional settlement and those who, although admitting of change within the existing system, defend existing constitutional arrangements. Both offer prescriptions for change that derive from different analyses of the political system and of the political culture that sustains it. At the root of the reform analysis is the collapse of the civic culture. It is, on the face of it, a plausible analysis, but one, I shall argue, that is both flawed and potentially dangerous.

THE STRENGTH OF THE POLITICAL CULTURE

Since the 1960s, Britain has faced various economic, political, and social problems. Economic growth has at times been slow and even nonexistent. There have been indecisive election outcomes, periods of political stalemate, clashes between government and different organized interests, political unrest in different parts of the United Kingdom, and clashes between different elected bodies. There have been outbreaks of violence in different parts of the country, with more sustained conflict in the province of Northern Ireland. There has been a more pervasive increase in crime. The criminal justice system has had difficulty coping, and the government has variously had difficulty raising resources to meet its commitments of public policy.

According to some analyses, these problems reflect and contribute to a decline, indeed a collapse, in the "civic culture" in Britain. This, as we noted in chapter 2, is the thesis advanced by Samuel Beer. In *Britain against Itself*, published in 1982, he argued that the growth of technocratic and populist attitudes had served to undermine the hierarchical and organic values that formed the civic culture in Britain, resulting in a greater degree of populism and distrust in government, with demands for a more radical participatory democracy. This, coupled with pluralist stagnation, served to explain political fragmentation and immobilism in Britain.[9] Other critics have similarly concluded that there has been a collapse of the civic culture. For them, the explanation is essentially structural. This argument we sketched in chapter 3. Political parties vie for the all-or-nothing spoils of election victory. Ultimate power to determine public policy rests with the party leadership enjoying a parliamentary majority. Power to determine public policy, though, is not the same as the power to implement it. The adversarial relationship between the parties has polarized society and made it more difficult for a party in government to mobilize group and mass support for its measures. To get its way, government has had to centralize power more and more, and the more it has done so the more it has undermined and divorced itself from a pluralist and responsive political process. The effect has been to stifle and erode respect for existing structures, deference giving way to apathy and opposition. Those offering this analysis share with Beer the view that "In an ironic sense, Britain is maintaining its leadership. As it once showed the way toward democratic success, today it blazes the trail toward democratic failure."[10] The solution is to mobilize what Beer calls the new populism through new structures. That necessitates a new constitution.

This thesis of a collapsed civic culture is supported by various empirical data. Beer, and more recently other writers, have drawn attention to surveys showing a lack of trust in government, with demands for constitutional change and more participatory politics. The data utilized by Beer suggested the decline in trust set in before the 1970s.[11] It was on the basis of survey evidence that Beer felt confident enough to conclude that there had been a collapse in the civic culture. More recent surveys have been used to show that the decline has been even greater since the 1970s. An extensive MORI poll for the Rowntree Reform Trust in 1991 found that almost two-thirds of those questioned believed the system of government needed quite a lot, or a great deal, of improvement, compared with almost half of those questioned in a poll in the early 1970s saying it mainly worked well and could be improved in only small ways. "This is not an isolated response. Rowntree's findings show that discontent runs deep."[12] Most respondents thought government power was too centralized (60%) and that rights were too easily changed (54%). There was overwhelming support for various items on the reform agenda, including a bill of rights and devolution, and with more respondents favoring electoral reform than opposing it (50% to 23%). Reformers thus have the basis both for asserting a collapse in trust in government and popular demand for a new constitution for the United Kingdom.

The thesis advanced by Beer and more recent critics of the Constitution thus appear highly plausible. Britain has demonstrably faced serious problems over the past 30 years. Does not a collapse of the civil culture underpin the nation's basic political problems—which themselves have consequences for the nation's social and economic welfare—and is not a, if not *the,* solution to those problems a new constitutional settlement, a settlement that enjoys popular support? The answer, on all counts, is no. My argument is simply stated. The claim that there has been a collapse in the civic culture if based on a misreading of history and is belied by recent events. The argument for a new constitution derives from survey data that are accorded a weight they cannot bear. The thesis, in short, derives from a misreading of both history and popular attitudes. The political culture remains relatively strong and is a culture consonant with existing constitutional arrangements. Indeed, there is a strong case to be made for the existing constitutional framework. Problems there indeed are, but the answer is not to be found in constitutional reform. The existing Constitution is part of the solution, not part of the problem.

Misreading History

Let me begin, as Samuel Beer begins, with a quotation from a distinguished U.S observer of British politics of the late nineteenth and early twentieth centuries, A. Lawrence Lowell. In *The Government of England,* published in 1908, Lowell opened with the following observation:

> Measured by the standards of duration, absence of violent commotions, maintenance of law and order, general prosperity and contentment of the people, and by the extent of its influence on the institutions and political thought of other lands, the English Government has been one of the most remarkable in the world.[13]

Beer contrasts this with the advice given to a student of his by the student's father: "Study England, a country on its knees. That is where America is going."[14] The contrast between the two quotations is stark. It is also misleading. Lowell's comment reflects the view he ascribes to "the typical Englishman"—that is, seeing the country from a somewhat rosy perspective. Though his description, viewed solely in comparative perspective, has some basis to it, the impression it conveys of domestic tranquility and contentment does not. Insofar as Britain has come close to witnessing an absence of violent commotions, it has done so in later decades than those covered by Lowell. The trend, in short, and insofar as there has been one, has not been in the direction implied by Beer.

The nineteenth century was strewn with occasions of "commotions." Lowell was writing of a country where the military had variously been used to maintain order and where the police were treated with suspicion and variously subjected to attack.[15] And the years following publication of his work hardly reinforced the impression he had conveyed. Consider the following quotation. It is a lengthy one but important for the purposes of my argument; it could have been longer:

> In 1919, following demobilisation, serious rioting occurred throughout the country. In May and June there were race riots in South Wales, the East End [of London,] and Liverpool when whites attacked blacks. In Cardiff three people were shot dead. In July the Peace Day celebrations were attended by riots in Wolverhampton, Salisbury, Epsom, Luton, Essex, Coventry and Swindon. In Luton the town hall was destroyed by arson. Police and firemen were attacked by bricks, stones and bottles and there was widespread looting. On the first of August the police in Liverpool went on strike, and severe rioting and widespread looting began, continuing for four days and nights. Steel helmeted troops and tanks were sent in. There were bayonet charges and shooting. In July and August there were also riots and battles between police and youths in London: in Greenwich, Hammersmith, Tottenham, Edmonton, Wood Green, Barking and Brixton.[16]

This was not an isolated period. There were clashes before the First World War between the police and the suffragettes (demanding votes for women) and between police and strikers. On a number of occasions troops were called out to assist the police. During a railway and dock strike in 1911, the home secretary, Winston Churchill, actually sent a gunboat up the River Mersey. He dispatched troops to guard Manchester railway stations. According to one newspaper, he sent troops "hither and thither as though Armageddon was upon us."[17] There was rioting on various occasions in the 1920s and 1930s. There were clashes between police and demonstrators during the General Strike of 1926. In 1931 thousands of unemployed demonstrators fought with the police in Glasgow; there was extensive damage. Violent clashes took place for two days between demonstrators and police in Birkenhead, resulting in many injuries.[18] Public disorder, in short, was far from unknown in Britain at the beginning of the twentieth century.

Nor has public disorder been unknown in recent years. There were race riots in the Notting Hill area of London in 1958, major clashes between anti–Vietnam War demonstrators and the police in the late 1960s, riots in a number of cities in the early and mid-1980s—most notably Bristol, Liverpool, Birmingham, and the Brixton and Tottenham areas of London—and more recently, in the early 1990s, clashes between groups of youths and the police in a number of towns and cities, including Oxford, Huddersfield, Blackburn, and Tynemouth. London witnessed its worst riot for decades in 1990 over the issue of the poll tax (see chapter 9). The disorder has resulted in some fatalities. One youth died after being hit by a police vehicle in Liverpool, two Asian shopkeepers died in a fire during riots in the Handsworth area of Birmingham, and a policeman was killed by a mob in Tottenham in 1985.

The landscape of British history, including throughout the twentieth century, has not been as settled as Lowell and many others have thought it to be. However, having established that the picture is not one of tranquility, let me now enter three significant qualifications.

First, violence and disorder in the twentieth century have been less pronounced than in the eighteenth and nineteenth centuries[19] and the decades since the Second World War have been relatively less violent than those at the beginning of the twentieth century. In recent decades, the police have coped with incidence of disorder without assistance from the military. Second, violence and disorder have been less extensive than in many other Western countries. As we saw in chapter 13 (Figure 13.3), despite an increase in the crime rate, England and Wales still fall some way behind the United States, Canada, Australia, Germany, and Holland—among others—in the incidence of violent crime. The United States continues to head the table. The United Kingdom has not witnessed anything on the scale of the race riots and the violence—including significant death tolls—following lock-outs and strikes that have been a feature of twentieth-century U.S. history.[20] Nor has Britain witnessed antistate demonstrations and violence on anything of the scale that has marred the experience of many other nations, such as France. Third, the occasions of disorder have been exceptional. They have been exceptional in a number of respects. One is obviously in terms of absolute numbers. Another is in comparative terms, both historically and internationally: As we have just seen, they are relatively less extensive than they were and less extensive than elsewhere. They are also exceptional in terms of what might be expected. The United Kingdom has a number of significant social and economic problems. There is the problem of an economic "underclass." There is the problem of high unemployment and of unemployment concentrated in certain age cohorts (notably school-leavers). The period since the early 1980s has seen unemployment at levels not witnessed since the depression of the 1930s. At the beginning of the 1990s the United Kingdom witnessed the most sustained recession of postwar years. Given the problems, why has public disorder, especially antistate behavior, not been even greater than it has been? Early in the 1970s, for example, many politicians believed unemployment could not be allowed to reach the 1-million mark because of the destabilizing effect it would have on government.[21] Yet in the 1980s, unemployment not only passed the 2-million figure, it peaked at a figure beyond 3 million. Government continued to govern; there were no major antistate demonstrations.

All three caveats, especially the final one, are central to my thesis. The landscape of British politics has not, *pace* Professor Beer, become more violent and unsettled. What is remarkable, given the problems faced by the nation, is that it has not been more unsettled. The explanation is to be found in the political culture. The orientations of that culture were identified in chapter 2. Throughout the twentieth century, a desire to reach agreement, "to work things out," and to accept established political authority has remained a predominant feature of that culture.

Despite clashes between police and demonstrators, most strikes and demonstrations have been peaceful. Attempts to use strikes as an economic weapon have been directed at employers and not at the state. Despite clashes during the General Strike of 1926, the most noteworthy feature of the dispute was its peacefulness and the desire to reach some form of agreement. "Paradoxically," wrote A. H. Halsey, "the General Strike of 1926, which may reasonably be described as a moment of tense confrontation between the two main classes, . . . provides unmistakable evidence of a consensual political culture."[22] He discerned this consensus as much in the actions of the political elite as in the activities of police and strikers. The union leaders were keen not to be seen as threatening the Constitution. Prime Minister Stanley Baldwin, for his part, was keen to heal any social wounds caused by the dispute. He discouraged his supporters from seeking further to restrict the unions once the strike was over, invoking in the House of Commons the prayer "Give Peace in our time, O Lord."[23] Similarly, when sailors (hit by a pay cut) refused to set sail on exercises, in the "Invergordon Mutiny" of 1931, there were no serious outbreaks of violence and force was not necessary to bring the incident to an end; a compromise was found and the ships were sent back to their home ports. The long-term effect of the action was an improvement in sailors' welfare.[24]

Though some unions were seen as pursuing more political goals in the 1970s and 1980s, industrial action has continued to take the form of wage militancy rather than political militancy.[25] The emphasis of the British union movement has been on employer-employee relationships and on the principle of free collective bargaining. Such bargaining has generally been conducted according to well-established procedures. And, indeed, attachment to procedures—especially procedures for resolving disputes by negotiation—remains an essential feature of the British political culture. Despite the emergence of different approaches to constitutional change over the past 20 years, there remains a consensus on the way in which favored change is to be brought about: that is, through the existing parliamentary process. Left-wing Labour MPs are among the most assiduous attenders of parliamentary debates and some of the most effective users of parliamentary procedures. Extra-parliamentary activity is generally decried as illegitimate. The elected nature of the House of Commons, as radical writer Ralph Miliband has noted, renders illegitimate any radical alternative, "for what it suggests above all to bring about fundamental change is a majority in the House of Commons."[26] The focus is thus Parliament, not the streets.

The most significant threat to this attachment to the parliamentary process came in 1990 with widespread demonstrations and rioting following the introduction of the poll tax (see chapter 9). The demonstrations and the extent of nonpayment created a major strain on the system. At the same time, it also demonstrated the attachment to, and workings of, that system. Though opposed totally to the poll tax, Labour party leaders nonetheless advised everyone to pay it—because it had been passed by Parliament. Demonstrations—and a riot in London—attracted the headlines. Less publicized was the extensive lobbying of MPs by constituents. Conservative MPs read their constituents' letters. They also read the opinion polls. Within seven months of the tax being levied in England and Wales, Conservative MPs had removed the one obstacle to its abolition: the party leader, Margaret Thatcher.[27]

The political culture has thus not "collapsed." Indeed, the strength of that culture is demonstrated when one considers those developments that Professor Beer identified as being responsible for its collapse. The culture has remained strong as the different variables identified by Beer have waned and sometimes disappeared. The romantic revolt—generating the waning of Toryism, less willingness to accept authority within the Labour party, a decline of leadership, and a weakening of parliamentary government—has not been sustained but rather, insofar as it ever existed, proved a short-term phenomenon. Margaret Thatcher as prime minister hardly proved a decline of leadership, and her failure to go even further than she wished signified the continuing strength of Toryism—as did her replacement by John Major. Neil Kinnock—elected to the labour leadership the year after *Britain against Itself* was published—asserted a control over the organization of the Labour party that was almost unprecedented. As we have touched upon, and as we shall see, attachment to parliamentary government remains a strong feature of the political culture. Finally, for Beer the parties most in tune with the new romanticism were the Liberal and Social Democratic parties. In alliance, they provided a significant third-party challenge in 1983 and, to a lesser extent, in 1987. In 1992, following their merger, they attracted less support than had the Liberal party in the mid-1970s, obtaining the vote of less than one in every five electors (see chapter 5). So much for the collapse of the civic culture.

It is possible that at this stage some readers, looking at the question from a U.K., rather than a British, perspective, may be getting irritated with this line of argument. What, they may well ask, is the position of Northern Ireland? Is that not an example of a nonconsensual society, one in which mutually exclusive stances are taken by different sections of the population, and one in which violence and strife occur, with significant antistate activity and sometimes political strikes, such as that by the Ulster Workers Council that brought down the new Northern Ireland executive in 1974? Indeed, yes, but this reinforces rather than undermines my argument. The *British* political culture is precisely that: British. The culture and history of Northern Ireland, as I sought to show in chapter 9, is distinct. It is precisely because of the gulf between the British and Northern Irish cultures that the problems of Northern Ireland are so incomprehensible to the British mind. It also helps explain why the British government has had difficulty knowing how to handle the problem, as policy is often premised on the British assumption that problems can be solved by discussion, by reasonable people gathering around a table to resolve their differences. The efforts to create a power-sharing executive and a "rolling consensus" (see chapter 9) reflect this assumption. The British political culture also helps provide a partial explanation for the continued presence of troops in Northern Ireland. Opinion polls, as we saw in chapter 9, reveal that a great many Britons would like to see troops withdrawn. They remain, in part because of a sense of responsibility shared by political leaders, who believe that to pursue a policy of withdrawal would result in a bloodbath.

The political culture—the British political culture—thus continues to exhibit the attributes outlined in chapter 2. Looked at in historical perspective, the twentieth century has witnessed not a collapse of that culture, but rather a reinforcement.

TABLE 15.1 Trust in government (1), 1970

Question: Which of these statements best expresses your opinion on the present system of running Britain?	
"Works extremely well and could not be improved"	5%
"Could be improved in small ways but mainly works well"	43%
"Could be improved quite a lot"	35%
"Needs a great deal of improvement"	14%
"Don't know"	4%

SOURCE: Royal Commission on the Constitution, Research Papers 7, reproduced in V. Hart, *Distrust and Democracy* (Cambridge University Press, 1978), p.60. Copyright 1978 Her Majesty's Stationery Office. Reprinted by permission.

Misreading Popular Attitudes

The thesis of a collapse is based on a misreading not just of history but also of contemporary attitudes. We are told that there has been a collapse in trust in government, that people believe that rights are too easily changed, and that there is popular pressure for reform.

The data for asserting a decline in trust we have referred to already. Let us look at those data in more detail. Tables 15.1, 15.2, and 15.3 show attitudes toward the system of government in 1970, 1978, and 1991. Clearly, the proportion believing the system needs quite a lot or a great deal of improvement is greater than in the 1970s, though the proportion believing it "mainly works well" appears to have increased in the years shortly before Beer penned his work. Nonetheless, there has been a shift in attitude toward the system of government.

Does this amount to a collapse in trust in government? It does not. First, the findings are given an interpretative weight that they simply cannot bear. The question in the tables is about whether the system of government can be improved or not. That is not an adequate surrogate for trust. I believe the system of government can be improved and in some respects considerably improved, and I have detailed ways in which Parliament in particular can be strengthened in order to meet popular expectations. That is independent of the question of trust. Do I have trust in the system of government? Yes. Do I believe that system can be improved? Yes. The latter answer cannot therefore be taken as proving a negative answer to the first question.

TABLE 15.2 Trust in government (2), 1978

Respondents were asked their opinion "on the present system of running the government of this country."	
"On the whole it works well and probably could not be improved"	4%
"It could be improved in small ways but mainly works well"	53%
"It could be improved a lot"	30%
"It needs a great deal of improvement"	11%

SOURCE: L. Moss, "Attitudes Towards Government," *SSRC Research Report HR 5427* (1980), Appendix, p. 28. Reprinted by permission.

TABLE 15.3 Trust in government (3), 1991

Question: Which of these statements best describes your opinion on the present system of governing Britain?

"Works extremely well and could not be improved"	4%
"Could be improved in small ways but mainly works well"	29%
"Could be improved quite a lot"	40%
"Needs a great deal of improvement"	23%
"Don't know"	4%

SOURCE: MORI, for the Joseph Rowntree Trust, 1991.

Second, attitudes to the system of government are closely related to voting intentions. In the 1991 MORI poll, for example, almost two-thirds of Conservative respondents believed the system worked well but only 20% of Liberal Democrats and 17% of Labour respondents gave the same answer. Third, and of particular significance, the 1991 MORI poll also quizzed respondents about the way in which they felt the system could be improved. The largest single response—given by 28%—was "abolish the poll tax." The poll tax ceased to exist on April 1, 1993. The second most frequently given response—by 14%—concerned the National Health Service. Very few of the responses were directed at the actual structures of government, but were concerned more with public policy, such as "better housing policy," "increase pensions," and "lower interest rates."

There is thus hardly a convincing case for a "collapse" in "trust" in the British system of government. This contention—that there has been no collapse—is reinforced by comparative data on how democracy works. Table 15.4 shows responses in the United Kingdom on the question of how satisfied people are with the way democracy works (in the United Kingdom), compared with the European Community average. That reveals an increase in confidence in the 1970s

TABLE 15.4 Satisfaction with the way democracy works

Q: On the whole, are you very satisfied, fairly satisfied, not very satisfied, or not at all satisfied with the way democracy works (in your country)?

	1973 UK %	1973 EC %	1978 UK %	1978 EC %	1983 UK %	1983 EC %	1990 UK %	1990 EC %
Very satisfied	7	8	6	6	12	8	8	9
Fairly satisfied	37	40	45	43	49	43	42	43
Not very satisfied	34	33	28	30	20	28	30	29
Not at all satisfied	20	13	12	14	12	14	14	14
No reply	2	6	9	7	7	7	6	5

EC = EC average
SOURCE: *Eurobarometer—Trends 1974–1990*, pp. 29-31.

and 1980s, actually exceeding—unlike early in the 1970s—the EC average, then falling back by 1990 but to a level basically matching the EC average and still higher than the levels of satisfaction in 1973.

Within the system we have seen much greater use made of existing channels, especially Parliament (see chapter 11). The British Social Attitudes Survey of 1984 found that, in a situation where an unjust or harmful measure was being considered by Parliament, a majority of respondents would contact their local MP; this constituted the most popular course of personal action and was also considered to be the most effective.[28] Later surveys elicited similar responses and the 1986 Social Attitudes Survey detected a "widespread and growing self-confidence on the part of the electorate to try to bring influence to bear on Parliament,"[29] a finding somewhat at variance with Beer's declaration four years before of the collapse of the civic culture. The 1991 MORI poll for the Rowntree Trust found that 59% of those questioned thought Parliament "did a good job," more than three times the number saying it did a bad job.

The data presented by those claiming a collapse in the civic culture are thus not sufficient to bear out their assertion. Indeed, what is remarkable about the data is the fact that they do not show the high negative levels that one might expect at times of economic and social problems.

What, then, are we to make of the finding that respondents believe that rights are too easily changed in Britain? Not a great deal, because that particular finding has to be contrasted with the finding of the Social Attitudes Survey conducted in 1990 that 85% of people think that rights are very or fairly well protected in Britain and 71% think Britain is an open society.[30]

What are we to make of the findings of the 1991 MORI poll and of others showing clear majorities for different constitutional reforms? Again, not too much. The findings themselves cannot be taken to show lack of trust in the existing system because the proportion of people believing constitutional reform is a significant issue virtually fails to register in opinion polls.[31] What support there is for specific items of change tends to be broad but neither deep nor well informed. Of respondents favoring proportional representation in the 1991 MORI poll, for example, more "tended" to support it than "strongly" support it, and the proportion claiming to know a "great deal" about it was half that saying they had "never heard of it."[32] Furthermore, support drops away when the consequences are considered. The proportion of people wanting a single-party government often exceeds those favoring parties forming a coalition government by a margin of two to one.[33]

Those arguing that there has been a collapse of the civic culture in Britain thus rely too heavily on data that will not bear the weight given them. Britain has not seen a collapse of attitudes and values from some golden age to a new dismal age. If there ever was anything approaching a "golden age" it was to be found in the quarter-century following the Second World War—certainly not before—and that period of stability and relative economic prosperity produced particularly high levels of pride in institutions, a pride tapped by Almond and Verba in *The Civic Culture*.[34] Those heady and exceptional days may be past, but the basic orientations toward cooperation and problem solving are not. The civic culture remains intact. Britain is a pluralist society, more pluralist than ever before.[35] The culture remains essentially a deferential one, but that deference—as we have argued—is contingent. If government goes beyond what is acceptable, various mechanisms still exist to check it. That is allied with the empirical approach to problem solving and cooperation. If things appear to be going too far, then efforts are made to find a practical solution.

It is this empirical approach that is emphasized by the traditional approach to the Constitution. There is no principled attachment to the status quo (the stand taken by the High Tory approach). There is a recognition that the system of government can be improved, and a belief that the way to improve it is to identify specific faults and address those faults. To produce grand blueprints—the stance taken by the liberal school—smacks too much of a rationalist approach and one that threatens to jettison the strengths of the existing system for the unknowns of another. Furthermore, to focus on the political system as a cause—wholly or partly—of Britain's economic and social ills is dangerous, in that it distracts attention from attempts to get at the root of those problems. For the traditionalist, therefore, the Constitution is not part of the problem, but rather part of the solution. The existing system offers coherence and accountability: a party system in which one party can be elected, implement a particular program of public policy, and then be held accountable at the next election—election day, in Karl Popper's words, constituting ''Judgement day'' (see chapter 11). The system may not be the ideal, but it is the real. Critics may find fault and there is room for improvement, but no convincing case has been made for sweeping it away.

CONCLUSION

At times of economic, social, or political difficulty, there has been a tendency—not confined to the United Kingdom—to look to constitutional change as a palliative or a means of dealing with the difficulty, of producing a system capable of being effective and resolving problems. At the time of the depression in the 1930s, for example, the implications for the Constitution were noted by Conservative leader Stanley Baldwin. ''There is bound to be unrest,'' he said, ''when more questions are being put than statesmen can answer. Within the House of Commons itself there is a growing sense of the need for overhauling the ship of state.''[36] Disappointment with the working of representative government, he observed, was no new thing. ''It recurs periodically and we are in one of the fermenting periods now. It may be uncomfortable but it is not surprising.''[37]

The years after the Second World War in Britain witnessed a period of stability and—especially in the 1950s—relative economic prosperity, with little debate consequently about constitutional arrangements. As the economic condition of the nation worsened in the 1960s, calls for change in structures began to be heard. Those calls became more strident in the 1970s and 1980s. By the beginning of the 1990s, there were various blueprints for constitutional reform—for a new constitution—on offer. Various approaches to change developed, with much of the recent debate focusing on the liberal and traditionalist approaches.

Constitutional debate has thus resumed in Britain after a relatively short lull. Many advocating a new constitution appear to mistake that lull for the norm of British history. Constitutional change is nothing new in Britain; neither is some element of unrest against a backdrop of relative stability. The current debate thus constitutes no grand departure but rather "business as usual."

NOTES

1. For critical works, see K. D. Ewing and C. Gearty, *Freedom under Thatcher* (Oxford University Press, 1990); and C. Graham and T. Prosser, *Waiving the Rules* (Open University Press, 1988). For the case identifying an extension of rights, see J. Patten, "Rolling Constitutional Change," in *Modernising British Government* (European Policy Forum, 1993), pp. 11–30; and J. Patten, *Political Culture, Conservatism and Rolling Constitutional Change* (Conservative Political Centre, 1991).
2. See especially J. Prior, *A Balance of Power* (Hamish Hamilton, 1986). Mrs. Thatcher even encouraged, albeit privately, her supporters in the House of Lords to support an amendment to a government bill to make the reforms stronger than they were. Confirmed to the author by one of the peers involved.
3. P. Norton, "Government Defeats in the House of Commons: Myth and Reality," *Public Law,* Winter 1978, pp. 360–378.
4. Examples of such works include, from the pen of a political scientist, N. Johnson, *In Search of the Constitution* (Methuen, 1980); and, from the pens of lawyers and political scientists, J. Jowell and D. Oliver (eds.), *The Changing Constitution* (Clarendon Press, 1985).
5. Most of these approaches are detailed in P. Norton, *The Constitution in Flux* (Blackwell, 1982), pp. 261–291.
6. Institute for Public Policy Research, *A Written Constitution for the United Kingdom* (Mansell, 1993).
7. Though favoring a free-market economy, Mrs. Thatcher never managed to divorce herself from her Tory antecedents. Though she was not adverse to "handbagging" certain institutions, she was never prepared to contemplate moving away from the existing constitutional framework and never managed to create a political framework— via the Conservative party—that would have allowed her to do so, even if she had wished to do so. On the latter point, see P. Norton, "Mrs. Thatcher and the Conservative Party: Another Institution 'Handbagged'?' in K. Minogue and M. Biddiss (eds.), *Thatcherism: Personality and Politics* (Macmillan, 1987), pp. 21–37.
8. See J. Major, *Scotland in the United Kingdom* (Conservative Political Centre, 1992); J. Patten, "Save Us from the Meddlers," *The Times,* December 4, 1991; and the works by J. Patten cited above in n. 1.
9. S. H. Beer, *Britain against Itself* (Faber, 1982).
10. Beer, pp. xiv–xv.
11. Beer, pp. 114–119.
12. P. Dunleavy and S. Weir, "Ignore the People at Your Peril," *The Independent,* April 25, 1991. See *State of the Nation* (MORI, 1991).
13. A. L. Lowell, *The Government of England* (1908), quoted in Beer, p. xi.
14. Beer, p. ix.
15. See R. D. Storch, "The Plague of the Blue Locusts," in M. Fitzgerald, G. McLennan, and J. Pawson (eds.), *Crime and Society* (Routledge & Kegan Paul, 1981), pp. 86–115.

16. S. H. Field and P. Southgate, *Public Disorder,* Home Office Research Study No. 72 (Her Majesty's Stationery Office, 1982), pp. 4–5.
17. A. G. Gardiner in the *Daily News,* quoted by S. Reynolds, book review, *Punch,* July 13, 1983, p. 60.
18. Field and Southgate, p. 5.
19. Ibid.
20. For example, in the three years of 1902, 1903, and 1904, about 200 people were killed and 2,000 injured in violence that accompanied strikes and lock-outs in the United States; there were 16 deaths in the Little Steel Strike of 1937. Race riots were a feature of various U.S. cities in the first half of the twentieth century—between 1915 and 1919 there were 22 racial disturbances in U.S. cities, with 15 whites and 23 blacks being killed in Chicago—and not just of the U.S. cities of the 1960s, Miami of the 1980s, and Los Angeles of the 1990s. See especially *To Establish Justice, To Insure Domestic Tranquility,* the Final Report of the National Commission on the Causes and Prevention of Violence (Bantam, 1970).
21. See, e.g., Prior, *A Balance of Power.*
22. A. H. Halsey, *Change in British Society,* 2nd ed. (Oxford University Press, 1981), p. 70.
23. Quoted in ibid., p. 71.
24. A. Ereira, *The Invergordon Mutiny* (Routledge & Kegan Paul, 1981).
25. A. W. Cox, "Strikes, Free Collective Bargaining and Public Order," in P. Norton (ed.), *Law and Order and British Politics* (Gower, 1984), pp. 115–133.
26. R. Miliband, *Capitalist Democracy in Britain* (Oxford University Press, 1984), p. 20.
27. See P. Norton, "The Conservative Party from Thatcher to Major," in A. King (ed.), *Britain at the Polls 1992* (Chatham House, 1993), pp. 43–45, 60.
28. R. Jowell and S. Witherspoon, *British Social Attitudes: The 1985 Report* (Gower, 1985), p. 12.
29. R. Jowell, S. Witherspoon, and L. Brook, *British Social Attitudes: The 1987 Report* (Gower, 1987), p. 58.
30. *The Guardian,* November 20, 1991.
31. Thus, for example, constitutional reform did not figure in MORI polls of the most important issues facing Britain in either 1992 or 1993. The most important issues were unemployment, the economy, the national health service, Europe, education, and law and order. MORI, *British Public Opinion,* 16 (5), June 1993, p. 2.
32. MORI, *British Public Opinion,* 14 (4), May 1991, p. 7.
33. Ibid.
34. G. Almond and S. Verba, *The Civic Culture* (Princeton University Press, 1963). See above, chapter 2.
35. See P. Norton, "In Defence of the Constitution," in P. Norton (ed.), *New Directions in British Politics?* (Edward Elgar, 1991), pp. 154–160.
36. S. Baldwin, *The Torch of Freedom,* 4th ed. (Hooder & Stoughton, 1937), p. 50.
37. Ibid.

Select Reading List

This is neither a bibliography of works used nor a comprehensive survey of available literature. Rather, it is a brief guide to the main and, in particular, the most recent texts available for student use. Chapter endnotes provide a pointer to further reading for students whose intellectual appetite is not satiated by what follows.

PART I: INTRODUCTION

Various reference works provide useful facts and figures on contemporary Britain. The most regular and helpful of these are *Britain: An Official Handbook,* published annually by Her Majesty's Stationery Office (HMSO), and *Social Trends,* compiled annually by the Central Statistical Office and also published by HMSO. There are now also annual volumes providing analyses of developments in institutions, politics, and policies in the preceding year. Edited by P. Catterall under the title *Contemporary Britain: An Annual Review,* they are published by Blackwell of Oxford. A similar, more student-oriented annual review is to be published by another Oxford publisher, Philip Allan, from 1994.

For a succinct introduction to political culture, see D. Kavanagh, *Political Culture* (Macmillan, 1972). The classic work is that of G. Almond and S. Verba, *The Civic Culture* (Princeton University Press, 1963). See also G. Almond and S. Verba (eds.), *The Civic Culture Revisited* (Little, Brown, 1980); and S. H. Beer, *Britain against Itself* (Faber, 1982). *British Social Attitudes,* published annually (Gower), provides analysis and the findings of the surveys conducted by Social and Community Planning Research. The volumes provide valuable material on contemporary attitudes on a range of issues and treat a number of the concerns covered in *The Civic Culture.* G. Parry, G. Moyser, and I. Day, *Political*

Participation and Democracy in Britain (Cambridge University Press, 1992) provides an extensive analysis of political participation and attitudes toward participation in Britain in the 1980s.

The history of Britain is treated in numerous works, including the 15-volume *Oxford History of England,* published by Oxford University Press. A recent and highly acclaimed political history, *The British Political Tradition,* by W. H. Greenleaf, has been published in three volumes: *Vol. 1: The Rise of Collectivism* (Longman, 1983), *Vol. 2: The Ideological Inheritance* (Longman, 1983), and *Vol. 3: A Much Governed Nation* (Longman, 1987).

A number of works also offer a historical perspective in analyzing political developments and the nation's problems. Among the more influential—written from different perspectives—are S. Brittan, *The Economic Consequences of Democracy* (Temple Smith, 1977; rev. ed. 1989); K. Middlemas, *Politics in Industrial Society* (Andre Deutsch, 1979); D. Marquand, *The Unprincipled Society: New Demands and Old Politics* (Fontana, 1988); S. Pollard, *Britain's Prime and Britain's Decline* (Edward Arnold, 1989); A. Gamble, *Britain in Decline,* 3rd ed. (Macmillan, 1990) and W. Rubinstein, *Capitalism, Culture and Decline in Britain* 1750–1990 (Routledge, 1993).

PART II: THE POLITICAL ENVIRONMENT

Since 1980, several publications have appeared putting the Constitution in a political context. Among the principal works are N. Johnson, *In Search of the Constitution* (Methuen, 1980 ed.); P. Norton, *The Constitution in Flux* (Martin Robertson/Blackwell, 1982); C. Harlow (ed.), *Public Law and Politics* (Sweet & Maxwell, 1986); R. Brazier, *Constitutional Practice* (Oxford University Press, 1988); and J. Jowell and D. Oliver (eds.), *The Changing Constitution,* 2nd ed. (Oxford University Press, 1989) R. Brazier, *Constitutional Reform* (Oxford University Press, 1991); and D. Oliver, *Government in the United Kingdom* (Open University Press, 1991) offer more prescriptive reform tracts. C. Munro, *Studies in Constitutional Law* (Butterworths, 1987) is also useful. Works that are central to the current debate on the Constitution—taking a particular stand on its strength and weaknesses—are listed under Part VI.

Election results, and details of candidates, are published after each general election in *The Times Guide to the House of Commons* (*The Times*). The standard works of analysis on British general elections are those published in the Nuffield election series, authored or coauthored by D. Butler and published after each election. The most recent edition is D. Butler and D. Kavanagh, *The British General Election of 1992* (Macmillan, 1992). A. King (ed.), *Britain at the Polls 1992* (Chatham House, 1993) provides an analysis of the 1992 election and of political developments since the preceding election. D. Butler, *British General Elections since 1945* (Blackwell, 1989) offers a short guide to elections from 1945 to 1987. The legal aspect of elections is well treated in H. F. Rawlings, *Law and the Electoral Process* (Sweet & Maxwell, 1988).

D. Denver, *Elections and Voting Behaviour in Britain* (Philip Allan, 1989) provides a brief introduction to the subject. The principal works offering explanations of voting behavior are D. Butler and D. Stokes, *Political Change in Britain,* 2nd ed. (Macmillan, 1974); B. Sarlvik and I. Crewe, *Decade of Dealignment* (Cambridge University Press, 1983); M. Franklin, *The Decline of Class Voting in Britain* (Oxford University Press, 1985); P. Dunleavy and C. T. Husbands, *British Democracy at the Crossroads* (Allen & Unwin, 1986); A. Heath, R. Jowell, and J. Curtice, *How Britain Votes* (Pergamon, 1985); R. Rose and I. McAllister, *Voters Begin to Choose* (Sage, 1986); R. J. Johnston, C. J. Pattie, and J. G. Allsop, *A Nation Dividing?* (Longman, 1988); R. Rose and I. McAllister, *The Loyalties of Voters* (Sage, 1990); A. Heath et al., *Understanding Political Change: The British Voter 1964–1987* (Pergamon, 1991); and H. Norpoth, *Confidence Regained: Economics, Mrs. Thatcher, and the British Voter* (University of Michigan Press, 1992). See also D. Sanders, "Why the Conservative Party Won—Again," in A. King (ed.), *Britain at the Polls 1992* (Chatham House, 1993).

In the debate on the electoral system, the seminal work for reformers has been S. E. Finer (ed.), *Adversary Politics and Electoral Reform* (Wigram, 1975). See also G. Smyth (ed.), *Refreshing the Parts* (Lawrence and Wishart, 1992); and *The Plant Report* (The Labour party, 1993). The defense of the existing system derives from more disparate pieces. See especially J. Chandler, "The Plurality Vote: A Reappraisal," in *Political Studies,* 30, 1982, pp. 244–275; Sir K. Popper, "The Open Society and Its Enemies Revisited," *The Economist,* April 23, 1988, pp. 25–28; and P. Norton, "Does Britain Need Proportional Representation?" in R. Blackburn (ed.), *Constitutional Studies* (Mansell, 1992). See also P. Norton, *The Constitution in Flux,* ch. 12; R. Rose, *What Are the Economic Consequences of PR?* (Electoral Reform Society, 1992); and "Electoral Reform," *The Economist,* May 1, 1993, pp. 23–26.

The classic but now dated work on political parties is R. McKenzie, *British Political Parties,* 2nd ed. (Heinemann, 1964). Recent introductory texts are S. Ingle, *The British Party System,* 2nd ed. (Blackwell, 1989); and A. Seldon (ed.), *UK Political Parties since 1945* (Blackwell, 1990). The best history of the Conservative party is R. Blake, *The Conservative Party from Peel to Thatcher* (Fontana, 1985). An overview of the party's history, philosophy, and organization is provided in P. Norton and A. Aughey, *Conservatives and Conservatism* (Temple Smith, 1981) and an extensive treatment is provided in A. Seldon and S. Ball (eds.), *The Conservative Party in the Twentieth Century* (Oxford University Press, 1994). R. Shepherd, *The Power Brokers* (Hutchinson, 1991) offers an introduction to the party and its leaders. On Margaret Thatcher and Thatcherism, see especially A. Gamble, *The Free Economy and the Strong State* (Macmillan, 1988); H. Young, *One of Us* (Macmillan, 1989); and P. Riddell, *The Thatcher Era and Its Legacy* (Blackwell, 1991).

For a history of the Labour party, see H. Pelling, *A Short History of the Labour Party,* 10th ed. (Macmillan, 1993). A more subjective approach is provided by A. J. Davies, *To Build a New Jerusalem* (Michael Joseph, 1992). On the party's political thought and recent developments, see G. Foote, *The Labour Party's Political Thought,* 2nd ed. (Croom Helm, 1986); P. Seyd, *The Rise and Fall of the Labour Left* (Macmillan, 1987); M. J. Smith and J. Spear (eds.), *The Changing Labour Party* (Routledge, 1992); and P. Seyd and P. Whiteley, *Labour's Grass Roots* (Oxford University Press, 1992). The party's relationship with the trades unions is covered in L. Minkin, *The Contentious Alliance* (Edinburgh University Press, 1991). On the Liberal party and its successor see C. Cook, *A Short History of the Liberal Party 1900–92,* 4th ed. (Macmillan, 1993); and J. Stevenson, *Third Party Politics since 1945: Liberals, Alliance and Liberal Democrats* (Blackwell, 1993). The way in which all three parties select their leaders is covered in R. M. Punnett, *Selecting the Party Leader* (Harvester Wheatsheaf, 1992). On developments within all three parties from 1987 to 1992, see especially the chapters by Norton, Seyd, and Denver in King, *Britain at the Polls 1992* (1993).

An invaluable study of the effect of political parties in office is provided by R. Rose, *Do Parties Make a Difference?* 2nd ed. (Macmillan, 1984), providing an effective rejoinder to the thesis of adversarial politics advanced by Finer in *Adversary Politics and Electoral Reform.*

On the development of group influence in British politics, see especially S. H. Beer, *Modern British Politics* (Faber, 1965; 3rd ed. 1982); Middlemass, *Politics in Industrial Society* (1979); J. Richardson and A. G. Jordan, *Governing under Pressure* (Martin Robertson, 1979); G. Jordan and J. Richardson, *Government and Pressure Groups in Britain* (Oxford University Press, 1987); and W. Grant, *Pressure Groups, Politics and Democracy in Britain* (Philip Allan, 1989). See also W. Grant, *Business and Politics in Britain,* 2nd ed. (Macmillan, 1993); and A. Taylor, *Trade Union Question in British Politics* (Blackwell, 1993). On the relationship of Parliament and pressure groups, see M. Rush, *Parliament and Pressure Politics* (Oxford University Press, 1990), and, on political lobbying, C. Miller, *Lobbying,* 2nd ed. (Blackwell, 1990); and G. Jordan (ed.), *Commercial Lobbyists* (Aberdeen University Press, 1991). The use of litigation by pressure groups is explored in C. Harlow and R. Rawlings, *Pressure through Law* (Routledge, 1992).

PART III: GOVERNMENTAL DECISION MAKING

Though there are a great many works on individual prime ministers, works on the premiership qua premiership are notable for their rarity. The principal works are A. King (ed.), *The British Prime Minister,* 2nd ed. (Macmillan, 1985); B. Donoughue, *The Prime Minister* (Cape, 1987); and J. Barber, *The Prime Minister since 1945* (Blackwell, 1991). P. Madgwick, *British Government: The Central Executive Territory* (Philip Allan, 1991) covers the role of the prime minister as well as the Cabinet. On the office itself, see R. Blake, *The Office of Prime Minister* (Oxford University Press, 1975). The premiership is considered in comparative perspective in G. W. Jones (ed.), *West European Prime Ministers* (Frank Cass, 1991).

For a good historical work on the Cabinet, see J. P. Mackintosh, *The British Cabinet,* 3rd ed. (Stevens, 1977). The most recent texts covering the Cabinet are P. Hennessy, *Cabinet* (Blackwell, 1986); P. Madgwick, *British Government* (cited above); and S. James, *British Cabinet Government* (Routledge, 1992). For a radical analysis, see B. Sedgemore, *The Secret Constitution* (Hodder & Stoughton, 1980). K. Theakston, *Junior Ministers* (Blackwell, 1987), explores a much neglected aspect of British government. Revelations about the workings of Cabinet and government departments are also provided by ministerial memoirs. Among the more useful of the many published in recent years are N. Fowler, *Ministers Decide* (Chapmans, 1991); N. Ridley, *"My Style of Government"* (Fontana, 1992); and N. Lawson, *The View from No. 11* (Bantam, 1992). The last of these provides an especially good—and extensive—insight into economic policy making.

The civil service is explored exhaustively in P. Hennessy, *Whitehall* (Secker & Warburg, 1989). More succinct analyses are offered by G. Drewry and T. Burton, *The Civil Service Today,* 2nd ed. (Blackwell, 1991); and R. Pyper, *The Evolving Civil Service* (Longman, 1991). Hennessy is valuable also for his coverage of the structure of government departments.

On subnational government, there are several introductory works on local government and center-local relationships. Among the more recent are J. Chandler, *Local Government Today* (Manchester University Press, 1991); G. Stoker, *The Politics of Local Government,* 2nd ed. (Macmillan, 1991); W. Hampton, *Local Government and Urban Politics,* 2nd ed. (Longman, 1991); and D. Wilson, C. Game, S. Leach, and G. Stoker, *Local Government in the UK* (Macmillan, 1993). See also S. Leach, J. Stewart, and K. Walsh, *The Changing Organisation and Management of Local Government* (Macmillan, 1993). On regional government, see R. A. W. Rhodes, *Beyond Westminster and Whitehall* (Unwin Hyman, 1988); and C. Gray, *Government beyond the Centre* (Macmillan, 1993).

For more on government and politics in Scotland, see the standard work by J. Kellas, *The Scottish Political System,* 4th ed. (Cambridge University Press, 1989); and also A. Midwinter, M. Keating, and J. Mitchell, *Politics and Public Policy in Scotland* (Macmillan, 1991). There is also an annual *Scottish Government Yearbook,* published by Edinburgh University Press. There are numerous works on the politics, problems, and future of Northern Ireland. Among the more recent are J. McGarry and B. O'Leary, *The Future of Northern Ireland* (Oxford University Press, 1990); J. Whyte, *Interpreting Northern Ireland* (Oxford University Press, 1991); M. J. Cunningham, *British Government Policy in Northern Ireland 1969–1989* (Manchester University Press, 1991); and B. Hadfield (ed.), *Northern Ireland: Politics and the Constitution* (Open University Press, 1992). See also the seminal work by R. Rose, *Governing without Consensus* (Faber, 1971).

There are also now numerous publications on the politics and institutions of the European Community and on Britain's position in the Community. See especially, among recent works, S. George, *An Awkward Partner* (Oxford University Press, 1990); S. George, *Britain and European Integration since 1945* (Blackwell, 1991); and, from a more policy-oriented perspective, S. Bulmer, S. George, and A. Scott (eds.), *The United Kingdom and EC Membership Evaluated* (Pinter, 1992). On the institutions and the future of the EC, see D. A. C. Freestone and J. S. Davidson, *The Institutional Framework of the European Communities* (Croom Helm, 1988); N. Nugent, *Government and Politics of the European Community,* 2nd ed. (Macmillan, 1991); and S. George, *Politics and Policy in the European Community,* 2nd ed. (Oxford University Press, 1991). The most useful work on the European Parliament is F. Jacobs and R. Corbett, *The European Parliament* (Longman, 1990).

PART IV: SCRUTINY AND LEGITIMATION

The most recent introductory work on Parliament is P. Norton, *Does Parliament Matter?* (Harvester Wheatsheaf, 1993). A large compendium of data is provided in J. A. G. Griffith and M. Ryle, *Parliament: Functions, Practice and Procedure* (Sweet & Maxwell, 1989; paper ed. 1990).

The principal work on Commons select committees is G. Drewry (ed.), *The New Select Committees,* rev. ed. (Oxford University Press, 1989); and, on Question Time and parliamentary questions, M. Franklin and P. Norton (eds.), *Parliamentary Questions* (Oxford University Press, 1993). Private members' bills are analyzed in D. Marsh and M. Read, *Private Members' Bills* (Cambridge University Press, 1988). Parliamentary parties are covered by P. Norton, ''The Organization of Parliamentary Parties,'' in S. A. Walkland (ed.), *The House of Commons in the Twentieth Century* (Oxford University Press, 1979); J. Brand, *British Parliamentary Parties* (Oxford University Press, 1992); and P. Norton, ''The Parliamentary Party,'' in Seldon and Ball, *The Conservative Party in the Twentieth Century* (1994). The constituency role and effect of individual members of Parliament is treated in B. Cain, J. Ferejohn, and M. Fiorina, *The Personal Vote* (Harvard University Press, 1987); and P. Norton and D. Wood, *Back from Westminster* (University Press of Kentucky, 1993). Biographical details of every MP and peer can be found in the annual edition of *Dod's Parliamentary Companion* (Dod's Parliamentary Companion Ltd.), which also contains a mass of useful data on Parliament and government departments.

The most recent and useful works on the House of Lords are D. Shell, *The House of Lords,* 2nd ed. (Harvester Wheatsheaf, 1992); and D. Shell and D. Beamish (eds.), *The House of Lords at Work* (Oxford University Press, 1993).

On the relationship of Parliament and pressure groups, see M. Rush (ed.), *Parliament and Pressure Politics* (Oxford University Press, 1990), and on its relationship with government in particular sectors of public policy, see D. Judge, *Parliament and Industry* (Dartmouth, 1990); and C. Carstairs and R. Ware (eds.), *Parliament and International Relations* (Open University Press, 1991).

There are many works dealing with the problems of the royal family but few good works putting the monarchy in a political context. F. Hardie, *The Political Influence of the British Monarchy* (Batsford, 1970); and C. Hibbert, *The Court of St. James* (Weidenfeld & Nicolson, 1979; Gill, 1983) provide valuable overviews. Basic material may be found in the HMSO monograph *The Monarchy* (HMSO, 1993). Radical critiques include T. Nairn, *The Enchanted Glass—Britain and Its Monarchy* (Century Hutchinson Radius, 1988); and E. Wilson, *The Myth of the British Monarchy* (Journeyman/Republic, 1989).

PART V: ENFORCEMENT AND FEEDBACK

There are several works, usually entitled *Constitutional and Administrative Law,* that provide introductions to the English (and sometimes the Scottish) legal system, as well as the broader constitutional context. One of the more useful and readable is S. de Smith and R. Brazier, *Constitutional and Administrative Law,* 6th ed. (Penguin, 1990).

On the debate surrounding judges, the courts, and the legal system, see M. Zander, *A Matter of Justice,* rev. ed. (Oxford University Press, 1989); J. Waldron, *The Law* (Routledge, 1990); J. A. G. Griffith, *The Politics of the Judiciary,* 4th ed. (Fontana, 1991); G. Drewry, "Judicial Independence in Britain," in P. Norton (ed.), *New Directions in British Politics?* (Edward Elgar, 1991); and J. A. G. Griffith, *Judicial Politics since 1920* (Blackwell, 1993). On the role of the law lords, see A. Paterson, *The Law Lords* (Macmillan, 1982). On the police, see M. Young, *An Inside Job: Policing and Police Culture in Britain* (Oxford University Press, 1990); and R. Reiner, *The Politics of the Police,* 2nd ed. (Harvester Wheatsheaf, 1992). Recent works on criminal justice include T. Morris, *Crime and Criminal Justice since 1945* (Blackwell, 1989); and A. Rutherford, *Criminal Justice and the Pursuit of Decency* (Oxford University Press, 1993).

There is a growing volume of literature on the role and effect of the mass media. Among the more recent publications are R. Negrine, *Politics and the Mass Media in Britain* (Routledge, 1989); J. Curran and J. Seaton, *Power without Responsibility: The Press and Broadcasting in Britain,* 3rd ed. (Routledge, 1991); and C. Seymour-Ure, *The British Press and Broadcasting since 1945* (Blackwell, 1991). See also the forthcoming work, C. Seymour-Ure, *Presidents, Prime Ministers and Media* (Blackwell, 1994).

PART VI: CONCLUSION

There are now several books and pamphlets that take a particular approach to constitutional change. Works that had a particular influence in the 1970s were S. E. Finer (ed.), *Adversary Politics and Electoral Reform* (Wigram, 1975); and Lord Hailsham, *Elective Dictatorship* (BBC, 1976). A dissection of the different approaches to reform was provided early in the 1980s by P. Norton, *The Constitution in Flux* (Martin Robertson/Blackwell, 1982). Recent critical literature has included R. Holme and M. Elliott, *1688–1988: Time for a New Constitution* (Macmillan, 1988); C. Graham and T. Prosser, *Waiving the Rules* (Open University Press, 1988); P. Hillyard and J. Percy-Smith, *The Coercive State* (Fontana, 1988); P. Thornton, *Decade of Decline* (Liberty, 1989); G. Robertson, *Street's Freedom, The Individual and the Law,* 6th ed. (Penguin, 1989); K. D. Ewing and C. Gearty, *Freedom under Thatcher: Civil Liberties in Modern Britain* (Oxford University Press, 1990); A. Wright, *Citizens and Subjects* (Routledge, 1993); and less critical but still reformist, F. Mount, *The British Constitution Now* (Heinemann, 1992). Draft written constitutions have been offered by the Institute of Public Policy Research (IPPR), *A Written Constitution for the United Kingdom* (Mansell, 1993) and by radical Labour politician Tony Benn, *Common Sense* (Hutchinson, 1993). See also *"We The People": Towards a Written Constitution* (Liberal Democrat Publications, 1990); and *The Charter of Rights* (Labour party, 1991).

The main defense of existing arrangements is offered in the conclusion to P. Norton (ed.), *New Directions in British Politics?* (Edward Elgar, 1991) and in various pamphlets published by the Conservative Political Centre (CPC), notably J. Patten, *Political Culture, Conservatism and Rolling Constitutional Change* (CPC, 1991); and P. Norton, *The Constitution: The Conservative Way Forward* (CPC, 1992). See also J. Patten, "Rolling Constitutional Change," in *Modernising British Government* (European Policy Forum, 1993).

Glossary

Backbencher. A member of either house of Parliament who is neither a government minister nor a spokesperson for the opposition. The name derives from where the members sit: on the back benches.

Barrister. A specialist lawyer who appears on behalf of clients in superior courts and is retained through a solicitor.

Bobby. Colloquial name for a policeman (not used much now) that was derived from the first name of the home secretary, Sir Robert Peel, responsible for the creation of the (metropolitan) police force in 1829.

Buckingham Palace. The official London residence of the queen. When the prime minister "goes to the palace" for an audience (i.e., meeting) with the queen, the reference is to Buckingham Palace.

By-election. The election to return a member of Parliament (MP) in a constituency in which a vacancy has occurred (usually because of the death or resignation of the incumbent). A vacancy can be filled only by means of an election. By agreement between the parties, the precise date of a by-election is usually determined by the party that previously held the seat. Like general elections, by-elections are traditionally held on a Thursday.

Chequers. The official country residence of the prime minister, located close to London, near Princes Risborough in Buckinghamshire. It was given to the nation by Lord Lee of Fareham in 1917.

Chief constable. The professional head of each police force, except in London, where the metropolitan and City of London forces are each headed by a commissioner.

The City. The City of London, occupying one square mile in the heart of London; it is the traditional home of the Bank of England, the Stock Exchange, and the nation's other financial institutions.

Collective ministerial responsibility. The answerability of all members of the government for decisions made by the Cabinet.

Commonwealth. A voluntary association of independent states and territories. The Commonwealth evolved from the British Empire and exists now to provide cultural, sporting, and some political links among member states. The queen is head of the Commonwealth.

Constituency. An electoral area equivalent in nature to a congressional district. Each is known by a geographical name rather than by number. Each constituency elects one member of Parliament.

Contest an election. To stand for election.

Conventions of the Constitution. Informal constitutional rules treated as binding by those to whom they are directed.

Devolution. The devolving of powers by national government to subordinate assemblies.

Dissolution. The dissolving of Parliament to prepare for a general election, that is, the election of a new Parliament.

Division lobbies. The voting lobbies in the two houses of Parliament. When members vote (divide), they enter lobbies on the two sides of the chamber; the "aye" lobby is to the right of the presiding officer, the "no" lobby to the left.

Downing Street. A small cul-de-sac off Whitehall housing three principal houses—numbers 10, 11, and 12. No. 10 is the official London residence of the prime minister, No. 11 the official London residence of the chancellor of the exchequer, and No. 12 houses the office of the government chief whip in the House of Commons.

Elector. A registered voter.

Empire. The British Empire comprised countries under British sovereignty (though some were self-governing) and in 1918 it encompassed well over a quarter of the human race and more than a quarter of the world's land surface. It began to wither as various dominions gained independence. From the 1920s onward, it came to be called the British Commonwealth of Nations, now known simply as the Commonwealth.

Erskine May. The manual of parliamentary procedure—"the parliamentary bible"—the full title of which is *Erskine May's Treatise on the Law, Privileges, Proceedings and Usage of Parliament.* Sir Thomas Erskine May was a nineteenth-century clerk of the House of Commons. The book is now in its twenty-first edition; new editions are compiled by clerks under the direction of the clerk of the house.

Field a candidate. To put up a candidate for election.

Fleet Street. A street in central London, a continuation of the Strand (off Trafalgar Square), that traditionally has housed the main national newspapers. The name is still used to refer to the British press, even though no national newspapers are still based there; the last newspaper left in 1989. Most have relocated in the docklands area of east London.

Free votes. Parliamentary votes in which parties have not formally requested their members to vote in a particular way.

Frontbenchers. The front bench on the government side of the House of Commons (known as the Treasury bench, and extending halfway down the chamber) is by custom reserved for ministers, and the equivalent bench on the opposition side of the house is reserved for spokesmen of the official opposition party. Hence, those who occupy them are known as frontbenchers. Front benches also exist in the House of Lords.

General election. The election of a new House of Commons.

Going to the country. The calling of a general election; hence "the prime minister has decided to go to the country" means that the premier has requested a dissolution and the election of a new House of Commons.

Head of government. Political head of the executive. In the United Kingdom, the prime minister.

Head of state. Ceremonial leader of nation. In the United Kingdom, the queen.

Individual ministerial responsibility. The answerability of ministers to the Crown (formally) and to Parliament (politically) for their official actions and those of civil servants within their particular departments.

Lord chancellor. A political appointee (a member of the Cabinet) who is head of the judiciary. He is also formally the presiding officer of the House of Lords, though this entails no significant powers.

Lord chief justice. A senior, professional judge who heads both the Queen's Bench Division of the High Court and the Criminal Division of the Court of Appeal.

Manifesto. A party's election platform, embodied in a written document.

Master of the rolls. A senior, professional judge who presides over the Civil Division of the Court of Appeal.

Member of Parliament (MP). A member of the House of Commons. No such designation applies to members of the House of Lords, who are known by their titles.

Ministry. A government department or the government collectively.

"New" Commonwealth countries. A term employed to refer to Asian and African countries that were granted independence by Britain in the 1940s, thus distinguishing them from the "old" Commonwealth countries of Canada, Australia, and New Zealand.

Officials. A reference usually, though not exclusively, to civil servants.

Oxbridge. The universities of Oxford and Cambridge.

Peer. A member of the peerage (i.e., a lord).

Premier. Alternative term used to refer to the prime minister.

Private members. All members of Parliament who are not ministers. The term is not synonymous with backbenchers, as opposition frontbenchers are private members.

Quango. Quasi-autonomous nongovernment organization.

Rt. Hon. (Right Honorable). This title—as, for example, the Rt. Hon. John Major MP— denotes a member of the Privy Council. The council, historically, was an important advisory body to the Crown but is now largely ceremonial in nature. However, membership in the council is still important because members can receive state secrets. All members of the Cabinet and other senior ministers are sworn in as members of the Privy Council. Once sworn, they remain members for life.

Scotland Yard. The headquarters of the metropolitan police force, presently titled New Scotland Yard. The name derives from the location of the original headquarters—Scotland Yard, Westminster (just off Whitehall). It now occupies a modern building in Broadway, Westminster, close to the Home Office.

Second reading. Parliamentary debate on the principle of a bill.

Speaker. The presiding officer of the House of Commons, selected by the house from among its members. The speaker has the power the select members for debate (through "catching the speaker's eye"), to select amendments for debate, and to discipline members, though all within fairly well-defined limits and procedures. After election to the post, the speaker ceases to be a member of a political party (seeking reelection at a general election simply as "the speaker"), operates as a nonpartisan figure, and leads an isolated parliamentary existence.

Swing. An average measure of the changes in the percentages of the vote received by the two major parties in successive elections.

Tabling a motion. The act of submitting a motion for debate. This is a positive move and should not be confused with the U.S equivalent, which means to shelve a motion.

Tory. A colloquial name for a member of the Conservative party, deriving from the name of the party, the Tory party, from which the Conservative party evolved in the 1830s. The term also refers to a specific strand of thought within British Conservatism.

Ulster. The northern nine counties of Ireland form the historic region of Ulster. However, the name (Ulster) is often used, especially by Unionists, to refer to the northern six counties that now constitute Northern Ireland. Since Northern Ireland was formed, it has been common to refer to it as a province of the United Kingdom.

Upper house. The House of Lords. (The House of Commons is the lower house, though it is rarely referred to as such.)

Vote of confidence. A formal motion expressing confidence (or no confidence) in the government, *or* a vote on a motion on which the government has declared that, if defeated, it will resign or request a dissolution. Such motions are discussed only in the House of Commons.

Wapping. An area in the docklands of London to which a number of national newspapers have relocated from Fleet Street.

Westminster. A district in London. The name is usually employed to refer to the Palace of Westminster, which houses the two houses of Parliament.

Whipped votes. Votes in Parliament in which the parties have requested their members to vote in a particular manner. Such requests are issued through a weekly written document known as the written whip. The request in the whip is given emphasis by underlining. The most important votes during which all party members are expected to be present and vote in unison are underlined three times. The term "three-line whip" derives from this practice. If there is a free vote (see above), there is no underlining.

Whips. Apart from the weekly written whip, there are members of each parliamentary party designated as whips. They act as channels of communication between party leaders and backbenchers, and largely as business managers. They are responsible for ensuring that party members know what business is being transacted and that they are present to vote when necessary and, on occasion, to speak when insufficient members have volunteered to take part in a debate. Contact between the whips' offices, especially the government and opposition chief whips, is known as contact "through the usual channels."

Whitehall. London street, between the Palace of Westminster and Trafalgar Square, traditionally housing government departments. The name is still employed to denote the environment occupied by ministers, and especially civil servants, even though most departments are now located elsewhere.

Whitehall Mandarins. The name employed on occasion to refer to the senior civil servants in government departments.

Index

Voting behavior. *See* Electors, voting
　　behavior of

Wade, E. C. S., 62, 64
Wales
　administrative devolution, 224–227
　electoral process in, 83
　integrated with England, 65
　political parties in, 137–138
　proposed devolution in, 227–230
Wales, prince of, 315–316, 317
Wales, princess of, 315–316, 317, 358
Walkland, S. A., 297
Wallace, George, 100
Wall Street Journal, 350
Walpole, Sir Robert, 177
Washington Post, 350
Watt, David, 313
Webber, Andrew Lloyd, 121
Wedderburn, Lord, 301
Welfare state, development of a, 43–46
Welsh Office, 193, 226–227
West Germany. *See also* Germany
　political system orientation in, 30

Westland, 117
Wheare, Kenneth, 62
Whigs, 40
Whitelaw, William, 233
Whiteley, Paul, 97, 145
White Paper on Full Employment (1944),
　　45
William and Mary of Orange, 39
Williams, Shirley, 134, 192
Wilson, Edgar, 317
Wilson, Harold, 46, 61, 110, 115
　election of, 125
　hereditary peerages and, 291
　image on television, 357
　interest groups and, 165
　relationship with monarchy, 310
　type of minister, 183
Windsor Castle, fire at St. George's Hall, 316
Witherspoon, S., 16
Worcester, R., 24
Working class, introduction of the term, 40
Works of authority, British Constitution and
　　the use of, 61–62